Quantitative Research Methods in Corporate Finance

Focused on empirical methods and their applications to corporate finance, this innovative text equips students with the knowledge to analyze and critically evaluate quantitative research methods in corporate finance and conduct computer-aided statistical analyses on various types of datasets. The chapters demonstrate the application of basic econometric models in corporate finance (as opposed to derivations or theorems), backed up by relevant research. Alongside practical examples and mini case studies, computer lab exercises enable students to apply the theories of corporate finance and make stronger connections between theory and practice, while developing their programming skills. All of the Stata code is provided (with corresponding Python and R code available online), so students of all programming abilities can focus on understanding and interpreting the analyses.

Taylan Mavruk is a Professor of Finance at the University of Gothenburg. His research focuses on corporate finance, investor behavior, home/local bias, insider trading, CSR/ESG, mutual fund performance, and economics of patents. His research has been published in leading finance journals. He has been teaching courses related to corporate finance and econometrics since 2006.

"This novel textbook fills a gap in corporate finance literature by focusing on the application of appropriate statistical methods when studying and analyzing the financial performance of businesses and investments. The book provides students and other readers with in-depth insights into how to apply basic and more advanced econometric models to their own empirical studies. Illustrative computer-based laboratory exercises as well as practical examples and mini-case studies support students' ability to conduct computational statistical analyzes and understand how to interpret the results."

Ted Lindblom, University of Gothenburg

"This technical book on empirical corporate finance methods is an excellent text for undergrads, Master's students, and even Ph.D. students. While it is a technical treatise, explanations of each concept are very carefully explained. Beginning students will find a ground-up discussion that assumes little more than a reasonable background in mathematics and statistics; in addition, students at all levels of math and statistical maturity will find useful guidance in the textbook. I find this book to be a "tour-de-force," and I plan to refer to it myself. I highly recommend it."

Russ Wermers, University of Maryland

Quantitative Research Methods in Corporate Finance

Exemplified by Stata, Python, and R

Taylan Mavruk
University of Gothenburg

CAMBRIDGE
UNIVERSITY PRESS

CAMBRIDGE
UNIVERSITY PRESS

Shaftesbury Road, Cambridge CB2 8EA, United Kingdom

One Liberty Plaza, 20th Floor, New York, NY 10006, USA

477 Williamstown Road, Port Melbourne, VIC 3207, Australia

314–321, 3rd Floor, Plot 3, Splendor Forum, Jasola District Centre, New Delhi – 110025, India

103 Penang Road, #05–06/07, Visioncrest Commercial, Singapore 238467

Cambridge University Press is part of Cambridge University Press & Assessment, a department of the University of Cambridge.

We share the University's mission to contribute to society through the pursuit of education, learning and research at the highest international levels of excellence.

www.cambridge.org
Information on this title: www.cambridge.org/highereducation/isbn/9781009307437

DOI: 10.1017/9781009307383

When citing this work, please include a reference to the DOI 10.1017/9781009307383

First published 2025

A catalogue record for this publication is available from the British Library

Library of Congress Cataloging-in-Publication Data
Names: Mavruk, Taylan, 1977– author.
Title: Quantitative research methods in corporate finance : exemplified by Stata, Python, and R / Taylan Mavruk, University of Gothenburg, Sweden.
Description: Cambridge, United Kingdom ; New York, NY, USA : Cambridge University Press, [2025] | Includes bibliographical references and index.
Identifiers: LCCN 2024021495 | ISBN 9781009307437 (hardback) | ISBN 9781009307383 (ebook)
Subjects: LCSH: Business enterprises – Finance – Research. | Econometrics. | Python (Computer program language) | R (Computer program language)
Classification: LCC HG4026 .M38 2025 | DDC 658.15–dc23/eng/20240612
LC record available at https://lccn.loc.gov/2024021495

ISBN 978-1-009-30743-7 Hardback
ISBN 978-1-009-30741-3 Paperback

Additional resources for this publication at www.cambridge.org/mavruk

Contents

Figures

Tables

Preface

The aim of this book is to improve readers' (mostly Bachelor, Master, and PhD students') understanding of empirical research in corporate finance studies and their ability to apply econometric methods in their own research and studies. It covers my lecture notes from the courses Quantitative Research Methods in Business Administration (PhD level), Research Methods in Accounting and Financial Management (Master level), and Corporate Finance (Bachelor/Master level) that I have been teaching at the University of Gothenburg since 2006.

One common characteristic of these courses is that the applications, the computer lab work, and mini case studies are practical and research-oriented. While the applications provide practical examples of the interpretations of the results, in the lab work students are able to apply the theories of corporate finance and thereby make a better connection between the theories and practice. Thus, in a sense, the applications in the selected chapters provide some examples of solutions and the interpretations of the questions asked in the lab work. The outcome of this applied approach has been successful in my own teaching. The quality and relevance of the applied lab work provides students with a dynamic and inclusive study environment, which has encouraged them to forge connections and exchange knowledge in group work. The outcome of these courses and the approach has not only enhanced students' knowledge and helped them to build long-term connections, but also yielded the writing of this book.

The book presents the most commonly used econometric methods in corporate finance studies, followed by an application of these studies, using observational data, related lab work, and mini case studies where students replicate the main findings in published research using the methods learned in the chapters. For the mini case studies, students can download the data and related software code from Harvard Dataverse: https://dataverse.harvard.edu. In Chapters 4–10, problem sets for the lab work and sample datasets are provided (on the book's webpage: www.cambridge.org/mavruk) so that students can work on data management and with the labs. Almost all data used in the applications and lab work come from my own research, obtained from databases provided at the Gothenburg University Library: https://databaser.ub.gu.se/?lang=en. At the time the research was published in journals, these datasets were freely available to download from databases like Harvard Dataverse. However, in the chapters there are some simulations provided as well. While the empirical methods and corporate finance theories are standard, the applications add new knowledge to the existing body of research. Also, the applications that aim to replicate the results of some previous studies enhance the reader's knowledge, as these replications are done using new data from a more recent period and another country. In a sense, these replications can also be seen as a robustness analysis, since they often use alternative measures to those used in the original studies.

The lab work, particularly the applications and mini case studies, allow students to become familiar with the structure of writing theses and research papers. Students also appreciate the datasets and code provided to reproduce both the applications and the lab work. Thus, the provided code gives solutions for the lab work. The main program used in the book is Stata; all the Stata code required is provided in the book. Thus, students can focus on understanding and interpreting the analyses rather than writing the code. But the provided code will also encourage students to develop their programming skills. In addition, the book offers an online resources page (www.cambridge.org/mavruk), including code for those who want to develop in Python and R. For the mini case studies, students download the data and Stata code from Harvard Dataverse: https://dataverse.harvard.edu. The provided code for Python and R software as an online source can be used to produce the results in the mini case studies, if students prefer to use these software programs instead. Students need to replace the variable names with the new variable names in the provided datasets in the mini case studies. Thus, students have the opportunity to compare how the analyses are run in different statistical software programs. It is valuable for students to learn how the code works and is applied to different datasets. The code will be helpful when students do their own research and write their thesis.

The book is written for Bachelor and higher-level students, so some basic statistical/econometrical knowledge, say a minimum of two courses in statistics, is necessary. It is possible to teach the chapters out of order, but it is most beneficial if instructors follow the chapter order. The first three chapters will prepare students for the rest of the book. The chapters begin with an introduction and outline of the book. They then cover hypothesis development, identification strategy, and the nature of sampling. This knowledge is necessary to read the rest of the book. Chapter 3 introduces Stata software and basic data management. Python and R code is provided on the online resources page (www.cambridge.org/mavruk). To complete the applications and lab work in the following chapters, students should follow the exercises in Chapter 3 closely.

The focus in Chapter 4 is on survey-data analysis, particularly principal component analysis. The idea behind this chapter is to combine the qualitative studies with the quantitative studies. The survey studies cover an important part of the corporate finance field and thus in this chapter students learn how to quantify and analyze survey data.

Chapter 5 can be seen as the core of the book. It covers the classical linear regression model and hence the ordinary least squares (OLS) estimator. The aim is to cover the assumptions and interpretation of this benchmark model, upon which more complex models are built. The model is applied to cross-sectional data, or the data are treated as cross-sectional, although it may have a time dimension.

Chapters 6 through 10 are related to Chapter 5, as the assumptions of OLS in these chapters are relaxed one by one and an appropriate model is proposed. For example, Chapter 6 covers alternative models where one of the important assumptions of OLS, exogeneity, does not hold in the data. The examples and analyses are based on the cross-sectional datasets, or they treat the data as cross-sectional. Chapter 7 focuses on time-series data, hence its analysis, and provides models where the OLS assumption of no autocorrelation in the error term is violated. Chapter 8 deviates a little from this structure by covering one of the most used methods in corporate finance studies, specifically, event study methods. However, the models provided count the OLS assumptions. The applications are on firm/stock-level time-series data. Chapter 9 covers linear panel-data models and focuses both on the no-autocorrelation and homoskedasticity assumptions of the OLS. Chapter 10 provides an overview of the non-linear models that are useful in studies where the dependent variable is binary or categorial instead of continuous. Thereby it provides models that relax the OLS assumption of linearity in the parameters. The cross-sectional datasets are used for the examples and applications. Chapter 11 gives some suggestions for writing empirical papers or thesis in corporate finance. Finally, Chapter 12 provides a future direction, a brief overview of the major types of machine-learning models, with a focus on the most commonly used methods in (corporate) finance.

It will be helpful for students if Chapters 1 through 6 are taught following the order in this book, but Chapters 7 through 12 can be taught in any order.

There are already many detailed and good-quality method books in finance for students. However, these books mostly cover more general finance topics, including asset pricing. The focus of this book is on empirical methods and their applications on corporate finance. Other books covering corporate finance are either theory books or apply corporate finance theories to companies and focus on case studies within the field. In contrast, this book covers more statistical and econometrical tools and applies them to corporate finance. As such, it is a good complement that brings additional insight to the already existing books by combining a wide range of statistical/econometrical methods and corporate finance studies. The main focus is on applications of the methods, using the statistical software Stata, but also providing Python and R code. The book stresses interpretation and assumptions of basic standard econometric models and thus may also reach out to a broader group of readers, students in economics, accounting, and other business studies, rather than those only interested in corporate finance – even though the applications mainly concern corporate finance studies. As the main focus is the practical applications of these models not the derivations or theorems, the book can also be valuable for practitioners and professionals. In sum, the book provides students, researchers, and practitioners with an in-depth understanding of the nature, advantages, and limitations of various quantitative methodological approaches used in the field of corporate finance.

Acknowledgments

There are many people who supported and encouraged me in writing this book. I would like to begin with especially thanking Ted Lindblom and Stefan Sjögren for their detailed and valuable review and comments, which I received in very short time. I am very grateful to them for always being there for me. I am grateful to Zelalem Abay for his assistance on R programming in Chapter 3. I am thankful to my editors at Cambridge University Press (CUP), Valerie Appleby, Emma Collison, and Melissa Shivers, for their useful comments, discussions, and assistance during the development process. I would also like to especially thank the many anonymous reviewers (I think a total of 17) arranged by CUP for their detailed and constructive comments, questions, and discussions on various drafts of each chapter. I believe that their input has helped to improve the quality of this book tremendously. I am grateful to language editor and translator Linda Pettersson for her high-standard language editing service to polish and simplify my academic writing in many drafts of the book – from proposal to final version. I have learned remarkably from teaching these topics and discussions with my colleagues at the IFEL and Centre for Finance at the School of Business, Economics and Law at the University of Gothenburg over the years. So, I am also very grateful to my students and colleagues. Finally, I am thankful for the incredible support of my family, Elvira, Erland, and Linda. Any remaining errors are mine alone.

Abbreviations

2SLS	two-stage least squares
AAR	average abnormal return
ACF	autocorrelation function
ADF	augmented Dickey–Fuller test
ADL	autoregressive distributed lag
AIC	Akaike information criterion
APT	arbitrage pricing theory
AR	abnormal returns
AR	autoregressive
ARCH	autoregressive conditionally heteroskedastic model
ARDL	autoregressive distributed lagged model
ARIMA	autoregressive integrated moving average
ARMA	autoregressive moving average
ATE	average treatment effect
ATT	average treatment effect of treated
ATU	average treatment effect of untreated
BHARs	buy-and-hold abnormal returns
BIC	Bayesian information criterion
BIRCH	method to build a hierarchy in the data
BLUE	best linear unbiased estimator
BZ	Banzhaf index
CAPM	capital asset pricing model
CAR	cumulative abnormal returns
CDF	cumulative density function
CFO	chief financial officer
Clogit	conditional logit model
CLRM	classical linear regression model
CLT	central limit theorem
CSR	corporate social responsibility
DBSCAN	density-based methods for clustering data
DF	Dickey–Fuller test
DiD	difference-in-difference
EG	Engle–Granger test
ESG	environmental, social, and governance disclosure
FA	factor analysis
FD	first difference

FDA	U.S. Food and Drug Administration
FE	fixed effects
GARCH	generalized autoregressive conditional heteroskedasticity
GDPR	EU General Data Protection Regulation
GICR	geo-industry cluster ratio
GICS	global industry classification standard
GLS	generalized least squares
GMM	generalized method of moments
HAC	heteroskedasticity and autocorrelation consistent
HC	heteroskedasticity consistent
HHI	Herfindahl index
HQIC	Hannan–Quinn criterion
IGARCH	integrated GARCH
IIA	assumption of independence from irrelevant alternatives
IPO	initial public offering
IV	instrumental variable
KMO	Kaiser–Meyer–Olkin measure of sampling adequacy
LAD	least absolute deviation
LASSO	least absolute shrinkage and selection operator
LATE	local average treatment effect
LDIV	long difference (higher than first difference) of the dependent variable as instruments
LM	(Breusch–Godfrey) Lagrange multiplier test
LP	linear probability
LPM	linear probability model
LSDV	least-squares dummy variable
M&M	Modigliani and Miller's irrelevance proposition
MA	moving average
ML	machine learning
ML	maximum likelihood
MLE	maximum-likelihood estimation
Mprobit	multinomial probit model
MSCI	Morgan Stanley Capital International
NPV	net present value
OC	ownership concentration
OLS	ordinary least squares
PACF	partial autocorrelation function analysis
PCA	principal components analysis
PSM	propensity score matching
R&D	research and development (expenditures)
RDD	regression discontinuity design
RE	random effects
RLE	relative effect
ROA	return on assets

SKF	Swedish bearing and seal manufacturing company
SS	Shapley–Shubik index
SUTVA	stable unit treatment value assumption
UCLA	University of California, Los Angeles
VAR	vector autoregressive
VECM	vector error-correction model

1 Introduction

The overall aim of this book is to deepen readers' (mostly Bachelor, Master, and PhD students') understanding of empirical research in corporate finance studies and improve their ability to apply econometric methods in their own research/studies. In this sense, the book may not be general enough for an econometrics course for all finance students, including those interested in asset pricing studies. However, some of the examples in the book cover studies on the behavior of individual/institutional investors and how this relates to the cost of capital of firms. This link is important to understand in empirical corporate finance studies that examine the investor base. In theory, a significant amount of increase in investor base should decrease the cost of capital because investors require a lower return through diversification, which increases the stock price.

This interpretation clarifies the notion of cost of capital to the owners of a firm. If the company uses a combination of debt and equity to finance the invested asset, then the cost of capital is the weighted average cost of debt and equity (WACC). The rational firm manager will keep investing in an asset until the marginal rate of return on the asset is equal to the WACC used to finance the asset. This proposition follows from either of two criteria of rational decision-making: (i) the maximization of profits and (ii) the maximization of market value (see Modigliani and Miller, 1958). The first criterion means that the firm manager should invest if the asset increases the net profit to the owners of the firm. The net profit will only increase if the marginal rate of return on the invested asset exceeds the WACC used to finance the asset.

The second criterion means that the firm manager should invest in an asset if it increases the value of the owners' equity. In other words, it is worth acquiring an asset if the asset adds more value to the market value of the firm than the cost of acquiring the asset. The key point here is that the additional value generated by the asset is given by discounting the stream of cash flows at the opportunity cost of capital, which is proxied by the market rate of return. This capitalized value will exceed the cost if the marginal rate of return on the asset exceeds the WACC used to finance the asset. These two criteria of rational decision-making are related, as both suggest that the cost of capital, in equilibrium, is equal to the marginal rate of return on the invested asset, regardless of whether the funds are acquired through equity issuance or through debt instruments. The practical examples in the book examine how firm managers' investment decisions influence the cost of capital and hence firm value by applying the empirical methods covered in the chapters.

The book may reach out to a broader group of readers, rather than those only interested in corporate finance, even though the applications mainly concern corporate finance studies. It covers my lecture notes from the courses Quantitative Research Methods in Business Administration (PhD level), Research Methods in Accounting and Financial Management (Master level), and Corporate Finance (Bachelor/Master level) that I have been teaching at the University of Gothenburg since 2006.

The book is a practical method book focusing on research covering essential basic econometric models to illustrate how to apply them to research by closely following some of the well-written and pedagogical books in econometrics, for instance, Wooldridge (2002), Brooks (2019), Stock and Watson (2019). However, this book provides applications and lab work on corporate finance studies, rather than from all sorts of fields of economics and business. The ideas in the examples are then summarized and interpreted in a simple way so that students and other readers can easily understand the applications to corporate finance.

1.1 Book Outline

The book begins with hypothesis development, identification strategy, and the nature of sampling. It then stresses the interpretation and assumptions of basic econometric models used in corporate finance studies, such as ordinary least squares, two-stage least squares, time-series models, event studies, panel-data models, and limited dependent-variable models. The main focus is on the application of these models, not the derivations or theorems. While presenting the models, each section also mentions why a particular empirical approach is most appropriate for a given dataset. This is complemented with applications, lab work, and mini cases, providing examples of the appropriateness of the empirical approach for different datasets.

However, students need to understand the regression equations to be able to interpret how the models work. Thus, the book also presents and step-by-step explains the regression equations behind the models. Each chapter ends with an application of the selected models presented, using collected data from our research by focusing on the interpretation of the results. The book provides detailed datasets and software code for these applications. Almost all data used in the applications and lab work come from my own research, obtained from databases provided at the Gothenburg University Library (https://databaser.ub.gu.se/?lang=en) or are simulated. At the time the research was published in journals, these datasets were freely available to download from databases like Harvard Dataverse: https://dataverse.harvard.edu.

In addition, at the end of the chapters (where appropriate), assignments (so-called "lab work"), the related sample datasets, and software code for the analyses are also provided via the book's online resources page (www.cambridge.org/mavruk), allowing students to apply the techniques easily. The selected chapters end with a mini case study, where students replicate the main findings in published research using the models that are covered in the chapters. For these mini case studies, students download the data and related software code from Harvard Dataverse: https://dataverse.harvard.edu.

The book introduces the software program Stata to replicate the studies in the chapters and to work with the labs, but to provide students with more alternatives, Python and R code are also given on the online resources page (www.cambridge.org/mavruk).[1] This code provides solutions for the applied work, the lab work, but also the mini cases. For example, the provided code for Python and R in the chapters can be applied to produce the results in the mini cases, if students prefer to use these software programs instead of Stata.

Particularly, in the introductory chapters, emphasis is put on how to interpret the empirical results generated by Stata code. The text proposes hands-on pedagogical features and offers plenty of data, code, tables, figures, and lab work, providing more student-focused materials. Both the quantity and quality of the code and datasets offered attempts to secure high quality in pedagogical features, which can be a significant value-added for Bachelor, Master and PhD students interested in corporate finance, but also for other students and readers.

Considering that students reading this book may have highly variable backgrounds, the introductory chapters cover a set of basic terminology and definitions in the econometric field. The chapters also include simple explanations and applications of the models to bring clarity and logic to the presented topics. Unlike standard econometrics textbooks, the main emphasis in this book is nevertheless on data, hypotheses, and adequate writing of a research project.

After reading this textbook, students will be able to identify a relevant quantitative methodological approach in relation to a research problem, as well as develop an appropriate research design applied to topics in corporate finance and business studies. Students will be able to analyze and critically evaluate quantitative research methods and conduct a computer-aided statistical analysis on various types of datasets. The book can also be valuable for practitioners and professionals in the field of corporate finance and business studies, as it focuses on the applications of the models, including data-collection methods, sampling techniques, survey design, analysis and interpretation of quantitative data. Taken together, the book provides students, researchers, and practitioners with an in-depth understanding of the nature, advantages, and limitations of various quantitative methodological approaches used in the field of corporate finance.

[1] For some of the analysis/models, the Python and R code produces slightly different results than those produced by Stata (and each other). The differences may depend on the different algorithms used in the programs and, sometimes, it is not possible to find exact matching code. Readers may use the Stata output as a benchmark.

1.2 Detailed Content of the Models Presented in the Chapters

The detailed content of the models presented in each chapter is as follows. Chapter 2 emphasizes the nature of sampling, non-parametric analysis, and hypothesis testing. During the hypothesis development and identification strategy part, the focus is on four major questions presented in Angrist and Pischke (2009):

- What is the causal relationship of interest?
- What would the ideal experiment look like?
- What is the identification strategy?
- What is the mode of statistical inference?

In the chapter, these questions are related to examples from corporate finance studies.

Thereafter, during the sampling section, it focuses on the following parts:

- Terminology.
- Data types.
- Unit of analysis.
- Data management.
- The nature of sampling (sample vs. census, sample design, sampling methods, sample size, sampling problems).

To be able to replicate the applications presented in the chapters, work with the assignments, and eventually carry on students' own studies, Chapter 3 introduces basic programming and data management in Stata. However, Python and R software codes are also provided on the online resources page (www.cambridge.org/mavruk) for those who prefer to develop in these programs. The book introduces the software program immediately after the introductory chapter, as the aim is to encourage students to replicate the studies and work with their labs. The learning-by-doing approach is an effective tool to learn from method books. Thus, the chapter provides plenty of practical information that might be missing from standard econometrics texts. In particular, the chapter provides details describing how to clean data, deal with outliers and missing observations, merge and sort, create dummy variables, prepare data for analysis, and so on. Hence, this chapter can also be seen as a supplement to other textbooks that can be recommended to students. Having said that, the chapter should not be seen as one standalone chapter on Stata; rather, it is an introductory read for the upcoming chapters, which embed the Stata materials parallel to the core content and models.

Chapter 4 covers survey-data analysis and the focus is on bivariate analysis (parametric, non-parametric, and semi-parametric tests) and principal component analysis. The chapter also briefly discusses factor analysis and its difference from principal component analysis. Although survey data may form a small part of financial research, there are some examples of capital structure decisions examined using survey data. Survey-data analysis also combines other fields of business administration with corporate finance studies by quantifying some of the qualitative information provided in the survey studies.

Chapter 5 introduces the classical linear regression model (CLRM) by emphasizing the assumptions and applications of the CLRM. OLS is a standard estimation method that is used to estimate the coefficients of a linear regression equation, examining the relationship between one or more independent variables and a dependent variable. Least squares means that the technique minimizes the sum of squared residuals. In other words, the technique measures the distance from each data point to the regression line (errors), calculates the square of these errors, and then sums all the squared errors. In this chapter, the assumptions of the CLRM are discussed in detail; the remaining chapters build on these assumptions by relaxing them one by one. So, the models presented in each of the remaining chapters can be seen as a remedy when one of the assumptions of the CLRM does not hold in the data.

Chapter 6 discusses the endogeneity problem by briefly covering the most used methods to deal with endogeneity bias in corporate finance studies. The following topics are covered:

- Sources of endogeneity bias.
- Two-stage least squares (2SLS), an instrumental variable (IV) approach.
- Treatment effects.
- Matching techniques.
- Regression discontinuity design (RDD).

Chapter 7 presents the basic time-series analysis models and discusses why some of the CLRM assumptions may be violated when using time-series data. The focus is on tests of autocorrelation, stationarity in time-series data, and cointegration. The models that are used to remedy problems with time-series data – such as autoregressive distributed lag (ADL) models, moving average (MA) models, autoregressive moving average (ARMA), autoregressive integrated moving average (ARIMA), generalized autoregressive conditional heteroskedasticity (GARCH), and vector autoregressive (VAR) models – are briefly presented.

Chapter 8 provides an introduction to different types of event studies, testing weak, semi-strong, and strong forms of market efficiency hypotheses. The chapter further discusses examples and models from: (i) the asset pricing literature, examining the weak form of market efficiency; (ii) the effects of firm-level and macro news on stock returns, testing semi-strong efficiency; as well as (iii) insider trading, testing the strong form of efficiency. The models covered include abnormal returns (AR) and cumulative abnormal returns (CAR) calculations, as well as statistical tests of AR and CAR.

Chapter 9 covers linear panel-data models by providing a wide range of examples within corporate finance. The models and sections covered include:

- Least-squares dummy-variable (LSDV) estimator.
- Fixed-effects (FE) model.
- First-difference (FD) model.
- Difference-in-difference (DiD) model.

- Random-effects (RE) model.
- Hausman–Taylor random-effects instrumental variable method.
- Stationarity in panel data.
- A short review of the generalized method of moments (GMM).
- Introduction to dynamic panel-data models.

Chapter 10 briefly introduces a selection of models with limited dependent variables. The focus is on how these models are used for firms' decision-making in general and their capital structure decisions in particular, but also for investors' decision-making and its connection to the cost of capital of firms. The chapter covers the following models:

- Linear probability (LP) model.
- Logit and probit models.
- Latent-variable model.
- Maximum-likelihood estimation (MLE).
- Multinomial logit and probit models.
- Conditional logit model.
- Ordered response models.
- Corner-solution models, tobit model.
- Censored and truncated models.
- Heckman selection model.
- Count-data models.

Chapter 11 provides some guidelines for writing empirical papers in corporate finance. It introduces a standard example for the structure of an empirical paper that can be useful for students studying various thesis courses. The chapter also provides some writing tips.

Finally, Chapter 12 discusses future directions and gives a brief overview of the types of machine learning (ML) models that are applied to (corporate) finance studies. ML is a growing multidisciplinary field and has broad applications, for example in finance studies but also other fields in business studies. The applications in corporate finance often seek to learn patterns from so-called training data and use the information to make predictions in the test data. The chapter briefly describes two major types of ML, supervised learning and unsupervised learning.

Besides ML methods, recently, the use of experimental methods in corporate finance has become more popular. One extension of the book could be to add experimental methods to its chapters. However, the use of experimental methods is a rather new phenomenon and may deserve more than a few chapters, perhaps a textbook on its own. Students and other readers are therefore referred to Gibbens (2012) for applications in finance and Stock and Watson (2019) for applications in economics.

KEY TERMS

The aim of the book; datasets; lab work; code in Stata, Python, and R; detailed chapter content.

REFERENCES

Angrist, J. D. and Pischke, J-S. 2009. *Mostly Harmless Econometrics: An Empiricist's Companion*. Princeton University Press, Princeton, NJ.

Brooks, C. 2019. *Introductory Econometrics for Finance* (4th ed.). Cambridge University Press, Cambridge.

Gibbens, J. C. 2012. *Experiments in Quantitative Finance*. Routledge, New York.

Modigliani, F. and Miller, M. H. 1958. The cost of capital, corporation finance and the theory of investment. *American Economic Review*, 48, 261–297.

Stock, J. and Watson, M. 2019. *Introduction to Economics (Global Edition)*. Princeton University Press, Princeton, NJ.

Wooldridge, J. M. 2002. *Econometric Analysis of Cross-Section and Panel Data*. MIT Press, Cambridge, MA.

2 The Nature of Sampling, Non-parametric Analysis, and Hypothesis Testing

INTRODUCTION

This chapter covers some terminology related to sampling and sampling bias, sampling techniques, and introduces hypothesis testing. It prepares the reader for the models and lab work in the coming chapters. The focus is on observational data. Although various databases offer a wide range of variables, covering firm and stock characteristics, observational data often have many missing values and accessible information is limited to listed, large, and well-known firms. Moreover, it is not uncommon to find some incorrect values of these variables. For a successful research project, it is therefore crucial to consider the expected outcome from the planned study before engaging in any data collection. Angrist and Pischke (2009) outline several steps for a successful research agenda.

As a first step, the casual relationship of interest in a study should be well thought out. The direction of the cause and effect has to be clear before you move to the next step. A casual relationship will lead to making predictions about an outcome when the circumstances or policies change. In other words, it will lead to drawing conclusions on what would happen in an alternative state of the world, called counterfactual. This step is so crucial that the book devotes the whole of Chapter 6 to descriptions and tests of causality.

Second, the expected outcome from the planned study in an ideal experiment should be considered. It is an experiment that could ideally be used to examine the casual relationship of interest. Thus, if you can describe the ideal experiment well, it will help you to better formulate your research questions. An ideal experiment is a study without practical, ethical, or resource-related constraints. It includes some treatments (or events) that are randomly assigned for a number of study units.

The third step is the identification strategy. Since an ideal experiment might be costly to conduct, you often use and draw conclusions from the observational data. A challenge is then to connect these conclusions to the expected outcome that could be drawn from an ideal experiment, so-called identification strategy. Thus, the way you use the observational data to approximate an ideal experiment is the identification strategy. The initial step to define a good identification strategy is how well the sample for the study is conducted and data managed. This chapter focuses on this initial step, sampling techniques, and hypothesis testing. More specifically, the chapter provides descriptions and explanations of the basic concepts in research design using observational data. The focus is on different data levels and types, units of analysis, sample design and methods, and hypothesis testing. Chapters 4 and 10 are concerned with different models for identification strategies.

Finally, you should consider the model of statistical inference. This step includes a description of the population, the sample to be drawn, and the assumptions made when making inferences on the population. This chapter provides a detailed description of these terminologies. When the data lack clusters or groups, the inference may be more straightforward. However, making inferences can be complex when the data are clustered or grouped. This chapter covers different sampling techniques and statistics applied to make inferences using the different samples.

In sum, the quantitative methods are essentially tools; if what is being studied is not important or interesting, the results will not have an impact on the field of study. Given that the research question is important, the method chosen – together with the quality of the analysis/interpretations – will also help with the identification strategy and to draw strong conclusions for the population of the study. The latter step includes statistical inference and covers estimation of standard errors. In this step, alternative explanations and mechanisms that drive the results are also provided.

2.1 Terminology Related to Sampling and Sampling Bias

2.1.1 Terminology Related to Sampling

It might be useful to review the levels of measurement or scales before presenting sampling techniques. These levels are helpful for identifying the actual unit of analysis in a study. There are four levels of measurement: nominal, ordinal, interval, and ratio. The first two can be grouped as qualitative (discrete) data and the last two can be classified as quantitative (continuous) data.

Nominal data. Nominal data include categories that cannot be arranged or ranked in any order. They are mutually exclusive.

Ordinal data. Ordinal data can be arranged in various orders, but the differences between the values do not matter. For example, according to one finance theory, if the risk and expected return of several investment portfolios are the same, and in the absence of behavioral biases, differences in the type of investment portfolio should not influence the portfolio value.

Interval level. The interval level is similar to the ordinal level, but the differences are meaningful. For instance, there may be no natural zero point in interval-level data; a stock return or relative price difference could be mentioned as an example.

Ratio level. The final level of data is ratio data, which is similar to interval data but has a natural zero point. Revenue without cost or any other deduction is a good example. If the ratio-level data is observed in natural units, it is said that the data is in absolute scale.

The choice of method depends largely on the statistical data type, covered next.

Cross-sectional data. Cross-sectional data are collected in a single time period. Classical linear regression models are based on such cross-sectional data.

Time-series data. Time-series data are collected over a specific time period and since, for an individual unit, it carries more information than the cross-sectional data, more advanced techniques are used to analyze these types of datasets.

Panel data. Finally, in panel data, the units (e.g., firms or stocks) are observed over time. The main difference between the time-series and panel data is that the units re-enter as observations in panel data, whereas you only observe the values of the units over time in time-series data. This feature of panel data makes it possible to study the changes in the characteristics of the units. These firm characteristics may or may not be observed, but since the information is richer, the applications of more advanced techniques in the analysis make it possible to capture the effects of such unobserved characteristics.[1]

To complete the basic concepts and definitions in sampling techniques, this chapter introduces some terminologies.

Unit of analysis. The unit of analysis is the level at which the analysis is conducted. This is important to carefully consider, as in some studies the unit of analysis may not be that clear. For instance, since the seminal work of Modigliani and Miller (1958), research on capital structure has focused on examining two different theories. The first is the static trade-off theory, in which firms have a leverage target that balances costs such as distress costs, stockholder–bondholder agency conflicts, and so on and benefits such as tax savings, mitigated manager–shareholder agency costs, and so on. The second theory is the pecking order (Myers and Majluf, 1984), which suggests that firms follow a financing hierarchy with the aim of minimizing the adverse selection costs of equity issuance (Graham and Leary, 2011). In a survey of capital structure that examines which of these capital structure theories firms follow, it is not clear whether the unit is the chief executive officer (CEO) or other director(s) making the capital structure decision, such as the chief financial officer (CFO), or the unit is the firm itself. It could also be that a financing decision is being made for a project, not for a firm. In that case, the unit of analysis would be the project. For a well-defined identification strategy, the connection between the research question and the unit of analysis should be clear.

Population. The population is the set of units that the study aims to examine, so it also needs serious consideration. If the population is not well considered, the researcher will neither be able to define the identification strategy well, nor make the correct inference to draw strong conclusions from the analysis. A variable is a measurable characteristic of the population.

[1] See Brooks (2019) for more details on data types.

Census. The analysis of the population, or variables in the population, is a census. It is uncommon to describe or apply more advanced statistical tools to examine a single population, since no inference is necessary. In a census study, since you already have the population, you do not need to collect and examine a sample in order to draw conclusions about the population. However, if the research questions are concerned with comparing two or more populations, making comparison tests is useful.

Sample. A sample is a selected subset of units in the population. There are several reasons why a study uses a sample in the analysis rather than conducting a census study. First, it might not be possible to obtain and analyze all the units in the population. Second, it might be costly and time consuming to analyze the whole population. Third, examining or conducting certain tests might be destructive for the population and may not be allowed by the regulations. Finally, because it is costly and time consuming, it may not be easy to rerun the analyses in the population for robustness or sensitivity analysis. However, if the population is small and the units (or characteristics of the units) are very different from each other, then the choice of a census study over a sample study is more plausible.

2.1.2 Terminology Related to Sampling Bias

Sampling error. If the characteristics of the units are quite different between the sample and the population, this will lead to (large) differences between the sample parameters and the population parameters. A pure random sampling should take into account these sampling errors. Besides the sampling errors, there might be non-sampling errors, which are not related to the sampling techniques.

Sample-selection bias. The study may wrongly select firms with certain characteristics. It could also be that firms in the sample get delisted or cease operation over time, leading to so-called survivorship bias. Such bias will lead to only examining the firms that survive in the market. This bias would overestimate the parameters. making the results unrepresentative for the population as a whole.

Self-selection bias. A self-selection bias occurs when individuals may influence the decision to be included in a certain study or program. It is then said that individuals "self-select" themselves into the study. Participating in the study may help improve the outcomes for these individuals.

Response bias. This bias is more related to survey studies in which data are collected by asking questions to potential respondents. For instance, in a survey of capital structure, some respondents may not state their true opinions, perhaps due to the firm having built a strong culture and it being difficult to make changes in the organization. A closely related bias is measurement error, where the respondent has an incentive to provide misleading responses.

Non-response bias. Respondents whose opinions deviate a lot from others may not respond to the survey. It is also possible that respondents who are unhappy with the current situation may respond to the survey, while those who are happy may ignore it.

While random sampling would take care of sampling errors, most of the biases arise because of non-sampling errors. The remaining chapters in the book cover quantitative methods that can correct some of the mentioned biases.

2.2 Sample Design

There are some steps involved before beginning the sampling for the analysis. The first step is to decide what information is required for the study. For instance, if the study involves hypothesis testing and regression analysis, you need to consider and determine the outcome of interest (dependent variable), the main variable of interest (main independent variable), and the control variables (other covariates). The second step is to consider the relevant population or a list of potential populations. The third step is the decision on the sampling technique and the sample size, which is the focus of the next section in this chapter. Finally, you need to decide on the statistical method(s) to infer population estimates from the sample data. The last step makes it possible to draw appropriate conclusions from the sample. The sampling methods can be classified into four categories: random sample, stratified random sample, cluster sample, systematic sample.

2.2.1 Simple Random Sampling

In a simple random sample, data of size n are selected from a population of size N, so that each unit in the population has an equal probability of being selected in the sample. Such a random sample can easily be produced in the statistical software Stata with the following code: `sample n, count`, where n is the sample size. In studies using sampling, it might be good to know how the standard error for the mean, *se*, is calculated. The standard error shows how different the population mean is likely to be from a sample mean. It is important because it shows an estimate of how well the sample data represents the whole population. In other words, standard errors are used to make an inference for the population. The standard error for the mean of a simple random sample is given in the Appendix for Chapter 2 at the end of the book.

2.2.2 Stratified Random Sampling

Stratified random sampling divides the population into non-overlapping groups, so-called strata or cohorts, of similar units. The technique then separately selects a random sample from each group (so-called stratum). Finally, it combines all these random samples in order to obtain the full sample. This technique is useful if there is a large heterogeneity among the groups in the population, and if the units within a group are quite homogenous. For example, it is often difficult to obtain detailed investor data with individual ID numbers, so that investors can be followed over time. One possibility is then to group investors, based on their age and gender in each period, into k number of strata and then randomly select investors from each stratum. Here, the number of investors i in each stratum is defined as n_i, where $i = 1, 2, \ldots, n_i$. The main variable of interest in the analysis is then averaged over each stratum, $\bar{x}_{\text{str}}$, either by equally weighting or value-weighting the investments in the stratum.

The sum of all investors in the k strata gives the total number of investors in the population, $N = \sum_{\text{str}=1}^{k} n_{\text{str}}$. One challenge is to determine the sample size of investors to be selected from each stratum. The most commonly used technique is proportional allocation, determined by the ratio $\frac{n}{N}$, where n represents the number of investors in a stratum, str, and N is the total number of investors in the data. Since this measure is a ratio, the resulting sample size needs to be rounded to the nearest integer. The overall mean calculated from the stratified random sample is the weighted average of the strata sample means, $\bar{\bar{x}} = \frac{1}{N} \sum_{\text{str}=1}^{k} n_{\text{str}} \, \bar{x}_{\text{str}}$, where the relative strata sizes are used as weights. The standard error for the mean of a stratified random sample is given in the Appendix for Chapter 2 at the end of the book.

2.2.3 Cluster Sampling

The main difference between stratified random sampling and cluster sampling is that, in the former, the units do not change groups over time. In the example above, investors in gender and age groups are in the same group over the entire study period. However, cluster sampling relaxes this assumption and groups, for instance, investors in clusters of c by geography, time, and so on. Note that within each cluster of c (e.g., geography), there are many investors with different age and gender, and these investors may move to different areas over time. Hence, the unit of analysis in such cluster samplings would be at the geography level. The next step is to draw simple random samples with size n from each cluster (you could also use a stratified random sampling technique at this stage). Each random sample would be a representative of the cluster and then finally the technique combines all the random samples. Cluster sampling is useful if the investors and firms in the example are spread over a large area and/or there are many different districts in an area. However, compared to stratified random sampling, there is less precision in cluster sampling as the technique makes it possible to draw samples from larger groups and, hence, excludes a significant number of units of the population from being selected in the sample. The standard error of the mean of a clustered random sample that assigns equal weights for each cluster is given in the Appendix for Chapter 2 at the end of the book.

2.2.4 Systematic Random Sampling

This method is favorable if the purpose is more administrative, since the technique follows a system in random sampling. The first step is to identify the total number of units in the population of N, then to identify the sampling ratio of m, which is the size of the sample in the subset, n, divided by the population size, $\frac{n}{N}$. The systematic part begins with identifying a random start and then drawing simple random samples. To continue the example of the investor behavior study, let's suppose that 10,000 investors are required for the study, which represents a sample size of n, and the study will draw a random sample of investors from Gothenburg, which has 42 districts d. Thus, the population size N will be the population size of Gothenburg (579,281 measured in 2019). The study will choose a random start of 1–10 blocks of b in each district d. The first district, say Gamlestaden, has a population size of 10,000, which means that the sampling ratio m from Gamlestaden is 1.7% ($10{,}000 \div 579{,}281$). Since the study uses 10,000 investors, you should draw 170 investors from Gamlestaden ($10{,}000 \times 0.017$). These 170 investors will be selected from the random start of 1–10 blocks. The same procedure continues until the samples are drawn from all 42 districts in Gothenburg. The standard error of the mean of a systematic random sample is given in the Appendix for Chapter 2 at the end of the book.

2.2.5 Determining Sample Size

Determining the sample size is not an easy task. Perhaps beginning with examining the sample size in closely related previous studies is a good idea. This strategy makes it possible to compare the current study's results with those obtained from previous studies. However, all data are different with regards to time and geography, and have their own defaults. Thus, considering a number of aspects before determining the sample size would save some time. First, the greater the variance of the units within the population, the larger the sample you should select in order to obtain a high estimation precision. A larger sample will lead to an increased precision of the estimate, since proxy variables are often used instead of exact measures of units due to lack of data availability. Using a larger sample will also satisfy the normality assumption (due to the central limit theorem[2]), which is the underlying assumption in many models. Second, the narrower the interval range (e.g., age groups in our example), the larger the sample that should be selected in order to avoid sample selection bias. Similarly, the greater the number of sub-units in the population, the larger the sample that should be selected.

[2] The central limit theorem (CLT) suggests that the distribution of sample means converges to a normal distribution when the sample size grows larger, regardless of the population's underlying distribution. A rule of thumb, although it might be a strong assumption, is that sample sizes equal to or greater than 30 are considered sufficient for this theorem to hold.

There are also statistical methods to determine the sample size. If the population can be assumed to be normally distributed and its variance σ is known, then the sample size is given by

$$n = \frac{z_{\alpha/2}^2 \sigma^2}{\text{ME}^2}, \tag{2.1}$$

where n is the sample size, z is the standardized normal distribution whose values can be obtained from the z-table, and α represents the significance level. $\alpha / 2$ means that both sides of the normal distribution (upper tail and lower tail) are being examined. For instance, with a 95% confidence level in examining both sides of the distribution, the z-value is 1.96. Finally, the margin of error (ME) is the mean sampling error, or put differently, it is the (self-determined) bound of the error of the estimation.

Equation (2.1) ignores the population correction factor by assuming that you can accept small n in the sample relative to the population size N. Let's apply this formula to an example and suppose that the aim is to estimate the investment cost of a project mean, μ. The standard deviation, σ, is \$30 and there are 500 projects (N) that have a similar risk and expected return to the project being considered. The task is to find how many samples of existing projects are needed to estimate μ for a given bound of the error of estimation ME = \$5 with 95% confidence level $(\alpha = 0.05, z = 1.96)$ using simple random sampling. Using Equation (2.1) above, n is calculated as

$$n = \frac{1.96^2 \times 30^2}{5^2} = 138. \tag{2.2}$$

The result suggests that the study requires about 138 samples that are randomly selected from the population size of 500 to estimate the investment cost of a project μ with a bound of the error of estimation ME = \$5. For the sensitivity analysis, let's vary ME by 5% and observe the results. If ME decreases by 5% to 4.75 (insert this value in the formula instead), then n becomes 153. If, instead, ME increases by 5% to 5.25 then n would be 125. The result explains how important it is to choose ME; a 5 percentage point variation in this assumption leads to about a 10 percentage point change, on average, in the sample size n. Also, note that decreasing ME will lead to a larger increase in n than the corresponding decrease in n when increasing ME, implying that the effects of a decrease and an increase in ME will have asymmetric effects on n.

Equation (2.1) assumes that the standard deviation of the population is known. If the standard deviation of the population is unknown (which is usually the case), then you can replace the standard deviation of the sample with the standard deviation of the population, σ. In this case, the t-distribution in the formula is used instead of the z-distribution. More formally:

$$n = \frac{t_{\alpha/2}^2 s^2}{\text{ME}^2}. \tag{2.3}$$

One difference between applying the t-distribution and the z-distribution is the number of degrees of freedom $(n-1)$ used for the t-distribution: $t_{\alpha/2}$, instead of the sample size n for the z-distribution. The degree of freedom represents the values that freely or independently (from each other) vary in the dataset. To provide an intuition, suppose that you have the values $i = 5,\ 10,\ 15$ in a dataset, which has an average value of 10. You could independently choose the first two digits of these values. However, the last digit is always fixed, given that you have already chosen the first two digits and, more importantly, you know the average value. For instance, if you have already chosen the digits 5 and 10, then the last digit has to be 15: it is fixed or not freely chosen, since the average is 10. So, in this simple example with $n = 3$ values (or observations), the number of values that freely vary is 2 $(n-1)$, because the last digit is always fixed. The t-distribution is similar to the standard normal distribution, symmetrical and bell-shaped, but it is more spread out depending on the number of degrees of freedom.

2.3 Hypothesis Testing

A hypothesis is often developed in a parametric analysis, which uses models that assume a functional form with one or more parameters. In a hypothesis, you make an assumption about a population mean (parameter). This assumption may or may not be true. The ideal way to test a hypothesis is to conduct a census study. However, it is often infeasible and in general a random sample from the population is examined to test the hypothesis. If the results obtained from the random sample are consistent with the hypothesis, you cannot reject the hypothesis. If not, it is rejected.

In a hypothesis test, the null hypothesis H_0 usually represents the status quo and cannot be rejected unless there is significant evidence against it. The alternative hypothesis, H_a, to the null hypothesis is supported only if H_0 is rejected. The alternative hypothesis is often the research hypothesis. If you find a significant relationship, for instance, between the main independent and dependent variable, the null hypothesis of no relationship is rejected, that is you find significant evidence that supports the research hypothesis. However, there are some exceptions; depending on the research, you can just as well formulate the null hypothesis as the research hypothesis. One example is the application of the capital asset pricing model (CAPM) to real data. If the research question concerns that, for instance, a particular (local) bias in individual investors' portfolios does not lead to inefficiency in the stock markets on aggregate, then the null hypothesis (suggesting that there are no abnormal returns for holding locally biased portfolios) would be the research hypothesis. Another example is examining the distributions of the variables. Such tests usually have the null hypothesis that a particular distribution that is being tested holds.

When testing the hypothesis, the analysis often encounters two types of error, so-called Type I and Type II errors. A Type I error means that you reject H_0 when it is true, while a Type II error means failing to reject H_0 when it is false. Table 2.1 provides a more formal presentation of these errors.

Table 2.1 Summary of Type I and Type II errors

	H_0 is true	H_0 is false
Reject H_0	Type I error (α)	Correctly tested $(1-\alpha)$
Do not reject H_0	Correctly tested $(1-\beta)$	Type II error (β)

Table 2.1 also presents the probability of making a Type I error (α) and a Type II error (β). Accordingly, the probability of not making a Type I error is $(1-\alpha)$ and the probability of not making a Type II error is $(1-\beta)$. The parameter α would also represent the size of the test. Since α is the probability of rejecting a true hypothesis, it is usually set to a low value to minimize the chance of rejecting a true hypothesis. In corporate finance studies, α is usually set to 5%, meaning that you need strong evidence to reject H_0. The parameter $(1-\alpha)$ is known as the power of the test; the probability of correctly rejecting H_0 when it is false. Note also that for a fixed sample size there is a trade-off between α and β; the lower we set α, the higher is the probability of making a Type II error (β) and vice versa.

To test a hypothesis, the custom is to use decision rules with reference to (i) a region of acceptance, (ii) the *p*-value, and (iii) the confidence interval. The region of acceptance refers to a range of values and if the test statistic (e.g., observed *t*-value) falls within this region of acceptance, the null hypothesis cannot be rejected. The values outside the region of acceptance are called the region of rejection. If the observed *t*-value falls outside the region of acceptance (hence, within the region of rejection), the null hypothesis is then rejected. The significance level α determines the region of acceptance (hence, rejection). If the null hypothesis is rejected, this means that it is rejected at the α level of significance.

When the standard deviation of the population is unknown, which is usually the case, a *t*-test to conduct a test about the population mean is used. When examining the population proportion, a *z*-test is used instead. You calculate the (observed) *t*-value by using the sample and compare it with the critical *t*-value that is obtained from the *t*-table. If the population standard deviation is unknown, the observed *t*-value can be calculated as

$$t_{\text{observed}} = \frac{\bar{x} - \mu_0}{s / \sqrt{n}}, \tag{2.4}$$

where $\bar{x}$ is the mean of a sample of size n with standard deviation s, and μ_0 is the estimated value of the population mean. The aim is to test whether this claimed value of μ_0 is true. In the test, s is used to estimate the population standard deviation of σ, since it is unknown. The observed *t*-value is then compared with the critical *t*-value obtained from the *t*-table for a given (or predetermined) α and $n-1$ degrees of freedom.

If the aim is to examine only one side of the sampling distribution, the rejection region is on only one side. The test is then a one-sided test. For example, testing the null hypothesis that the mean investment cost is less than or equal to $100 million.

The alternative hypothesis is that the mean investment cost is greater than \$100 million. In this example, the region of rejection would cover the values located on the upper side of the sampling distribution, values greater than \$100 million. If the aim is to examine the lower side of the sampling distribution instead, the null hypothesis is the mean investment cost being greater than, or equal to, \$100 million. In this case, the alternative hypothesis would be that the mean investment cost is less than \$100 million. The region of rejection would cover the values less than \$100 million, the lower tail of the sampling distribution.

Finally, if the aim is to examine both sides of the sampling distribution, the region of rejection would lie on both sides of the sampling distribution, which is called a two-sided test. In the example, the null hypothesis would then be formulated as the mean investment cost being equal to \$100 million. The alternative hypothesis would be that the mean investment cost is not equal to \$100 million (less than \$100 million or greater than \$100 million). The region of rejection would cover the values both less than \$100 million and greater than \$100 million. Table 2.2 presents the rejection principles.

The Stata code to make a (one-sample) *t*-test is `ttest` and the program provides both one-sided (for either of the sides) and two-sided *t*-tests along with their probabilities or *p*-values. These *p*-values can be used as a second or alternative decision rule to test the hypothesis, since it also measures the strength of evidence in support of the null hypothesis. Suppose that the critical *t*-value obtained from the *t*-table is t_{critical}. The obtained *p*-value would then represent the probability of observing the test statistics, t_{observed} as high as t_{critical}, assuming that the null hypothesis holds. In other words, the *p*-value measures how likely the observed result is due to chance. Since this is a probability, its values vary between 0 and 1. Lower *p*-values indicate that the observed result is unlikely to be due to chance. The decision rule is as follows: if the obtained *p*-value is less than the preset significance level α, the null hypothesis can be rejected. Approximate probabilities or *p*-values are provided for one-sided tests in Table 2.2. Similarly, regression outputs in Stata usually provide two-sided *p*-values, which can be used to calculate one-sided probabilities following the approximate approach in Table 2.2. You could also use the confidence interval

Table 2.2 Hypothesis rejection principles

Hypothesis	Reject if	Reject if (approximate)
Upper-tail test $H_0 : \mu \le \mu_0$ $H_a : \mu > \mu_0$	$t_{\text{observed}} > t_\alpha$	$p/2 < \alpha$
Lower-tail test $H_0 : \mu \ge \mu_0$ $H_a : \mu < \mu_0$	$t_{\text{observed}} < -t_\alpha$	$(1-p)/2 < \alpha$
Two-sided test $H_0 : \mu = \mu_0$ $H_a : \mu \ne \mu_0$	$\lvert t_{\text{observed}} \rvert > t_{\alpha/2}$	$p < \alpha$

as a decision rule: if the confidence interval includes zero, the null hypothesis cannot be rejected; if not, the null hypothesis is rejected. In a regression analysis, the Stata output provides the same result for all three decision rules. It is probably easier to use the p-values as a decision rule, but some researchers use the region of acceptance approach or the confidence intervals.

When testing hypotheses about population proportion, you can make an approximation to the normal distribution if the sample size n is large.[3] Table 2.3 presents the rejection principles for a test of the population principle.

Table 2.3 Hypothesis rejection principles for population proportion

Hypothesis	Reject if	Reject if (approximate)
Upper-tail test $H_0 : p \leq p_0$ $H_a : p > p_0$	$z_{\text{observed}} > z_\alpha$	$p/2 < \alpha$
Lower-tail test $H_0 : p \geq p_0$ $H_a : p < p_0$	$z_{\text{observed}} < -z_\alpha$	$(1-p)/2 < \alpha$
Two-sided test $H_0 : p = p_0$ $H_a : p \neq p_0$	$\lvert z_{\text{observed}} \rvert > z_{\alpha/2}$	$p < \alpha$

The test statistic z is given by

$$z = \frac{\hat{p} - p_0}{\sqrt{\frac{p_0(1-p_0)}{n}}}, \tag{2.5}$$

where $\hat{p}$ is the estimated proportion in the sample, p_0 is the claimed proportion in the population, and n is the sample size.

2.4 Summary

The quality of research depends on, among other aspects of the research design, how representative the sample of the population is. Thus, it is essential to use the most relevant and appropriate sampling techniques in a research design. Once the sample is selected, the study should then focus on how well the expected outcome from the planned research design matches the expected outcome from an ideal experiment. This is an experiment where the researcher can control all aspects of the research design without any practical, ethical, or resource-related constraints. A well-formulated and described ideal experiment will lead us to better formulate research questions, develop hypotheses, and eventually examine the causal relationship of interest. In corporate finance research, it is important that the hypothesis is closely tied to economic theory

[3] See Dewhurst (2006) and Stock and Watson (2019) for more details.

and previous literature. It is only then that we can draw meaningful conclusions from the studied relationships and deductions will follow from the hypothesis.

This chapter focuses on sample selection, identification strategy, and hypothesis development. It is an introductory chapter aimed at preparing the reader for the models and the lab work in the coming chapters. The sample selection part explores the steps for a well-structured sample design. The chapter first covers some terminology and then discusses data types, the unit of analysis, data management, and different sampling methods. The identification strategy part covers the causal relationship of interest, ideal experiments, and statistical inference. Software Stata codes are provided for the examples. The chapter ends with a hypothesis development section that details some decision/rejection rules.

KEY TERMS

Terminology; sampling techniques; non-parametric analysis; semi-parametric analysis; hypothesis tests.

REFERENCES

Angrist, J. D. and Pischke, J-S. 2009. *Mostly Harmless Econometrics: An Empiricist's Companion*. Princeton University Press, Princeton, NJ.

Dewhurst, F. 2006. *Quantitative Methods for Business and Management* (2nd ed.). McGraw-Hill, London.

Graham, J. R. and Leary, M. T. 2011. A review of empirical capital structure research and directions for the future. *Annual Review of Financial Economics*, 3, 309–345.

Modigliani, F. and Miller, M. 1958. The cost of capital, corporation finance and the theory of investment. *American Economic Review*, 48, 261–297.

Myers, S. and Majluf, N. 1984. Corporate financing and investment decisions when firms have information that investors do not have. *Journal of Financial Economics*, 13, 187–221.

Stock, J. and Watson, M. 2019. *Introduction to Econometrics (Global Edition)*. Princeton University Press, Princeton, NJ.

3 Basic Data Analysis in Stata

INTRODUCTION

A research project is more likely to be a success if the research data management is executed properly. It is not only important for the current research project but also if you need to go back to the information and data after several years of work. Also, you need to be able to explain the steps taken in the data-management process to your supervisors and colleagues, possibly across multiple disciplines, and the journals in a simple way. In order to execute successful research data management, you first need to understand your data well. Thus, understanding the units, levels, dimensions of the data, and so on that are discussed in Chapter 2 of this book is crucial. Then you need to be good at programming, which is part of the aim with this chapter. It will provide some tools to learn and develop your programming skills, along with providing basic data analysis.

It might be wise to create a data-management plan, documenting how the data are managed and the steps taken, until you obtain the final version of a dataset for the study. Most of the programming and data management can easily be forgotten if you ignore detailing them in a document. It is important that you update this document throughout the project to reflect any changes. In group work, such a document becomes even more important as there might be more than one member collecting and managing the data. The data-management document also makes it possible for all the group members to work with the data collection and management in a consistent way. It is also essential that previous versions of the data are saved so that you can go back to them if necessary. Try to save the data on more than one hard drive in case the drive gets damaged. Also, be aware of the restrictions and permissions when, for example, saving and storing proprietary data.

This chapter focuses on data-management techniques, with applications in Stata software. It is oriented towards writing theses and research papers, so the main focus is on handling missing values and outliers. In addition, the chapter covers how to do some basic data management and data analyses in Stata. Although not listed explicitly, the main text of the chapter provides some exercises by walking the reader through the solutions. The exercises cover the analysis and tests presented in Chapter 2. They also prepare the reader for reproducing the applications and working on the labs and mini cases provided in Chapters 4–10.

The analysis emphasizes the use of the do file editor to write the code and programs, although all the code can be run on the menu bar. Using the do files means that it is possible to save the programs and reuse them in the future. You could also note some details about the data-management process and how and why you are using a particular code in the do files. It then becomes a part of your data-management document. Thus, do files, by allowing for the continuous implementation of a series of commands in sequence without interruption, make it possible to replicate analysis and results. This chapter offers a snippet of do files, by demonstrating their power through basic operations like opening and saving datasets.

For the exercises and applications, the dataset MTB.dta is available on the book's webpage (www.cambridge.org/mavruk).[1] A summary of the Stata code will also be provided on this webpage. For those who are interested in doing the exercises in Python and R, the webpage also includes the full code in these software programs. In the text, all the code for Stata will be marked in bold to allow for easier identification and to copy and paste into the do file.

It is good practice for beginners in Stata to follow the exercises in this chapter and run the code in their own do file. Readers are encouraged to interpret and discuss the results with their associates. All the code presented in this chapter can be found via the **help** command in Stata, along with more technical descriptions and examples for how to use the commands. In your own research, the help command assists you only once you know the name of the command. Otherwise, you can use Google™ to search for the name of the command to begin with. These help documents can also be seen online via Stata's webpage (see Stata recourses and support). The University of California, Los Angeles (UCLA) Institute for Digital Research and Education is a useful source to learn the commands and resulting analysis (see UCLA resources to learn and use Stata).

This chapter is divided into four main sections. The first section introduces importing, reviewing, and saving files. The second section covers summarizing, variable transformations, and analysis of missing values and outliers. The third section focuses on bivariate analysis and the final section presents appending and merging datasets.

3.1 Importing, Browsing, and Saving Datasets

3.1.1 Help and findit

It might be helpful to begin with the most important commands in Stata that are used for looking up commands: **help** and **findit**. If you want to write a code but do not know how, search engines like Google™ work well but the **help** command name will pull up Stata's documentation for the command. It is difficult to remember all the commands, even for more advanced programmers. The command

[1] The extension ".dta" indicates that it is a Stata dataset.

help will also search the documentation for keywords and give explanations of commands and some examples of how to use them. Readers can just copy the examples, paste them into their do files, and modify the names of the variables to their own dataset.

If a new function that is not built into Stata is needed, just use **findit** and follow the instructions. This can be done for a new statistical test. The command **findit** will search the internet and install the function. Let us try **findit winsor2**, a command that will be used shortly. If any of the commands used in this chapter (or in the book) do not already exist in Stata, just use **findit** and install them in seconds.

3.1.2 Importing, Reviewing, and Saving a New Stata Dataset

Stata has the capability to display data in various formats without altering the underlying format types. It allows for presenting data in different formats and modifying data into different formats. Most of the commands presented in this section do not change the format of the underlying data. However, users can modify data and change variables' formatting as needed. For example, when presenting descriptive statistics, you do not need to specify the display format since Stata will make reasonable assumptions when displaying the variables. However, you always have the option to display them in a desired format.

To import a new dataset in Stata, the command **use** is applied. Insert the following code into the do file editor:

```
use "C:\Your own directory\MTB.dta"
```

In the command, "Your own directory" refers to the directory that includes MTB. dta, which is a quarterly dataset on firm and stock characteristics that covers an average of 262 firm stocks in each quarter between 2010 and 2014. The standard firm and stock characteristics include market-to-book value, average stock return during the quarter, volatility of the stock return, liquidity of the stock, market cap, tangibility, stock beta and size, defined as a natural logarithm of total assets. In this chapter, the basic data-management and analysis code is applied to this dataset.

Prior to performing the analysis, a review of the data is necessary. If there are input errors, clean them before proceeding. There are several ways to review the data. Examining the codebook, listing the data, performing range checks with the **tabulate** command, and graphing the data with histograms are some of the means that are helpful. The codebook displays the coding for each variable. Type, for instance, **codebook size**. This command will provide basic information about the data type, variable label, and value labels. It will also provide the value range and the number of missing values. In addition, the codebook output presents the mean, standard deviation, and percentile distribution for numeric variables. In large datasets, browsing the variables and/or certain values of the variables saves time. Typing **browse** opens the data to view (in an Excel-style view) without changing the format, while using **edit** it is possible to make changes. The command **edit** can be used conditionally, for instance, type **edit if size>=15**, which opens only observations where the variable called "size" is 15 or more. If, for instance, the size variable shows negative values, which is unlikely to occur, you can examine the problem values by typing **edit if size<0**.

In large datasets with many variables and many observations, it might be useful to find variables by using the code **lookfor**, which searches for variables with a given word. The word can appear in either the variable name or its description (variable label). The code **lookfor name** will list variables with "name." When searching for more than one word, more than one variable, the code will find variables with any of the words. For instance, **lookfor name ret** (short for return) in MTB.dta will find variables with "name" or "ret." This is useful for tracking down data from documentation or observing what is in the dataset.

To save a new dataset in Stata, the command **save** is used. Insert the following code in the do file editor:

```
save "C:\Your own directory\MTB.dta"
```

3.2 Summarizing, Variable Transformation, Missing Values and Outlier Management

3.2.1 Summarizing

Univariate analysis explores each variable separately. To observe the distribution, summarize the data with the code **sum X** or look at a more detailed distribution by using the code **sum X, detail**, where X represents the variable(s) to be analyzed. Run the code **sum size, detail** and discuss the average firm size, median, minimum, maximum, and standard deviation. Do the values make sense? For the nominal and ordinal levels of the data, examine the frequency distribution (it makes less sense to examine the standard deviation of nominal or ordinal level data, since this data is discrete).

3.2.2 Summarizing Based on Groups: Variable Transformations

Sometimes you need to transform a variable from its original form to, for example, a different name or unit or category, while keeping the original variable in the dataset. Some examples of such transformations are as follows. The command **rename** changes the old name of the variable to a new variable name. For instance, command **rename _rsq_ idiorisk** will rename the variable called _rsq_ (squared residuals) to idiorisk (idiosyncratic risk). A variable can be recoded; for example, a variable x with a range of 10 may be collapsed into a dummy variable with two categories. One category can be 5 or below. The other category can be above 5 with the following command: **recode x 0/5=0 6/10=1**. Let us apply this to the MTB.dta dataset. To categorize the variable called size in the dataset, first find its distribution with the following code: **sum size, detail**. Writing only **sum size** will give the basic statistics for size. If **detail** is included after a comma in the code, it will give a more detailed distribution that can be used to determine the interval values for the variable size. Table 3.1 presents the original Stata output along with the code at the top of the table.

Table 3.1 Stata output for detailed summary of size

. sum size, detail

	Percentiles	Smallest		
1%	17.589	16.799		
5%	18.345	16.799		
10%	18.881	16.799	Obs.	5100.000
25%	19.900	16.799	Sum of Wgt.	5100.000
50%	21.072		Mean	21.405
		Largest	Std. Dev.	2.046
75%	23.052	26.404		
90%	24.367	26.404	Variance	4.186
95%	24.881	26.404	Skewness	0.325
99%	26.009	26.404	Kurtosis	2.312

The table presents the smallest (16.8), mean (21.4) and median (50%: 21.0), and largest (26.4) values, along with some percentile values in the dataset. The variance (4.2), standard deviation (2.0), skewness (0.3), and kurtosis (2.3) are provided. The number of observations (5100), which shows the same value as the sum of the weights, is also given. By default, Stata gives a weight of 1 for each observation in the data, then the sum of the weights will equal the number of observations.

Once categories are determined (perhaps based on a statistical distribution). The following code will create the new variable size1, which is a category variable: **`recode size 0/19=1 19/23=2 23/27=3, gen(size1)`**. Note that it is important to keep the original variables in the dataset when transforming them, as you may need to go back to the original variables for another transformation. Thus, the optional part in the code **`gen(size1)`** will create a new variable called size1 by transforming the original variable size for given categories.

To analyze the frequency distribution of the variables, use the code **`tab size1`**. This will present the frequency distribution of size1 that is at ordinal level. Table 3.2 shows the Stata output. Examine the outcome. Does it make sense? Does it correspond to the distribution of the variable that was analyzed earlier?

Table 3.2 Stata output for tab size1

. tab size1

RECODE of size	Freq.	Percent	Cum. Percent
1	567	11.120	11.120
2	3218	63.100	74.220
3	1315	25.780	100
	5100	100	

Sometimes, **if** statements can be applied in tab: **tab size1 if icbname="Financials"**, which will tabulate size1 if industry is equal to Financials. Some analyses require the study of adjusted statistics. It is not uncommon that surveys have samples that are not purely random. Recall the selection bias from Chapter 2; data may include only firms with certain characteristics, for example, large firms. Such surveys usually have a weight variable to adjust for the sampling, which would weigh down a high proportion of large firms. This can be done by adding **[aweight=X]** after the commands, just before the comma, to use analytical weights. *X* in the code represents the weighting variable. Stata also allows other kinds of weights, for instance, **[pweight]**, which stands for probability or sampling weight and is less commonly used. Generally, which one to specify is less important; all will do the desired weighting in the sample. The following code will weigh the variable liabilities by size: **sum liabilities [aweight=size]**.

It is also common to summarize data based on groups. **If** statements are useful here as well. For instance, the code **sum if size>15 & icbname=="Financials"** will provide summary statistics for all financial firms that have size greater than 15. The groups make it possible to split the file, which means performing an analysis by sorting categorical variables. Running the command **by size1** will make it possible to perform one analysis for each size category in the dataset. Here is the code for summarizing market value by size categories: **by size1, sort: sum marketvalue**. Using bars, graphs, or histograms, depending on the level of the data, will make it possible to learn about the structure and patterns of the variables. This section covers such descriptive analysis. Table 3.3 shows Stata output for summary statistics on market value by size categories.

Table 3.3 Stata output for descriptive on market value by size

. by size1, sort: sum marketvalue

Variable	Obs.	Mean	Std. Dev.	Min	Max
size1 = 1					
marketvalue	567	2.52E+08	2.96E+08	28750	2.15E+09
size1 = 2					
marketvalue	3210	2.14E+09	4.41E+09	3112.5	5.23E+10
size1 = 3					
marketvalue	1315	2.72E+10	4.20E+10	2.08E+07	2.45E+11
size1 = .					
marketvalue	140	1.29E+11	9.46E+10	9776522	3.80E+11

Let's do another exercise by recoding the year variable and naming it "trend." The command is as follows: **recode year (2010=1) (2011=2) (2012=3) (2013=4) (2014=5), gen(trend)**. Use the code **tab trend** to examine the frequency distribution of the variable. The command **if** can be used for a conditional recode that transforms the variable based on a certain condition. For example, **recode size 0/19=1 19/23=2 23/27=3 if year==2010,**

gen(size2). This example creates categories for size only for the year 2010 and names the new variable as size2. Examine the frequency distribution of size2 with the following code: **tab size2**.

The command **gen newvarname=x** generates a new variable based on the existing variable. For instance, let us create a new variable based on industry names in the MTB dataset. The code is as follows: **gen icbname_new=icbname**. Additional exercises are as follows. The code **gen log_TA=log(total_assets)** will generate a new variable, log_TA, by taking the logarithm of total assets. The code **gen vol2=vol*vol** will generate the variance named vol2 by taking the square (or multiplying it with itself) of the volatility (vol). There are many operations the code **gen** can do. For the desired operation, write the code **findit** followed by the desired operation name and run it. Stata will provide a description of the operation and present some examples. Copy and paste the examples into the do file and modify the variable names if necessary. The command **egen** is an extension of the **gen** command that can handle variable lists for its arguments. For example, the following **egen** code calculates firm value by adding up debt and equity values: **egen Firm_Value=rowtotal (liabilities marketvalue)**. Note that the **egen** command with the **rowtotal()** option treats missing values as zero, unlike the **gen Firm_Value=liabilities+marketvalue** command. The code **sum Firm_Value** summarizes the variable to learn about its distribution. Table 3.4 presents the Stata output.

Table 3.4 Stata output for sum Firm_Value

. egen Firm_Value=rowtotal(liabilities marketvalue)
. sum Firm_Value

Variable	Obs.	Mean	Std. Dev.	Min	Max
Firm_Value	5240	1.82E+10	4.47E+10	5007400	3.90E+11

Try altering the name of the existing variables using the command **replace**, for instance, **replace icbname_new=icbname**, although replacing the variable is not recommended. Try keeping the original variables if there is enough space in the data. For some data-management purposes, a replacement is plausible, but creating (or copying) a new variable with a slightly different name will make it possible to get back to the original variable.

3.2.3 Missing Values

In a dataset there are two types of missing values. Those missing values shown as dots are for numeric variables and those shown as blanks are for character (string) variables. The command **missing()** can flag both types and return 1 for missing and 0 for non-missing values. For numeric variables, they are placed as very large numbers; Stata treats missing values as a very large value. If this is not properly accounted for, it may lead to serious errors. For example, keeping **size>20** will generate a dataset with size larger than 20 and all the observations with missing values of size. Using the command **mdesc**, Stata can provide detailed information on the missing values. Run the code for total assets, total liabilities, and market value in the MTB.dta dataset, **mdesc total_assets liabilities marketvalue**, and discuss the result. Table 3.5 presents the Stata output.

Table 3.5 Stata output for mdesc total_assets liabilities marketvalue

. mdesc total_assets liabilities marketvalue

Variable	Missing	Total	Percent Missing
total_assets	140	5240	2.670
liabilities	148	5240	2.820
marketvalue	8	5240	0.150

The code **mvpatterns** will provide the pattern in the values of the variables: **mvpatterns total_assets liabilities marketvalue**. See Table 3.6.

Table 3.6 Stata output for mvpatterns total_assets liabilities marketvalue

. mvpatterns total_assets liabilities marketvalue

Variable	Type	Obs.	mv
total_assets	double	5100	140
liabilities	double	5092	148
marketvalue	double	5232	8

Patterns of missing values

_pattern	_mv	_freq
+++	0	5084
..+	2	140
++.	1	8
+.+	1	8

To convert Stata missing values to new values, such as 999, use the **mvencode** command. For example, **mvencode size, mv(999)**. However, it is not suggested to replace missing values with such numbers as it is easy to forget about this replacement, which will affect the results. The common practice is to first find out why they are missing; that is, to find out whether it is a measurement error or the data is actually missing. If the explanation is satisfying, first conduct one analysis with all the missing values remaining in the dataset. In a regression analysis (that will be covered in Chapter 5), Stata ignores the missing values. If there are five variables in a model and say one of the variables has a missing value in row 10, and the remaining variables have full information (non-missing) in row 10, Stata will remove the whole of row 10 and ignore the information in the other variables. This may have substantial effects on the results. Once the results from the original data are observed, you could then replace the missing values with the mean or median (or with some other statistics of the variable) and observe the results again. If the results differ substantially, replacing the missing values with the mean or median is perhaps not the correct solution. Hopefully, collecting more data and solving the issue before applying some more advanced data-management techniques will work.

3.2.4 Missing Values in Time-Series and Panel Data

In time-series data, a variable may have some missing values in the middle of the series. In this case, some studies carry the last observation forward. To do that you first need to declare the data to be a time series with the time variable say date; the command is **tsset date**. Double check that the values of the variables for the same date enter only once in the dataset. Otherwise, the dataset cannot be declared as a time series. If this is not the case, collapse the data on variable and date. Here is the code: **collapse size roa, by(date)**, which collapses both size and return on assets (ROA) by date. Note that by default, the collapse command collapses both size and ROA to their mean, respectively. Once the data are in the correct shape and sorted by date (when declared as a time series the data are automatically sorted by date, otherwise simply use the command **sort date**), apply the following code, assuming that size has missing values in the middle of the series:

```
gen size1 (drop the variable first if it already exists)
replace size1=size1[_n-1] if size==.
```

The notation **[_n-1]** in the command refers to the previous observation given the current sort order; in other words, it is the lagged value in a time series. If instead **_n** is used, it represents any given observation. If **_n+1** is used, it refers to the following observation, leading observation, and so on. Note that this exercise would not work in MTB.dta, since MTB is a panel dataset. However, Chapter 7 will provide time-series data and hence plenty of exercises on time-series analysis methods. For the panel dataset, declare the data as a panel. All the exercises done so far treated MTB.dta as cross-sectional data, which is the focus of this chapter. Chapter 9 will focus on panel data and its techniques. However, if the aim is to carry the last observation forward in a panel dataset, first use the code **xtset isin_id period** to declare the data as a panel. If the id variable is a string as in MTB.dta, such as isin, the code will not work; transform the id variable to a numeric variable. The following code will do the trick:

```
egen isin_id=group(isin)
xtset isin_id period
```

where isin_id is the unit of analysis, in this case the firm stock, and the period could be daily, monthly, quarterly, yearly, and so on. In this example it is quarterly. Similar to the time-series data, the same firm cannot enter the data more than once in the same time period. If such a pattern is observed, collapse it on isin_id and the period. The following codes will fill the gaps in size by carrying the last non-missing observation forward. First use **tsfill** to expand the data. If a balanced panel is desired where each unit enters the data in all periods, use **tsfill, full**. Then use the code **bysort isin_id: carryforward size, gen(size1)**. Again, if the variable size1 already exists, either drop it or use another name for the new variable. All these examples carry the last observation forward and do not carry observations backwards. If there is no last observation with non-missing information in the data (e.g., stock gets delisted), not all the missing values will be filled. If the aim is to carry observations backwards (although not suggested), use an additional carryforward command. Note that in the fourth line of the command below, the code uses size1 to generate size2:

```
tsfill, full
bysort isin_id: carryforward size, gen(size1)

gsort isin_id period
bysort isin_id: carryforward size1, gen(size2)
```

There are also more advanced techniques to deal with missing data. One example uses conditional mean imputations and weighted least squares, generated in a generalized method of moments (GMM) framework, which is beyond this book. Interested readers should consult Freyberger et al. (2022) for these techniques.

3.2.5 Outliers

Outliers are observations that deviate significantly from the normal observations in the data, and they are different from the noise data (random error in the measurement). The basic rule is to delete the noise data but analyze and understand the outliers. So, how to detect outliers? The first approach is to eyeball the distribution. After running the **sum X, det** code for each variable in X, examine min, p1 (first percentile), p25 (equivalent to quartile 1, q1), mean, median, p75 (q3), p99, max, and standard deviation of the variable. As a first step, focus on whether the mean and median values deviate quite a lot from each other. Then look at the deviation between min and p1 and the deviation between p99 and max. Larger deviations between these values are reflected in the standard deviation. The code also provides skewness and kurtosis values of the distribution, which are helpful to examine whether and how the distribution deviates from the normal distribution. The more formal tests for normality when testing the assumptions of the classical linear regression model will be provided in Chapter 5.

To detect outliers, you could also use parametric methods, for instance, the Grubbs test – also called the maximum normalized residual test (Grubbs, 1969). The Grubbs test computes a z-score for each value (observation) of a variable in a dataset based on the normality assumption. The normality assumption suggests that about 68.28% of the observations of a normally distributed variable lie within one standard deviation of the mean (1σ). About 95.44% of the observations lie within 2σ of the mean and about 99.74% of the observations lie within 3σ of the mean. If the z-score is greater than its benchmark (determined by the Grubbs formula based on normality), a dummy variable is assigned to the observation. This would help with further examination of the outliers. The code for the Grubbs test is as follows: `grubbs size, level (99)`. The option `level (99)` sets the confidence interval to 99%. Stata will automatically add a new variable called grubbs_size, which assigns 1 for the outliers, else 0. Run the code for the other variables (e.g., total assets), `grubbs total_assets, level(99)`, and tabulate it as `tab grubbs_total_assets` to examine the percentage of outliers in the total assets. Table 3.7 shows the Stata output for the frequency distribution of the dummy grubbs_total_assets.

Table 3.7 Stata output for frequency distribution of dummy grubbs_total_assets

. tab grubbs_total_assets

grubbs_total_assets	Freq.	Percent	Cum. Percent
0	6508	96.560	96.560
1	232	3.440	100
Total	6740	100	

Non-parametric methods include the use of histograms or box-and-whisker plots. The code `histogram size` and the code `graph box size` will produce these plots for the variable size. Figure 3.1 shows the output from the `graph box size` command.

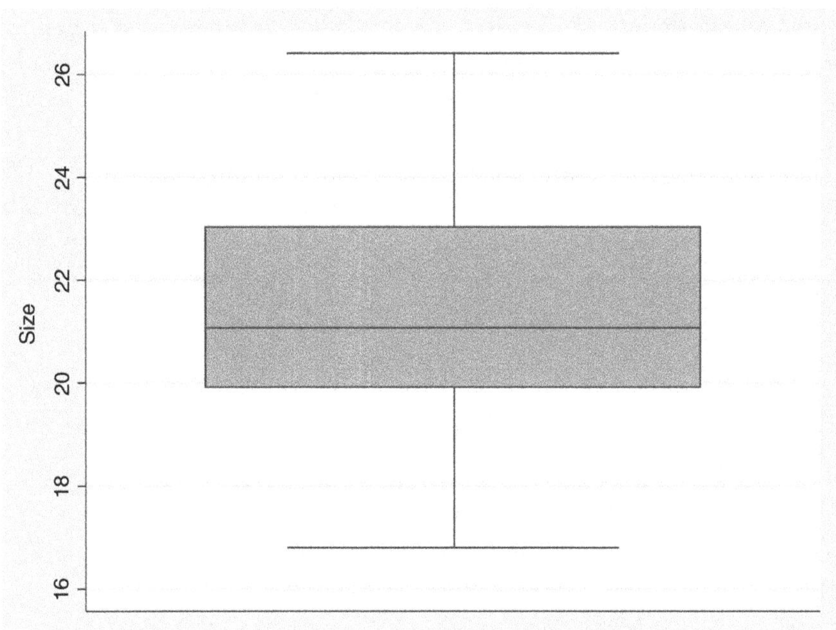

Figure 3.1. Stata output from the graph box size command

3.2.6 Conditional Replacement

Conditional replacement is useful if there are many missing values or outliers. For instance, the code **replace icbname_new="missing" if icbname_new==" "** inserts the text "missing" for those observations of industry name that are missing. Use **tab icbname_new** to check the frequency distribution. Note that one equal sign "=" is used to change variable values and two "==" to check for equality. So, after **if** in the previous code, use "=="; this is a very common error. In case of any problems, check whether this is the cause. Additional examples of the **replace if** command are as follows:

```
sum size, detail
generate size3=size
replace size3=1 if (size<19)
replace size3=2 if (size>=19) & (income<23)
replace size3=3 if (size>=23) & (income<27) & (size<.)
```

The new size variable is named size3 since there are already size1 and size2 in the data. Deleting (so-called dropping in Stata language), for instance, size1 and regenerating would also work. The code would be **drop size1**. To drop more than one variable, simply add them after the drop command with a space between: **drop size1 size2 size3**. These codes drop the entire column. If the aim is to drop a certain value or, say, missing values of the variable, use the following code: **drop if size==.** for numeric variables of such size. To drop the missing values of a string variable, say industry names, run the following code: **drop if icbname==" "**. Quotation marks are used to indicate the values of a string variable. In a large dataset, to keep only a few variables, it is more efficient to use the command **keep** instead. For instance, the code **keep firm_id size roa** keeps only these three variables while dropping the others. Note that this is a dangerous procedure as it keeps only the variables that are listed. If the code is already run, to get back to the original data, the data should be imported again.

In the code **varname!=x**, the exclamation mark means the variable *does not equal x*. Here is an example: **replace icbname_new="non-missing" if icbname_new!="missing"**. Let's examine the frequency distribution again, **tab icbname_new**. Table 3.8 presents the Stata output from the latest command.

Table 3.8 Stata output for tab icbname_new

. tab icbname_new

icbname_new	Freq.	Percent	Cum. Percent
missing	819	15.630	15.630
non-missing	4421	84.370	100
Total	5240	100	

3.2.7 Trimming and Winsorizing

How to proceed once outliers are detected? First, examine the outliers and try to understand them. If they are just noise, drop (trim) them as discussed above or winsorize them. The latter means replacement of the outliers with other values of the variable. This is similar to the missing value analysis above. Replacing could be done with mean, median, or lagged lead values. The most common replacement method is to winsorize with respect to confidence interval, for instance, at the 1% level. This means replacing all values lower than the p1th percentile value with the value of the p1th percentile. Similarly, replacing all values higher than the p99th percentile value with the value of the p99th percentile. Winsorizing is usually done for both sides of the distribution, otherwise you would impose censoring on one side, which may not be appropriate for the analysis if normality is assumed for the variables (or the combination of the variables; standard errors). The value of 1% is arbitrary, other thresholds are also possible to use – like 0.5% or sometimes as high as 2%. However, be careful not to lose too much information. The following code will winsorize the total assets at the 1st and 99th percentile levels:

```
gen total_assetsM=total_assets/1000000
sum total_assetsM
winsor2 total_assetsM, suffix(_wins) cuts(1 99)
sum total_assetsM_wins
```

The code above first generates a new variable, total assets in millions (total_assetsM) and then applies **winsor2** code to the variable. If this command does not exist in the software, just use **findit winsor2** and install it. The **suffix** option generates a new variable and inserts "_wins" at the end of the variable that is winsorized automatically, total_assetsM_wins. Study the distribution of the winsorized variable and compare it to its unwinsorized version. It is a good exercise to apply this code to the variable market value and observe what happens to the mean and median values. Let us practice this by trimming the values instead of winsorizing. Use market value in MTB.dta for the exercise, following this code:

```
sum marketvalue
winsor2 marketvalue, suffix(_wins) trim by(icbname)
  cuts(1 99)
sum marketvalue_wins
```

The difference between the last two codes is that **trim** is used in the latter, the default is winsorization. The code **by(icbname)** does trimming by industry name. Change it to other groups or trim by more than one group as the latest versions of Stata allow. Note that if observations are deleted or winsorized in the analysis, they should be stated clearly and the reason for such treatment should be well explained.

3.3 Bivariate Analysis

3.3.1 Cross-Tabulations and the Mean Comparison Test

Once the univariate analysis is done, consider a bivariate analysis that is simply mean or frequency comparisons of the variables, which is useful for understanding the pairwise relations between variables. Such an analysis may also help with model selection for the regression analysis. The **tab** command can be used for cross-tabulations between two variables. For instance, **tab size1 icbname, row nofreq chi2** gives a 2×2 of size1 vs. industry along with χ^2 statistics, testing the independence between size and industry categories; a χ^2 test of whether the rows and columns are independent. This is useful for a simple examination of the size distribution within the industry. It is also helpful for the data-management process when cleaning the data. Run the code and check whether size1 has inconsistent (with ideal) values, for instance, whether the sample contains very small firms in industries such as basic materials.

Typing **ttest x y** will produce a *t*-test for the mean comparison of variables that are continuous. You can also run a *t*-test by group, but the groups are limited to only two. The example creates a new variable size2 (drop the variable if you already have a variable with the same name), which has only two groups and provides a *t*-test for the volatility by size group. Table 3.9 shows the Stata output:

```
recode size 0/21=0 21/27=1, gen(size2)
ttest vol, by(size2)
```

The code will test whether the volatility in the sample of large and small firms is the same. One-sided (upper and lower) and two-sided *t*-test results can be observed at the bottom of Table 3.9. Observe that the volatility seems to be larger for small firms.

Table 3.9 Stata output for *t*-test

. ttest vol, by(size2)

Two-sample *t*-test with equal variances

Group	Obs.	Mean	Std. Err.	Std. Dev.	[95% Conf.	Interval]
0	2494	0.427	0.001	0.049	0.425	0.429
1	2517	0.410	0.002	0.076	0.407	0.413
combined	5011	0.419	0.001	0.065	0.417	0.420
diff		0.018	0.002		0.014	0.021
diff = mean(0) − mean(1)						
t-value	9.696					
Ha: diff < 0						
Pr(T < t)	1.000					
Ha: diff != 0						
Pr(|T| > |t|)	0.000					
Ha: diff > 0						
Pr(T > t)	0.000					

Pairwise relations can be studied by correlation tables. When cleaning the data, some variables may covary in particular ways. If the variables are at interval or ratio scale, the Pearson correlation test, which is the parametric version of the Spearman correlation test (used for non-parametric tests), can be used. The Appendix for Chapter 3 at the end of the book gives details on non-parametric analysis. Such tests are also useful to detect so-called multicollinearity, which will be discussed along with the classical regression model in Chapter 5. The following code will produce the correlation tables between the pair(s) of stated variables:

```
corr size total_assets liabilities marketvalue, means
pwcorr size total_assets liabilities marketvalue, obs sig
```

Table 3.10 presents the Stata output from the **pwcorr** command.

Table 3.10 Stata output for Pearson correlation test

. pwcorr size total_assets liabilities marketvalue, obs sig

	size	total_assets	liabilities	marketvalue
size	1			
	5100			
total_assets	0.660	1		
	0.000			
	5100	5100		
liabilities	0.630	0.918	1	
	0.000	0.000		
	5092	5092	5092	
marketvalue	0.496	0.631	0.640	1
	0.000	0.000	0.000	
	5092	5092	5084	5232

The **pwcorr** command with options **obs** and **sig** will provide additional information on the number of observations used and the significance level or *p*-values of the correlation (see Table 3.10). If the observed *p*-value is less than 5%, a significant correlation between the pair of variables exists – see, for instance, the significant correlation (at the 1% level) between total assets and size (0.66). For the Spearman correlation test, just replace the **corr** command with **spearman** in the code (the code beginning with **pwcorr** would not work with the Spearman correlation test). The code would provide Spearman's rho correlation coefficient.

In a regression analysis, one of the variables is dropped if there is a high correlation between the two. Two important questions arise. First, what counts as high? It is common to use 0.8 or 0.7 as a cut-off value but that is arbitrary. Second, which one should be dropped? It is usually the least important one for the model, but if the variable was not important, it would not have been in the sample in the first place. In this case you may turn to the previous literature in your study for a solution. Since your results should be compared to the results in the previous literature, it will be helpful to use similar variables in your analysis when you make a comparison.

3.3.2 Curve Linearity

If the relation between the two variables is curve linear, a Pearson correlation test does not capture the curve linearity as it tests the linear correlation between the variables. If there is curve linearity in the relationship, a scatterplot between the two variables can be examined. Type the following command to examine, for instance, the average return during the period in MTB.dta:

```
egen mean_return=mean(mean_return), by (icbname year)
twoway scatter mean_return year
twoway (scatter mean_return year) (lfit mean_return year)
```

Figure 3.2 shows the output from the last command.

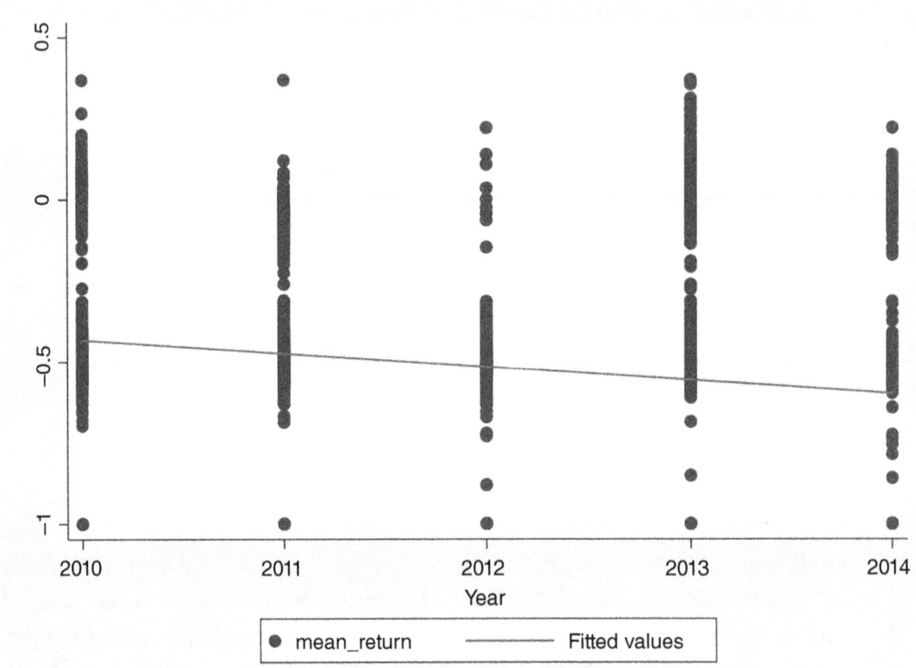

Figure 3.2. Stata output for mean return by year

3.4 Appending and Merging Datasets

3.4.1 Appending

Suppose there are two datasets a.dta and b.dta that contain the same variables, but different observations. One example is a split dataset by time. To append observations from these two datasets, first import data a.dta: **`use "C:\Your own directory\a.dta"`**. The next step is to type **`append using b`**. This command completes the appending of the observations in dataset b to those of dataset a.

The current dataset containing the observations of both datasets a and b can be saved under a different dataset name. Here is the full code:

```
use "C:\Your own directory\a.dta"
append using "C:\Your own directory\b.dta"
save "C:\Your own directory\ab.dta"
```

3.4.2 Merging

Suppose the aim is to merge two datasets (a.dta and b.dta) with different variables, but the values of the variables are measured in the same time period. These two datasets contain a unique identifying variable and for the purposes of this example, the identifier will be called international security id number, ISIN. The original dataset, say a.dta, is called the *master dataset* and b.dta, which is to be merged with a.dta, is called the *using dataset* in Stata language. As a first step, sort both datasets by ISIN and period and then save the datasets. The code for sorting is **sort ISIN period**. For saving, type **save "C:\Your own directory\a.dta", replace**. The option **replace** needs to be added as it will not replace the original dataset otherwise. This also means you need to be careful when replacing the original datasets. The second step is similar to the appending process but uses the **merge** command instead. The simplest way is to type the following code:

```
use "C:\Your own directory\a.dta"
merge 1:1 ISIN period using "C:\Your own directory\b.dta"
```

In the code, term 1:1 indicates a one-to-one merging, meaning that both datasets have an equal number of units and observations. Stata allows us to merge many-to-one (m:1), one-to-many (1:m), and many-to-many (m:m) datasets. If the datasets fit into the other forms, replace 1:1 with the relevant term that is stated within parentheses. Let's apply this code, one-to-one merge, to our dataset MTB.dta for merging together with a using dataset called ROA1.[2]

```
use "C:\Your own directory\MTB.dta", clear
sort ISIN period
merge 1:1 ISIN period using "C:\Your own directory\ROA1.dta"
tab _merge
keep if _merge==3
```

[2] The using dataset ROA1 is not directly provided. We generate it using the code below and save it for merging:

```
use "C:\Your own directory\MTB.dta"
keep roa ISIN period
rename roa roa1
sort ISIN period
save "C:\Your own directory\ROA1.dta", clear
```

In your research you will have two genuinely legitimate datasets for merging, and thus this step is not necessary.

In the code, **`rename`** is an additional step, since the aim is to generate a new dataset (the *using dataset*) from the existing one for the sake of this exercise. The variable ROA already exists in the *master dataset*, MTB.dta. If new data are used, the variables preferably have new names that do not exist in the master data, otherwise merging may produce inconsistent results. There is a remedy for this inconsistency, but it is better to keep things simple and use new names for the variables. Stata will automatically produce a category variable called "_merge" that contains the source of each observation. _merge has five categories: category 1 means that the observation exists in the master dataset only; category 2 means that the observation exists in the using dataset only; category 3 indicates that the observation exists in both datasets; category 4 means that the observation exists in both datasets and missing values are updated; finally, category 5 means that the observation exists in both datasets, but that the values are inconsistent. For a convenient merge, category 3 is the most interesting one – those observations that exist in both datasets, and hence these observations should be kept.[3]

The main message in this chapter is that it is all about how correct the data are and how well prepared for the analysis. For each new project, try to learn about all the details of the data and try to understand the data-generating process. This is time-consuming (according to my research experience, depending on the project, the minimum time taken is about 3 months), but it is definitely worth the effort. It is often the case that your thesis or paper will be rejected when you send it to your supervisor or to a journal. A referee rejection may result in a return to the data-management process and it is not motivating to go back to this stage after years of work on a project. However, a rejection by referee or advisor is the name of the game. Projects are more often rejected than accepted, but hopefully the comments received will not mean that you need to build the entire dataset from scratch. Surely you will still learn something – perhaps not to make the same mistakes repeatedly – but it is more motivating to collect and build a new dataset for each new project.

3.5 Summary

Data management concerns collecting, processing, analyzing, organizing, storing, and maintaining the data you collect for a research design. Successfully organized and managed data lead to detailed and structured pieces of information as an input in detailed analysis applied to answer the research question(s). Most importantly, carefully managed data saves time. Data management has grown tremendously, which can be seen as an asset to any research institution. Along with this development comes the regulatory compliance requirements, including data privacy and

[3] For a detailed discussion and common merging problems, see www.princeton.edu/~otorres/Merge101.pdf.

protection laws such as the EU General Data Protection Regulation (GDPR). The GDPR was adopted in 2016 and applied in 2018. The regulation defines individuals' fundamental rights, the obligations of the analysts who process the data, methods for ensuring compliance, and sanctions for those in breach of the rules. The GDPR has proved essential since analysts, research institutions, and companies manage and maintain larger volumes of data, so-called big data. Without appropriate data management, such big data are difficult to control, maintain, and thus make informative in a research design.

The focus in this chapter is on learning how to use Stata and applying data-management techniques to a provided dataset, MTB.dta. No previous knowledge is required. The chapter goes through the basic operations for data management, including missing-value analysis and outlier analysis, from the start. It then covers descriptive statistics (univariate analysis) and bivariate analysis. Finally, it ends with discussing how to merge and append datasets. This chapter is important to proceed with the lab work in upcoming chapters, since it is a means to become familiar with the software. Stata codes are provided in the main book. For those who are interested in using Python and R software instead, the corresponding codes are provided on the online resources webpage (www.cambridge.org/mavruk).

KEY TERMS

Data management; variable transformations; conditional replacement; missing values; outliers; basic data analysis; descriptive statistics; bivariate analysis; dropping; winsorizing; appending; merging; Stata; Python; R.

REFERENCES

Freyberger, J., Höppner, B., Neuhierl, A., and Weber, M. 2022. Missing data in asset pricing. Working Paper, Booth School of Business, University of Chicago, Chicago, IL.

Grubbs, F. 1969. Procedures for detecting outlying observations in samples. *Technometrics* 11, 1–21.

Stata recourses and support. www.stata.com/support/

UCLA resources to learn and use Stata. https://stats.idre.ucla.edu/stata/

4 Survey-Data Analysis

INTRODUCTION

This chapter concerns survey-data analysis. The main focus is on principal components analysis (PCA), as the use of PCA is common in corporate finance and business studies. Although other econometric methods that will be covered in Chapters 5–10 can also be applied to survey data, depending on the nature of the data and the research question, PCA is a common technique. This chapter also discusses factor analysis (FA) and provides a comparison between the two methods. Survey-data analysis is an important part of corporate finance studies and other subjects in business administration. Surveys (and interviews) are often used to understand the decision-making process of firm managers and directors in these studies. For instance, in capital structure studies, surveys are sent to firm managers to understand the choice of financing particular projects in the firm. Observational data covering such details at the project level are scarce or too expansive to obtain for students/researchers.

Similar to observational data, the primary issue in surveys is related to sampling, which was covered in Chapter 2. One difference is that while simple random sampling is a more common technique when using observational data, it is possible that more complex sampling techniques are used in surveys, including, for instance, stratified random sampling or cluster sampling. This means that the underlying population structures of these samples could be more complex than those used for simple random sampling. These features of the population should be accounted for carefully if other than simple random sampling is used to obtain the survey data. Further discussion of the complexity of the sampling structure of the survey data and the complexity in the referred population is beyond the scope of this chapter.

In this chapter, it is therefore assumed that the sample data are generated directly from the population using a simple random sample. In this sense, standard formulations of many of the econometric models that are covered in Chapters 5–10 can also be applied to the survey data. On the other hand, if it is reasonable to assume a simple random sample (or the sampling scheme is ignorable), the survey-data analysis techniques can also be applied to observational data. In this case, the techniques are used for analytic purposes rather than descriptive ones. Analytic uses are related to the estimation of the parameters and the inference for the population.

This chapter provides an example of the application of PCA to observational data, more specifically, ownership concentration measures. The technique is applied to examine different dimensions of ownership concentration. The results can be used to relate these dimensions to, for instance, firm performance. There are many measures of ownership concentration that have been proposed in the corporate finance and corporate governance literature, and they lead to different results and interpretations related to firm performance. Survey-data analysis techniques can group these different ownership concentration measures, allowing them to be linked to ownership theories that can explain observed empirical results.

Another reason for including survey-data analysis techniques in this book is to connect qualitative studies with quantitative studies, as such techniques can help to quantify and measure the output of qualitative research. The techniques make it possible to measure and quantify the qualitative information into measurable variables that can be used in the regression models for further analysis. In this sense, this chapter can be seen as a transition between the basic introductory chapters of sampling and hypothesis development and the coming chapters, mainly focusing on different details in regression analysis. To understand the mechanics behind concepts such as eigenvalues and eigenvectors, some previous knowledge of matrices and vectors is required. Readers may consult Brooks (2019) to review a simple matrix algebra, although this book focuses on the applications of these methods rather than mathematical explanations. Students/researchers who understand simple matrix algebra are likely to gain most from this chapter. The chapter ends with lab work and a mini case.

4.1 Principal Components Analysis

In general, both factor models and PCA are used as dimensionality reduction methods in datasets that have many correlated variables. The techniques group the variables into principal components that are common to the variables. If the dimensions are known/observable before the analysis, it is called factor analysis. Suppose that the aim is to test an economic theory and there are many proxies (variables) in the dataset that can be used to test this theory. The factor analysis can group the variables into a factor, s. If you instead do not know which theory the variables in the dataset proxy, you can use principal components analysis. Sometimes factor models are called economic factor models because they rely on economic theory, while PCA is known as a mathematical factor model because it relies purely on the statistical distribution of the variables. In this sense, PCA can also be used as a first step in a multivariate analysis to examine the outliers, multicollinearity, and whether the distribution of predictor variables is a multivariate normal distribution. These are all important properties that need considering before running any regression analysis. If there are severe outliers in the data, they may affect the results of the regression analysis. The existence of multicollinearity will substantially affect the interpretation of the results from a regression model. If the distribution of the variables is not normal, you may need to consider transforming the variables.

PCA mathematically transforms a set of correlated (response) variables into a smaller number of uncorrelated variables, so-called principal components. Put differently, PCA makes it possible to identify the dimensions of the data but does not eliminate the number of original variables. PCA uses the original variables to group them into principal components. Since the original variables in a dataset are likely (highly) correlated, the actual dimensionality is likely to be less than the number of original variables. If true, then you can replace the original variables by a smaller number of underlying variables (components) without losing any information. These components can then be used in further analysis, such as in regression models, but also for verifying the results of clustering experimental analysis and discriminant analysis. However, if the correlation among the original variables is close to zero, you will not be able to group the variables into a smaller number of principal components and there is no point running PCA.

There are some other important aspects to keep in mind regarding the original variables. The variables should be in comparable units. Since PCA uses the variance (and covariance) of the variable to determine the principal component, if the original variables are in different units, this will affect the variables that constitute the principal component.[1] This aspect also means that you should have variables with similar variances in PCA. If you rescale one of the variables and keep the other related variables in their original scale, the rescaled variable will have less variance than the other variables. If one variable has much larger variance than the others, it will dominate the first principal component regardless of the covariance structure in the data. In this case, the standard way of performing PCA on the variance–covariance matrix will not work. Instead, PCA can be applied on the correlation matrix. If the values of the variables are in different units and you have significant differences in the variance of the variables, you should either standardize the variables or apply PCA on the correlation matrix. The Appendix for Chapter 4 at the end of the book describes the eigenvalues and eigenvectors of the variance–covariance matrix and mathematically explains how PCA works.

4.1.1 PCA Applied on the Correlation Matrix

Apart from experimental data where you have total control over the variables and their units, it is often the case that the values of the variables in survey data and observational data come in different units and have different variances. For this reason, it is more plausible to apply PCA on the correlation matrix rather than on the variance–covariance matrix. One drawback with this approach is that it does not permit us to differentiate whether the original variables in the PCA have different importance for the analysis. However, newly developed software programs can make it possible to assign weights to those variables that are more important when applying PCA on the correlation matrix.

[1] For example, one variable could be in SEK and the other variable in million SEK, or a percentage.

Most of the notations and explanations discussed in the Appendix for Chapter 4 at the end of the book also apply for PCA of a correlation matrix. For example, to compute the ith principal component, using the correlation matrix, z-scores are used. Consider the mth observation of the ith principal component, then the principal component score using the correlation matrix is defined as $y_{m,i}^{z} = \mathbf{b}_i^{z'} \mathbf{z}_m$, where the principal component $i = 1,2,\ldots,p$ and the observation $m = 1,2,\ldots,N$. The superscript z indicates that the principal component score is computed using the z-scores. The component correlation vectors $\mathbf{c}_i^z$ represent the correlations between the ith principal component and the original variable, $c_{m,i}^{z} = \text{corr}(x_m, y_i^z)$. PCA is usually applied to a sample correlation matrix not the population correlation matrix, and thus the eigenvalues and eigenvectors are the estimated values of the correlation matrix. The easiest way to determine the number of principal components is to select eigenvalues that are greater than 1. Since PCA is applied on the standardized data, the variance of the standardized variable is 1. The intuition is that you are selecting the principal components that account for more variation than a single variable by itself can account for.

There are also some arguments against this method. In Monte Carlo analyses (computer algorithms that generate repeated random sampling), Costello and Osborne (2019) show that 36% of the samples retained too many factors/principal components using this method. The authors therefore suggest the scree test, which makes it possible to examine the graph of the eigenvalues. In the analysis, the break point in the data where the curve levels off is key to determine the number of principal components. However, it can be difficult to determine the break point if the data points are clustered together around the curve. Next, we present an application of PCA on an ownership dataset where further details of the PCA, such as rotation, are also discussed.

4.1.2 Application of PCA on Ownership Data

This exercise uses 1 year's worth of data from a study exploring different ownership concentration measures. Mavruk, Overland, and Sjögren (2020) (henceforth MOS) examine the distributional properties of ownership concentration measures and document that measures come from different underlying statistical distributions. Using PCA, MOS group ownership concentration measures into different dimensions to represent a monitoring dimension or shareholder conflict dimension. The monitoring dimension concerns the conflicting interests between managers and owners, so-called agency costs, and the shareholder conflict dimension relates to the interplay between owners. According to Jensen and Meckling (1976), decisions taken by utility-maximizing managers may result in agency costs that could be reduced by stronger ownership concentration in the firm, since large owners would have stronger incentives to engage in costly monitoring. MOS call this dimension the monitoring dimension. There is also a possibility that conflicting interests occur among the owners regarding how and which crucial decisions should be taken to manage the firm. In this case, concentrated ownership may allow large shareholders to expropriate minority shareholders (see, e.g., Burkart, Gromb, and Panunzi,

1997; Claessens, Djankov, and Lang, 2000; Shleifer and Vishny, 1997). MOS call this dimension the shareholder conflict dimension.

MOS, in their main model, apply PCA to 20 ownership measures based on voting rights to 240 firms listed on Nasdaq Stockholm in 2008. In contrast, this exercise applies PCA to eight ownership measures, calculated based on cashflow rights instead of voting rights, to 235 firms listed on Nasdaq Stockholm in 2009. This is because some of the measures based on cashflow rights are not available for the year 2009. Thus, the results might differ slightly from those presented in the original article; however, the overall conclusions are the same.

4.1.2.1 Definition of Ownership Measures

In this exercise, eight ownership concentration measures represent the various measures within the following categories.

Simple ownership concentration measures

- Largest owner (largest_owner, or LO): The cashflow rights of the largest shareholder.
- Sumfive (sum_five): The cashflow rights of the five largest shareholders.
- First/Second (first_second): The largest owner's cashflow rights divided by the second largest owner's cashflow rights.

Herfindahl index

- Herfindahl index (herfindahl_index, or HI): The sum of the squared sums of all shareholders' cashflow rights.

Power indices

- The power indices show the ability to form winning coalitions. Both the Shapley–Shubik index and the Banzhaf index used in the analysis are measures based on game theory, treating shareholders as players, and their indices measure the probability of individual players affecting the decision-making. The variables are as follows: SS and BZ indicate Shapley–Shubik and Banzhaf indices, respectively; C and D show concentrated ownership and dispersed ownership, respectively; 5 and 5% indicate whether the major shareholders are defined as the five largest owners or owners holding 5% or more of the voting rights; and L and O show whether it is the index value of the largest owner or the index value of the ocean. For instance, ssd5_l represents the Shapley–Shubik index of the owners with more than 5% cashflow rights as major owners and considers minor shareholders (those who own less than 5% cashflow rights) to be dispersed. If the notation does not include an underscore (e.g., ssd5l), it means that the five largest owners are considered as major owners instead of those who own more than 5% of the cashflow rights in the firm. The analysis in this exercise uses two BZ indices (bzd5l and bzd5_l) and two SS indices (ssd5_l and ssd5_o). Readers interested in more details on these measures, as well as in the ownership concentration measures that are not covered in this chapter, are referred to Mavruk et al. (2020). Table 4.1 presents descriptive statistics of these measures.

Table 4.1 Descriptive statistics

. sum HI LO first_second sum_five bzd5l bzd5_l ssd5_l ssd5_o

Variable	Obs.	Mean	Std. Dev.	Min	Max
HI	238	0.117	0.122	0.007	0.733
LO	236	0.336	0.213	0.055	0.930
first_second	238	4.168	6.708	0.380	46.875
sum_five	238	0.490	0.176	0.145	0.941
bzd5l	236	0.721	0.318	0.200	1.000
bzd5_l	236	0.800	0.298	0.185	1.000
ssd5_l	236	0.475	0.339	0.058	1.000
ssd5_o	236	0.385	0.274	0.000	0.941

Table 4.1 shows Stata output for descriptive statistics for eight ownership concentration measures between 236 and 238 firms along with the codes above. The mean HI is approximately 12%, the largest owner has 34% cashflow rights in an average firm, and the sum of the five largest owners have cashflow rights of 49%, on average. Both the Shapley–Shubik index and the Banzhaf index, which represent dispersed ownership in the table, have larger mean values when the measures concern the largest five owners' power rather than oceans' (smaller owners') power. One important observation in Table 4.1 is that the units of these ownership concentration measures – and thus the standard deviations – are quite different. Hence, it is more plausible to use PCA of a correlation matrix (not a covariance matrix), which will make it possible to use standardized ownership measures. Table 4.2 shows the Pearson correlation matrix between the ownership variables, along with the Stata code.

Table 4.2 Pearson correlation matrix

. pwcorr HI LO first_second sum_five bzd5l bzd5_l ssd5_l ssd5_o, sig

	HI	LO	first_second	sum_five	bzd5l	bzd5_l	ssd5_l	ssd5_o
LO	0.778	1.000						
	0.000							
first_second	0.587	0.545	1.000					
	0.000	0.000						
sum_five	0.817	0.693	0.293	1.000				
	0.000	0.000	0.000					
bzd5l	0.413	0.699	0.358	0.334	1.000			
	0.000	0.000	0.000	0.000				
bzd5_l	0.289	0.506	0.275	0.116	0.771	1.000		
	0.000	0.000	0.000	0.077	0.000			
ssd5_l	0.660	0.955	0.487	0.616	0.748	0.548	1.000	
	0.000	0.000	0.000	0.000	0.000	0.000		
ssd5_o	−0.654	−0.889	−0.414	−0.746	−0.539	−0.242	−0.906	1.000
	0.000	0.000	0.000	0.000	0.000	0.000	0.000	

Table 4.2 shows that most of the correlation coefficients are significant at the 1% significance level (see that *p*-values < 1% right under the coefficients). This result indicates that data are suitable for PCA, since these highly correlated ownership concentration measures are likely to load onto the same principal components that are uncorrelated with one another. Note also that some measures are positively correlated (e.g., HI and LO) and some measures are negatively correlated (e.g., HI and ssd5_o).

4.1.2.2 PCA Analysis

Table 4.3 begins the analysis by performing a basic PCA for eight ownership measures. In the Stata code, the default is PCA of a correlation matrix. If you want to run PCA of a covariance matrix, you need to add the covariance option to the code (after the comma).

Table 4.3 PCA output

. pca HI LO first_second sum_five bzd5l bzd5_l ssd5_l ssd5_o

Principal components/correlation				
			No. obs.	235
			No. comp.	8
			Trace	8
Rotation: (unrotated = principal)			Rho	1

Component	Eigenvalue	Difference	Proportion	Cumulative
Comp1	5.110	3.795	0.639	0.639
Comp2	1.316	0.550	0.165	0.803
Comp3	0.766	0.307	0.096	0.899
Comp4	0.458	0.278	0.057	0.956
Comp5	0.180	0.068	0.023	0.979
Comp6	0.113	0.078	0.014	0.993
Comp7	0.034	0.012	0.004	0.997
Comp8	0.023		0.003	1.000

Variable	Comp1	Comp2	Comp3	Comp4	Comp5	Comp6	Comp7	Comp8	Unexplained
HI	0.366	−0.300	0.214	0.517	−0.127	0.544	−0.387	−0.055	0.000
LO	0.430	−0.016	−0.063	−0.152	−0.256	0.306	0.737	−0.291	0.000
first_second	0.268	−0.037	0.885	−0.215	0.142	−0.274	0.048	0.024	0.000
sum_five	0.332	−0.443	−0.239	0.437	0.270	−0.532	0.248	0.167	0.000
bzd5l	0.334	0.482	−0.128	0.011	0.765	0.225	−0.042	−0.053	0.000
bzd5_l	0.247	0.655	0.013	0.400	−0.430	−0.372	−0.094	−0.133	0.000
ssd5_l	0.420	0.078	−0.159	−0.327	−0.228	0.073	−0.124	0.783	0.000
ssd5_o	−0.389	0.212	0.263	0.454	0.063	0.241	0.466	0.500	0.000

The first output in the table is the summary of the estimated eigenvalues (e.g., $\hat{\lambda}_1 = 5.11$ and $\hat{\lambda}_2 = 1.32$). The number of firm observations is 235. There are eight ownership measures, so the total number of components (equal to the trace) is eight in the analysis. The trace is the sum of all eigenvalues of the components, which also means that the eigenvalues represent the sum of the diagonal elements (characteristic roots) in the underlying diagonal matrix. Since the table shows results from all the components, Rho, the fraction of explained variance, is 1 (100%). This is also evident in the bottom output showing the eigenvectors. To illustrate, the eigenvector of component 1 is $\hat{\mathbf{b}}_1' = [0.366, 0.430, \ldots, -0.389]$. The unexplained variation is 0, because the table presents eigenvectors for all eight components. If you only chose to present results from the first and second principal components, Rho would be 80.33%, which is the cumulative variance explained in the data by these two principal components.

The components are ranked based on their eigenvalues; the ability to explain the variance in the component. They can be ranked because the correlation matrix is a symmetric matrix and thus the eigenvalues are real numbers, meaning that they can be ordered from largest to smallest. The first component has the largest eigenvalue of 5.11, which explains as much as 63.9% of the variation in the data alone. The second component has the eigenvalue of 1.32 and explains 16.5% of the variation in the data. The first and second principal components together explain 80.3% of the total variance in ownership concentration measures (see the cumulative column). The column difference presents the difference in the eigenvalues of the respective components. For instance, the difference between the eigenvalues of component 1 and component 2 is 3.80. To determine the number of principal components we use the Kaiser rule, a commonly used criterion suggesting that those principal components with eigenvalues greater than 1 should be selected. Accordingly, the analysis suggests a two-component model, meaning that components 1 and 2 will be selected, and the rest will be ignored in the analysis because of their limited explanatory power of the variance in the data.

Figure 4.1 presents a scree plot of the eigenvalues for all the components, obtained by simply running the code **scree plot** after **pca** in Stata.

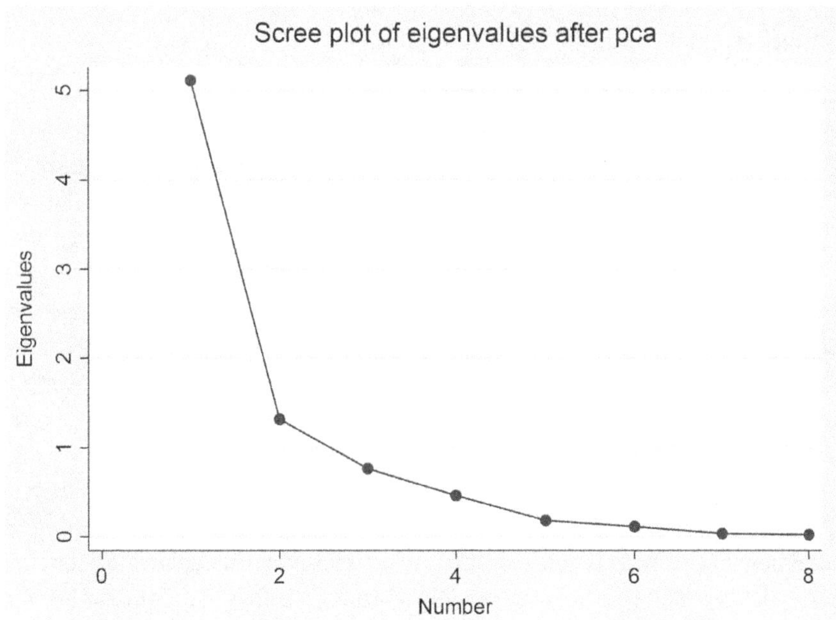

Figure 4.1. Scree plot

The scree plot basically provides the same information as in Table 4.3. The first two components have eigenvalue greater than 1 and will be selected as principal components by the Kaiser rule. After point 2 the eigenvalues level off, indicating that they are close to 0, and hence will be ignored.

Table 4.3 also presents eigenvectors at the bottom of the table. These are the loadings that describe each ownership concentration's contribution to a particular principal component. In other words, loadings are the correlations between the underlying ownership measures and the principal components. They are (just as any other correlation coefficients) given in absolute terms and show whether the measure has a strong or weak correlation with the principal component. The important question is to assess which ownership concentration measures have a strong relationship to which component, and thus can be grouped in the principal component. To determine this, you need to have a cut-off value for the loadings, which is arbitrary. The usual practice is to follow the previous literature and determine the cut-off value accordingly. MOS, following the previous literature, use 0.2 (in absolute terms) as a cut-off value. There are also some examples that ignore cut-off values (due to their arbitrary nature) and group the variables into principal components based on highest loading/correlation. A rule of thumb is that a principal component should have a minimum of three variables. For a given cut-off value, say 0.2, the first two principal components (1 and 2) in the table satisfy this condition. However, it is also evident that the ownership concentration measures are highly correlated with more than one component, making it difficult to assess which measure can be grouped into which principal component. For instance, the ownership concentration measure bzds5l loads highly on both principal component 1 and 2, with both loading coefficients exceeding the cut-off value of 0.2 (in absolute terms).

4.1.2.3 Rotation

In the case of high correlation between the variables, a rotation can be used to better assess the ownership concentration measure in a principal component. A rotation will improve the interpretability of the loadings by obtaining a simpler structure; if the ownership measure loads high on one principal component it will not do so on the other principal component. Note that a rotation will not change the position of the ownership measures relative to each other, meaning that the correlations between the measures will remain the same. However, it will change (rotate) the coordinates of the ownership measures, allowing a better match between the ownership measure and the principal component. This means that you are simply redefining the axis for the same loadings and therefore less likely to observe one measure loading highly on more than one principal component.

There are two main types of rotation method. Orthogonal rotation assumes that principal components are independent of each other, while oblique rotation assumes that principal components are correlated with each other. The most common orthogonal rotation method is varimax, which maximizes the sum of the variance of the squared loadings. The method is useful for determining the most important ownership concentration measures of a principal component, given that you can assume (or expect) zero correlation between the principal components. If this assumption does not hold, you may use a promax rotation, which is an oblique rotation that allows for dependence between the principal components. These two rotation techniques, varimax (among orthogonal rotation techniques) and promax (among oblique rotation techniques), are the most used techniques. The choice between the two depends on whether you can assume or expect independent or correlated principal components in the analysis.

It is more common to use orthogonal rotation since results obtained from, for example, varimax are easier to interpret than results obtained using an oblique rotation technique. However, Costello and Osborne (2019) argue that most studies expect some correlation structures among the principal components, since the studied variables representing the underlying behavior do not function as independently of one another. Thus, using orthogonal rotation may result in a loss of valuable information if the principal components are correlated, and oblique rotation should be used instead. If the principal components are uncorrelated, both types of rotation method should produce nearly identical results and the interpretations are essentially the same. For details and other types of rotation technique, the reader may consult Johnson (1998).

Table 4.4 presents the results from varimax rotation.

Table 4.4 Results from varimax rotation

. rotate, varimax blanks(.2)

Principal components/correlation			No. obs.	235
			No. comp.	2
			Trace	8
Rotation: orthogonal varimax (Kaiser off)			Rho	0.803

Component	Variance	Difference	Proportion	Cumulative
Comp1	4.244	2.062	0.531	0.531
Comp2	2.182		0.273	0.803

Rotated components (blanks are abs(loading)<.2)

Variable	Comp1	Comp2	Unexplained
HI	0.464		0.199
LO	0.385		0.057
first_second	0.253		0.633
sum_five	0.503	−0.231	0.179
bzd5l		0.583	0.124
bzd5_l		0.693	0.123
ssd5_l	0.331	0.269	0.093
ssd5_o	−0.443		0.168

After the rotation eigenvalues are changed, the first two components still explain the same amount (percentage) of variance – 80.3% – in the ownership concentration measures. This is because rotation does not influence the total explained variance, but simply redistributes the variance among the principal components. Using the option **blanks(.2)** in the code ignores those loadings between 0.2 and −0.2. You can observe that ownership variables HI, LO, first_second, sum_five, and ssd5_l positively load on principal component 1 and the measure ssd5_o negatively loads on principal component 1. Moreover, the measures bzd5l and bzd5_l positively load on principal component 2. These results, besides HI and first_second, are consistent with those obtained by MOS, who find three principal components using 20 ownership concentration measures and voting rights instead of cashflow rights. However, MOS also relate their third principal component to the first one and suggest that components 1 and 3 represent a monitoring dimension, while the second principal component represents a shareholder conflict dimension. The results from Table 4.4 support their conclusions by grouping those ownership concentration measures that represent the monitoring dimension into the first principal component, and grouping those that represent the shareholder conflict dimension into the second principal component.

4.1.2.4 The Kaiser–Meyer–Olkin Measure of Sampling Adequacy

One interesting post estimation is the Kaiser–Meyer–Olkin (KMO) measure of sampling adequacy. This test should be run directly after the **pca** command and before pursuing the predictions of principal component scores. The KMO reveals how suitable the data are for PCA. In this case, the analysis shows the sampling adequacy for the ownership concentration measures in PCA. The sampling adequacy is larger if the proportion of variance in the ownership measures, which can be derived from the common variance, is larger. The value of KMO is bounded between 0 and 1, with the higher value indicating that the data are suitable for PCA. Again, the threshold to determine what is a high value is arbitrary, but the literature suggests that a KMO value less than 0.50 is unacceptable. Table 4.5 shows the results from KMO.

Table 4.5 KMO measure of sampling adequacy

. estat kmo

Variable	kmo
HI	0.690
LO	0.877
first_second	0.745
sum_five	0.659
bzd5l	0.873
bzd5_l	0.668
ssd5_l	0.786
ssd5_o	0.707
Overall	0.755

The results from KMO show that 75.5% of the variance in the ownership concentration measures can be derived from the common variance in the data, meaning that there is enough (a KMO value between 0.7 and 0.8 is considered "average") information overlap among the ownership concentration measures in the data. Hence, data are suitable for PCA. Along with KMO, Cronbach's alpha can also be computed and presented. The measure refers to reliability (internal consistency); in other words, it measures how the variables in PCA reliably represent the same underlying variable. The value of Cronbach's alpha ranges from 0 to 1. Zero means that there is no correlation between the variables. The general rule of thumb is that a value of Cronbach's alpha greater than 0.7 indicates a good reliability in PCA.

4.1.2.5 The Predicted Principal Component Scores

The final step in PCA can be to predict the two principal component scores for later use in regression analysis. The predicted principal component scores are computed by using the eigenvectors as coefficients. More formally, following our notations, the principal components y_i are computed using eigenvectors and z-scores for the ownership concentration variables x_i, since PCA is run on the correlation matrix, that is the ownership concentration measures are standardized:

$$\begin{aligned}
\hat{y}_1 &= \hat{b}_{1,1}z_1 + \hat{b}_{1,2}z_2 + \cdots + \hat{b}_{1,p}z_p, \\
\hat{y}_2 &= \hat{b}_{2,1}z_1 + \hat{b}_{2,2}z_2 + \cdots + \hat{b}_{2,p}z_p, \\
&\vdots \\
\hat{y}_p &= \hat{b}_{p,1}z_1 + \hat{b}_{p,2}z_2 + \cdots + \hat{b}_{p,p}z_p.
\end{aligned} \tag{4.1}$$

Note that principal components are estimated using the (original) eigenvectors in Table 4.3, not by using the rotated components in Table 4.4. Descriptive statistics and the Pearson correlation matrix for the predicted principal components are given in Table 4.6.

Table 4.6 Descriptive statistics and Pearson correlation matrix for predicted principal components

Panel A. Descriptive statistics

. sum pc1 pc2

Variable	Obs.	Mean	Std. Dev.	Min	Max
pc1	235	0.000	2.261	−3.456	6.162
pc2	235	0.000	1.147	−2.900	2.239

Panel B. Pearson correlation matrix

. pwcorr pc1 pc2, sig

	pc1	pc2
pc1	1.00	
pc2	0.00	1.00

Panel A shows that the mean values of the principal component scores are 0, because they are scaled to have zero mean. Note that the squared values of the standard deviations of principal component scores will be equal to the eigenvalues. (For pc1, $2.26^2 = 5.11$.) Panel B shows zero correlation between the predicted principal components 1 and 2. These predicted principal components seem to be appropriate to use in a further (regression) analysis, which will not be covered in this chapter.

4.2 Factor Analysis

FA is similar to PCA in many aspects. FA results in a smaller set of uncorrelated variables, so-called underlying factors, from a set of correlated variables. Thus, it simplifies large datasets and allows for better understanding of the variables by reducing the dimensions without losing information in the original variables. It aims to explain the covariance or correlation structure among the variables. FA differs from PCA because it depends on the underlying model. Unlike PCA, FA permits us to eliminate some of the original variables that are less important for creating underlying factors. There are two types of factor analysis. The first type is explanatory FA, which is similar to PCA since it aims to examine the relations among the variables without having theoretical assumptions or a hypothesis for the analysis. The second type is confirmatory FA, which is based on theoretical assumptions and thus aims to test some hypotheses.

This book will not go into the details of FA because, relative to FA, there are more applications of PCA in corporate finance. The main reason for this is that there are some subjectivities involved in the applications of FA that are difficult to motivate when explaining the determined factors. It is unclear how the number of underlying factors is determined to begin with. It is also ambiguous how the resulting factors should be interpreted and evaluated in relation to the theory, which is also true for PCA. Having said that, there are also some valid examples of the use of FA in the closely related field of risk management literature.

4.3 Lab Work: Survey-Data Analysis

Problem set

1. Briefly explain the following concepts:
   (a) Factor analysis
   (b) Principle components analysis
   (c) Eigenvalue
   (d) Factor loadings

(e) Factor scores
(f) Uniqueness
(g) Communalities
(h) Rotated factor loadings
(i) Varimax rotation
(j) Promax rotation

Use Chapter_4_OC_Y2009.dta on ownership concentration (OC) measures for firms in Sweden in the year 2009. The dataset is available on the book's webpage (www.cambridge.org/Mavruk). The OC measures of interest are as follows: HI LO first_second sum_five bzd5l bzd5_l ssd5_l ssd5_o. Copy and paste these measures into your do file.

You can find the definitions of these measures in Mavruk et al. (2020). Alternatively, you can download the publicly available version from the following link: https://papers.ssrn.com/sol3/papers.cfm?abstract_id=3498145. This is the latest version before the published version, so all the definitions and table numbers in this version match exactly the published version at *European Financial Management*.

2. Analyze principal components, eigenvalues, and proportion of variance. Interpret your results. Run a scree plot and interpret the figure.

   Useful Stata commands:

```
describe, summarize, corr, pca, screeplot
```

3. Compute the component loadings and focus on loadings above +0.2 or below −0.2. Interpret the results. Run component loadings with (i) no rotation, (ii) varimax, and (iii) promax. Explain and compare the results.

   Useful Stata commands:

```
pca, rotate, varimax, promax
```

   For example: **`rotate, varimax comp(3) blanks(.2)`**

4. Predict the components and show their descriptive statistics. What do you observe? Why do the scoring coefficients for orthogonal varimax rotation show zero values in Stata output?
5. What is a KMO measure of sampling adequacy? Explain. What is the KMO in your PCA analysis?
6. Run a Pearson correlation test on the predicted components and interpret the significance, the sign, and the magnitude of the correlation coefficients. Explain how these predicted components could be used in further analysis (see Mavruk et al., 2020).

   Useful Stata commands:

```
predict, sum, estat kmo, pwcorr
```

7. Run steps 2–6 again by making a factor analysis instead.
   Useful Stata commands:

   replace **`pca`** with **`factor`** in the Stata command above

   ```
   loadingplot, scoreplot, predict, pwcorr
   ```

8. What are the differences between PCA and FA? What differences do you observe in your data? Which method is more useful for your own research? Explain the reason(s).

Good luck!

4.4 Mini Case

Homroy, Mavruk, and Nguyen (2023) built a General Managerial Ability Index to classify CEOs as generalists or specialists. The authors closely follow the method introduced by Custodio, Ferreira, and Matos (2013) and run a PCA where they predict the principal component scores to define the index. The CEO characteristics that are used in the PCA include: (i) the number of positions that the CEO has had in his career (nlistpos_total); (ii) the number of firms that the CEO has worked for (nlistfirm_total); (iii) the number of industries (at four-digit SIC level) where the CEO has worked (nlistsic_total); (iv) an experience dummy, equal to 1 if the CEO has held a position as CEO in another firm (ceoinother); and (v) a conglomerate experience dummy, equal to 1 if the CEO has worked in a multi-division firm (multi_segment). The exact variable names in the dataset are presented within parentheses. These variables are used as proxies for human capital in the PCA.

Task

1. Go to the link: Replication data for: ESG-Linked Compensation, CEO Skills, and Shareholder Welfare – Review of Corporate Finance Studies Dataverse (harvard.edu)
   Download the dataset: General_ability_index.tab
   Download the do file: Stata_codes_main_results.do
2. Note that the first part of the do file is for the PCA. Present and describe the summary statistics for the variables that are used in the PCA.
3. Run a Pearson correlation test and explain the results.
4. Run a PCA and explain your results.
5. Rotate your results using varimax. Explain your findings.
6. Run a KMO analysis and explain your results.
7. Predict the principal component score(s).
8. Present and describe summary statistics for the principal component score(s).

4.5 Summary

Studies based on large samples are common in empirical research and they have several advantages over other studies. Analysis conducted on large samples tends to have more statistical power and cross-sectional variation. One caveat with these studies, however, is the variable specification. It is common to use so-called proxy variables instead of the true measures of variables, as the information in large samples is often noisy. It is also difficult to find information on qualitative questions in large sample studies. Using small samples – focusing on particular companies – may provide more detailed information on the unique aspects of corporate behavior, but the results from such studies are often not generalizable.

Survey studies offer a balance between large-sample analysis and more sample-specific studies, since they can be based on a large sample of cross-sectional companies but at the same time they allow us to ask specific qualitative questions of the respondents. Survey studies also allow us to measure and quantify decision-making processes and beliefs (qualitative information), not just the actions taken by managers (quantitative information). Thus, survey-data analysis can be seen as a bridge connecting qualitative studies to quantitative studies in corporate finance. This chapter covers the most commonly used technique in survey-data analysis. It focuses particularly on the assumptions and applications of PCA (principal components analysis), but also briefly explains FA (factor analysis). The chapter also briefly discusses the similarities and differences between these two methods. It includes an example of an application of PCA to ownership concentration by examining the different dimensions of ownership concentration. Finally, lab work on PCA and a mini case are provided.

KEY TERMS

Principal components analysis; eigenvalue; rotation; KMO measure of sampling adequacy; predicted principal component scores; application of ownership concentration measures.

REFERENCES

Brooks, C. 2019. *Introductory Econometrics for Finance* (4th ed.). Cambridge University Press, Cambridge.

Burkart, M., Gromb, D., and Panunzi, F. 1997. Large shareholders, monitoring, and the value of the firm. *Quarterly Journal of Economics*, 112, 693–728.

Claessens, S., Djankov, S., and Lang, L. H. P. 2000. The separation of ownership and control in East Asian corporations. *Journal of Financial Economics*, 58, 81–112.

Costello, A. B. and Osborne, J. 2019. Best practices in exploratory factor analysis: Four recommendations for getting the most from your analysis. *Practical Assessment, Research, and Evaluation*, 10, 1–9.

Custodio, C., Ferreira, M. A., and Matos, P. (2013). Generalists versus specialists: Lifetime work experience and chief executive officer pay. *Journal of Financial Economics*, 108, 471–492.

Homroy, S., Mavruk, T., and Nguyen, V. D. 2023. ESG-linked compensation, CEO skills, and shareholders' welfare. *Review of Corporate Financial Studies*, 12, 939–985.

Jensen, M. C. and Meckling, M. 1976. Theory of the firm: Managerial behavior, agency costs and ownership structure. *Journal of Financial Economics*, 3, 305–360.

Johnson, D. E. 1998. *Applied Multivariate Methods for Data Analysis*. Duxbury Press, Pacific Grove, CA.

Mavruk, T., Overland, C., and Sjögren, S. 2020. Keeping it real or keeping it simple? Ownership concentration measures compared. *European Financial Management*, 26, 958–1005.

Shleifer, R. and Vishny, A. 1997. A survey of corporate governance. *Journal of Finance*, 52, 737–783.

5 Classical Linear Regression Model

INTRODUCTION

Regression analysis is powerful and the most common technique when analyzing multiple variables to answer complex research questions. It allows us to estimate the parameters that can be used to infer to the population. To this end, sampling techniques, covered in Chapter 2, are essential to make an inference on the population. The coefficient estimates obtained from the regression equation are assumed to be the estimates of the population parameters. For this assumption to hold, the coefficient estimates should be unbiased, on average. However, the estimates are almost never precisely correct, so there is often some deviation between the estimated coefficient and the population parameter.

While the aim is to minimize this deviation, the main focus is on the causal relationship of interest (see Angrist and Pischke, 2009), examining how the dependent variable y is influenced by changes in the independent variable x. Roughly speaking, the principal components analysis covered in Chapter 4 can be thought of as a regression analysis without the dependent variable. In a standard regression analysis, y is the outcome variable (endogenous) that potentially varies with the independent variable x, which is assumed to be exogenous. It is probably difficult to find a direct relationship between these two variables, and to think that you will obtain any robust significant results from such a simple model. Usually, it is necessary to include so-called control variables in the model to isolate the effects of x on y. A control variable is not of main interest to test a hypothesis in a regression model. It is included in the model because it could potentially affect the dependent variable, or it could affect the relationship between the main variable of interest and the dependent variable. These control variables are held fixed when examining and interpreting the relationship between y and x, which is the main variable of interest.

Because the estimates are based on a sample regression function, an inference needs to be made on the true population regression function, which is not observed. In order to obtain the best possible inference, you need a framework that is provided by the classical linear regression model (CLRM). Ordinary least squares (OLS) is a method that is used to estimate the CLRM.[1] It is important

[1] For more details the reader may consult Wooldridge (2002), Kennedy (2008), Verbeek (2017) and Stock and Watson (2019).

to emphasize that the CLRM will make it possible to infer the population only if several assumptions of the model hold. Thus, the main focus of this chapter is on these assumptions.

OLS is the most commonly used minimization method for linear models, and thus, this chapter can be seen as the core of the book. The CLRM is often applied to cross-sectional data, or data is treated as cross-sectional, although it may have a time dimension. Chapters 6–10 are related to this chapter as the assumptions of the CLRM in these coming chapters are relaxed one by one and an appropriate model is proposed. Thus, in the remaining chapters (besides Chapters 11 and 12), the book presents some alternative regression models where one or more of the CLRM assumptions do not hold in the data. The OLS method is still used in the alternative models in Chapters 6–9, but Chapter 10 mainly focuses on the maximum likelihood estimation that is used for non-linear models.

Taken together, this chapter begins with a presentation of a simple linear regression model. This is followed by a presentation of the multiple linear regression model, which also includes some control variables in the model. The assumptions of the CLRM are examined in detail, and the application of an OLS method to corporate finance is provided. The chapter ends with lab work and a mini case.

5.1 Linear Regression Model

In a linear regression model, the estimated values of the dependent variable y (the variable that is explained) are calculated using the values of the independent variable(s) $\mathbf{x}$ (the variables that can explain the dependent variable) in the dataset. If there is one independent variable explaining the dependent variable, it is called a simple linear regression model.

5.1.1 Simple Linear Regression Model

A simple linear regression model is given by

$$y_i = \beta_0 + \beta_1 x_i + e_i, \forall i = 1, \ldots, N, \tag{5.1}$$

where y_i is the dependent variable, β_0 is the intercept, and β_1 is the slope of the regression function, showing the effect of x on y. The notation β is used for a population (true) parameter. To indicate that the parameters are estimated using a sample, the notation b is often used:

$$y_i = b_0 + b_1 x_i + e_i. \tag{5.2}$$

The estimated values of the dependent variable are denoted as $\hat{y}$, and the differences between the actual values of the dependent variable and the estimated values are called the residuals, $e = y - \hat{y}$. The residuals are the estimated values of the dependent variable that are unexplained by the independent variables, factors. More formally, they are disturbances (disturbance term) or errors (error term) in the model, and all the assumptions concern disturbances or errors.[2] Figure 5.1 illustrates the residuals.

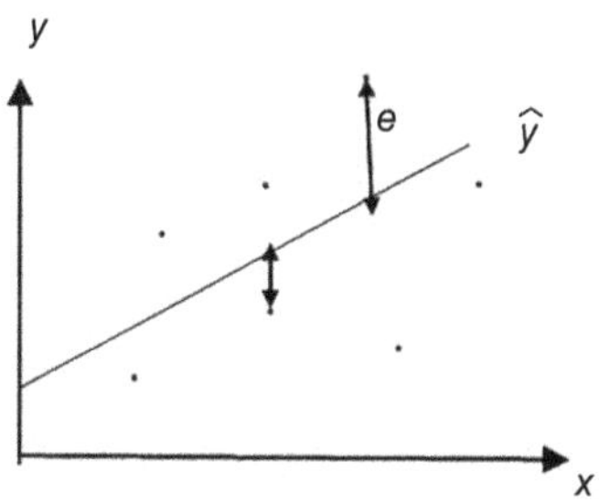

Figure 5.1. Residuals

The straight line represents the estimated values $(\hat{y})$ of the dependent variable y; the dots represent the correlations between y and the independent variable x. The deviations from the estimated value (straight line in Figure 5.1) are the residuals, e. Obviously, you have a good estimator if the deviations from the estimated values are small. Thus, the aim is to minimize the weighted sum of all these residuals. If equal weights for the residuals are assumed, the sum of the absolute values of the residuals is minimized. The method implicitly describes the minimization method of least absolute deviations (LAD). There may be other methods to minimize the residuals as well, for instance, if you are worried about data errors, you may assign a constant weight (a threshold) on the squared values of large residuals. However, minimizing the sum of the squared values of the residuals has been the most common method among the alternative approaches, which is discussed next.

5.1.2 Ordinary Least Squares Estimation Method

To calculate b in Equation (5.2), the most common estimation method, OLS, is used. The intercept b_0 in Equation (5.2) is the average of y when x is 0. The slope b_1 is calculated by taking the derivative of $E(y)$ with respect to $x : b_1 = \frac{dE(y|x)}{dx}$. Figure 5.2 shows the intercept and slope of the regression function.

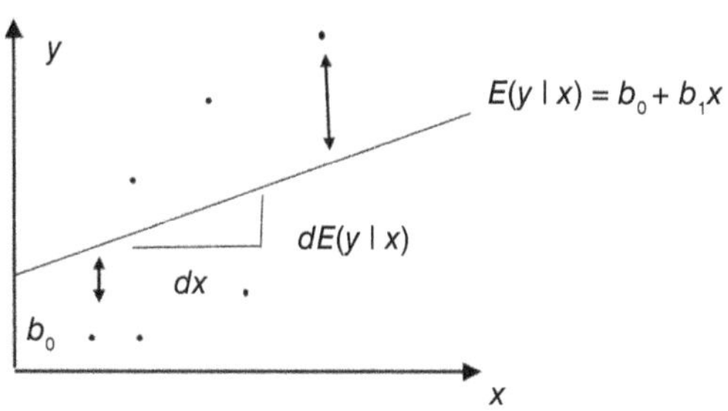

Figure 5.2. Intercept and slope

[2] Estimated residuals/errors/disturbances are just a by-product of the estimation process. The literature uses different names but they all refer to e in the model. Hence, this book uses these names interchangeably.

The OLS method, used to calculate the intercept b_0 and the slope b_1, suggests that the regression line fitted to the data minimizes the sum of squares of distance from each point to the line. In other words, the OLS method minimizes the residual sum of squares. The intercept and slope that best fit the data, using this principle, are denoted b_0 and b_1. The OLS estimate b_1 is the observed marginal effect that represents the unknown population parameter β_1. The OLS residuals that are minimized are given by

$$\hat{e}_i = y_i - \hat{y}_i = y_i - b_0 - b_1 x_i, \tag{5.3}$$

where $\hat{e}_i$ are the estimated residuals and $\hat{y}_i$ is the estimated dependent variable, $E(y_i \mid x_i)$. The residual sum of squares is given by

$$\sum_{i=1}^{N} \hat{e}_i^2 = \text{RSS}(b_0, b_1) = \sum_{i=1}^{N} (y_i - b_0 - b_1 x_i)^2. \tag{5.4}$$

Appendix A for Chapter 5 at the end of the book shows how to minimize the residual sum of squares (RSS) in a simple linear regression model.

As an example, Table 5.1 illustrates 10 observations for a Capital Asset Pricing Model (CAPM) regression, $R_p - R_f = b_0 + b_1\text{MTR} - R_f + e_i$, where the dependent variable $R_p - R_f$ is the equally weighted return on a portfolio of stocks minus the risk-free rate. The independent variable is the market risk premium $\text{MTR} - R_f$. For the dependent and the independent variables, the table also shows the deviation of each observation from its own mean (demeaned variables), $(y_i - \bar{y})$ and $(x_i - \bar{x})$, respectively. Finally, a squared demeaned independent variable $(x_i - \bar{x})^2$ and the multiplication of these demeaned variables $(x_i - \bar{x}) \times (y_i - \bar{y})$ are shown. The sums of the values of these variables are used to calculate b_0 and b_1.

Table 5.1 Intercept and slope in CAPM regression

Year	Month	E return AB	Rf	MKT	y:Ri-Rf	x:MKT-Rf	$(x_i - \bar{x})$	$(x_i - \bar{x})^2$	$(y_i - \bar{y})$	$(x_i - \bar{x}) \times (y_i - \bar{y})$
2010	Feb	−0.0016	0.0001	0.0247	−0.0017	0.0246	−0.0076	0.0001	−0.0495	0.0004
2010	Mar	0.0938	0.0002	0.0714	0.0937	0.0713	0.0391	0.0015	0.0459	0.0018
2010	Apr	0.0263	0.0001	0.0376	0.0261	0.0375	0.0053	0.0000	−0.0216	−0.0001
2010	Maj	−0.0617	0.0001	−0.1406	−0.0618	−0.1407	−0.1728	0.0299	−0.1096	0.0189
2010	Jun	0.0068	0.0001	0.0194	0.0066	0.0193	−0.0129	0.0002	−0.0411	0.0005
2010	Jul	0.3017	0.0001	0.1233	0.3016	0.1232	0.0911	0.0083	0.2538	0.0231
2010	Aug	−0.0357	0.0001	−0.0535	−0.0359	−0.0537	−0.0858	0.0074	−0.0836	0.0072
2010	Sep	0.1044	0.0001	0.1929	0.1043	0.1928	0.1607	0.0258	0.0565	0.0091
2010	Okt	0.0062	0.0001	0.0068	0.0061	0.0067	−0.0254	0.0006	−0.0417	0.0011
2010	Nov	0.0109	0.0001	−0.0342	0.0107	−0.0343	−0.0664	0.0044	−0.0370	0.0025
2010	Dec	0.0759	0.0001	0.1069	0.0758	0.1068	0.0747	0.0056	0.0280	0.0021
Avg.					*0.0478*	*0.0321*				
Sum								*0.0838*		*0.0665*

The numerator and denominator for b_1 are these aggregated values obtained from the bottom of the table. Finally, b_0 is computed using the averages of the dependent and independent variables (shown at the bottom of the table) and b_1. Although the data in the example are time series, it is treated as cross-sectional data. In other words, a static regression equation is used in the presence of time-series data, where dynamic regression equations are often used. The values obtained from the table are inserted into the formula for b_0 and b_1, more formally: $b_1 = \frac{0.0665}{0.0838} = 0.7940$ and $b_0 = 0.0478 - 0.7940 * 0.0321 = 0.0223$.

Note that 10 is a small number of observations for regression analysis. Also, by just calculating b_0 and b_1, you cannot draw meaningful conclusions; you need to examine both the statistical and economic significance of these coefficients, which will be covered in this chapter.

5.1.3 Multiple Linear Regression Model

The discussion so far has focused on a model with a single independent variable. Thus, the regression model in Equation (5.1) may have trouble with so-called omitted variables, which often lead to the OLS estimator of the effects of b_1 on the dependent variable y_i being biased, so-called omitted variable bias. This means that the mean of the sampling distribution of the OLS estimator is not equal to the true effect β_1. Omitted variable bias in the OLS estimator occurs if the independent variable is correlated with an omitted variable, which is a determinant of the dependent variable in the model. In this case, including the omitted variable that potentially affects the dependent variable (if data is available) can eliminate the omitted variable bias. This leads to the multiple linear regression model, in which the dependent variable y_i depends on more than one independent variable. More formally, the multiple regression model is described as follows:

$$y_i = b_0 + b_1 x_{1i} + b_2 x_{2i} + b_3 x_{3i}, \ldots, b_k x_{ki} + e_i, \forall i = 1, \ldots, N, \tag{5.5}$$

where the variables $\mathbf{x}$ represent all the independent variables that potentially explain the dependent variable, and e_i are the residuals. One or more of the independent variables are sometimes called control variables. As mentioned in the Introduction, the control variables are included in the model because it is assumed that they potentially affect the relationship between the main variable of interest and the dependent variable. The control variables are held fixed when interpreting the relationship between the independent variable and the main variable of interest.

The terminology of OLS used so far for the simple linear regression model is the same in the multiple linear regression model. Also, the formulas for the OLS estimators in a multiple regression model are similar to those in a simple regression model. The OLS residual is the difference between the dependent variable y_i and the predicted value $\hat{y}_i$; that is, $\hat{e}_i = y_i - \hat{y}_i$. The estimated coefficients that minimize the sum of squared errors are the OLS estimators. For more details on the derivation of the OLS estimators in a multiple regression model, the reader may consult Stock and Watson (2019).

The regression model in Equation (5.5) assumes that the functional form of the model is known and is correct. In other words, it is assumed that the function is linear (the model is linear in parameters) and the residual term follows the normal distribution. This makes the model parametric. In contrast, in non-parametric models, the functional form is not specified a priori; instead, it is determined from the data at hand. Semi-parametric models are a hybrid of parametric and non-parametric models. In such models, some of the independent variables take on predetermined functional forms (as in parametric models) and others do not take predetermined forms. Appendix C for Chapter 5 at the end of the book briefly covers the approach applied to semi-parametric models.

5.2 Assumptions of the Classical Linear Regression Model

The parameters in the CLRM are estimated based on a sample. To be able to make an inference on the population parameters, the assumptions of the CLRM that are based on the residuals have to hold in the empirical data. This section describes these assumptions.

5.2.1 Assumption 1: Linearity in Parameters

This assumption is about the linearity in parameters not in the variables. You could have inverse or squared values of the variables in the model, but you will be estimating a constant parameter for each of the independent variables. This assumption is necessary to make an assumption about the population parameter, otherwise it would be difficult to know what is being examined or estimated. Ignoring the linearity assumption will require us to use other estimation methods than OLS. However, the linearity assumption seems to provide a reasonable description of the data and it is easy to interpret.

5.2.2 Assumption 2: The Expected Value of the Residuals is Zero

This assumption, $E(e_i) = 0$, means, for instance, that the linear regression function in Equation (5.2) equals $b_0 + b_1 x_i$, on average; in other words, the regression line should be correct and thus the regression equation is deterministic. This assumption is a special case of Assumption 6 that will be covered in Section 5.2.6, implying that the independent variable and the residuals are uncorrelated. That is, the values of the independent variable do not provide any information about the expected values of the residuals or their covariances. Assumption 2 means that the residuals are zero, on average, while Assumption 6 implies that the residuals are zero conditional on the independent variable(s), on average. Assumption 2 provides a meaningful interpretation of the relation between the dependent and independent variables. In a sense, if this relation is incorrect on average, there is no reason to estimate the regression function. The assumption also implies that b_0 and b_1 are unbiased estimates of β_0 and β_1. Note that, if there is an intercept in the model, you cannot test this assumption, as the sum of the estimated residuals will be zero, $\sum_{i=1}^{N} \hat{e}_i = 0$. Appendix B for Chapter 5 at the end of the book provides an illustration of this assumption.

5.2.3 Assumption 3: Homoskedasticity

The homoskedasticity assumption, $\sigma_{e_i}^2 = \sigma^2, \forall i$, suggests that the variance of the residuals is constant for all i. If this assumption holds, e_i is said to be homoskedastic; in other words, the variance of e_i does not depend on the independent variable x_i. If this assumption is violated, then e_i is said to be heteroskedastic. The applied section of this chapter will examine the estimated residuals $\hat{e}_i$ to determine whether they are heteroskedastic or homoskedastic.

If heteroskedasticity is evident in the regression analysis, it will cause two serious problems. First, a number of desired properties of the OLS estimator will not hold. These properties will be covered shortly. Second, if the conventional standard errors that are obtained from OLS are incorrect (i.e., meaning that the standard test cannot be used), the z-statistics will not have variance equal to 1. This also means that OLS is ineffective. However, this is less of a problem since you can remedy the problem of heteroskedasticity by transforming the regression model, as long as the other assumptions of the CLRM hold.

Let's revisit Equation (5.2) in the presence of heteroskedasticity, so that $\sigma_{e_i}^2 = \sigma_i^2$, the variance changes for each i, and transform the regression equation by assuming that σ_i^2 is known. The transformation is done by dividing the variables by σ_i:

$$\frac{y_i}{\sigma_i} = b_0 \frac{1}{\sigma_i} + b_1 \frac{x_i}{\sigma_i} + \frac{e_i}{\sigma_i}. \tag{5.6}$$

For simplicity, write the equation as

$$y_i^* = b_0 + b_1 x_i^* + e_i^*. \tag{5.7}$$

The variance of the residuals in this transformed equation is given by

$$\sigma_{e_i^*}^2 = \text{var}\left(\frac{e_i}{\sigma_i}\right) = \frac{1}{\sigma_i^2}\text{var}\left(e_i\right) = \frac{1}{\sigma_i^2}\sigma_i^2 = 1. \tag{5.8}$$

Equation (5.8) shows that the residuals in the transformed equation are homoskedastic because it equals a constant, 1. When the regression equation is transformed, the generalized least squares (GLS) estimator is obtained. GLS is more efficient than OLS since it has resulted in homoskedastic residuals, but the assumption that σ_i^2 is known is very strong and may not hold in real data. Researchers can make other assumptions about the structure of the heteroskedasticity to make GLS feasible. One example is to assume that the residual variance develops with x_i.

5.2.3.1 Test for Heteroskedasticity

How can you test for heteroskedasticity? One commonly used method is the Breusch–Pagan test. The basic idea behind this test is as follows. Consider Equation (5.2) again and assume that the residuals are heteroskedastic; the variance of the estimated residuals is determined by some other variables than x_i. The problem is that you either do not know what these other variables are, or have difficulty obtaining and including them in the regression model. In this situation you can predict the dependent variable $\hat{y}_i$ and add some powers, then include it in the regression model. If the residuals from the original regression equation are already homoskedastic, the additional variables that are added to the model should not produce significant parameters, and thus the structure of the regression equation should be correct. This also means that if you add powers to $\hat{y}_i$ and include them in the regression equation, the parameters of these powered $\hat{y}_i$s should not be significant.

5.2.3.2 Remedy for Heteroskedasticity

The most common remedy for the problem caused by heteroskedasticity in regression models is to use heteroskedasticity-consistent (HC) standard errors, or simply White (1980) standard errors:

$$se_{\text{HC}}(b_1) = \sqrt{\left(\sum_{i=1}^{N} x_i x_i'\right)^{-1} \sum_{i=1}^{N} \hat{e}_i^2 x_i x_i' \left(\sum_{i=1}^{N} x_i x_i'\right)^{-1}}, \tag{5.9}$$

where $\hat{e}_i$ is the estimated OLS residual. Indeed, regardless of the result from the Breusch–Pagan test, you are better off using HC standard errors, which will alter the standard errors and hence the t-values while the coefficients will remain the same. This estimation is still conducted by OLS. HC standard errors use the estimated variance of residuals $\hat{e}_i^2$ instead of unknown residual variance σ_i^2; however, the use of $\hat{e}_i^2$ relies on N being large. When N is large, the HC standard errors will merge with the conventional standard errors that are homoskedastic. This means that you may use HC standard errors even if you do not have a problem with heteroskedasticity. This approach also gives a simple examination for heteroskedasticity, first running OLS with the conventional standard errors and then running it again with HC standard errors. In the absence of heteroskedasticity, the results from the two regression models should produce roughly similar standard errors. Taken together, using HC standard errors is easier than assuming a structure for the unknown variance σ_i^2 to transform the regression equation and thus using GLS.

5.2.3.3 Heteroskedasticity and Risk

There is a significant relationship between heteroskedasticity and total risk, measured as the volatility of stock returns (Schwert and Seguin, 1990). Black (1976) suggests that high-volatility stocks tend to be more sensitive to market volatility changes than low-volatility stocks. It seems that when stock volatilities change, they tend to change in the same direction. Evidence from Schwert and Seguin (1990) is consistent with the results from Black (1976), and suggests that the proportional changes in volatility are not the same for all firms. Particularly, the authors show that small-firm variances are approximately four times more sensitive to market volatility changes than large-firm variances.

This result also has implications for calculating betas (systematic risk) in CAPM regressions. If heteroskedasticity is non-proportional, the beta coefficient in CAPM regressions varies with the level of aggregate volatility. As a remedy for this problem (Schwert and Seguin, 1990), add the term market risk premium (see Section 5.1.2 for the definition of market risk premium) divided by its estimated variance, which is referred to as the heteroskedastic market model. In addition, using equally weighted market portfolio return in the market risk premium calculations and applying a weighted least squares approach also seems to work. However, it is common to use generalized autoregressive conditional heteroskedasticity (GARCH) models, which represent a set of time series whose variances and covariances change over time. These models make it possible to calculate time-varying betas as they approximate the time-varying behavior of the conditional variances. Schwert and Seguin (1990) show that the heteroskedastic model applied to CAPM and GARCH models yields similar results. The overall conclusion from these analyses is that heteroskedasticity is important when examining stock returns and their volatility. Chapter 7 will briefly cover GARCH models.

5.2.4 Assumption 4: Serially Uncorrelated Residuals

If the assumption of serially uncorrelated residuals, more formally $\mathrm{cov}(e_i, e_j) = 0$, $\forall i \neq j$, does not hold, then it is said that e_i is serially correlated or autocorrelated. This is related to the time-series data, which have a natural ordering across time, meaning that you cannot change the place of two observations that depend on time while aiming at maintaining the structure of the data. If there is such dependency, it is likely that there is autocorrelation in the data. What could be the remedy if the data suffer from autocorrelation? The most common model to use is an autoregressive (AR) one, which also gives a test of autocorrelation. The notation for time series is usually t, then Assumption 4 can be rewritten as $\mathrm{cov}(e_t, e_{t-1}) = 0$ and the first-order AR model would be as follows:

$$e_t = \rho e_{t-1} + u_t. \tag{5.10}$$

Here the residuals u_t are assumed to satisfy the CLRM assumptions and the parameter ρ is the autocorrelation coefficient that is assumed to be $-1 < \rho < +1$. If $\rho > 0$, then e_t shows a positive autocorrelation, meaning that a positive value at time $t-1$ is followed by a positive value at time t. If, instead, $\rho < 0$, then e_t shows a negative autocorrelation: if the value at time $t-1$ is below average then the value at time t is likely to be above average. Finally, if $\rho = 0$, then e_t is not autocorrelated. The general pattern for autocorrelation can be written as $\mathrm{corr}(e_t, e_{t-k}) = \rho^k$ for $k \geq 1$. The interpretation of ρ is as follows. If $|\rho| < 1$, then the effects on u_t will disappear over time. For $k \geq 1$, the effects of ρ on u_t will be smaller. This is the most common autocorrelation structure. Consider the 2008 financial crisis; its effects on individual firms and the market were greater in 2009 than in 2012. The case of $|\rho| > 1$ is not that common in financial markets.

In the presence of autocorrelation, the conventional formula for standard errors is not correct. Similar to HC standard errors, in the presence of autocorrelation you can use heteroskedasticity and autocorrelation-consistent (HAC) standard errors:

$$se_{\text{HAC}}(b_1) = \sqrt{\sum_{j=1}^{m} \sum_{t=1}^{T} w_t \hat{e}_t w_j \hat{e}_{t-j}}, \tag{5.11}$$

where w is the weight and m is the lag order or bandwidth parameter, which increases with T but at a lower rate. A conventional choice of lag order is $m = 0.75T^{1/3}$. For instance, if you have 10-month data, m would be approximately 2 $(m = 0.75 * 10^{1/3} \approx 2)$. Using HAC standard errors is also superior to GLS as you need to make an additional assumption for the autocorrelation structure to use GLS. It sounds too good to be true, but HAC standard errors can be used even in the absence of heteroskedasticity and autocorrelation. If there is no heteroskedasticity and/or autocorrelation, the HAC standard error formula will merge to the conventional OLS standard error formula (see Verbeek, 2017 for details).

To test for autocorrelation, the Breusch–Godfrey Lagrange multiplier (LM) test can be used. Consider a standard simple regression equation where the residuals are assumed to follow an AR(1) process:

$$y_t = b_0 + b_1 x_i + e_t. \tag{5.12}$$

The residuals in Equation (5.12) can be replaced by $e_t = \rho e_{t-1} + u_t$ and, since is unknown, you can use its estimate $\hat{e}_{t-1}$ instead:

$$y_t = b_0 + b_1 x_i + \rho \hat{e}_{t-1} + u_t. \tag{5.13}$$

The Breusch–Godfrey LM test in Equation (5.13) tests the null hypothesis that $\rho = 0$ by using a t-test. If the null hypothesis cannot be rejected, it indicates that $e_t = u_t$, and the residuals in Equation (5.12) do not follow an AR(1) process. If the aim is to test AR for a higher-order process, AR(p) errors, you can implement the Breusch–Godfrey LM test by using an F-test for the null hypothesis that $H_0 : \rho_1 = \rho_2 = \cdots = \rho_p = 0$. The regression Equation (5.13) would be modified by

$$y_t = b_0 + b_1 x_i + \rho_1 \hat{e}_{t-1} + \rho_2 \hat{e}_{t-2} + \ldots + \rho_p \hat{e}_{t-p} + u_t. \tag{5.14}$$

5.2.5 Assumption 5: Normality in Residuals

The assumption of normality in residuals, $e_i \sim N(0, \sigma^2)$, suggests that the residuals are normally distributed. This assumption also implies that large outliers are unlikely. If this assumption does not hold, the results obtained from the OLS estimator can be unreliable (Stock and Watson, 2019). If the data contain large outliers, you should examine these outliers to make sure that they are not mistakes. Readers are referred to Chapter 3 for data management techniques for outliers.

If N is small, the distribution of t and F (to be covered shortly) used to test the significance of the coefficients is complicated, because it depends on an unknown population distribution. There is no point using small-sample t- and F-distributions to test the hypothesis. If N is large, this assumption will hold. Because of the central limit theorem, the residuals will be approximately normally distributed. You can then use a large-sample distribution, for example, Student's t-distribution instead. The importance of the normal distribution stems from the central limit theorem, hence from large-sample considerations. A valid question (without an exact answer) is, then, what is large for N? Conventional textbooks use a threshold of 30 in the calculations for some examples, but this may not be enough for estimation using empirical data.

5.2.6 Assumption 6: Exogeneity

The assumption of exogeneity means that the independent variables in the model should be uncorrelated with the residuals. More formally, $E(e_i \mid x_i) = 0$; that is, the expected value of the residuals is zero conditioned on the independent variable(s). As mentioned, this is a special case of Assumption 2, which implies that residuals are zero, on average. If Assumption 6 does not hold, it is said that x_i is endogenous and the OLS parameters b are biased. This assumption makes less sense with fixed regressors. However, in corporate finance studies you typically have observational data and random regressors. Thus, if x_i is random then the assumption of exogeneity should hold. This assumption is so crucial, particularly in corporate finance studies, that this book will devote the next chapter to discuss endogeneity concerns in OLS regressions. It will cover how to test endogeneity and what kind of methods can be used to remedy the endogeneity problem.

5.3 Properties of the OLS Estimator

The OLS method may do a good job of minimizing the sum of the squared values of the residuals, but this does not necessarily mean that it estimates a parameter that reflects the true population parameter β well.[3] To provide some intuition, assume that you use OLS to estimate the parameter b in a repeated sample by keeping the values of the independent variable unchanged, but obtain new observations for the dependent variable and re-estimate the parameters 1000 times. From each estimation you will obtain, and since the samples differ, the bs are also likely to be different. The distribution of these estimated bs is called the sampling distribution, and its properties will be discussed next.

[3] Also, not all estimation criteria may optimize an objective function – for example, in the case of the generalized method of moments (GMM), which will be discussed briefly in Chapter 7.

If the assumptions of the CLRM hold, the estimators obtained using OLS will have a number of required properties that lead to the so-called best linear unbiased estimator (BLUE). In this acronym, "best" represents that the OLS estimator b has the minimum variance within the class of linear unbiased estimators. This holds under the condition that the residuals in the linear regression model are uncorrelated, residuals have equal variances, and the expected value of the residuals is zero. This theorem is known as the Gauss–Markov theorem (Wooldridge, 2002). "Linear" in the acronym indicates that b is a linear estimator. "Unbiased" means that on average, the estimated b is equal to the population parameter β. Finally, "estimator" in the acronym stands for b being an estimator of the population parameter β.

5.3.1 Consistency

Consistency means that the probability that the estimated b is more than a fixed value of distance away from its true value β goes to zero as the sample size gets larger. This is an important asymptotic property. Asymptotic properties of estimators relate to the distribution of an estimator when the sample size gets large and approaches infinity. The word asymptotic refers to an infinitely large sample, or means that the sample size goes to infinity. The bias and standard error of an estimator tend to decrease as the sample size goes to infinity. For a very large sample size, the estimated coefficients tend to be effectively unbiased with high precision. Also, for a large sample the central limit theorem suggests that the estimated function can often be approximated by a normal distribution. Since, in reality, infinitely large samples do not exist, the word "approximate" is used; that is, results obtained based on asymptotic properties are only approximations. This means that estimated coefficients can be assumed asymptotically normally distributed. Assumptions 2 and 6 of the CLRM, described above, are sufficient for consistency of the OLS estimator (see Kennedy, 2008 for more details).

5.3.2 Unbiasedness

Under Assumptions 2 and 6 of the CLRM, the OLS estimator is unbiased. This means that the OLS estimator is unbiased as long as the residuals have mean zero and are independent of all regressors, even if heteroskedasticity or autocorrelation is present. This property is related to the mean of the sampling distribution. The estimated b is said to be an unbiased estimator of the population parameter β if the average value of its sampling distribution is β. This means that there is no systematic bias in the estimation of the coefficients. The property of unbiasedness is a stronger condition than the consistency property because it holds even in small samples. If you do the exercise of estimating b in a repeated sample, say 1000 times, you are more likely to obtain a mean value of b that is closer to the true parameter β. In this example you may have the consistency condition and the unbiasedness condition if the distance between the estimated b and its true value β eventually goes to zero. However, not all unbiased estimators are consistent, unless the variance decreases as the sample size gets larger.

5.3.3 Efficiency

The OLS estimator, by only minimizing the sum of the squared values of the residuals, does not necessarily lead to an unbiased estimate. Another property concerns the variance of the sampling distribution, so-called efficiency. Under Assumptions 1–6 of the CLRM, the OLS estimator is efficient (best). This means that the OLS method leads to the lowest variance among any other linear unbiased estimators. Examining an arbitrary alternative unbiased estimator, the Gauss–Markov theorem proves that the OLS estimator has the lowest variance among the class of linear unbiased estimators.

5.4 Tests for Parameters and Goodness of Fit in Ordinary Least Squares

This section begins with a test of a single hypothesis using Student's t-test and then discusses how to test multiple hypotheses using an F-test. It also covers goodness-of-fit statistics R^2 and the F-statistics for goodness of fit, which differ from the above-mentioned F-test as the latter refers to the F-statistics used as a specification test for the overall model.

5.4.1 The *t*-Statistic

The t-statistic is used to test whether the estimated single parameter is significant or not. The parameter is often tested against zero, but it can be tested against any constant. The test statistics for parameter b are given by the t-value $\frac{b-b^*}{\text{SE}(b)}$, where SE($b$) is the standard error of the parameter b and b^* is the value of β under the null hypothesis, H_0. It is common to set $b^* = 0$, so that we test whether b is significantly different from zero in a two-sided test that aims to test whether the variable has a significant effect on the dependent variable y_i. As discussed in Chapter 2, the test could also be one sided (e.g., b smaller or larger than zero, or a certain value). You need some distribution for the t-value to compare the estimated t-values with the critical t-values obtained from the (Student's) t-distribution table. It is shown that the t-value follows a t-distribution with $T-2$ $(n-k-1)$ degrees of freedom, where n is the number of observations and k is the number of parameters estimated in the model, including the intercept. For the comparison you need to choose a significance level, usually denoted α, a so-called size of the test, which determines the rejection region. α is often set to 5% in business and economics studies, but setting $\alpha = 1\%$ is not uncommon. On the other hand, $\alpha = 10\%$ is known as partial significance and interpreted cautiously or preferably not at all. If the estimated t-value, in absolute terms, is greater than the critical t-value obtained from the t table at predetermined significance level α and $T-2$ degree of freedom, you can reject H_0; otherwise, H_0 cannot be rejected.

5.4.2 The *F*-Statistic for Multiple Hypotheses

While the t-statistic is used to test a single hypothesis, a single parameter, you sometimes need to test the significance of more than one parameter simultaneously, or want to make a joint test, in which case you use the F-statistic, testing multiple hypotheses. For the F-test you are actually estimating two regressions. One is an unrestricted regression, where the parameters are determined by the empirical data as in Equation (5.5). The other is a restricted regression, where some parameters (those you want to test) are restricted. For instance, if you impose $b_1+b_2=1$ in Equation (5.5) (because you have some theory suggesting this restriction), then Equation (5.5) becomes a restricted regression. This means that you can substitute $b_1=1-b_2$ into the regression.

The F-test statistics can be calculated as $F=\frac{\text{RRSS}-\text{URSS}}{\text{URSS}} * \frac{N-k}{m}$, where RRSS is the restricted residual sum of squares, URSS is the unrestricted residual sum of squares, N is the number of observations, k is the total number of estimated parameters including the intercept, and m is the number of imposed restrictions. For instance, in the example above, you have imposed one restriction, $m=1$. As in the t-test, you compare the calculated F-value with the critical F-value obtained from the F-distribution. The critical F-value has two degrees of freedom parameters. In the F-distribution table, column m (the number of restrictions) will show the first degrees of freedom, and row $N-k$ will show the second degrees of freedom, which will help in obtaining the critical F-value. Unlike the t-distribution, the F-distribution has only positive values, so you will reject the null hypothesis (e.g., $H_0: b_1+b_2=1$) if the calculated F-value is greater than the critical F-value. The t-distribution is directly related to the F-distribution. In a single hypothesis, the F-value would roughly equal the square of the t-value.

5.4.3 Goodness-of-Fit Statistics, R^2

To measure how well the variables explain the variation in the dependent variable, how well the proposed model fits the data at hand, the coefficient of determination, R^2, is used. The total variation in the dependent variable y_i is given by the *total sum of squares*, $\text{TSS}=\sum_{i=1}^{N}(y_i-\bar{y})^2$. The total variation has two parts, one that the model can explain, the *explained sum of squares*, $\text{ESS}=\sum_{i=1}^{N}(\hat{y}_i-\bar{y})^2$, and one that the model cannot explain, the *residual sum of squares*, $\text{RSS}=\sum_{i=1}^{N}\hat{e}_i^{\,2}$. The coefficient of determination, R^2, is defined by the fraction of explained variance to total (explained and unexplained) variance in the dependent variable, $R^2=\frac{\text{ESS}}{\text{TSS}}$ – a ratio taking values between 0 and 1. The higher ESS is, the higher R^2. Using cross-sectional datasets, models with R^2 above 0.8 are rare, but using time-series data you can find models that have R^2 above 0.8 (see Brooks, 2019).

If R^2 is 1, all the correlation points between x and y in Figure 5.1 would lie on the regression line. If R^2 is 0, the regression line would be flat, and the correlation points between x and y would randomly lie around this flat regression line.

The main problem with deciding the goodness of fit based on R^2 is that it does not decrease if we include new independent variables that do not add much to the model. It either remains the same or increases if the new variables are meaningful. Thus, a modified goodness-of-fit measure is used instead, adjusted R^2 or $\overline{R}^2$, which modifies R^2 with loss of degrees of freedom due to adding new independent variables in the model: $\overline{R}^2 = 1 - \left[\frac{N-1}{N-k}(1-R^2)\right]$. The equation indicates that if you add a new independent variable, k increases, but if R^2 is unaffected by an offsetting amount, then $\overline{R}^2$ would decrease. It is still problematic to use $\overline{R}^2$ alone as a measure of goodness of fit as it is not a test statistic, merely showing the fraction of explained variance in the dependent variable. Thus, the F-statistic for goodness of fit in a model can be used to test whether the regression model fits the empirical data at hand, which is explained next.

5.4.4 The *F*-Statistics for Goodness of Fit

The test statistics based on F-statistics for goodness of fit compare ESS to RSS: $F = \frac{\text{ESS}/(k-1)}{\text{RSS}/(N-k)}$ and as before the F-distribution has two degrees of freedom. In the numerator, is adjusted for the total number of parameters in the model, k, minus 1, which excludes the intercept (unlike the F-test for multiple hypotheses described in Section 5.4.2). In the denominator, RSS is adjusted for the total number of observations N in the model, minus the total number of parameters k in the model (including the intercept). If the calculated F-value is greater than the critical F-value obtained from the F-distribution table, then the model is a good fit for the empirical data. Intuitively, this F-test tests whether R^2 is significantly different from 0, or high enough in the model. Again, a valid question (without a concrete answer) is what is high enough. By only examining the result of the F-test and looking at R^2 in the current model, you will not obtain an answer to the question of what is high. You need to compare R^2 from the model to R^2 from a similar model in the previous literature that you strictly follow. Note also that the F-statistic mentioned here is different from the F-statistic used to test multiple hypotheses, as explained in Section 5.4.2. The applied section of this chapter will provide an example of an interpretation of a t-test, an F-test, and R^2.

5.5 Interpreting the Parameter Estimates

The main reason why OLS has been the most popular estimator is because it is easy to apply to the empirical data at hand. It is easier to examine (and interpret) a linear relationship between the variables of interest, regardless of how complicated the relation among the variables can be. The focus is on the economic significance, but of course statistical significance is necessary. Empirical researchers tend to perform OLS to begin with and use the outcome as some sort of benchmark in a more detailed analysis. It is also easier to find the OLS estimator in most software packages. Researchers aim to find alternative estimators when the OLS estimator does not meet the desired estimation criteria. OLS is used in cross-sectional data to examine how the independent variable(s) affect the dependent variable. Suppose that Assumptions 1–6 of the CLRM hold and that you want to examine the effect of an independent variable on the dependent variable. Three outcomes would be interesting to examine.

First, whether the parameter or the coefficient of the independent variable is significant. As seen in Section 5.4, this could be done by a t-test to examine a single hypothesis, or by an F-test to examine multiple hypotheses. The software packages produce a t-test and an F-test for goodness of fit for the overall model (see Section 5.4.4), but not an F-test of multiple hypotheses (see Section 5.4.2). You need to run a post-estimation for an F-test to examine multiple hypotheses. For a single hypothesis test, the software packages also produce the confidence interval and a p-value, indicating the significance of the coefficient. If the p-value is less than our predetermined significance level of 5%, this means that the coefficient is significant at the 5% level (in a two-sided test).

This result also indicates that the calculated t-value in absolute terms is greater than the critical t-value obtained from the t-distribution table with the corresponding degrees of freedom. This also means that the corresponding confidence interval, produced by the software package, does not include 0. If it does, then the coefficient would not be significantly different from 0; relatedly, the calculated t-value would be lower than the critical t-value, and the p-value would be greater than the predetermined significance level of 5%. Thus, all three statistics – t-value, p-value, and a confidence interval for the coefficient – tell the same story, whether the coefficient is significant or not. This means that it would be enough to look at only one of these statistics, preferably the p-value because of its simple interpretation. If the calculated (produced by the software) p-value is less than 5%, then the coefficient is significant at the 5% level (in a two-sided test). For a one-sided test, roughly half of the p-value produced by the software can be used to determine the significance of a coefficient, but to be absolutely sure about the p-value you can run a post-estimation.

Second, once you establish that the coefficient is significant, the sign of the coefficient should be examined. The sign will indicate the direction of the effect of the independent variable on the dependent variable. It will tell whether the variation in the independent variable increases or decreases the dependent variable. If the hypothesis is directional, a one-sided test is useful. Finally, the magnitude (size) of the effect of the independent variable should be examined. All three outcomes should be discussed in the analysis, but of course the last two outcomes become important only if the coefficient is significant. Otherwise, there is no point in interpreting the sign and size of the coefficient.

5.5.1 Marginal Effects

Suppose that the coefficient is significant, how then to interpret the effects? The most common and important (depending on the research question) interpretation is the so-called marginal effects of continuous variables, or relative effects of dummy variables. Assume that x_i is continuous and b_i is the estimated coefficient, then the straightforward interpretation of the marginal effects is that if x_i increases by one unit, the dependent variable y_i will change (an increase or decrease depending on the sign) by b_i units. If instead x_i is a dummy variable taking the value 1 for one category and 0 for another category, then the interpretation of the relative effect would be as follows: the dependent variable y_i will change by b_i units for the given category 1 relative to category 0, it is a relative effect. The intercept from the regression model, b_0, is the conditional mean when the independent variables equal 0. The important point is the unit of the dependent and (for continuous variables) independent variables. This must be crystal clear before we perform OLS.

5.5.2 Elasticity

Besides the marginal or relative effects, it would be interesting to examine the elasticity, ε. The elasticity of the dependent variable y_i with respect to the (continuous) independent variable x_i is given by the ratio of the percentage change in y to the percentage change in x, $\varepsilon = \frac{dy}{dx} * \frac{x}{y}$. The elasticity is interpreted as follows: if x changes by 1%, then y on average will change by ε%. In the OLS regression, the elasticity is evaluated at the mean value of the variables, so that the equation becomes $\varepsilon = \frac{dE(y)}{dx} * \frac{x}{E(y)} = b * \frac{x}{E(y)} = b * \frac{\bar{x}}{\bar{y}}$, where the mean values of the dependent and independent variables ($\bar{x}$ and $\bar{y}$) substitute for x and $E(y)$. You can also evaluate the elasticity at a certain value of x if the hypothesis suggests a certain value.

The semi-elasticity could also be interesting, in which case the interpretation would be such that if x changes by one unit then y on average will change by b%. The calculations of marginal/relative effects or elasticities depend on the functional form of the regression equation. For instance, the calculation of the marginal effects will be different if the model is a log–log model, in which both the dependent variable and the independent variable are in logarithmic form. It could be a log–lin model, in which the dependent variable is logarithmic but the independent variable is linear, or a lin–log model, reciprocal model, or polynomial model, in which the independent variable enters the model with various powers. Of course, you can also combine these features and have a multiple regression model, in which, for instance, the dependent variable is in log form and some of the **x** variables are in log form, while others are in linear form. Table 5.2 presents marginal effects and elasticity calculations for common functional forms in OLS regressions. For simplicity, the index on dependent and independent variables is dropped and population parameters β are used instead of parameters estimated from a sample b.

Table 5.2 Summary of common functional forms

Model	Form	Slope = $\frac{dY}{dY}$	Elasticity = $\frac{dY}{dX} \times \frac{X}{Y}$
Linear	$y = \beta_0 + \beta_1 x + e$	β_1	$\beta_1 \frac{x}{y}$
Log–log	$\ln y = \beta_0 + \beta_1 \ln x + e$	$\beta_1 \frac{y}{x}$	β_1
Log–lin	$\ln y = \beta_0 + \beta_1 x + e$	$\beta_1 y$	$\beta_1 x$
Lin–log	$y = \beta_0 + \beta_1 \ln x + e$	$\beta_1 \frac{1}{x}$	$\beta_1 \frac{1}{y}$
Reciprocal	$y = \beta_0 + \beta_1 \left(\frac{1}{x}\right) + e$	$-\beta_1 \frac{1}{x^2}$	$-\beta_1 \frac{1}{xy}$
Log-inverse	$\ln(y) = \beta_0 - \beta_1 \left(\frac{1}{x}\right) + e$	$\beta_1 \frac{y}{x^2}$	$\beta_1 \frac{1}{x}$

When the values of x and y are not specified, the elasticity is often evaluated at the mean values $\bar{x}$ and $\bar{y}$.

5.6 Interaction Effects in Dummy Variable Regression Models

In some analyses, if the independent variables are qualitative in nature (nominal level), such as gender and nationality of CEO, then dummy variables are used, indicating the category in which the study subject belongs. The dummy variables take the value 1 for one category and 0 for the reference category. The alternative names used for the dummy variables are indicator variable, binary variable, categorical variable, and dichotomous variable. A simple dummy variable regression equation is given as follows:

$$y_i = b_0 + b_1 D_i + e_i. \tag{5.15}$$

The relative effect of $D_i = 1$ on y_i is b_1. The mean value of y_i for $D_i = 1$ is calculated as $E(y_i \mid D_i = 1) = b_0 + b_1 \times 1 = b_0 + b_1$. Finally, the mean value of y_i for $D_i = 0$ is given by $E(y_i, D_i = 0) = b_0 + b_1 * 0 = b_0$.

Let us introduce an interaction term into Equation (5.15). A clear understanding of how the interaction model with two dummy variables works will make the interpretations a lot easier in the analysis of the model that has an interaction term with one dummy variable and one continuous variable. Thus, this analysis provides an interpretation of an interaction model with two dummy variables:

$$y_i = b_0 + b_1 D_{1i} + b_2 D_{2i} + b_3 D_{1i} \times D_{2i} + e_i. \tag{5.16}$$

For the sake of interpretation, assume that the dependent variable y is corporate social responsibility (CSR) activity, D_1 (indicating financial constraint of the firm) takes the value 1 for financially constrained firms and 0 otherwise. D_2 is a dummy taking the value 1 for large firms and 0 for small firms. In the interaction model, these dummy variables D_1 and D_2 are called the main effects, and $D_1 \times D_2$ is the interaction effect, which is the main variable of interest in this exercise. The interaction effect gives the joint (or simultaneous) effect of these two dummy variables. Equation (5.17) provides a more formal description (note that the subscript i is dropped from the dummy variables for simplicity):

$$y_i = b_0 + b_1 \text{Fconst.} + b_2 \text{Large} + b_3 \text{Fconst.} \times \text{Large} + e_i. \tag{5.17}$$

The interpretations below are based on Equation (5.17).

1. b_1 is the differential effect of financially constrained firms for small firms.
2. b_2 is the differential effect of large firms for financially unconstrained firms.
3. b_3 is the incremental effect of being large conditional on the firm switching from being financially unconstrained to financially constrained.

To better understand the interpretations below, let's write the expected CSR activity for financially constrained firms:

$$E\left[\text{CSR}_{\text{Fconst.}}\right] = b_0 + b_1 + b_2\text{Large} + b_3\text{Large} = (b_0 + b_1) + (b_2 + b_3)\text{Large}, \quad (5.18)$$

and the expected CSR activity for large firms is given by

$$E\left[\text{CSR}_{\text{Large}}\right] = b_0 + b_1\text{Fconst.} + b_2 + b_3\text{Fconst.} = (b_0 + b_2) + (b_1 + b_3)\text{Fconst.} \quad (5.19)$$

4. $(b_2 + b_3)$ is the differential effect of large firms for financially constrained firms (see Equation (5.18) for details).
5. $(b_1 + b_3)$ is the differential effect of financially constrained firms for large firms (see Equation (5.19) for details).
6. The difference between points 5 and 1 = $b_1 + b_3 - b_1 = b_3$ is the interaction effect.
7. The difference between points 4 and 2 = $b_2 + b_3 - b_2 = b_3$ is the interaction effect.
8. Total effect: $E(y_i \mid D_1 = 1, D_2 = 1) = b_0 + b_1 + b_2 + b_3$.

If an additional continuous independent variable x_i is included in the model, this would not affect the interpretation of points 1–7 but the total effect would be different. You would add $b_4 \times \bar{x}$ to the calculation in point 8. If one of the dummy variables was a continuous variable instead, say the variable Large is a continuous variable, then the main interest of the interaction term b_3 is called the differential slope coefficient and b_1 would be the differential intercept coefficient since it is still a dummy for financially constrained firms. The interaction effect b_3 would be interpreted as the marginal effect of a one unit increase in size for financially constrained firms.

The use of three-way interaction models is increasing in corporate finance studies, although their interpretation is somehow more complicated than the two-way interaction models as described above. For simplicity, suppose you want to include the geographic aspect in regression Equation (5.17) and thus include a dummy for urban firms (headquartered in urban areas). You would have three regressors in a model: Fconst., Large, and Urban. You can think of the variable Fconst. as the main independent variable and the variables Large and Urban as the two moderator variables whose relationship you want to examine with the dependent variable y, CSR activity. In the three-way interaction model: (i) all three variables are included separately; (ii) a pairwise combination of these variables is included – Fconst.Large, Fconst.Urban, LargeUrban; and (iii) triple interaction of these variables is included in the model, Fconst.LargeUrban. It is easier to interpret them when one or more of these variables is discrete (in this example, all three variables are discrete), but there are also examples where all three variables are continuous. The main interest in the three-way interaction model is to examine the triple interaction effects. That is, you examine whether the studied two-way interaction relationship in Equation (5.17) is different across urban firms versus rural firms.

5.7 Application of OLS Method to Capital Asset Pricing Model

This section applies the analysis in Table 5.1 to individual stocks in a larger dataset. The analysis examines whether the CAPM holds for the return of the Swedish bearing and seal manufacturing company (SKF) stock in a weekly dataset between week 35 in 2004 and week 35 in 2010. The CAPM is an equilibrium model that can be used to estimate the expected return for any risky asset given the risk-free rate, the expected return on the market portfolio, and the asset's relative risk to the market portfolio. The model is introduced in work by Treynor (1961) and Sharpe (1964), developed further by Lintner (1965), Mossin (1966), and Black (1972). Although the dataset used in CAPM regressions is time series, a static regression equation is used instead of dynamic regression equations. Table 5.3 provides descriptive statistics for the dependent variable risk premium on the SKF stock ($R_{\text{skf}} - R_f$) and the independent variable risk premium on the Nasdaq OMX30 market ($R_m - R_f$). The risk-free rate is the 3-month Treasury bill rate obtained from Riksbanken (the central bank of Sweden) and represented as a simple weekly return. The Treasury bill rates are often presented as simple annual rates and thus the annual rate is divided by 52 to represent a weekly rate. The regression model is as follows:

$$\left(R_{\text{skf},t} - R_{f,t}\right) = b_0 + b_1\left(R_{m,t} - R_{f,t}\right) + e_t. \tag{5.20}$$

Table 5.3 presents the Stata code at the top of the table and descriptive statistics showing that the average weekly risk premium on SKF is 0.4%, whereas the average weekly market risk premium is 0.1%. Observe the slightly higher standard deviation of the risk premium on SKF. Figure 5.3 plots these risk premiums over time.

Table 5.3 Descriptive statistics

```
. sum rp_skf rp_omx_30
```

Variable	Obs.	Mean	Std. Dev.	Min	Max
rp_skf	312	0.004	0.047	−0.162	0.178
rp_omx_30	312	0.001	0.032	−0.202	0.130

The figure shows that the variation in the risk premium on SKF is larger than the market, however, the opposite is observed in 2009 (what could be the reason?). Table 5.4 shows the Pearson correlation between the risk premium on SKF and the market. This analysis is usually made for independent variables to test multicollinearity, but the CAPM is a simple linear model with a single independent variable, and thus the analysis shows the correlation between the risk premium on SKF and the market, just for an example. You will have plenty of exercises to correlate independent variables in a multiple regression model in the upcoming chapters.

The table shows that the risk premiums on SKF and the market are significantly and highly (78%) correlated at the 1% level. If these were two independent variables, you would probably drop one of them from the regression analysis.

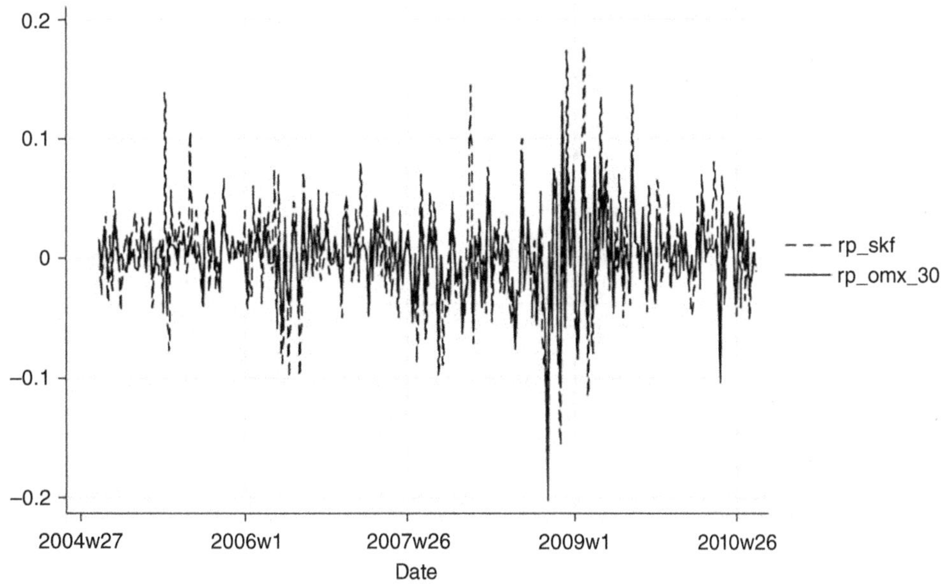

Figure 5.3. Risk premiums over time
Code: `twoway line rp_skf rp_omx_30 date`

Table 5.4 Pairwise correlation analysis

. pwcorr rp_skf rp_omx_30, sig

	rp_skf	rp_om~30
rp_skf	1	
rp_omx_30	0.7833	1
	0.000	

5.7.1 Results

Table 5.5 shows the Stata regression output. The Stata code `outreg2` or `estout` can be used to produce more quality tables, which will be an exercise in the lab work at the end of this chapter. At the bottom of the table, the coefficient b_1 is tested against 1 as the theory of the CAPM suggests that if the stock follows the market – has the same (systematic) risk as the market – then b_1 should not be significantly different from 1. Note that Stata tests the coefficients against 0, unless otherwise imposed. The intercept b_0 in CAPM regression shows whether the stock outperforms or underperforms the market – an abnormal return. The theory of the CAPM suggests that the market return explains the return on the individual stock and thus there should be no abnormal return (any additional return over and above what the market explains). Investors can only be compensated by taking systematic risk, which is reflected in b_1. Hence, b_0 should not be significantly different from 0.

Table 5.5 CAPM regression

. reg rp_skf rp_omx_30

Source	SS	df	MS		No. obs.	312
					F(1, 310)	492.050
Model	0.4227	1	0.4227		Prob > F	0.000
Residual	0.2663	310	0.0009		R-squared	0.614
Total	0.6890	311	0.0022		Adj R-squared	0.612
					Root MSE	0.029
rp_skf	Coefficient	Std. Err.	t	P > |t|	[95% conf. interval]	
rp_omx_30	1.1405	0.0514	22.1800	0.0000	1.0393	1.2416
_cons	0.0022	0.0017	1.3300	0.1860	−0.0011	0.0055

.test rp_omx_30=1

rp_omx_30 = 1	
F(1, 310)	7.470
Prob > F	0.007

Let's begin by interpreting the specifications in the table. The model SS at the top represents the explained sum of squares, $ESS = \sum_{i=1}^{N}(\hat{y}_i - \overline{y})^2$, while residual SS is the residual sum of squares, $RSS = \sum_{i=1}^{N}\hat{e}_i^{\,2}$. Because there is one independent variable, there are two parameters k, the intercept and the slope of the independent variable, hence the model degree of freedom is $k-1$. The residual degree of freedom is the number of observations N minus the total number of parameters k being estimated $(312-2=310)$. The mean of sums MS value at the top is SS divided by the number of degrees of freedom, which is the numerator and the denominator of the F-value for goodness of fit, $F\text{-value} = \frac{\frac{ESS}{k-1}}{\frac{RSS}{N-k}} = \frac{0.4227111832}{0.00085908} = 492.05$, which is also reported in Table 5.5, $F(1, 310)$. Prob > F is less than 5% (0.00), indicating that the model is a good fit of the empirical data at hand. The total SS adds values of explained (model) sums of squares ESS and residual sums of squares RSS. Total SS divided by the total number of degrees of freedom (311) is total MS (0.02). R-squared is given by $R^2 = \frac{0.4227111832}{0.689026761} = 0.6135$. The adjusted R-squared is not much different from R-squared because there is only one independent variable in the model, $\overline{R}^2 = 1-\left[\frac{N-1}{N-k}(1-R^2)\right] = 1-\left[\frac{312-1}{312-2}(1-0.6135^2)\right] = 0.6122$. Thus, the model explains as much as 61% of the variation in the dependent variable. The final specification is root MSE, that is the squared root of the mean residual sum of squares (MS residual in the table):

$$\sqrt{MRSS} = \sqrt{0.00085908} = 0.02931.$$

Let's interpret the marginal effects, coefficients. In the table b_0 is shown as _cons, that is the intercept. Observe that the p-value, $P > |t|$, in the table is larger than 5%

(0.186), indicating that the intercept is not significantly different from 0. Hence, the t-value (1.33) would be smaller than the critical t-value observed from the t-distribution table with corresponding degrees of freedom and the 95% confidence interval includes 0. Thus, it would be enough to observe the p-value to conclude significance. The insignificant intercept b_0 in a CAPM model suggests that the stock does not outperform or underperform the market. Thus, there is no point interpreting the magnitude of b_0. The coefficient b_1, also called beta in a CAPM model, is shown as rp_omx_30 in the table (this, of course, depends on how you name the variable) and tested against 0, which is not interesting. The theory suggests that it should be tested against 1, and the F-test below the table shows the result. Prob $> F = 0.0066$ suggests that beta is significantly different from 1 at the 5% level, and since the results show that it equals 1.14 in the estimation table, you can conclude that the SKF stock is riskier than the market. A clearer interpretation is that if the market increases by 1%, SKF stock will rise, on average, by 1.14%. The assumptions of the CLRM are tested next.

5.7.2 Testing the Assumptions of the CLRM

Figure 5.4 shows that the relationship between the risk premium on SKF and the market is roughly linear. This is suggestive evidence that CLRM Assumption 1 is satisfied.

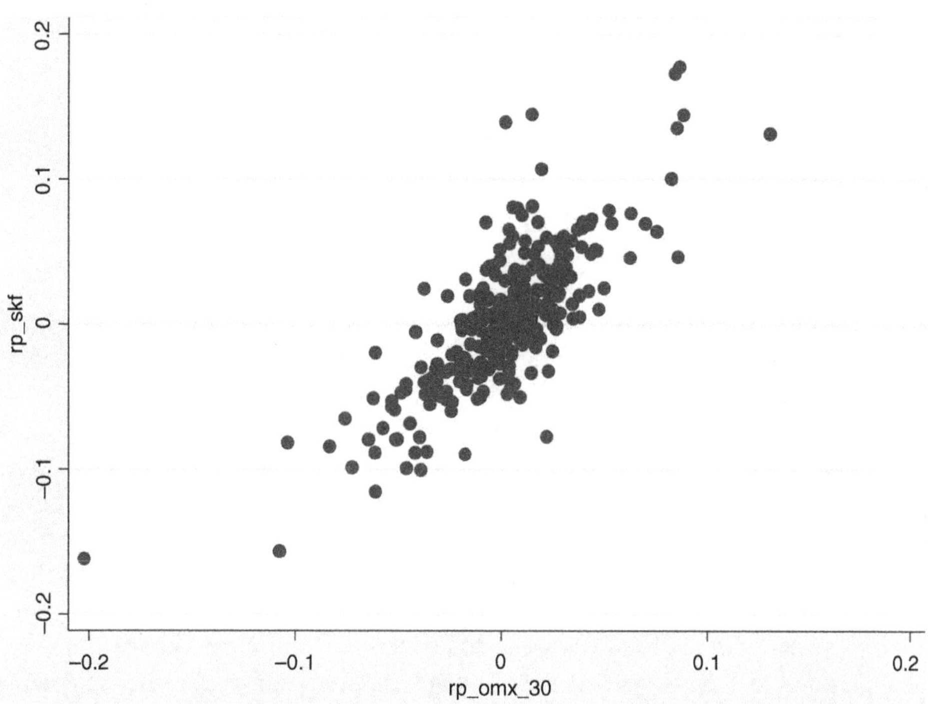

Figure 5.4. Linear relationship between the risk premiums

```
Code: twoway (scatter rp_skf rp_omx_30)
```

Figure 5.5 plots the fitted value $\hat{y}$ from the CAPM regression.

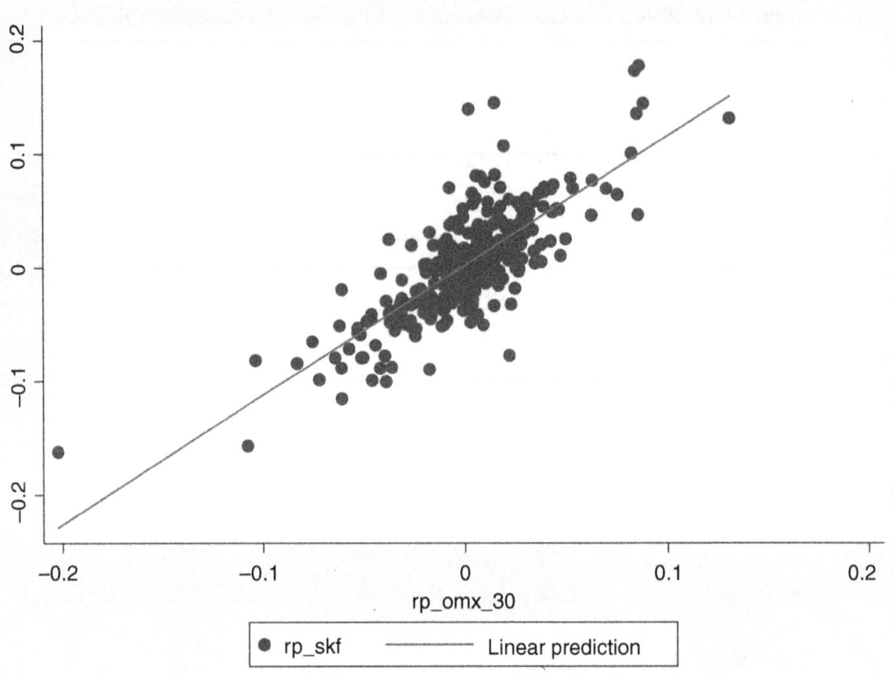

Figure 5.5. Fitted value from CAPM regression

```
Code:
reg rp_skf rp_omx_30
predict yhat, xb
twoway (scatter rp_skf rp_omx_30) (line yhat rp_omx_30)
```

The regression includes the intercept, so the regression line passes through the middle of the data, meaning that the residuals will sum to zero. Figure 5.6 plots the residuals.

Figure 5.6a shows that the residuals do not seem to be normally distributed, which is also evident in Figure 5.6d, testing the null hypothesis that residuals are normally distributed using the Shapiro–Wilk test. The high z-value shows that you can reject the null hypothesis of normality. The residuals seem equally dispersed around the values of the market risk premium in Figure 5.6b, indicating that the homoskedasticity assumption holds. This result is also evident in Figure 5.6c: the variance of the residuals seems to be constant over time. Let's test this assumption, the null hypothesis that the residual variance is constant using the Breusch–Pagan test. The results are shown in Figure 5.7 and the code is provided at the top of the figure.

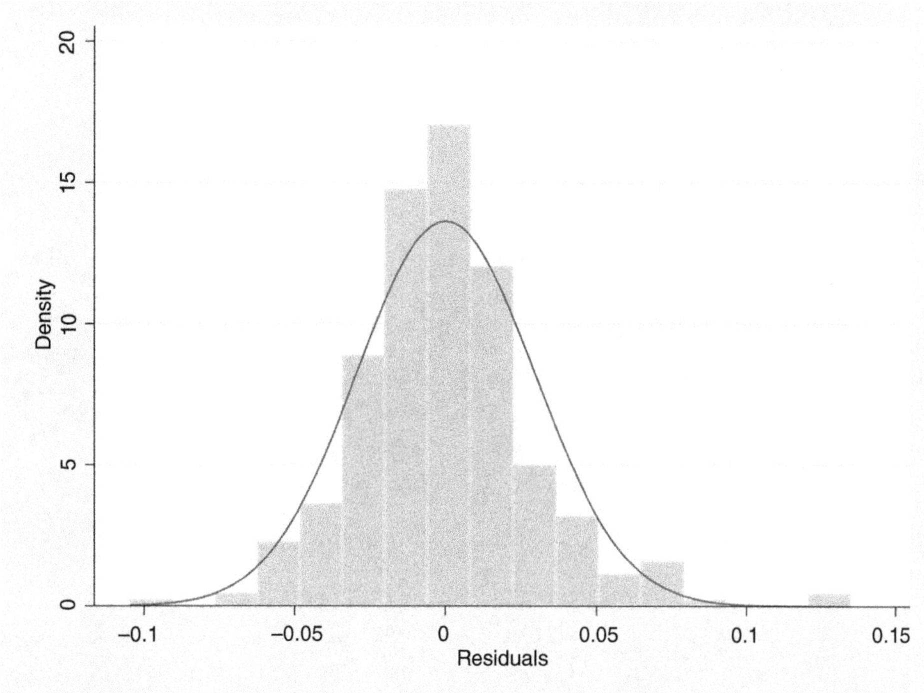

Figure 5.6a. Residuals

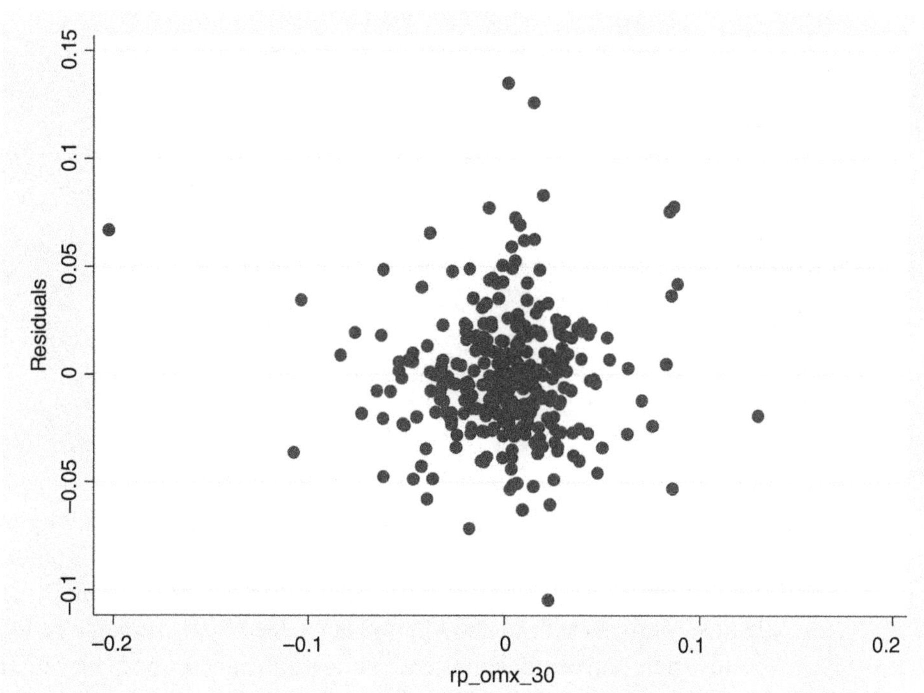

Figure 5.6b. Residuals and market risk premium

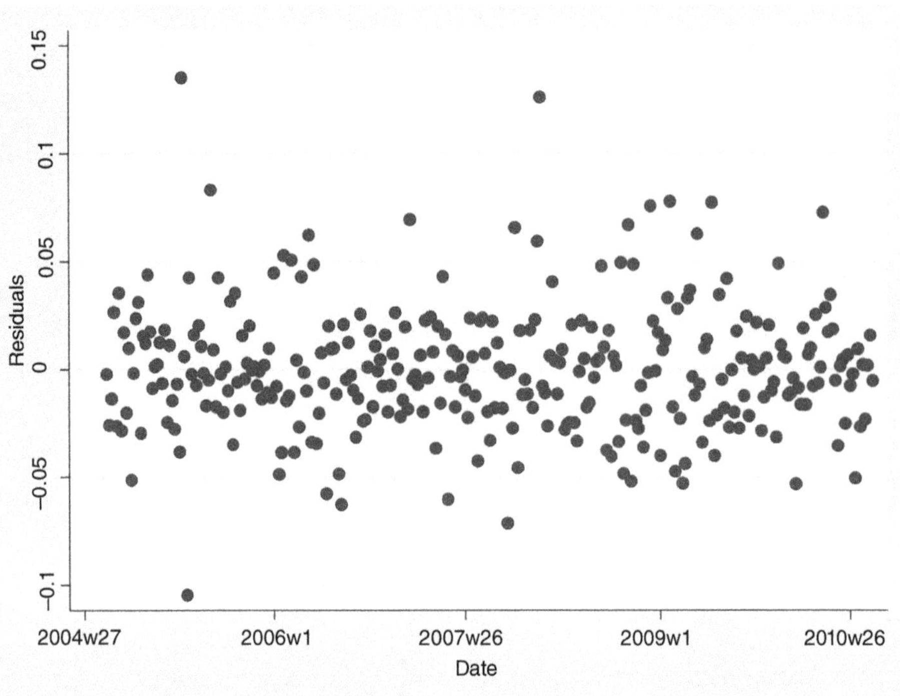

Figure 5.6c. Residuals over time

```
. swilk ehat

                   Shapiro-Wilk W test for normal data

    Variable |        Obs       W           V         z       Prob>z
-------------+------------------------------------------------------
        ehat |        312    0.96223      8.332     4.986    0.00000
```

Figure 5.6d. Normality test

```
Code:
reg rp_skf rp_omx_30
predict ehat, residuals
histogram ehat, normal
twoway (scatter ehat rp_omx_30)
twoway scatter ehat date
```

The results from the F-test suggest that you cannot reject the null hypothesis of constant residual variance, indicating that there is no need to use HC standard errors in this regression. Figure 5.8 provides a quick test for autocorrelation by correlating the estimated residuals with the one-period lag value of the estimated residuals.

The autocorrelation coefficient is −0.17 and significant at the 5% level. This result shows that if the value at time $t-1$ is above average, it is likely to be below average at time t, indicating a mean reversion, but the degree of mean reversion is not high enough. Chapter 7 on time-series analysis will cover autocorrelation and its remedy.

```
. estat hettest, fstat

Breusch-Pagan/Cook-Weisberg test for heteroskedasticity
Assumption: i.i.d. error terms
Variable: Fitted values of rp_skf

H0: Constant variance

F(1, 310) =    0.20
 Prob > F = 0.6539
```

Figure 5.7. Test for homoskedasticity

```
. pwcorr ehat lag_ehat, sig /*autocorrelation at lag 1*/

             |     ehat lag_ehat
-------------+------------------
        ehat |   1.0000
             |
             |
    lag_ehat |  -0.1674   1.0000
             |   0.0031
             |
```

Figure 5.8. Autocorrelation test

5.7.3 Interaction Model

Finally, let's see how an interaction model works. For this exercise, define a financial crisis dummy taking the value 1 after 2008 and 0 before 2008. You can exclude the assumed event year of 2008 from this analysis. The event studies will be discussed more in the upcoming chapters. Figure 5.9 provides the frequency distribution of the crisis dummy along with Stata codes that generate the dummy and the frequency table.

The output shows 87 return observations in the crisis period and 174 return observations before the crisis. The results from the interaction model are given in Table 5.6.

The coefficient on the interaction dummy D_crises_rp_omx_30 is negative but not significant, indicating that SKF's stock return does not move differently with the market return before and after the financial crisis. The slope is not different before and after the crisis. D_crises alone does not affect the risk premium on SKF, as the coefficient on the crisis dummy is also insignificant. However, beta (the coefficient

```
. gen D_crises=0

. replace D_crises=. if date>= tw(2008w1) & date <=tw(2008w52)
(52 real changes made, 52 to missing)

. replace D_crises =1 if date >= tw(2009w1)
(87 real changes made)

. tab D_crises
```

D_crises	Freq.	Percent	Cum.
0	174	66.67	66.67
1	87	33.33	100.00
Total	261	100.00	

```
. gen D_crises_rp_omx_30= D_crises*rp_omx_30
(53 missing values generated)
```

Figure 5.9. Frequency distribution of crisis dummy

Table 5.6 Interaction effects model

. reg rp_skf rp_omx_30 D_crises D_crises_rp_omx_30

Source	SS	df	MS		No. obs.	260
					F(1, 310)	108.98
Model	0.26241056	3	0.0874702		Prob > F	0
Residual	0.20546669	256	0.0008026		R-squared	0.5609
Total	0.46787725	259	0.0018065		Adj R-squared	0.5557
					Root MSE	0.02833

rp_skf	Coefficient	Std. Err.	t	P > |t|	[95% conf. interval]	
rp_omx_30	1.206	0.099	12.220	0.000	1.011	1.400
D_crises	0.001	0.004	0.180	0.855	−0.007	0.008
D_crises_rp_omx_30	−0.003	0.134	−0.020	0.983	−0.267	0.261
_cons	0.001	0.002	0.630	0.529	−0.003	0.006

.test rp_omx_30=1

rp_omx_30 = 1	
F(1, 310)	4.34
Prob > F	0.0381

on rp_omx_30) is 1.21 and (tested against 1 at the bottom of the table) significant at the 5% level, indicating that a 1% increase in the market return increases the return on SKF by approximately 1.21% before the financial crisis. Again, the decrease of −0.0028817 after the financial crisis is not significant. That the F-value of the model is 108.98, or Prob > F less than 1%, suggests that the model is a good fit for the data. But observe the explained variation R^2 or $\overline{R}^2$ of 56%, which has decreased from 61% in the CAPM model without the interaction effect. This is further evidence that the interaction effect does not add much to the model for SKF returns.

5.8 Lab Work: Classical Linear Regression Model

Problem set

Use Chapter_5_CLRM.dta (available at www.cambridge.org/Mavruk) to answer the questions below. Data include weekly prices on the OMX 30 index, Ericson, H&M (hm), SEB, and SKF stocks and the risk-free rate; 3-month Treasury bill rate obtained from Riksbanken presented as a simple annual rate. Section 5.7 has examined SKF. In this lab work you are supposed to examine the stock returns of Ericson, H&M (hm), and SEB and compare them to the findings from SKF.

Begin by generating a weekly date variable.

Stata commands:

```
gen date=w(2004w35)+_n-1
format date %tw
tsset date
```

1. Calculate the return on the Nasdaq OMX index and the (arithmetic) return, $\frac{(P_t - P_{t-1})}{P_{t-1}}$, on **each** stock. Plot the returns against the time variable, date. Interpret the graphs. Construct the risk-premium measure for each company and the overall market risk premium. Note that the risk-free rate is presented **annually** in the data, while your analysis window is **weekly**. You need to divide the risk-free rate by 52. If you use the return on the stocks in decimal form, then you also need to use the risk-free rate in decimal form. Remember that the units of the return variables need to match.
2. Plot these risk premiums over time and describe what you see.

   Useful Stata commands:

   ```
   gen, twoway
   ```

3. Recalculate the return using logarithmic returns. To compare your results with the arithmetic returns, run descriptive statistics on both arithmetic and logarithmic returns and test the mean differences. What do you observe? What is the difference between arithmetic return and logarithmic return? Which one would you suggest using in regressions and why?

4. Useful Stata commands:

```
sum, mvtest means
```

For the rest of the questions, use only arithmetic returns.
Run descriptive statistics and Pearson correlation analysis on all the return variables (not the risk premium) in the data. Explain your results.
Useful Stata commands:

```
sum, pwcorr
```

5. Estimate the CAPM model for each company. Interpret the intercept b_0, CAPM beta, b_1, R^2, and F-value.

   (a) Is b_0 significantly different from 0?
   (b) Is b_1 significantly different from 1? Why are you testing b_1 against 1?

   When answering these questions, formulate the null and alternative hypotheses. State the test statistics, find the rejection region, calculate the observed value of the test statistic, and state your conclusion.
   Useful Stata commands:

```
reg, test, outreg or outreg2
```

   Note that the last two commands (**`outreg`**) will be helpful to present your regression results in the assignment or in your thesis later on. Use `findit outreg2` to find out more about the details and presentations.

6. Find the residuals from each regression model (for each stock) and plot them in a histogram. Do you have normally distributed error terms in the model? Test for normality (for each residual) by using a Shapiro–Wilk test. Explain what you observe.
   Useful Stata commands:

```
reg, predict, resid, histogram, swilk
```

7. Plot the residuals from the regression over time. Do you see any pattern in the residual plot, or do you regard it as random? Calculate the correlation coefficient of the residual and lagged residual. Is the correlation coefficient significantly different from zero? What does that imply?
   Useful Stata commands:

```
twoway, gen, pwcorr
```

   Example for lag residual (lag_ehat):

```
gen lag_ehat=l.ehat
pwcorr ehat lag_ehat, sig /*autocorrelation at lag 1*/
```

8. Test for homoskedasticity of residuals from each regression. Explain how the test works and interpret your results.
   Useful Stata commands:

```
rvfplot, estat hettest
```

9. Check for multicollinearity by examining the variance inflation factor. For the sake of this exercise, include the risk premium of the other stocks as independent variables in the model and run the tests. Interpret your results.
   Useful Stata commands:

   ```
   pwcorr, reg, vif
   ```

   Note that if any of the code does not exist in your version of Stata you need to install the code. Just write for example "findit vif" in the command box and click install, which should take just a few seconds.

10. Interaction effects: In your CAPM regression include a crisis dummy variable, D_crises, by assuming that the crisis begins in 2008 and you treat the whole year as event time (exclude it from the analysis).
    Use the following codes:

    ```
    gen D_crises=0
    replace D_crises=. if date>= tw(2008w1) & date
    <=tw(2008w52)
    replace D_crises =1 if date >= tw(2009w1)
    tab D_crises
    ```

    Next, generate an interaction term between D_crises and the market risk premium (OMX return minus the risk-free rate):

    ```
    gen D_crises_Rm_rf= D_crises*Rm_rf
    ```

    Include D_crises and the interaction term in your CAPM regression for each stock and run the regression again. Interpret your results.

Good luck!

5.9 Mini Case

Lé and Vinas (2022) examine how companies finance their investments depending on firms' listing status, their size, and the nature of the investments. They use 2.2 million financial statements from around 177,000 firms operating in France over the last 25 years and examine the unconditional contributions of various funding sources (bank credit, financial debt, equity, retained earnings, and cash holdings) to the financing of both fixed-asset and working-capital asset accumulation. They estimate their regressions using OLS weighted by firm size, because the data are skewed towards large firms. The main findings in the study are that bank credit, other financial debt, equity, retained earnings, and cash holdings all contribute to the financing of investment. The dependent variables in the study are the changes in bank credit, the changes in other debt, the changes in equity, the changes in retained earnings, the changes in cash holdings, and the changes in residual liabilities. The main independent variables are the changes in fixed assets, the changes in net working capital assets, and the changes in residual assets. The control variables include the share of equity over total assets, the share of cash holdings over total assets, the share of bank credit over total assets, the growth rate of sales, the ratio of dividends to sales, and the log of total assets. Standard errors are clustered at the firm level.

Task

1. Go to the link: Replication code and pseudo data for: Firm Listing Status, Firm Size, and the Financing of Investment – Review of Corporate Finance Studies Dataverse (harvard.edu)
   Download the dataset: PseudoData_LE_VINAS_FirmInvestment_RCFS_v4.tab
   Download the do file: Code_LE_VINAS_FirmInvestment_RCFS_v4.do
   Go to the link: Firm Listing Status, Firm Size, and the Financing of Investment | The Review of Corporate Finance Studies | Oxford Academic (oup.com)
   Download the paper. Alternatively, you can download the most recent working paper version: The Financing of Investment: Firm Size, Asset Tangibility and the Size of Investment | Publications (banque-france.fr)
2. Replicate Table 9 (Table 8 in the working paper version). Present and explain your results. (Table 7 in the working paper version corresponds to the unweighted regression.)
3. It is a panel dataset but ignore the panel structure by removing the firm fixed effects and year fixed effects. Apply pooled OLS. Present and explain your results. How do your results differ from step 2? Explain.
4. Revise your analysis using conventional standard errors instead of clustering. How do your results differ from step 2? Explain.
5. Revise your analysis using robust standard errors instead of clustering. How do your results differ from step 2? Explain.

5.10 Summary

Regression analysis is a central part of corporate finance studies. The aim of regression analysis is to summarize the observed data and study how the response of a dependent variable varies as the values of the independent variables change. There are many models that examine this relationship by obtaining the estimates of parameters in a regression model. The classical linear regression model (CLRM) is the basis of all other models discussed in this book. However, estimating a CLRM model does not simply provide a reliable relationship between the dependent and independent variables. To reliably estimate the relationship, it is essential to understand the properties and assumptions behind this model. The most commonly used CLRM that efficiently obtains estimates of parameters is OLS (ordinary least squares), where parameter estimates are chosen to minimize the residual sum of squares. OLS is the most commonly used technique mainly because of its simplicity and high interpretability. The least-squares calculations are based on averages, sums of squares, and sums of cross-products.

This chapter discusses CLRM in detail using an OLS estimation method. Empirical studies often tend to perform an OLS to begin with and use the outcome as some sort of benchmark in a more detailed analysis. The focus in this chapter is on the assumptions and applications of this technique, starting from a single regression model with one independent variable and then covering the multiple linear regression model with many independent variables. The chapter provides an application to the Capital Asset Pricing Model and ends with lab work on CLRM and a mini case.

KEY TERMS

Classical linear regression model; assumptions; the OLS estimation method; tests for parameters; goodness of fit; interpretation of the estimates; interaction effects; application to CAPM.

REFERENCES

Angrist, J. D. and Pischke, J-S. (2009). *Mostly Harmless Econometrics: An Empiricist's Companion*. Princeton University Press, Princeton, NJ.

Black, F. 1972. Capital market equilibrium with restricted borrowing. *The Journal of Business*, 45, 444–455.

Black, F. 1976. Studies of stock price volatility changes. In *Proceedings of the 1976 Meeting of the Business and Economic Statistics Section*. American Statistical Association, Washington, D.C., pp. 177–181.

Brooks, C. 2019. *Introductory Econometrics for Finance* (4th ed.). Cambridge University Press, Cambridge.

Kennedy, P. 2008. *A Guide to Econometrics* (6th ed.). Wiley, Hoboken, NJ.

Lé, M. and Vinas, F. (2022). Firm listing status, firm size, and the financing of investment. *Review of Corporate Finance Studies*. https://doi.org/10.1093/rcfs/cfac038

Lintner, J. 1965. The valuation of risky assets and the selection of risky investments in stock portfolios and capital budgets. *Review of Economics and Statistics*, 47, 13–37.

Mossin, J. 1966. *Theory of Financial Markets*. Prentice Hall, Englewood Cliffs, NJ.

Schwert, G. and Seguin, P. J. 1990. Heteroskedasticity in stock returns. *Journal of Finance*, 45, 1129–1155.

Sharpe W. F. 1964. Capital asset prices: A theory of market equilibrium and conditions of risk. *Journal of Finance*, 19, 425–442.

Stock, J. and Watson, M. 2019. *Introduction to Econometrics: Global Edition*. Princeton University Press, Princeton, NJ.

Treynor, J. L. 1961. Market value, time, and risk. Unpublished manuscript.

Verbeek, M. 2017. *A Guide to Modern Econometrics* (5th ed.). Wiley, Hoboken, NJ.

White, H. 1980. A heteroskedasticity-consistent covariance matrix estimator and a direct test for heteroskedasticity. *Econometrica*, 48, 817–838.

Wooldridge, J. M. 2002. *Econometric Analysis of Cross-Section and Panel Data*. MIT Press, Cambridge, MA.

6 Endogeneity Bias

INTRODUCTION

Most studies in corporate finance aim to examine a causal relationship rather than correlations. Examining a causal relationship requires knowledge of the data-generating process and is often not possible using only the empirical data at hand. Hanoi's Rat Massacre of 1902 is a good example, emphasizing the importance of understanding the data-generating process (see Marton and Sjögren, 2022). The French Governor-General of Indochina, Paul Doumer, aimed to transform the Vietnamese city of Hanoi into a modern and civilized city, just like the ones in France during the 1900s. His plan included introducing a sewer system to Hanoi, but the sewer system also led to an increase in the number of rats. The French administration employed Vietnamese workers as rat hunters, however, despite their efforts the number of rats continued to increase. The administration came up with a program that offered one cent per rat tail, hoping for a solution to the city's rat problem. However, the plan did not work. Although there were many reported rat tails, which suggested rat deaths, the number of rats kept increasing. The administration discovered that the hunters simply cut the tails off the rats and let them live, so they could earn more profits. The hunters even tried to raise rats in farms (Culture trip, 2022).

This story suggests that without some knowledge of the data-generating process, the conclusion would be that the program did not help reduce the number of rats. The story also emphasizes the importance of considering the strategic behavior of, in this case, rat hunters. It is not uncommon to observe similar strategic behavior by firms in the current business world. Firms act strategically and make investment decisions depending on what other firms are doing in the market. In a competitive market, the strategic behavior of one firm should not affect market prices and the presence of other firms. However, deviation from full competition is common in the real business world, one example being the oligopolistic market condition.

Consider the music streaming applications – such as Spotify, Apple music, and Amazon music – that dominate the music industry today. The decisions made by one of these firms are likely to be strategic, depending on other firms within the industry. Ignoring such strategic decision-making in a study will generate endogeneity concerns. More specifically, it will lead to an omitted bias problem, which will cause a correlation between the independent variable(s) and the error term in a regression model. As discussed in Chapter 5, such a correlation will violate one important assumption of the classical linear regression model (CLRM), namely exogeneity. Endogeneity leads to biased and inconsistent parameter estimates, which will prevent the study from making reliable inference in the analysis.

This chapter first examines the causes of endogeneity and then discusses some techniques that can address the endogeneity problem using cross-sectional data. Roberts and Whited (2013) map these techniques into two categories. The first one includes techniques that use a clear source of exogenous variation for identifying the parameters: instrumental variables (IVs), difference-in-differences (DiD) estimators, and regression discontinuity design (RDD). Particularly, the last two mentioned models are known as quasi-experimental methods, used to overcome the difficulties of selecting appropriate IVs. A brief definition of IVs is that they are variables which are highly correlated with the endogenous independent variable but uncorrelated with the dependent variable. As these techniques do not necessarily rely on time-series information, they can be applied to cross-sectional data. Thus, this chapter will focus on these techniques.

The second category includes techniques that rely on modeling assumptions, for instance, panel-data methods (covered in Chapter 9) that are based on time-series information. These techniques will be covered in the upcoming chapters, after the book provides a brief review of time-series data and its analysis in Chapter 7. This chapter ends with a practical application of the methods on observational data, with a focus on interpretations, lab work, and finally a mini case.

6.1 Sources of Endogeneity

The standard definition of an endogenous variable is that the variable determined within the context of the model is called endogenous, generating a correlation between the independent variable and the residuals in a regression model (Stock and Watson, 2019; Woolridge, 2002). Recall that the assumptions of the CLRM concern the residuals and in the case of endogeneity (Assumption 6 discussed in Chapter 5), x_i is exogenous, $E(e_i \mid x_i) = 0$, is violated. In such a case you should know which variable(s) are endogenous and why. Once the source is clear, the aim is to remedy the problem of this important assumption. It is common to face the endogeneity problem when using observational data, where it is uncertain which variable is driving which variable. There are three known sources of endogeneity: omitted variables, measurement errors, and simultaneity. This section will elaborate on each of them and explain how the estimated ordinary least squares (OLS) coefficient b_1 is determined in the presence of endogeneity and type of bias (upward or downward). But first, let's examine the OLS coefficient b_1 in the presence of endogeneity in general.

Recall the rat-tail example above, the program introduced by the French Governor-General could not stop the increase in the number of rats in a traditional OLS estimation method. The omitted variable, representing that hunters handed in only tails but let the rats go to breed more, was not known to the model. This means that the model should include and control for one or more variables, but since this information is unknown, these additional variables cannot be controlled. In this case, the OLS method is not likely to be a consistent estimator and the direction of the bias in the estimation tends to be upward. Consider a single regression population model:

$$y_i = \beta_0 + \beta_1 x_i + e_i. \tag{6.1}$$

Recall the definition of the OLS estimator b_1 from Chapter 5:

$$b_1 = \frac{\Sigma(x_i - \bar{x})(y_i - \bar{y})}{\Sigma(x_i - \bar{x})^2}. \tag{6.2}$$

In the presence of endogeneity, the OLS estimator is as follows (the Appendix for Chapter 6 at the end of the book provides more details on the derivation):

$$\text{plim}\,\hat{b}_1 = \beta_1 + \frac{\text{cov}(x_i, e_i)}{\text{var}(x_i)}. \tag{6.3}$$

The notation plim refers to probability limit. In this context, it means that the probability that $\hat{b}_1$ is very different from the term on the right-hand side, $\beta_1 + \frac{\text{cov}(x_i,e_i)}{\text{var}(x_i)}$, becomes very small as the sample size increases. Think of it as if you have a sequence of estimates of bs for different sample sizes. Since probabilities are real numbers between 0 and 1, the definition of plim means that $\hat{b}_1$ is the probability limit of $\beta_1 + \frac{\text{cov}(x_i,e_i)}{\text{var}(x_i)}$ if the probability that the difference between the estimated bs and $\beta_1 + \frac{\text{cov}(x_i,e_i)}{\text{var}(x_i)}$ becomes very small as the sample size gets large. Note that this is related to the consistency property of the OLS estimator, covered in Section 5.4.1. However, the consistency condition holds in the absence of endogeneity, where the covariance term is zero, $\text{cov}(x_i, e_i) = 0$. Thus, in the presence of endogeneity even, $\text{plim}\,\hat{b}_1$ will not converge to β_1 (as the sample size increases). The numerator, the covariance, in the second term in Equation (6.3) can be negative or positive or zero, but the denominator is positive. If the covariance is zero, there would not be an endogeneity problem. Research shows that the covariance tends to be positive and thus the OLS estimate would be upward biased in the presence of endogeneity (see Stock and Watson, 2019; Woolridge, 2002). Taken together, because the numerator is a covariance between the independent variable and the residuals, the bias would not disappear when the number of observations increases in a dataset. The aim is to estimate the causal effects, and thus the OLS estimators are unreliable because they will produce a true parameter β_1 and something else.

6.1.1 Omitted-Variable Bias

Omitted-variable bias is a common problem in corporate finance. For instance, studies examining manager decisions have difficulty observing and quantifying all the manager-specific characteristics. If there are some important determinants missing, which thus cannot be included as independent variables in the model, they will enter the residual term in the model. Because these determinants are considered important, they will be correlated with the independent variables, causing endogeneity bias. If the unobserved variables are not correlated with the independent variables, there would be no problem with endogeneity bias. Consider that x_{2i} represents the omitted variable that should be controlled for and thus the population model will be as follows:

$$y_i = \beta_0 + \beta_1 x_{1i} + \beta_2 x_{2i} + e_i. \tag{6.4}$$

If x_2 cannot be controlled for, it enters the residuals $e_i = \beta_2 x_{2i} + \varepsilon_i$. Let's examine how the estimation b_1 is affected by omitted-variable bias:

$$\text{plim}\,\hat{b}_1 = \beta_1 + \text{plim}\frac{\sum x_{1i}'(\beta_2 x_{2i} + \varepsilon_i)}{\sum x_{1i}'^2}, \tag{6.5}$$

$$\text{plim}\,\hat{b}_1 = \beta_1 + \beta_2 \frac{\text{cov}(x_{1i}, x_{2i})}{\text{var}(x_i)}. \tag{6.6}$$

In Equation (6.6), $\hat{b}_1$ would be a consistent estimator of a population parameter β_1 if either β_2 is 0 or $\text{cov}(x_{1i}, x_{2i}) = 0$. If the second term is non-zero, then the type of bias (whether upward or downward) depends on the sign of β_2 and the covariance.

6.1.2 Measurement Error in the Independent Variable

In corporate finance studies you often use proxy variables to quantify a phenomenon or a study object. If the variables are "true" measures, measuring exactly what you want to study, there is no measurement error. In fact, if you have "true" measurements, having fewer observations in an OLS estimation would also be fine as you would not need the consistency property. However, particularly in observational data, measurement errors are inevitable and unfortunately, if there is measurement error in the independent variable, it will result in endogeneity bias. Measurement error in the dependent variable may have similar implications to omitted-variable bias, but is considered less of a concern in OLS estimation, although it is important for the study per se. It is more difficult to examine the measurement error in a dependent variable as in another study the same variable could just as well be used as an independent variable (depending on the research question).

For instance, in capital structure studies it is common to observe the market leverage ratio, defined as the market value of debt divided by the market value of the firm, that is debt plus equity, as a dependent variable. It is easy to obtain the market value of equity, but the market value of debt is difficult to obtain since debt is usually privately held by financial institutions, so there is no observed market value of debt. Researchers may use public debt, but there is not much liquidity in public debt so it will make a poor proxy for the market value of debt. Thus, it is common to use the observed book value of debt as a proxy for the market value of debt in capital structure studies. Further, the measurement error that arises from using the book value of debt is assumed to be uncorrelated with the independent variable in most studies. Thus, the effect of a measurement error in the dependent variable will be on the error variance and the parameter covariance. However, empirically this assumption may be too strong given that the market value of debt seems to decrease more than the book value of debt with financial distress, which is also correlated with some determinants of capital structure (e.g., profitability; see Roberts and Whited, 2013).

To examine how $\hat{b}_1$ is affected by a measurement error in the independent variable, and hence the endogeneity bias, consider Equation (6.1) again and assume that you do not observe x_i but use a proxy variable, a noisy measure of x_i called x_i^{proxy}:

$$y_i = \beta_0 + \beta_1 x_i^{\text{proxy}} + \varepsilon_i. \tag{6.7}$$

The proxy variable is equal to what you want to measure, x_i plus a noisy residual term $v_i : x_i^{\text{proxy}} = x_i + v_i$. Here the assumption is that $\text{cov}(x_i^{\text{proxy}}, \varepsilon_i) = 0$ but you also need to assume that the CLRM assumptions hold for the true measurement x_i, particularly $\text{cov}(x_i, v_i) = 0$ as well as $\text{cov}(x_i, \varepsilon_i) = 0$, otherwise x_i will be endogenous. This also means that ε_i must be uncorrelated with v_i, $\text{cov}(\varepsilon_i, v_i) = 0$. Replacing $(x_i + v_i)$ with x_i^{proxy} gives the following equation:

$$y_i = \beta_0 + \beta_1 (x_i + v_i) + \varepsilon_i = \beta_0 + \beta_1 x_i + (\beta_1 v_i + \varepsilon_i). \tag{6.8}$$

This equation is similar to Equation (6.1) but note that the residual term in Equation (6.1) in the presence of a measurement error is $e_i = (\beta_1 v_i + \varepsilon_i)$. This also means that the residual term in Equation (6.7) is $\varepsilon_i = (e_i - \beta_1 v_i)$. Let's examine $\hat{b}_1$ by following Equation (6.34) in the Appendix for Chapter 6; the difference here is that you do not observe x_i but observe x_i^{proxy} and thus the residual term is ε_i, just as in Equation (6.7):

$$\text{plim}\, \hat{b}_1 = \beta_1 + \text{plim} \frac{\Sigma x_i^{\prime\text{proxy}} \varepsilon_i}{\Sigma x_i^{\prime\text{proxy}2}}. \tag{6.9}$$

Recall that $x_i^{\text{proxy}} = x_i + v_i$ and $\varepsilon_i = (e_i - \beta_1 v_i)$. Also recall that $x_i' = (x_i - \bar{x})$:

$$\text{plim}\, \hat{b}_1 = \beta_1 + \text{plim} \frac{\Sigma (x_i' + v_i)(v_i - \beta_1 v_i)}{\Sigma (x_i' + v_i)^2}. \tag{6.10}$$

The assumption that the measurement error v_i is uncorrelated with x_i, $\text{cov}(x_i, v_i) = 0$, is called a classical error-in-variables (CEV). Further, if CEV holds then x_i^{proxy} and v_i must be correlated. Thus, the covariance between x_i^{proxy} and the measurement error v_i is equal to the variance of the measurement error: $\text{cov}\left(x_i^{\text{proxy}}, v_i\right) = E\left(x_i^{\text{proxy}}, v_i\right) = E(x_i, v_i) + E\left(v_i^2\right) = \sigma_v^2$. Given this result, you can examine the numerator in Equation (6.10). The covariance between x_i^{proxy} and e_i is assumed to be 0. Thus, $\text{cov} = ((x_i + v_i), (e_i - \beta_1 v_i)) = -\beta_1((x_i + v_i), v_i) = -\beta_1 \sigma_v^2$ (see Woolridge, 2002, p. 74 for more details). The denominator in Equation (6.10) is the sum of two variances, σ_x^2 and σ_v^2:

$$\text{plim}\, \hat{b}_1 = \beta_1 + \frac{-\beta_1 \sigma_v^2}{\sigma_x^2 + \sigma_v^2}. \tag{6.11}$$

We multiply the denominator by β_1 to rewrite the equation:

$$\text{plim}\, \hat{\text{b}}_1 = \beta_1 \left(\frac{\sigma_x^2}{\sigma_x^2 + \sigma_v^2} \right), \tag{6.12}$$

Here, σ_x^2 represents the variance of the "true" independent variable that you want to examine and σ_v^2 is the variance of the measurement error. The term within parentheses is bounded between 0 and 1. In sum, in the presence of measurement error, $\hat{b}_1$ is an inconsistent estimator of the true parameter β_1. Equation (6.12) leads to three interesting results.

First, because the variation in the measurement error lies in the denominator, the OLS estimator will be downward biased in the presence of measurement error. This is called attenuation bias. Second, the size of the attenuation bias will depend on the ratio σ_x^2 / σ_v^2, the so-called signal-to-noise ratio. The larger the variance of the measurement error σ_v^2, the larger is the attenuation bias. Finally, because the terms in parentheses are variances (non-negative), the sign of β_1 will not change in the presence of measurement error. The example of measurement error has covered a single regression model. If you have a multiple regression model and particularly have measurement error in more than one variable, it will be difficult to analyze the size and direction of the endogeneity bias caused by measurement error. Unfortunately, this situation is not uncommon in corporate finance studies. You usually assume that a measurement error (or omitted variable bias) exists but is uncorrelated with the independent variables. However, in empirical data, the measurement error may produce inconsistent estimates for all the parameters in a multiple linear regression model, depending on how the unobserved variable is correlated with the independent variables in the model.

6.1.3 Simultaneity and Reverse Causality

Simultaneity is another source of endogeneity. In the presence of simultaneity, there is a system of equations and independent variables that are simultaneously determined together with dependent variables. Roberts and Whited (2013) provide a good example to help clarify simultaneity and its corporate finance applications. Research has established that the index of anti-takeover provisions is negatively related to firm value measured, for instance, by market-to-book value. The interpretation of this result is not clear as it does not imply that the index of anti-takeover provisions causes a decrease in firm value. Managers of low-value firms may use anti-takeover provisions to entrench themselves in the firm. In this case, the market-to-book value and anti-takeover provisions are determined simultaneously, leading to reverse causality.

Equations (6.13) and (6.14) provide an example. Skip index i for simplicity:

$$y_1 = \beta_0 + \beta_1 x_1 + \beta_2 y_2 + e_1, \tag{6.13}$$

$$y_2 = \gamma_0 + \gamma_1 x_2 + \gamma_2 y_1 + e_2. \tag{6.14}$$

Suppose you want to estimate Equation (6.14) in which y_2 depends on y_1 but in Equation (6.13) y_1 depends on y_2, which results in y_1 and e_2 being correlated and hence endogeneity bias arises. An example of the demand and supply equation in Brooks (2019) can be consulted for the derivation of a reduced form of equation.

If you ignore simultaneity and estimate these regressions by OLS, you will obtain a biased coefficient estimate of, for instance, γ_2. This bias will not disappear as the sample size gets larger, so the OLS coefficient γ_2 will also be inconsistent. The OLS estimation of Equation (6.14) is given by

$$\text{plim}\,\hat{\gamma}_2 = \gamma_2 + \frac{\text{cov}(y_1, e_2)}{\text{var}(y_1)}, \tag{6.15}$$

$$\text{plim}\ \hat{\gamma}_2 = \gamma_2 + \frac{\beta_2(1-\beta_2\gamma_2)\text{var}(e_2)}{\beta_2^2\,\text{var}(e_2)+\text{var}(e_1)}. \tag{6.16}$$

As can be seen in Equation (6.16), the sign and size of the simultaneity bias depend on the sign and size of the coefficients β_2 and γ_2 that enter both the numerator and the denominator, and thus it is difficult to interpret.

6.2 Remedy for Endogeneity Bias

Empirically you cannot test whether an independent variable is correlated with the residual term since the residual term is not observed to begin with. This means that it is difficult to ensure that the endogeneity bias has been solved. However, this section will go through some of the standard methods that may help to decrease the magnitude of the endogeneity bias. These methods either rely on a clear source of variation for identifying the parameters, such as the IV approach, proxy-variable solution, DiD estimators, and RDD, or methods that rely on modeling assumptions, such as panel-data methods and matching methods. Most of these methods will be covered in this chapter, but DiD estimators and panel-data methods will be covered in the upcoming chapters, as you need to have knowledge of time-series data to understand these methods.

6.2.1 Proxy-Variable Solution to Omitted-Variable Bias

The proxy-variable approach may itself cause problems with measurement error, but it is a common approach in corporate finance when an instrument (explained in the next section) is not available for the endogeneity problem. Consider the following model:

$$y_i = \beta_0 + \beta_1 x_{1i} + \beta_2 x_{2i} + \cdots + \beta_k x_{ki} + \gamma q_i + e_i, \tag{6.17}$$

where q is an (unobserved) omitted variable causing an endogeneity problem if it is correlated with other independent variables since it will enter the error term (skip the index i for simplicity). The proxy-variable approach here is that you do not observe q, but have a proxy variable z that is highly correlated with q and can be used in the model instead. Perhaps the main aim is not to test γ, although it is important, but to reduce or eliminate bias in β_j when including the proxy z in the model. To be able to use z as an independent variable, two conditions should be satisfied.

First, the proxy z should be redundant in the structural Equation (6.17). The second condition is a bit more difficult. Once you use the proxy variable z, the correlation between the omitted variable q and the other independent variables x_j should go to 0. Since the underlying regression equation for the omitted variable is also an OLS: $q = b_0 + b_1 z + u$, the CLRM assumptions should hold in this regression too.

In addition, b_1 should be significantly different from 0, otherwise you cannot use z as a proxy. However, it is also important that the residuals in this regression and the independent variables in the structural regression model should not be correlated, $\text{cov}(x_j, u) = 0$. To see this, replace q in Equation (6.17) with $b_0 + b_1 z + u$. You will see that the residual term in this regression would be $(\gamma u + e)$ and thus it is crucial that the condition $\text{cov}(x_j, u) = 0$ holds, otherwise the use of proxy z will generate an endogeneity itself. In corporate finance studies it is also common to use more than one proxy variable; hopefully the linear combination of these proxies (residual term from regressing the omitted variable on these proxies) is not correlated with x_j. This condition is difficult to satisfy in most studies, as you do not observe the omitted variable q to begin with. Note also that you do not observe the residual u directly. So, when using a proxy, it is important that the CLRM assumptions hold, otherwise using a proxy will not help solve the omitted-variable bias problem.

6.2.2 Instrumental Variable Approach

The IV approach, sometimes called two-stage least squares (2SLS), is the most common but also the most difficult approach to remedy the endogeneity problem. In this approach you find an instrument that is correlated with the endogenous variable in the model.[1] One major difference between the proxy-variable approach and the IV approach is that a good proxy is correlated with the omitted variable (redundant in the structural equation, which is the main model based on some underlying economic theory) while a good instrument is correlated with the endogenous independent variable (not redundant in the structural equation). The difficulty is to find an instrument that will satisfy the conditions of this approach. Consider the following model:

$$y_i = \beta_0 + \beta_1 x_{1i} + \beta_2 x_{2i} + \cdots + \beta_k x_{ki} + e_i. \tag{6.18}$$

Assume that the independent variable x_{ki} is correlated with the residuals $\text{cov}(x_{ki}, e_i) \neq 0$, causing endogeneity bias. There could be more than one endogenous variable in a model (common in corporate finance studies), but it is easier to explain how the IV approach works if one of the independent variables is endogenous. Otherwise, finding instruments for all the endogenous variables that satisfy the IV conditions is difficult.

The instrument, z_i, should satisfy two important conditions. First, exclusion restriction: z_i should be redundant in the structural regression equation,

[1] The IV approach was first introduced by Wright (1928) in an appendix. Import tariffs appeared to be a major source of tax revenue in the 1920s and the study examined import tariffs on animal and vegetable oils and fats. It focused on estimates of the demand and supply curves.

$\text{cov}(z_i, e_i) = 0$. Again, this is difficult to test as residuals in the structural equation are unobserved to begin with. The assumption suggests that the instrument z_i has no direct relation with the dependent variable in the structural equation, and thus the only relation goes through the endogenous variable.

Second, the instrument should be relevant, (partially) correlated with the endogenous variable in the first stage of the analysis. This condition is easier to test. In the first stage you regress the endogenous variable x_{ki} on the instrument(s) plus all the other independent variables that are used in the structural equation:

$$x_{ki} = \gamma_0 + \gamma_1 x_{1i} + \gamma_2 x_{2i} + \cdots + \gamma_{k-1} x_{k-1i} + \delta z_i + u_i, \tag{6.19}$$

where the residual term u_i satisfies the CLRM assumptions. The relevance condition can be tested by testing (t-test) whether the coefficient δ on the instrument z_i is significantly different from 0. Although it may seem odd to include all the (exogenous) independent variables here, it is a reduced-form equation for the endogenous variable x_{ki} and thus you do not expect a structural relationship between the independent variables and the endogenous variable. If you are able to find more than one instrument, you can test the relevance condition with a test of the joint null hypothesis (F-test). Using Equation (6.19), the structural equation in reduced form is given as

$$y_i = \alpha_0 + \alpha_1 x_{1i} + \alpha_2 x_{2i} + \cdots + \alpha \gamma_{k-1} x_{k-1i} + \theta z_i + v_i. \tag{6.20}$$

If the IV conditions hold, all the independent variables in Equation (6.20) are uncorrelated with the residuals v_i. You can estimate the equation by OLS and the coefficients from this reduced form of Equation (6.20) will be functions of the coefficients in the structural equation.

If there are multiple instruments, say more than the endogenous variables in the model, it is said that the model is overidentified. With only one endogenous variable you need only one valid instrument to identify the coefficients. It is then said that the coefficient is exactly identified. It is not possible to test the exogeneity assumption when the coefficients are exactly identified. However, in the case of multiple instruments, you can test whether the model is overidentified. You test the hypothesis that additional instruments are exogenous under the assumption that there are enough valid instruments to identify the coefficients. The test gives an analysis of whether all possible subsets of instruments provide the same estimates of the coefficient. If the subset of instruments is valid and exogenous, they should lead to the same estimates. If the estimates differ, then you can conclude that there is something wrong (not exogenous) with one or more of the instruments. However, using more instruments might be better from an asymptotic perspective (the bias introduced by endogeneity will converge to zero as the sample size increases), but it may introduce even more bias in the estimation from a finite-sample perspective (a small sample or moderate in size).

Together, there is no point including more instruments if there is already a good one. It is probably best to intuitively explore the economics behind the research question to find a good instrument. The main intuition is that the instrument should affect the outcome variable only indirectly via the endogenous variable. Another important condition to consider is whether the instrument is weakly correlated with the endogenous variable or not. If the correlation is weak, it can lead to a bias in finite samples (Stock, Wright, and Yogo, 2002). Particularly if the coefficient δ on the instrument z_i in Equation (6.19) is close to zero, the normal approximations to the distribution of IV estimates may be poor. That is, the normal approximation to the sampling distribution of the 2SLS estimator fails if the instrument is weak.

To test whether the instrument is weak, you can use a test suggested by Stock and Yogo (2005), which is based on the Cragg–Donald F-statistic. Lower values of this F-statistic would indicate a weak instrument. When there is a single endogenous independent variable but more than one instrument, the F-statistic tests that the coefficients on all the instruments are zero in the first stage of 2SLS. Higher values of the F-statistic will allow you to reject the null hypothesis of weak instruments. There is also a simple rule of thumb that if the F-statistic is greater than 10, then you can reject the null hypothesis of weak instruments. In this Stock–Yogo test, the strong instruments are those for which the bias in the 2SLS estimator is at most 10% of the bias in the OLS estimator. The first-stage F-statistic is compared to a critical value depending on the number of instruments. For a 5% significance level, this critical value ranges between 9.08 and 11.52. Thus, the rule of thumb of a critical F-value of 10 seems a good approximation to this test. Note that these tests refer to cases with homoskedastic residuals.

If it turns out that you have many weak instruments but a few strong instruments, it is probably best to drop the weak instruments from the model, although this may lead you to obtain larger standard errors. If the coefficients are exactly identified, then you cannot afford to drop the weak instruments. If the coefficients are overidentified and you do not have strong instruments, then you need to keep searching for strong instruments, which is difficult but worth the effort. Alternatively, you may move on with the weak instruments but you need to use other estimation methods that are less sensitive to weak instruments than 2SLS. One example of such an estimator is the limited information maximum-likelihood estimator (see Stock and Watson, 2019 for details). We cover maximum-likelihood estimators in Chapter 10.

6.2.3 Treatment Effects

Studies using methods of treatment effects often examine the effect of a (hopefully exogenous) event on an outcome variable. We discuss how the standard event studies work and can be examined in Chapter 8, but studies of a treatment effect are also a type of event study. The interest lies in the causal effect of a binary variable indicating the event on an outcome variable. The standard notations explaining the treatment effects follow Robert and Whitted (2013) in this section. The treatment indicator d shows whether a study group is treated or not, the so-called treatment group. To compare the outcome of interest y for those treated and not treated, you need a control group. The outcome for the treated group is denoted as $y(1)$ and for the control group $y(0)$. The treatment effect would be the difference between these two outcomes. You can compute three (main) treatment effects: (i) average treatment effect (ATE); (ii) average treatment effect of treated (ATT); and (iii) average treatment effect of untreated (ATU). More formally:

$$\text{ATE} = E\left[y(1) - y(0)\right], \tag{6.21}$$

$$\text{ATT} = E\left[y(1) - y(0) \mid d = 1\right], \tag{6.22}$$

$$\text{ATU} = E\left[y(1) - y(0) \mid d = 0\right]. \tag{6.23}$$

To compute unbiased (and consistent) average treatment effects it is important that you select the treated and control groups randomly. This means that study subjects are equally likely to be selected in the treatment group and in the control group. Thus, ATE represents the difference between the expected outcome of randomly selected treated and control groups. Similarly, ATT and ATU represent the effect for randomly selected subjects within each group. If the study subjects are not randomly selected, it is difficult to rely on the results from these simple average treatment effects; the study will be faced with so-called selection bias (see Heckman, 1997). Thus, more sophisticated models are needed. This indicates the importance of a random selection.

As a first step in examining more sophisticated methods, one concept that should be considered is the counterfactual. In the data, you observe one outcome for each study subject, either treated or untreated. Thus, the observed outcome is $y(1)$ for $d = 1$ and $y(0)$ for $d = 0$. The unobserved outcome for each group, $y(0)$ for $d = 1$ and $y(1)$ for $d = 0$, is called the counterfactual. That is, for a participant in the treatment group, a counterfactual is the potential outcome under the condition of control. For a participant in the control group, a counterfactual is the potential outcome under the condition of treatment. These are the outcomes that would have happened (to the outcome) if a participant was in the other group. This framework is sometimes referred to as the Neyman–Rubin counterfactual framework of causality (Neyman, 1923; Rubin, 1974, 2005).

Since counterfactuals are unobserved, they will be missing in the real data, the so-called fundamental problem of causal inference (Holland, 1986). It is indeed an omitted-variable bias problem and the challenging task is to use the data at hand to impute a missing value for this unobserved outcome. This is key for examining a causal relationship between the outcome and the treatment. That is, examining what would have happened to the outcome if a treated participant was not treated. The Neyman–Rubin counterfactual framework is based on the assumption that you can estimate the counterfactual by examining the average outcome of the treated group and the average outcome of the untreated group in the population. The difference in the mean outcomes of these two groups defines the average treatment effect.

One disadvantage with using this approach is that the outcome is the average treatment effect, it does not vary across the study units. If the treatment effect is heterogenous, exhibits a large variability over the units, it will not be a representative statistic for the causal effect of a specific unit. In many studies the main interest lies in the treatment effects of certain units. Heterogeneity in treatment effects will also affect the accuracy of the estimated treatment effect. Regarding inference between units, apply the "Stable Unit Treatment Value Assumption" (SUTVA) (Smith, 2022). This assumption means that there are no spillovers across units, that is, treated and untreated outcomes for a given unit are independent of the treatment choice of any of the other units.

Studies that concern treatment effect heterogeneity use various averages of treatment effects, besides ATE. The average treatment effect of the treated group, ATT, was already mentioned. In cases where the control group can be substituted, studies use a random assignment to the treatment group as an instrument for being treated, which defines the so-called local average treatment effect (LATE). LATE is the average effect of treatment on the units that receive the treatment if assigned to the treatment group but do not receive it if assigned to the control group (Smith, 2022). It will be covered in more detail, along with RDD, below. Imbens and Angrist (1994) provide details on how such instruments can be applied to overcome the problem of treatment effect heterogeneity.

However, some studies still criticize the use of averages in the presence of treatment effect heterogeneity, although it is conventional to present an average. Heckman and Vytlacil (2005) suggest that using other statistics of the distribution of counterfactuals, might be more representative than averages. For example, studies can show: (i) the proportion of participants who benefit from a treatment program relative to another treatment program; (ii) the proportion of the total population who benefit from a treatment program relative to another program; and (iii) selected quantiles of the treatment effects.

Besides presenting different statistics for the treatment effect, some studies partition treatment effect heterogeneity into a systematic part and an unsystematic (idiosyncratic) part (see Djebbari and Smith, 2008). In this context, systematic heterogeneity is captured by the observed characteristics of the units and the treatment program. These variables are sometimes called moderators, observable characteristics. Idiosyncratic heterogeneity in the treatment effect refers to factors that are not captured by these observable characteristics. Thus, the division of systematic and idiosyncratic heterogeneity depends on which characteristics you can observe and include in the analysis. More observable characteristics increase the systematic part and decrease the idiosyncratic part of heterogeneity.

Including these observable characteristics in the model will also alleviate the selection bias caused by counterfactual effects. An easier way of handling the selection bias caused by counterfactual effects is to find independent variables that are correlated with the treatment and relevant for the outcome of interest and include them in the model. These independent variables, so-called control variables, control for observable differences between the treated group and the control group. The ATE would then be $E(y \mid d=1,\mathbf{x})-E(y \mid d=0,\mathbf{x})$. However, this will not eliminate selection bias completely. Let's see why by inserting the counterfactuals for each group in the ATE equation. The bold terms below are the counterfactuals:

$$E(y \mid d=1,\mathbf{x})-E(y \mid d=0,\mathbf{x})=E\left[\left(y(1) \mid d=1,\mathbf{x}\right)\right]-\boldsymbol{E}\left[\left(\boldsymbol{y}(0) \mid \boldsymbol{d}=1,\mathbf{x}\right)\right] \\ +\boldsymbol{E}\left[\left(\boldsymbol{y}(0) \mid \boldsymbol{d}=1,\mathbf{x}\right)\right]-E\left[\left(y(0) \mid d=0,\mathbf{x}\right)\right], \tag{6.24}$$

where the first term $(E[(y(1) \mid d=1,\mathbf{x})] - \boldsymbol{E}[(\boldsymbol{y}(0) \mid \boldsymbol{d}=1,\mathbf{x})])$ is the ATT and the second term $(\boldsymbol{E}[(\boldsymbol{y}(0) \mid \boldsymbol{d}=1,\mathbf{x})] - E[(y(0) \mid d=0,\mathbf{x})])$ is the selection bias. Including **x** to control for factors that are related to both treatment and the outcome of interest does not eliminate the selection bias completely, because there are still unobservable differences between the treatment group and the control group that cannot be included in the model. Note that this is similar to the problem of omitted-variable bias. However, if you use a random rotation of the study subjects, randomly assign those who are treated as untreated, and vice versa, then you could eliminate the selection bias. This implies that the treatment is independent of the expected outcomes. The second term would look like $\boldsymbol{E}[(\boldsymbol{y}(0) \mid \boldsymbol{d}=1,\mathbf{x})] - E[(y(0) \mid d=1,\mathbf{x})] = 0$, since those untreated are now randomly assigned as treated. If the treatment is independent of the expected outcome, then the first term in the equation, which is ATT, will equal ATE: $E[(y(1) \mid d=1,x) - \boldsymbol{E}(\boldsymbol{y}(0) \mid \boldsymbol{d}=1,\mathbf{x})] = E[(y(1) \mid \mathbf{x}) - \boldsymbol{E}(\boldsymbol{y}(0) \mid \mathbf{x})]$.

Taken together, including the control variables in these calculations may make the measurement of ATE more complicated, but it could be achieved by running a linear regression with some assumptions. The main assumption is that the treatment is independent of the expected outcomes for given control variables. In addition, the assumptions of the CLRM should hold. Implementation of a random assignment or mentioned random rotation might be easier with experimental data. However, in observational data you often seek exogenous variation in the assignment of treatment to be able to identify its causal effects. As discussed, it is also possible that treatment effects vary across study subjects, heterogenous effects, which will cause additional bias to selection bias in the regression. Again, one easier remedy is either the random assignment or exogenous variation in the treatment assignment.

6.2.4 Matching Techniques

Matching techniques are useful in particular when examining treatment effects. Although it is not necessary to apply a matching technique to examine the treatment effects, it is particularly useful when the number of treated and untreated study subjects is very different from each other. For instance, if your treated group covers only 1% or 2% of the data, then matching technique could be used to obtain a more balanced sample. As a control group you can match each treated study subject to one (or several) untreated study subjects, based on some similar characteristics. There are different matching techniques, and this section will focus on the most common ones. Although matching treated subjects to untreated ones eliminates some of the selection bias discussed above, since matching permits us to examine counterfactuals, it will not eliminate the selection bias and hence the endogeneity entirely. This is because the matching technique provides neither a clear exogenous variation in the treatment, nor a random rotation between those who are treated and untreated (Smith and Todd, 2005).

There are two important assumptions behind the matching techniques. The first assumption has already been discussed. It is the identification of treatment effects;

that the potential outcomes are independent of the treatment assignment conditional on the observable characteristics of the study subjects (conditional independence assumption). The second assumption, referred to as overlap, suggests that there is a probability of being selected in the treatment group and in the control group for given observable control variables. If this assumption does not hold, you cannot find a match for treated subjects.

6.2.4.1 Propensity Score Matching

One important aspect to consider when matching observations is the choice of variables. Even if the data are available, using all relevant variables may not be possible in situations with high-dimensional data. When the number of observations is small, you cannot include as many variables in a model (the curse of dimensionality). Instead, Rosenbaum and Rubin (1983) suggest the use of balancing scores; that is, functions of the relevant observed variables. You can use these variables if the conditional independence assumption holds; that is, if their conditional distribution is independent of assignment into treatment. One example of a balancing score is the propensity score, which is defined as the probability of participating in a treatment program given the observed variables. The matching techniques that use such a balancing score are called propensity score matching (PSM).

Propensity scores are computed based on observable characteristics of treated and untreated groups, instead of using all the control variables themselves in the model. The assumption would then be that the potential outcomes are independent of treatment assignment conditional on propensity score. Although using propensity scores instead of the control variables would lead to unbiased coefficient estimates, in some corporate finance studies you still find examples of using some of the control variables together with propensity scores in the regressions to increase the efficiency of the coefficient estimates. This is partly because it is difficult to find a perfect match for all the treated subjects in the control group, particularly if there are many continuous control variables in the model. The next section provides a brief explanation of the mechanism behind PSM.

The propensity score is an index l_1 that assigns observation i of variable x_1 in the treatment group to the closest observation (in terms of a distance metric) of x_1 in the control group. Suppose this closest matched observation is m_1. The index l_2 assigns the next closest observation of x_1 in the control group, m_2, and so on. So, there are M close observations where the propensity score index $L_M(x_i) = l_1(x_i) + l_2(x_i) + \cdots + l_M(x_i)$ points to the observation in the treatment group. There is no rule for stating the optimal number of matches; many matches are good for efficiency, but then you may sacrifice precision. There are several different matching alternatives. Nearest-neighbor matching chooses the closest m matches only, where the number m is subjective. In caliper matching the treated observations are matched by using a predetermined interval of the propensity score. The interval is often determined as a fraction of the standard deviation of the propensity score. For example, you assign an interval and choose all matches with, say, $\mp 0.5\%$ of the propensity score.

The matching technique will make it possible to observe the counterfactual outcome. For instance, for the predicted outcome $y(1)$, you will observe y_i if $d_i = 1$. However, you will also observe an outcome for the counterfactual $d_i = 0$, that is the predicted outcome $y(1)$ will equal the average outcome observed from all the matched observations in the control group, $\frac{1}{M}\sum_{j=1}^{M} y_j$, where M is the number of close observations matched to the treated group. Similarly, matching will make it possible to observe the counterfactual outcome for prediction of $y(0)$ when $d_i = 1$. This means you can now compare the actual outcome to its counterfactual and compute ATE, ATT, and ATU (assume one-to-one matching, so $M = N$):

$$\text{ATE} = \frac{1}{N}\sum_{i=1}^{N}\left(\hat{y}_1(1) - \hat{y}_1(0)\right), \tag{6.25}$$

$$\text{ATT} = \frac{1}{N}\sum_{(d_i=1),\, i=1}^{N}\left(y_1 - \hat{y}_1(0)\right), \tag{6.26}$$

$$\text{ATU} = \frac{1}{N}\sum_{(d_i=0),\, i=1}^{N}\left(\hat{y}_1(1) - y_i\right). \tag{6.27}$$

Because the counterfactual outcome is unobservable, it is not possible to test the conditional independence assumption. You can use a falsification test as robustness, in which case you falsely assign a treatment where there should not be any treatment. This can be done if there are multiple control groups. To examine the second assumption, overlap, you can plot the distribution of the independent variables by treatment and control groups. It is also possible to examine how the worst matched observations deviate from the observation of the treated group. If there is a large deviation, the match is perhaps not a good one. Similarly, you can examine the distribution of propensity scores in the treatment and control groups. It might be a good idea to drop the bad matches, those with estimated propensity score below a threshold, but this threshold is arbitrary.

The discussion so far has ignored whether matching should be done with or without replacement. The interest is often in ATT; in this case, matching with replacement means that the same observation from the control group can be matched to more than one observation in the treatment group. This is particularly useful if there is a smaller number of observations in the control group. The technique decreases bias but at the expense of precision. For ATT you try to find matches for the treated group. If the interest is in ATE, you need to find matches for both treatment group and control group. In corporate finance research it is common to use matching with replacement even if there is a large enough sample size in the control group. The control variables are important as they are used in the matching process. Unlike the control variables in the treatment effects mentioned above, in matching techniques the control variables or observable differences are assumed uncorrelated with the treatment effect. Having a large set of independent variables that measure the observable differences will help mitigate the selection bias.

6.2.4.2 Propensity Score Matching Implementation Steps

This section briefly covers PSM implementation steps. For a detailed review, readers are referred to Caliendo and Kopeinig (2005).

(i) *PSM estimation.* Propensity scores can be estimated by OLS, maximum likelihood, or using non-parametric methods. Empirical evidence seems to show that the underlying estimation method is relatively less important when it comes to a binary model, where the dependent variable is either 1 or 0. In this case, OLS or a probit model that relies on the maximum likelihood estimation method can be used. Estimation methods using maximum likelihood will be covered in Chapter 10. The choice of the estimation method and the variables that are included in the model are key in PSM. The decision on the variables should be based on theory and previous literature.

(ii) *Choose matching algorithm.* The suggestion here is difficult, as there is no one algorithm that can be useful for all data. The choice often depends on the sample and its size. For example, nearest-neighbor matching or caliper matching depends on the sample size; the number of observations in the treatment and control group.

(iii) *Check overlap/common support.* Treatment effects can only be estimated in the region of common support, defined as the range of propensity scores for units in both the treatment and control groups. So, there should be an overlap in the propensity score distribution to find a match between a treatment unit and a control unit. Otherwise, it is not possible to find a match between these groups. To determine the common support region, you may start by visually examining the distribution of propensity score in the treatment and control groups. The result of this examination yields a strategy that can be used to implement the common support condition. For example, minima and maxima comparison or trimming can be used.

(iv) *Check matching quality.* PSM is performed on the propensity score not on all the observable variables in the data. Thus, you need to check whether the matching procedure can balance the distribution of the variables in the treatment and control group. This can be done using, for example, a t-test and pseudo R^2 (see Caliendo and Kopeinig, 2005). If the matching quality is not acceptable, you may consider the functional form of the model by including, for example, interaction terms or higher-order variables and rerunning the propensity score regressions.

(v) *Sensitivity analysis.* Sensitivity analysis is necessary for the validity of the results. Caliendo and Kopeinig (2005) suggest several approaches. For example, using Rosenbaum bounds makes it possible to examine how strongly an unobserved variable must affect the selection process to weaken the implications of matching analysis. Using Lechner bounds makes it possible to evaluate the sensitivity of the treatment effects with respect to the common support problem.

6.2.5 Regression Discontinuity Design

RDD is a quasi-experimental technique. In studies where it is not possible to randomly assign study subjects to treatment and control groups, the treatment is assigned based on some continuous (observed) independent variable or the variables crossing an explicit threshold. This variable is often called the forcing or running variable. There are two types of regression discontinuity design: a sharp design where the probability of treatment changes from 1 to 0 at the threshold value and a fuzzy design where the probability of treatment is discontinuous at the threshold value. This section briefly covers these two techniques.

6.2.5.1 Sharp RDD

In Sharp RDD, assignment to treatment is based on a deterministic decision rule (Assumption 1); the probability of treatment moves from 1 to 0 at the threshold value. Again, let d be the assignment to treatment, x is the forcing variable, and x' is the threshold. If the values of x are equal to or greater than the threshold value, $x \geq x'$, then $d = 1$, else $d = 0$. The threshold value is given exogenously, for instance by a regulation. The notations in this section closely follow the notation and explanations in Roberts and Whited (2013), to which the reader is referred for further details. Once the assignment dummy d is determined, you can simply run a regression to examine the slope differential for treated and control groups, including the forcing variable x:

$$y_i = \beta_0 + \beta_1 d_i + \beta_2 x_i + e_i. \tag{6.28}$$

If the assumptions of the CLRM hold, β_1 would reveal the average treatment effect. However, you already know that the treatment assignment is based on the forcing variable, so it is likely that d_i is correlated with e_i, although you have included the forcing variable and may even include some other observed control variables in the model. This is mostly because the overlap assumption in the treatment effects is violated; each value of forcing variable is either assigned to a treated or a control group. In this case the decision rule is clear, but this violates the assumption of positive probability of any observations being both in the treatment and control groups.

Turning to the second assumption of the model, the local continuity assumption: both potential outcomes (in estimating ATE), $E(y(1) \mid d = 1, x)$ and $E(y(0) \mid d = 0, x)$, are continuous in the forcing variable at the threshold value x'. This assumption means that the average outcomes for treatment and control groups are similar around the threshold. In the absence of treatment there would be no change in the outcome. Thus, any difference in the potential outcome (ATE) of the treated and control groups is only due to the treatment effect. This also means that ATE can be identified just above and below the threshold values of the forcing variable, because the difference in the expected value of the residuals will go to 0 as you approach the threshold from above and from below. More formally:

$$\lim_{x_i \downarrow x'} E(y_i \mid x_i) - \lim_{x_i \uparrow x'} E(y_i \mid x_i) = \left[\lim_{x_i \downarrow x'} E(\beta_1 d_i \mid x_i) + \lim_{x_i \downarrow x'} E(e_i \mid x_i)\right] - \left[\lim_{x_i \uparrow x'} E(\beta_1 d_i \mid x_i) + \lim_{x_i \uparrow x'} E(e_i \mid x_i)\right]. \tag{6.29}$$

Here, the notation $\lim_{x_i \downarrow x'}$ means values of x_i approach the threshold x' from above and $\lim_{x_i \uparrow x'}$ denotes that the values approach the threshold from below. The local continuity assumption suggests that $\lim_{x_i \downarrow x'} E(e_i \mid x_i) - \lim_{x_i \uparrow x'} E(e_i \mid x_i) = 0$. Thus, ATE is correctly identified as β_1:

$$\text{ATE} = \lim_{x_i \downarrow x'} E(\beta_1 d_i \mid x_i) - \lim_{x_i \uparrow x'} E(\beta_1 d_i \mid x_i) = \beta_1.$$

One potential problem with this approach is to define what is local, as this approach identifies ATE only for those subjects around the threshold. This could be the small sample of the study subjects, and hence limits the external validity of the study. It is possible to increase the interval, define a larger locality around the threshold, to observe whether the results hold in a robustness analysis. Figure 6.1a provides an example of discontinuity in the outcome variable around a cut-off value. In Figure 6.1b, a bandwidth window of 5% is chosen to examine the local discontinuity around the cut-off value.

The choice of bandwidth window or size depends mostly on data availability. It could involve a variance versus bias trade-off. If the sample size is large enough, the observations that are very close to the cut-off can be used. The advantage of

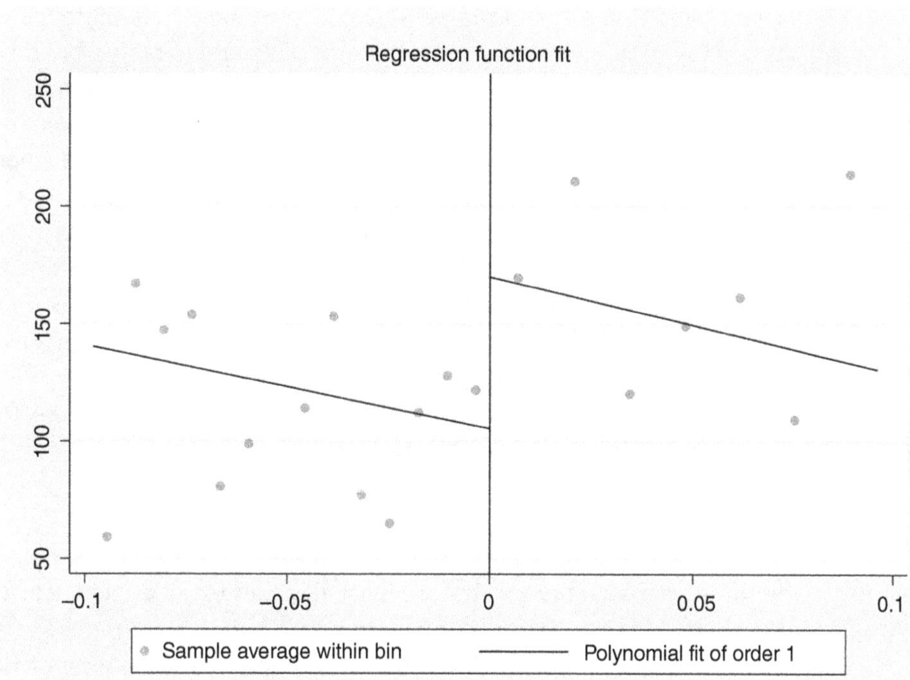

Figure 6.1a. RD plot

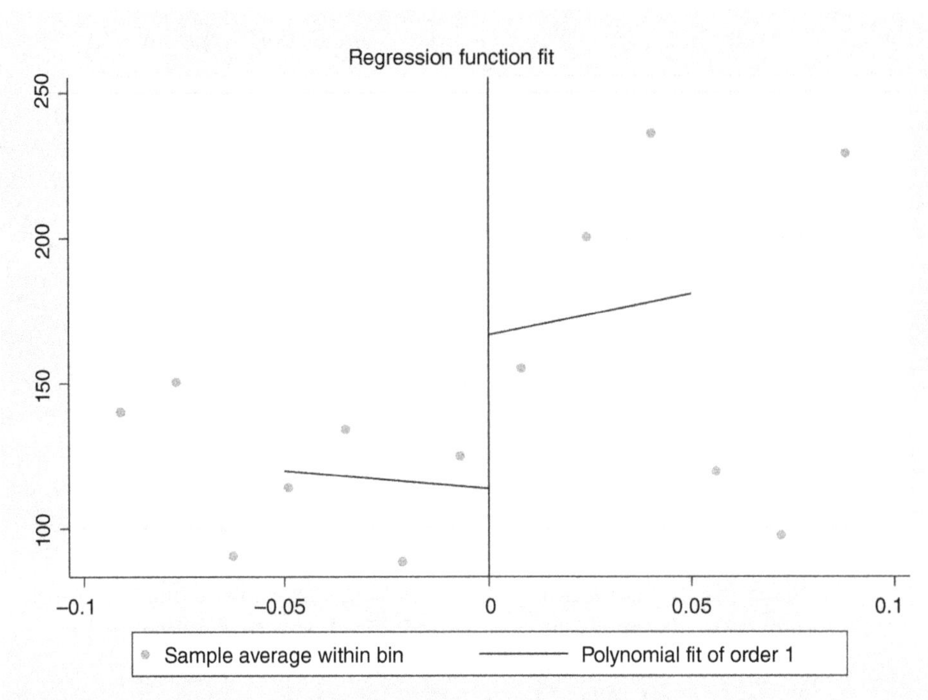

Figure 6.1b. RD plot with bandwidth 0.05

this approach is that the functional form of the regression equation would be less problematic and thus you can run parametric regressions to compute the treatment effects. However, there are some disadvantages of using a narrower bandwidth window as well. Schochet (2008) suggests that a narrower bandwidth window could lead to less precise estimates if there is a possibility of using a wider bandwidth window. Using a wider window could also help with external validity when extrapolating results to units that are far away from the threshold value.

There are several methods suggested for the choice of bandwidth window. To select a bandwidth, Ludwig and Miller (2007) use an approach that minimizes the average squared distance between actual outcome and predicted outcome from a regression model. Similarly, Porter (2003) estimates weighted regressions that use kernel functions, assigning larger weights to those observations that are closer to the cut-off than those further away. As selection criteria, the goodness-of-fit statistics based on the cross-validation models could be used.

6.2.5.2 Fuzzy RDD

In the fuzzy approach there is not a binary decision for treatment, but the treatment probability is a function of the forcing variable x. Thus, the ATE is the difference between two probabilities of outcomes: $\lim_{x_i \downarrow x'} P(d_i = 1 | x_i) - \lim_{x_i \uparrow x'} P(d_i = 1 | x_i)$ Since both are probabilities, they are bounded between 0 and 1. Since these are probabilities, assignment to treatment may occur both above and below the threshold values, although it is more likely that the values above will be assigned as treated. Note that this feature of the fuzzy approach satisfies the overlap condition in the treatment effects but may lead to a misassignment of treatment. The reason for having a threshold is to assign the values to the treated group correctly. The misassignment is more likely to occur if treatment depends on some unobserved variables. The resulting ATE in a fuzzy approach can be calculated as the ratio of the average difference between the expected outcome of the treated and control groups near the threshold to the difference in the probability of assignment to treated and control groups. More formally:

$$\lim_{x_i \downarrow x'} E(y_i \mid x_i) - \lim_{x_i \uparrow x'} E(y_i \mid x_i) = \left[\lim_{x_i \downarrow x'} E(\beta_1 d_i \mid x_i) + \lim_{x_i \downarrow x'} E(e_i \mid x_i)\right] - \left[\lim_{x_i \uparrow x'} E(\beta_1 d_i \mid x_i) + \lim_{x_i \uparrow x'} E(e_i \mid x_i)\right], \tag{6.30}$$

$$\lim_{x_i \downarrow x'} E(y_i \mid x_i) - \lim_{x_i \uparrow x'} E(y_i \mid x_i) = \beta_1\left[\lim_{x_i \downarrow x'} E(d_i \mid x_i) - \lim_{x_i \downarrow x'} E(d_i \mid x_i)\right],$$

$$\beta_1 = \frac{\lim_{x_i \downarrow x'} E(y_i \mid x_i) - \lim_{x_i \uparrow x'} E(y_i \mid x_i)}{\lim_{x_i \downarrow x'} E(d_i \mid x_i) - \lim_{x_i \uparrow x'} E(d_i \mid x_i)},$$

where, because of the local continuity assumption, the expected value of the residuals goes to 0 as the values of the forcing variables approach the threshold from above and below, just as in the sharp design. If you are certain about the assignment to treatment, as in the sharp design, then the denominator of the second term would be 1 and you are back to the sharp design.

ATE in the fuzzy RDD approach can also be calculated using an IV technique (see Hahn, Todd, and Van Der Klaauw, 2001) by implementing a 2SLS method. In the first stage, the assignment to treatment, d, is predicted using an indicator variable T, where the values of x are equal to or greater than the threshold value, $x \geq x'$. Note that the indicator T is not equal to d in the fuzzy RDD approach because there is not a binary decision for treatment due to misassignment or some unobservable factors. Thus, d is predicted in the first stage by using T as an instrument along with the function of subtracting the threshold from the forcing variable, $g(x_i - x')$. This is the same as the first stage of 2SLS in a standard IV approach. The instrument is included along with the other independent variables in the first stage. In the second stage, the predicted values of d are included in the regression. The result yields LATE if (Imbens and Angrist, 1994) the local monotonicity condition holds. In addition, the previously mentioned IV conditions should hold.

6.2.5.3 Difference between Sharp and Fuzzy Designs

In sharp designs, as already discussed, the probability of treatment switches from 0 to 1 at a cut-off point. In real-life examples, treatment is often partially determined by the forcing variable and a cut-off value. Thus, it is more plausible that the probability of treatment changes less than 1 as the forcing variable exceeds the cut-off value. This feature leads to the fuzzy design. To provide more intuition for how it works, Matsudaira (2008) gives an example by using data from a large school district in the United States. The sample covers 338,608 students enrolled in the third grade (about 8 years old) of elementary school and the fifth grade (about 10 years old). Student scores are reported for math and reading tests in the spring of 2001 and 2002.

In the example, students move to the next class if their grade exceeds a predetermined threshold. Students with grades below the threshold need to attend a 4- to 6-week summer school, otherwise they need to repeat the grade. So far, this fact generates a sharp discontinuity in the probability of attending summer school as a function of both math and reading test scores. Students who barely fail either exam are more likely to attend the summer school than those students who barely pass the exam. The observed characteristics of students around the thresholds are almost identical. Thus, the difference in academic achievement between students just below and just above the threshold captures the causal effect of the summer school.

One important fact in the example is that some students who had scores below the threshold did not attend the summer school. Likewise, some students who had scores above the threshold did attend the summer school. This situation leads to the link between the year-end test scores and attendance at the summer school not being deterministic, and thus the discontinuity design is fuzzy rather than sharp. Overall results from the study suggest that students in higher grades gain more from summer school attendance than students in the third grade. For example, the results from the fuzzy RDD method suggest that the scores of fifth-grade students increased by 24.1% the following year, while the scores of third-grade students increased by 12.8% the following year after summer school attendance.

6.2.5.4 Local Average Treatment Effects

In the case of heterogenous treatment effects, β is not constant for each individual and thus the conditional independence assumption is less likely to hold; the treatment effect for individuals is not independent of the treatment assignment. This can happen, for instance, if study subjects self-select themselves to treatment (Heckman and Sedlacek, 1985). We cover alternative methods for selection bias in the coming chapters, but one way to remedy such bias in this context is to calculate local average treatment effects (see Imbens and Angrist, 1994).

LATE would show the ATE of compliers, those subgroups of study subjects that are near cut-off and would switch (treatment vs. control) groups if their value of x crosses the threshold. In addition to the assumptions made for ATE, two additional assumptions are necessary for LATE. First, the treatment effect β and the deterministic treatment assignment d that varies across the study subjects are jointly independent of the forcing variable x around the threshold x'. Second, the likelihood of treatment assignment is weakly greater above the threshold than below. These assumptions are related to the bandwidth, which is subjective. On the one hand, a wide bandwidth increases the precision of the estimate of $E(y \mid x)$ as it includes more observations in the analysis, but it introduces bias in the estimation of ATE. On the other hand, a narrow bandwidth decreases the bias in ATE but introduces inefficiency as it uses a smaller number of observations. So, there is a trade-off between bias and efficiency.

6.2.5.5 Robustness for the Local Continuity Assumption

The local continuity assumption suggests that study subjects just below and above the threshold should be similar (have similar potential outcomes). Regardless of whether it is a sharp design or a fuzzy design, it is important to check the robustness of this assumption. Although there is no clear test for it, you need to make sure that the study subjects do not manipulate the forcing variable to be included in the treatment group (or control group). If they do, then the local continuity assumption is violated. At best you can discuss in the analysis whether there is any possibility for study subjects to manipulate the forcing variable. The assumption is that these study subjects around the threshold are comparable on both observable and unobservable characteristics. Examining whether these groups are similar on observable characteristics is relatively easy. One way to do it is to replace the dependent variable with each characteristic of x and repeat the RDD analysis. There should be no treatment effects in this analysis.

To examine whether the groups are similar on unobservable characteristics, there is not much choice but you can try to find more control variables that may reflect (or proxy) these unobservable characteristics and include them in the model. This approach should absorb the variation in residuals but not influence the treatment effect, increasing the precision of the estimate. Including more (relevant) covariates may also help with bias in finite samples.

Another approach, as suggested by Lee (2008), is a two-step procedure. First, regress the dependent variable on the observable characteristics and predict the residuals, then run RDD using the residuals as a dependent variable in the model. It is also possible to do falsification tests as a robustness check by changing the cut-off point. The treatment effect from the actual cut-off should be significantly larger than the treatment effect from any of the falsely assigned cut-offs.

Some standard tests can also help in detecting violations of the assumptions underlying the RDD model. McCrary (2008) uses a test for continuity in the density of the forcing variable. It is important to use regression discontinuity (RD) graphs to examine if discontinuities appear for other values of the forcing variable. If there are discontinuities for unknown reasons, then it is difficult to claim a causal interpretation associated with differences at the primary discontinuity of interest. RD graphs will encourage thinking, because observing some discontinuity may not mean that you can make a causal claim.

6.3 Application of the IV Approach

The analysis uses a dataset from a recent study on firms' corporate social responsibility (CSR) activities. Using firm data from Sweden, Mavruk (2023) examines how CSR activity-induced local ownership affects firm performance. This section will replicate his first set of analyses and focus on the IV approach. As a first step, the study examines whether more global CSR activity increases the public image of firms and thereby increases remote ownership, thus decreasing local ownership. As one measure of global CSR activity, Mavruk (2023) uses firms' local community score obtained from Thomson. The community score indicates firms' CSR activities in particularly underdeveloped countries. In the study, local ownership is measured as a percentage of total ownership. A decrease in local ownership means an increase in remote ownership. The standard OLS estimations in the study suffer from endogeneity bias caused by reverse causality, because both firm-level and market-wide factors may influence a firm's decision to engage in CSR activities. In other words, firms that perform well may undertake CSR activities. Also, firms may engage in local CSR activities if they have more local owners.

The study applies the IV technique as one of the solutions to this type of endogeneity problem, although lagged values of community score are used in the model. The proposed instrument is the percentage of involvement by the Green Party in the governance of the municipality where the firm has its branches. Perhaps the perspectives of the political parties in Sweden regarding environmental issues do not differ much, however, there is a clear effect of this instrument on CSR activity in the first-stage regressions. Also, there is no reason to believe that the Green Party should directly influence the dependent variable (local ownership) either. So, any effect on local ownership should come indirectly via firms' CSR activities.

Table 6.1 shows the results from the **`ivreg2`** (or **`ivreghdfe`**) command. Panel A shows that the percentage of involvement by the Green Party increases the lagged values of the community score in the first-stage analysis (t-value: 7.04). The result remains unchanged if the community score is used instead of the lagged values. This is empirical evidence that the instrument is relevant. The specification tests in Figure 6.2 indicate that the null hypothesis of underidentification or weak identification can be rejected (Sanderson–Windmeijer F-test: 49.52). The test result from the Cragg–Donald Wald F-statistic (71.22) suggests a rejection of weak identification. Comparing the Cragg–Donald Wald F-statistic with the Stock–Yogo critical values provided in the table suggests that you can reject the null hypothesis that the maximum relative bias due to weak instruments is 10%. So, the maximum relative bias seems to be less than 10%. However, you may need at least two overidentifying restrictions for one endogenous variable to rely on these critical values. Thus, in this case at least three instruments are necessary. In addition, these critical values may work for independent and identically distributed (i.i.d.) standard errors, not for clustered standard errors. However, not clustering standard errors,

Table 6.1 IV approach

Panel A. First-stage regression

No. obs.	2548
No. clusters (yq)	54

lcom_score	Coefficient	Robust Std. Err.	t	P > |t|	[95% conf.	interval]
environ_party	8.039	1.142	7.040	0.000	5.799	10.279
leverage	6.642	4.634	1.430	0.152	−2.445	15.729
roa	0.101	0.160	0.630	0.526	−0.212	0.415
market_capT	−0.019	0.022	−0.880	0.379	−0.061	0.023
return	1.118	2.690	0.420	0.678	−4.158	6.394
return_sd	−16.131	6.227	−2.590	0.010	−28.342	−3.921
tangibility	−0.751	7.912	−0.090	0.924	−16.267	14.765
total_revenueT	−0.349	0.137	−2.550	0.011	−0.616	−0.081
firm_age	18.185	1.150	15.810	0.000	15.929	20.442

Panel B. Second-stage regression

No. clusters (yq)	54	No. obs.	2548
		F(9, 53)	18.950
		Prob > F	0.000
Total (centered) SS	4.287	Centered R2	0.057
Total (uncentered) SS	4.287	Uncentered R2	0.057
Residual SS	4.043	Root MSE	0.041

Lo	Coefficient	Robust Std. Err.	t	P > |t|	[95% conf.	interval]
lcom_score	−0.0004069	0.0001762	−2.310	0.025	−0.0007603	−0.0000536
leverage	−0.029	0.009	−3.430	0.001	−0.046	−0.012
roa	0.000	0.000	−1.120	0.269	−0.001	0.000
market_capT	0.000	0.000	3.440	0.001	0.000	0.000
return	−0.001	0.006	−0.190	0.852	−0.014	0.011
return_sd	0.033	0.015	2.150	0.036	0.002	0.063
tangibility	−0.002	0.017	−0.140	0.891	−0.037	0.032
total_revenueT	−0.001	0.000	−4.510	0.000	−0.002	−0.001
firm_age	−0.015	0.004	−3.590	0.001	−0.024	−0.007

the results are the same and even stronger. Also, the Kleibergen–Paap F-statistic (49.52) reported under Panel A is robust against these violations (see Baum, 2006) and provides qualitatively the same results.

In Panel B,, in the second stage of 2SLS, the results show that the instrumented lagged community score decreases local ownership and increases remote ownership (t-value: −2.31). In Figure 6.3, the Hansen J-statistic that tests whether the instruments are overidentified is 0. This is because there is only one instrument; in other

```
F test of excluded instruments:
  F(  1,     53) =     49.52
  Prob > F       =    0.0000
Sanderson-Windmeijer multivariate F test of excluded instruments:
  F(  1,     53) =     49.52
  Prob > F       =    0.0000
Summary results for first-stage regressions


                                         (Underid)             (Weak id)
Variable     | F(  1,     53)  P-val | SW Chi-sq(  1) P-val | SW F(  1,     53)
lcom_score   |      49.52    0.0000 |       53.19    0.0000 |       49.52
NB: first-stage test statistics cluster-robust
Stock-Yogo weak ID F test critical values for single endogenous regressor:
10% maximal IV size            16.38
                                   15% maximal IV size                  8.96
                                   20% maximal IV size                  6.66
                                   25% maximal IV size                  5.53

Source: Stock-Yogo (2005).  Reproduced by permission.
NB: Critical values are for i.i.d. errors only.


Underidentification test
Ho: matrix of reduced form coefficients has rank=K1-1 (underidentified)
Ha: matrix has rank=K1 (identified)
Kleibergen-Paap rk LM statistic          Chi-sq(1)=33.41    P-val=0.0000
Weak identification test
Ho: equation is weakly identified
Cragg-Donald Wald F statistic                                          71.22
Kleibergen-Paap Wald rk F statistic                                    49.52
Stock-Yogo weak ID test critical values for K1=1 and L1=1:
                                   10% maximal IV size                 16.38
                                   15% maximal IV size                  8.96
                                   20% maximal IV size                  6.66
                                   25% maximal 24IV size
5.53 Source: Stock-Yogo (2005).  Reproduced by permission. NB:
Critical values are for Cragg-Donald F statistic and i.i.d. errors.
```

Figure 6.2. Specification tests after the first stage

words, the model is exactly identified. If there was more than one instrument in the model, a low Hansen J-statistic would still be required, because a high Hansen J-statistic (rejecting overidentification) indicates that the instrument does not work. Finally, the analysis has used an additional option for the endogeneity test of lagged community score, which showed no endogeneity issue to begin with, but this positive result is difficult to justify theoretically. One intuition is using the lagged values of community score, which to a certain extent helped to mitigate the endogeneity bias. Another observation is that the results from 2SLS are qualitatively similar to those from OLS reported by Mavruk (2023), indicating less of an endogeneity concern when using lagged values of CSR variables in the regression model. However, the 2SLS analysis would rationalize the concern with this type of endogeneity bias posed by a referee.

```
Underidentification test (Kleibergen-Paap rk LM statistic):              33.413
                                                    Chi-sq(1) P-val =    0.0000

Weak identification test (Cragg-Donald Wald F statistic):                71.217
                         (Kleibergen-Paap rk Wald F statistic):          49.518
Stock-Yogo weak ID test critical values: 10% maximal IV size              16.38
                                         15% maximal IV size               8.96
                                         20% maximal IV size               6.66
                                         25% maximal IV size               5.53
Source: Stock-Yogo (2005).  Reproduced by permission.
NB: Critical values are for Cragg-Donald F statistic and i.i.d. errors.

Hansen J statistic (overidentification test of all instruments):          0.000
                                             (equation exactly identified)
-endog- option:
Endogeneity test of endogenous regressors:                                0.001
                                                    Chi-sq(1) P-val =    0.9723
```

Figure 6.3. Specification tests after the second stage

6.4 Application of the RDD Approach

This section will replicate a study by Abay (in press) who examines stock market reaction to the recently adopted European Union (EU) Directive 95/2014 on mandating certain entities to disclose non-financial information, such as environmental, social, and governance (ESG) disclosure. According to the directive, firms with more than 500 employees are required to disclose information on environmental, employee, anti-corruption, human rights, and bribery-related matters. Thus, it is an exogenously determined size-based EU directive on mandatory non-financial disclosure with a clear cut-off point of 500 employees, indicating the applicability of a sharp design. Firms above are considered as affected (treated group) and firms below are considered as unaffected (control group) by the EU directive. The EU adopted the mandate in April 2014 and it became effective from fiscal year 2017. However, the proposal to enhance business transparency on social and environmental matters came in April 2013, which is the first event in Abay (in press), who examines stock market reaction to a total of four related events that cover procedural stages. This exercise will focus on the first event, but all the analyses are rerun for the other events as robustness analyses. In addition, Abay (in press) examines cumulative abnormal returns (CARs) as an outcome variable, but the analysis in this section will focus on return on assets (ROA) and revenue (as robustness) to examine the sensitivity of Abay's results using a more short-term accounting performance than CARs. The forcing variable, the rating score R for firms, is determined as $R = \left(\frac{x_i - \bar{x}}{\bar{x}}\right)$, where x_i is the number of employees and $\bar{x}$ is the cut-off point of 500 employees.

To examine the potential problem of agent migration around the cut-off, the analysis first examines the smoothness of the forcing variable near the cut-off point by drawing a histogram. Second, the analysis covers a threshold manipulation test as proposed by McCrary (2008). Table 6.2 shows results from this test and Figure 6.4 shows a histogram for the forcing variable R. The idea behind the manipulation test is that, in the absence of systematic manipulation of the forcing variable around the cut-off, the density of units should be continuous. Thus, the aim is to examine whether there is any evidence of discontinuity in the density of units around the cut-off. The null hypothesis in this t-test is that there is no discontinuity. Rejecting the null hypothesis means that there is evidence of self-selection or non-random (endogenous) sorting of units into affected and unaffected firms. The results from Table 6.2 show that you cannot reject the null hypothesis of no discontinuity in the density of units around the cut-off (t-value: 1.27). This is also evident in the histogram in Figure 6.4. The conclusion is that the firms in the sample do not systematically manipulate their employment levels to be on either side of the cut-off. The results from the binomial count test show that for smaller window lengths, less than $\mp 3.6\%$ around the cut-off value, you can reject the null hypothesis that firm observations are equally likely assigned to treatment and control groups, $(H_0 : 0.5)$. However, for window length above $\mp 3.6\%$, you cannot reject that the firm observations are equally likely assigned to the groups.

Table 6.2 RD density

. rddensity R if Event == 1

c=0.000	Left of c	Right of c		No. obs.	118
				Model	unrestricted
Numberofobs	63	55		BW method	comb
Eff.Numberofobs	52	45		Kernel	triangular
Orderest.(p)	2	2		VCE method	jackknife
Orderbias(q)	3	3			
BWest.(h)	0.08	0.08			
Runningvariable:R.					
Method	T	P > |T|			
Robust	1.270	0.204			

P-values of binomial tests. (H0: prob = .5)

Window Length / 2	<c	>=c	P > |T|
0.004	4	22	0.001
0.008	16	40	0.002
0.012	18	52	0.000
0.016	28	60	0.001
0.02	34	68	0.001
0.024	48	72	0.035
0.028	50	88	0.002
0.032	56	90	0.006
0.036	70	96	0.052
0.04	80	102	0.119

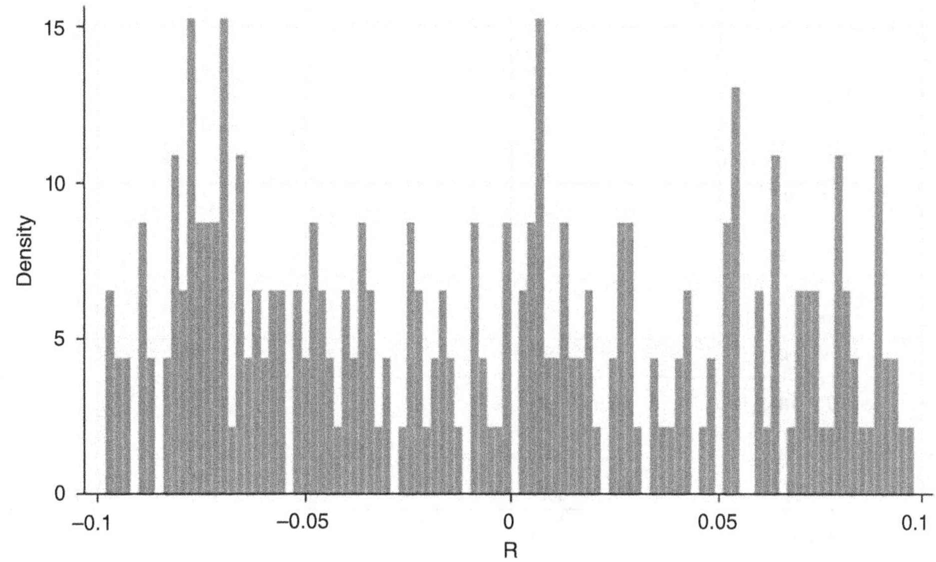

Figure 6.4. Histogram on R

Table 6.3 examines whether the output variable ROA is the same for affected and unaffected firms. The result from a non-parametric test, the Wilcoxon rank-sum test, shows that there is no difference in ROA between affected and unaffected firms (z-value: −0.019).

Table 6.3 Wilcoxon rank-sum test

. ranksum ROA if Events == 1, by(affected)

Two-sample Wilcoxon rank-sum (Mann–Whitney) test			
Affected	Obs.	Rank sum	Expected
0	63	3745	3749
1	55	3276	3273
Combined	118	7021	7021
Unadjusted variance	34361.250		
Adjustment for ties	−0.500		
Adjusted variance	34360.750		
H0: ROA(affected==0)	ROA(affected==1)		
z	−0.019		
Prob > |z|	0.985		
Exact prob	0.9871		

The RD plots in Figures 6.5a (the full sample) and 6.5b (bandwidth of 5% around the cut-off) show some evidence of discontinuity when ROA is examined graphically. However, the result from a formal test, RD robust, reveals in Table 6.4 that the observed discontinuity around the cut-off is not statistically significant, regardless of whether you use conventional standard errors (z-value: 1.29) or robust standard

Table 6.4 RD robust test

. rdrobust ROA R if Event == 1, p(1)

Cut-offc=0	Left of c	Right of c	No. obs.	118
			BW type	mserd
Numberofobs	63	55	Kernel	Triangular
Eff.Numberofobs	12	21	VCE method	NN
Orderest.(p)	1	1		
Orderbias(q)	2	2		
BWest.(h)	0.029	0.029		
BWbias(b)	0.045	0.045		
rho(h/b)	0.633	0.633		

Outcome: ROA
Running variable: R

Method	Coeff.	Std. Err.	z	P > |z|	[95% conf.	interval]
Conventional	11.546	8.959	1.289	0.197	−6.014	29.106
Robust			1.394	0.163	−5.919	35.050

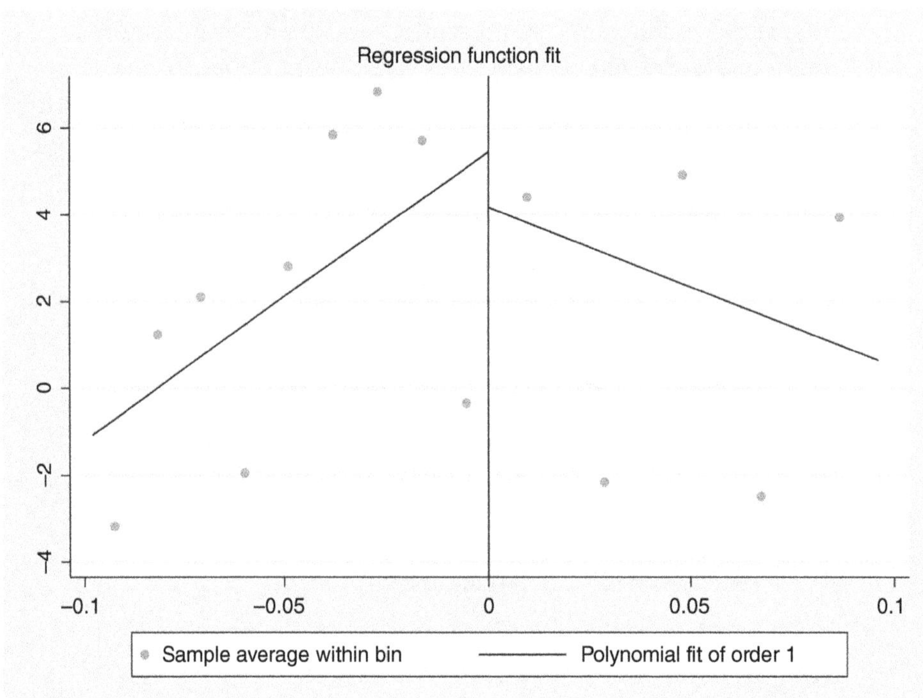

Figure 6.5a. RD plot of ROA

errors (z-value: 1.39). By default, the **`rdrobust`** command uses an optimal data-driven bandwidth selection, but the results are robust if you alter the bandwidth. The results are also consistent when using quadratic, cubic, or a higher-order polynomial.

Table 6.5 Parametric RD estimates

. reg ROA affected_event1 affected_event2 affected_event3 affected_event4 affected_R R PTBV Totalassets CAPEX Revenue LEVERAGE, vce(cluster NRIC)

					No. obs.	468.000
					F(9, 174)	
					Prob > F	
					R-squared	0.130
					Root MSE	11.213

ROA	Coeff.	Robust Std. Err.	t	P > |t|	[95% conf.	interval]
affected_event1	−0.653	2.835	−0.230	0.818	−6.249	4.943
affected_event2	−0.653	2.835	−0.230	0.818	−6.249	4.943
affected_event3	−0.374	2.762	−0.140	0.892	−5.826	5.078
affected_event4	−0.374	2.762	−0.140	0.892	−5.826	5.078
affected_R	−70.918	45.801	−1.550	0.123	−161.315	19.479
R	48.940	38.366	1.280	0.204	−26.783	124.664
PTBV	0.395	1.188	0.330	0.740	−1.951	2.740
Totalassets	0.000	0.000	0.120	0.904	0.000	0.000
CAPEX	0.000	0.000	−0.080	0.933	0.000	0.000
Revenue	0.012	0.005	2.530	0.012	0.003	0.021
LEVERAGE	−0.157	0.051	−3.090	0.002	−0.257	−0.057
_cons	6.066	2.091	2.900	0.004	1.939	10.193

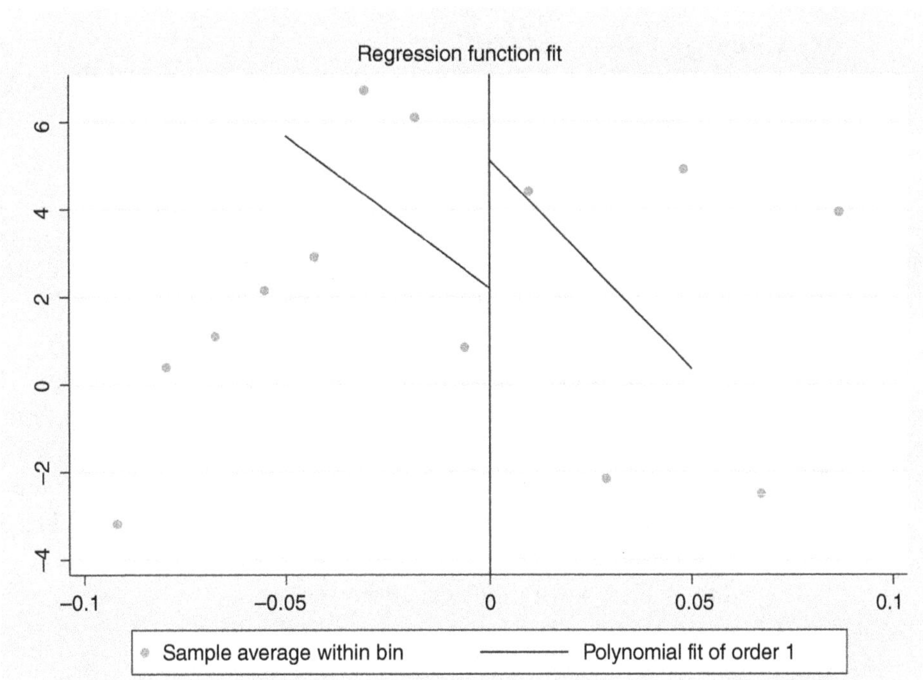

Figure 6.5b. RD plot of ROA with bandwidth 0.05.

Finally, in Table 6.5 the analysis replicates Abay's (in press) results for ROA in a parametric test using an OLS estimation method, in which all events are included. In the model the forcing variable, as well as an interaction term between each event and whether the firm is affected by the EU directive, is included. The coefficient on these interaction terms will show whether the ROA is different for affected and unaffected firms after each event. The interaction term between all affected firms and the forcing variable will show if there is any discontinuity in ROA, regardless of which event is examined. The forcing variable *R* and the control variables – total assets, price-to-book value, capital expenditure, revenue, and leverage – are also included in the model. Standard errors are clustered at the firm level. The results show that none of the interaction terms are significantly related to ROA, indicating the absence of statistical and economical discontinuity in ROA around the events of the EU directive. These results are consistent with non-parametric tests, and also with the inclusion of various fixed effects, such as firm, industry, and time fixed effects. Overall, the EU directive of mandating on ESG disclosure does not seem to affect firm performance, either measured as ROA in this exercise or as CARs in Abay (in press).

6.5 Lab Work: Endogeneity Bias

In this lab work you will use a sample dataset from my students on the course Master's Degree Project in Accounting and Financial Management.

Will Good Deeds Redeem Your Sins?

A Quantitative Study of the Effects of Corporate Charitable Donations in a Sin Stock Setting

By
Herman Weber
Fredrik Mattsson
Spring 2019
Master's Degree Project in Accounting and Financial Management

This study examines CSR activities in sin stocks, and specifically explores corporate donations. Using a sample of listed sin stocks from the North American and European markets, from the period 2009 to 2018, the study tests two main hypotheses: (1) corporate donations are negatively related to abnormal returns in sin stocks; and (2) corporate donations decrease idiosyncratic risk in sin stocks.

The thesis can be downloaded at: Will Good Deeds Redeem Your Sins? A Quantitative Study of the Effects of Corporate Charitable Donations in a Sin Stock Setting (gu.se).

The data for this lab work are available on the book's webpage (www.cambridge.org/Mavruk). To download, apply the following code:

```
Use Chapter_6_Sinstocks.dta
```

We treat this data as pooled data and focus on the endogeneity analysis.

Dependent variables:

1. IR: idiosyncratic risk.
2. Alpha: abnormal return.

Independent variables:

1. Donationstorevenue: percentage of revenue donated by an entity in a given fiscal year.
2. Sin_Dummy: whether an entity is a sin stock.
3. Sin_don: an interaction variable between independent variables 1 and 2.
4. GROWTH_5Y_CAGR: growth rate.
5. DE: debt-to-equity ratio.
6. ROA: return on assets.
7. Reinvestment: reinvestment ratio.
8. O_lev: operating leverage.
9. DebtEBITDA: debt-to-EBITDA ratio.
10. Log_mktcap: log of market cap.

Problem set

1. Replicate Table 3.3, Panels A and B in the Weber and Mattsson dataset and explain your results.

   Useful Stata commands:

   ```
   Sum, pwcorr
   ```

2. (a) Run the following regression:

   ```
   y=IR
   X= Donationstorevenue Sin_Dummy Sin_don
   ```

   Cluster the standard errors on company id (e.g., cluster(company_id)).

   (b) Include the other independent variables: GROWTH_5Y_CAGR DE ROA Reinvestment O_lev DebtEBITDA Log_mktcap.

   Cluster the standard errors on company id again.

   (c) Run the following regression with clustered standard errors:

   ```
   y= Alpha
   X= Donationstorevenue Sin_Dummy Sin_don
   ```

   (d) Include the other independent variables: GROWTH_5Y_CAGR DE ROA Reinvestment O_lev DebtEBITDA Log_mktcap.

   Cluster the standard errors on company id again.

   Use the **outreg2** command to present your results from these four regressions, so you should have four columns for the results in the table. Interpret your results.

   Useful Stata commands:

   ```
   reg, cluster(company_id), outreg2
   ```

3. Explain what clustered standard errors are. Run the full model for each regression (IR and Alpha regressions) again: (i) without the clustered standard errors; (ii) with the robust standard errors. What do you observe? What are robust standard errors? (You do not need to show the results from these regressions. Just explain the differences from these models in the text.)

   Useful Stata commands:

```
reg, robust
```

4. Treat variable Sin_don as endogenous. Using the **ivreg2** command, estimate the model in Question 2(b) and (d) using 2SLS with Sin_ind_avg (industry average sin variable) as an instrument and robust standard errors. Describe the results and contrast them to those obtained from OLS (you may have to install the **ivreg2** command). Note that the "first" option in **ivreg2** is used to show the first stage of the regression. Interpret the coefficient on Sin_ind_avg in the first stage. What are the assumptions behind the model using 2SLS? Explain.

   What is the potential problem with using Sin_ind_avg as an instrument? Explain briefly.

   Useful Stata commands:

```
ivreg2, robust, first
```

5. What is the overidentification test? Explain. Test the overidentifying restrictions associated with using Sin_ind_avg as an instrument. Interpret the result from the Hansen *J*-statistic (overidentification test of the instrument). Note that the **ivreg2** command produces the Hansen *J*-statistic. You may use the model in Question 2(b) (y = IR) for this exercise.
6. Perform a Durbin–Wu–Hausman (DWH) test of the null that Sin_don is exogenous using Sin_ind_avg as the instrument and using the **ivendog** command. What exactly is the null hypothesis of this test? Can you reject the null? Compare the DWH test from the **ivendog** command to that produced by the **endog** option for **ivreg2**. Note that you need to remove the **robust** command to be able to run a DWH test using the **ivendog** command. What is the difference between these two endogeneity tests? You may use the model in Question 2(b) (y = IR) for this exercise.

   Stata codes:

   Durbin–Wu–Hausman

```
ivreg2 IR Donationstorevenue Sin_Dummy GROWTH_5Y_CAGR
DE ROA Reinvestment O_lev DebtEBITDA Log_mktcap (Sin_
don=Sin_ind_avg)
ivendog Sin_don
```

7. For IR regression, obtain the predicted residual from the first-stage regression that you estimated in Question 4 and call it resid1. Note that you may need

to run the first-stage regression manually to obtain the predicted residuals (use the **reg** command). Run the full regressions for IR by adding resid1 among the other independent variables. Use robust standard errors in the regressions. Describe and interpret your results.

Useful Stata commands:

```
reg, predict, robust
```

8. What is simultaneous equations bias? Explain.
9. Revise the analyses in Question 2(b) by using a basic simultaneous equations model and assume non-zero covariance between the disturbance terms. You may drop the interaction term in this exercise and use industry average donation as identifying variable, Don_ind_avg. Interpret your results.

   Stata codes:

```
sem (IR <- Donationstorevenue Sin_Dummy GROWTH_5Y_
CAGR DE ROA Reinvestment O_lev DebtEBITDA Log_mktcap)
(Donationstorevenue <- IR Sin_Dummy GROWTH_5Y_CAGR
DE ROA Reinvestment O_lev DebtEBITDA Log_mktcap Don_
ind_avg), cov(e.IR*e.Donationstorevenue) nocapslatent
iterate(100)
```

   Note that when you copy and paste this code into your do file, it may create a gap between "e" and the following variables in the command **cov(e.IR*e. Donationstorevenue)**, just remove the gap and the code will work.

Good luck!

6.6 Mini Case

Quan et al. (2023) examine the corporate site visits by mutual funds to Chinese firms and show that firms with more visits are associated with lower mutual fund herding than those with fewer visits. The authors explain their findings with the information cascade theory. The study uses data on mutual funds' corporate site visits to firms listed on the Shenzhen Stock Exchange from 2013 to 2021. The herding measure is standard and follows that introduced by Lakonishok, Shleifer, and Vishny (1992), which is used as a dependent variable. The main variables of interest are dummy: (i) whether the mutual fund visits the corporate site; (ii) the natural logarithm of the times the corporate site is visited by mutual funds; and (iii) the logarithm of the number of mutual funds that visit the corporate site. The study then implements an IV approach to examine causality between the negative relation between herding and corporate site visits. The visit measure is instrumented with the travel convenience scores of the cities in which the firms are headquartered. The assumption is that convenient transportation facilitates mutual funds' visits to a firm and is exogenous to their herding propensity.

Task

1. Go to the link: Replication Data for: To see is to believe: Corporate site visits and mutual fund herding – Financial Management (harvard.edu)
   Download the dataset: HerdingData1.dta.xlsx
   Download the do file: FMDataSharing.do
2. Go to the link: To see is to believe: Corporate site visits and mutual fund herding – Quan – 2023 – Financial Management – Wiley Online Library.
   Download the paper. Alternatively, you can download the paper from the following link, which provides the full text to the published version: To see is to believe: Corporate site visits and mutual fund herding (researchgate.net)
3. Replicate Table 2 in the paper. Present and explain your results.
4. Explain why there might be an endogeneity problem in the analysis obtained from Step 3.
5. Replicate Table 3 in the paper. Present and explain your results.
6. Explain and motivate why the instrument used is relevant and valid.

6.7 Summary

Corporate finance research requires close consideration of the assumptions underlying the econometric models that are applied to test the hypothesis. This is partly because, as the field has evolved, more complex relationships in corporate finance have been examined – some of which pose a problem of endogeneity. Thus, in research, it is useful to carefully clarify the problems associated with endogeneity and examine how these problems can be addressed. Endogeneity is likely to occur when studies include another outcome variable on the right-hand side of an equation, to examine how this variable influences the dependent variable (outcome variable of the model). Consequently, this creates validity problems in the model. The key to addressing this problem is first to understand the source of endogeneity. Second, it is essential to realize that endogeneity leads to biased and inconsistent estimators in the models used to test the hypothesis. This leads to inaccurate inferences and drawing wrong conclusions from the research.

Endogeneity is also one problem that violates the assumptions of the CLRM. It is so central in corporate finance studies that this book devotes a whole chapter to discussing it. The chapter covers the sources of endogeneity bias and the most commonly used methods that can be applied to cross-sectional data to deal with them. The methods cover the 2SLS (so-called IV approach), treatment effects, matching techniques, and RDD. An application is provided for an IV approach and an RDD approach. The chapter ends with an application of the most common methods to real data, lab work, and a mini case.

KEY TERMS

Endogeneity; sources of endogeneity; remedy for endogeneity bias; proxy variable; instrumental variable approach; 2SLS; treatment effects; matching techniques; RDD; application of IV approach; application of RDD approach.

REFERENCES

Abay, Z. in press. Does the market react to mandating ESG disclosure? A regression discontinuity based evidence. *International Journal of Accounting, Auditing and Performance Evaluation.*

Baum, C. F. 2006. *An Introduction to Modern Econometrics Using Stata.* Stata Press, College Station, TX.

Brooks, C. 2019. *Introductory Econometrics for Finance* (4th ed.). Cambridge University Press, Cambridge.

Caliendom, M. and Kopeinig, S. 2005. Some practical guidance for the implementation of propensity score matching. IZA Discussion Paper No. 1588.

Culture trip. 2022. The story behind Hanoi's rat massacre of 1902. https://theculturetrip.com/asia/vietnam/articles/the-story-behind-hanois-rat-massacre-of-1902/

Djebbari, H. and Smith, J. 2008. Heterogeneous impacts in PROGRESA. *Journal of Econometrics*, 145, 64–80.

Hahn, J., Todd, P., and Van Der Klaauw, W. 2001. Identification and estimation of treatment effects with a regression discontinuity design. *Econometrica*, 69, 201–209.

Heckman, J. 1997. Instrumental variables: A study of implicit behavioral assumptions used in making program evaluations. *Journal of Human Resources*, 32, 441–462.

Heckman, J. and Sedlacek, G. 1985. Heterogeneity, aggregation and market wage functions: An empirical model of self-selection in the labor market. *Journal of Political Economy*, 93, 1077–1125.

Heckman, J. and Vytlacil, E. 2005. Structural equations, treatment effects, and econometric policy evaluation. *Econometrica*, 73, 669–738.

Holland, P. W. 1986. Statistics and causal inference. *Journal of the American Statistical Association*, 81, 945–960.

Imbens, G. and Angrist, J. 1994. Identification and estimation of local average treatment effects. *Econometrica*, 62, 467–475.

Lakonishok, J., Shleifer, A., and Vishny, R. W. 1992. The impact of institutional trading on stock prices. *Journal of Financial Economics*, 32, 23–43.

Lee, D. S. 2008. Randomized experiments from non-random selection in U.S. House elections. *Journal of Econometrics*, 142, 675–697.

Ludwig, J. and Miller, D. 2007. Does Head Start improve children's life chances? Evidence from a regression discontinuity design. *Quarterly Journal of Economics*, 122, 159–208.

Marton, J. and Sjögren, S. 2022. Kvantitativ forskning som underlag för policy, Debattartikel.

Organisation & Samhälle – Svensk företagsekonomisk tidskrift. https://org-sam.se/kvantitativ-forskning-som-underlag-for-policy/

Matsudaira, J. D. 2008. Mandatory summer school and student achievement. *Journal of Econometrics*, 142, 829–850.

Mavruk, T. 2023. Local CSR activities, local ownership and firm performance. Working Paper, University of Gothenburg.

McCrary, J. 2008. Manipulation of the running variable in the regression discontinuity design: A density test. *Journal of Econometrics*, 142, 698–714.

Neyman, J. 1923. Sur les applications de la theorie des probabilites aux experiences agricoles: Essai des principes. Master's Thesis (1923). Excerpts reprinted in English. *Statistical Science*, 5, 463–472.

Porter, J. (2003). Estimation in the regression discontinuity model. Working Paper, Harvard University Department of Economics.

Quan, X., Xiang, C., Li, D., and Tan K. J. K. 2023. To see is to believe: Corporate site visits and mutual fund herding. *Financial Management*, 52, 711–740.

Roberts, M. R. and Whited, T. M. 2013. Endogeneity in empirical corporate finance. In *Handbook of the Economics of Finance*. Elsevier, New York.

Rosenbaum, P. and Rubin, D. 1983. The central role of the propensity score in observational studies for causal effects. *Biometrika*, 70, 41–50.

Rubin, D. 1974. Estimating causal effects of treatments in randomized and nonrandomized studies. *Journal of Educational Psychology*, 66, 688–701.

Rubin, D. 2005. Causal inference using potential outcomes. *Journal of American Statistical Association*, 100, 322–331.

Schochet, P. 2008. Statistical power for random assignment evaluations of education programs. *Journal of Educational and Behavioral Statistics*, 33, 62–87.

Smith, J. 2022. Treatment effect heterogeneity. IZA Discussion Paper No. 15151.

Smith, J. and Todd, P. 2005. Does matching address Lalonde's critique of nonexperimental estimators? *Journal of Econometrics*, 125, 305–353.

Stock, J. and Watson, M. 2019. *Introduction to Econometrics: Global Edition*. Princeton University Press, Princeton, NJ.

Stock, J., Wright, J., and Yogo, M. 2002. A survey of weak instruments and weak identification in Generalized Method of Moments. *Journal of the American Statistical Association*, 20, 518–529.

Stock, J. and Yogo, M. 2005. Testing for weak instruments in linear IV regression. In Andrews, D. W. K. and Stock, J. H. (Eds.), *Identification and Inference for Econometric Models*. Cambridge University Press, New York, pp. 80–108.

Wright, P. G. 1928. *The Tariff on Animal and Vegetable Oils*. Macmillan, New York.

7 Time-Series Analysis

INTRODUCTION

The time-series data show how the study subjects have been behaving in the past. The data display the value of the variable at various points in time, for instance, each year, quarter, month, and so on for some past years. These values are observed over fixed sampling intervals. In corporate finance studies you observe revenues, cost figures, cash flows, interest rates, and stock prices in various frequencies. The motivation for the choice of frequency and the time period is important to learn the patterns in the time-series data, as sampling intervals may differ depending on the data-generating process. In other words, data may have been aggregated or sampled.

Consider, for instance, the capital asset pricing model (CAPM) regressions. To calculate the daily returns, closing prices may have been selected. If the stock is illiquid, information on the closing price of the stock is likely to be missing for that closing day. In this case the sampling interval should be short enough to find a close approximation, if keeping the particular day observation is important in the analysis. Time-series analysis provides such opportunities that if a series has a regular pattern, then the value could be used as a function of previous values.

The aim with the time-series analysis is first to understand observed patterns in the data. You then try to model the stochastic mechanism behind the series to be able to predict or forecast future values of the data, based on the historical values. Overall, the aim of the time-series analysis is similar to the aim with traditional models. That is, to build a model that minimizes the error between the predicted value and the actual value. Thus, the ordinary least squares (OLS) estimation method covered in Chapter 5 is essential in time-series analysis as well. One difference between the time-series models and the traditional models using cross-sectional data is that the time-series models use the lag values of the dependent variable as an independent variable. In contrast, the traditional models – for example, classical linear regression models – use the other independent variables, since there is no time dimension in the cross-sectional data.

This chapter will briefly examine basic problems with time-series data and some time-series models. The main characteristics of the time-series data are trends, seasonal fluctuations, and that values which are close in time tend to be serially correlated (so-called dependence). Most of the models in time-series analysis are centered around explaining this dependence using econometric methods. The key focus is dependence, as values (close in time) of the variables in time-series data are unlikely to be independent.

The dependence of the values in a series is related to the violation of Assumption 4 of the CLRM. That is, the residual terms are uncorrelated: $\text{cov}(e_i, e_j) = 0, \ \forall i \neq j$. This was examined in Chapter 5. Recall that if this assumption does not hold, then it is said that e_i is serially correlated or autocorrelated. This chapter will examine this property using many plots and figures, as time-series analysis is about how variables develop over time. Studies using time-series analysis rely on graphical analysis to describe and examine the data. The method is helpful for understanding a time-series process but more sophisticated methods are often applied for predictability and forecasting.

Time-series analysis is also essential for the coming chapters covering event study methods (Chapter 8) and panel-data methods (Chapter 9). Understanding the systematic patterns in the data can make it possible to evaluate the effects of some event, which could be either firm-specific or a macro event that affects the whole economy. As for all the models discussed in this book, one chapter on time-series models will not do the subject justice. The chapter will therefore focus on some basic concepts needed to understand time-series models. It will describe the problems with time-series data, cover the tests used to detect these problems, and, in turn, introduce some basic time-series models as a remedy for these problems. Those readers who are interested can carry on to more advanced courses/books in order to further develop their knowledge of time-series models and analysis. The chapter ends with some applications of the most common time-series models, as the focus is more applied, lab work, and a mini case.

7.1 Autocorrelation

If the assumption $\text{cov}(e_i, e_j) = 0, \ \forall i \neq j$ does not hold, you need to remedy this problem using some other structure of the residual terms. Consider the following population model with autoregressive AR(1) residuals. Note that this is not to be confused with the first-order autoregressive models, in which you lag the dependent variable (we will get back to these models shortly). In Equation (7.1) the residuals follow an AR(1) process:

$$y_t = \beta_0 + \beta_1 x_t + e_t, \tag{7.1}$$

$$e_t = \rho e_{t-1} + v_t, \tag{7.2}$$

where e_t is the residual term from a population model, e_{t-1} is the one-period lagged values of the residual term, and v_t is the new residual term in the current model that satisfies the CLRM assumptions. The coefficient ρ is known as the autocorrelation coefficient and measures the degree and direction of the autocorrelation (Stock and Watson, 2019). The interpretation of ρ is as follows:

(i) If $\rho > 0$, then e_t shows positive autocorrelation.
(ii) If $\rho < 0$, then e_t shows negative autocorrelation.
(iii) If $\rho = 0$, then e_t does not show any autocorrelation.

7.1.1 The Breusch–Godfrey Lagrange Multiplier Test for Autocorrelation

To be able to make the interpretations, it is necessary to test whether the observed autocorrelation is significantly different from 0. The Breusch–Godfrey Lagrange multiplier (LM) test can be used to test for autocorrelation (see Baum, 2006; Breusch, 1978; Godfrey, 1978). To see how the Breusch–Godfrey LM test works, replace e_t in Equation (7.1) with Equation (7.2). Since e_t is an estimate, it can be rewritten as $\hat{e}_t$:

$$y_t = \beta_0 + \beta_1 x_t + \rho \hat{e}_{t-1} + v_t, \tag{7.3}$$

where the Breusch–Godfrey LM test tests the null hypothesis that the autocorrelation coefficient is 0, $H_0 : \rho = 0$. In the model presented in Equation (7.1), the residuals follow an AR(1) process. If the residuals exhibit higher-order autoregressive AR(p), you can test the second or higher-order (up to p) (lagged) autocorrelation as follows:

$$y_t = \beta_0 + \beta_1 x_1 + \rho_1 \hat{e}_{t-1} + \rho_2 \hat{e}_{t-2} + \cdots + \rho_p \hat{e}_{t-p} + v_t. \tag{7.4}$$

Then the Breusch–Godfrey LM test is an F-test testing the joint hypothesis that all the autocorrelation coefficients equal 0, $H_0 : \rho_1 = \rho_2 = \cdots = \rho_p = 0$. The Breusch–Godfrey LM test is widely used in empirical work. The Appendix for Chapter 7 at the end of the book provides an alternative test, a Durbin–Watson test, based on small samples (bounded test) for those who are interested.

7.1.2 Remedy for Autocorrelation

Similar to the use of heteroskedasticity-consistent standard errors, in the presence of autocorrelation it is possible to use heteroskedasticity and autocorrelation-consistent standard errors (HAC), regardless of whether there is an autocorrelation present in the data.

7.1.2.1 Newey–West Variance Estimator

In the presence of autocorrelation, the conventional standard error formula is not valid and needs to be adjusted by multiplying it by a weighted factor that adjusts for autocorrelation (see Newey and West, 1987). The weights are determined by the lags and the factor reflects the autocorrelation coefficient. Consider the following model:

$$y_t = \beta_0 + \beta_1 x + e_t. \tag{7.5}$$

In the case of autocorrelation, the conventional variance formula is biased by the factor f_T, which is unknown in advance and hence needs to be estimated:

$$\operatorname{var}\left(\widehat{\beta}\right)=\left[\frac{1}{T}\frac{\sigma_{v}^{2}}{\left(\sigma_{x}^{2}\right)^{2}}\right]f_{T}, \tag{7.6}$$

where $v_t=\left(x_t-\overline{x}\right)e_t$. Newey–West is an estimator for f_T, which is commonly used in studies of time-series data:

$$\hat{f}_T=1+2\sum_{j=1}^{m-1}\left(\frac{m-j}{m}\right)\tilde{\rho}_j, \tag{7.7}$$

where $\tilde{\rho}_j$ is an estimator of ρ_j and m is the truncation parameter. As a rule, it is determined by $m=0.75T^{1/3}$.

Besides this method, there are two common methods that are applied in corporate finance studies to correct for autocorrelation: the autoregressive (AR) model and the moving average (MA) model. Time series that have no problems with autocorrelation and stationarity (a property that this chapter will examine shortly) are said to follow a process called white noise. White noise has a constant mean and a constant variance. Figure 7.1 is an example of a simulated univariate white-noise process. Observe how quickly the process reverts to the mean.

If the time-series data deviate from this process, you can use the following two most common methods to correct for autocorrelation.

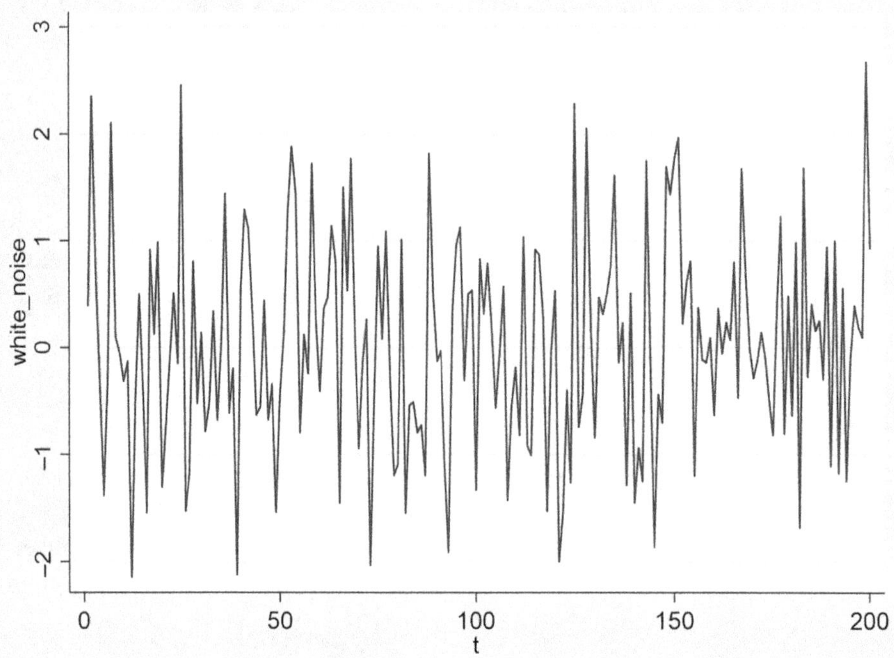

Figure 7.1. A white-noise process

7.1.2.2 Autoregressive Model

In the autoregressive model, lagged values of the dependent variable are included in the model, so that the dependent variable at time t depends on the lagged values, say at time $t-1$. A model with lagged values on the right-hand side will account for the autocorrelation. The AR(1) model can then be written as follows:

$$y_t = \beta_0 + \beta_1 y_{t-1} + e_t. \tag{7.8}$$

If the model is an autoregressive model with p lags, then the model can be written as

$$y_t = \beta_0 + \sum_{i=1}^{p} \beta_i y_{t-i} + e_t. \tag{7.9}$$

Figure 7.2 provides two examples of an autoregressive process with $\beta_1 = 0.9$ and $\beta_1 = -0.9$.

Observe that the mean reversion in Figure 7.2b is faster than the mean reversion in Figure 7.2a.

7.1.2.3 Moving Average Model

In the moving average model, you include the lagged values of the residuals in the model instead of the lagged values of the dependent variable. This is another

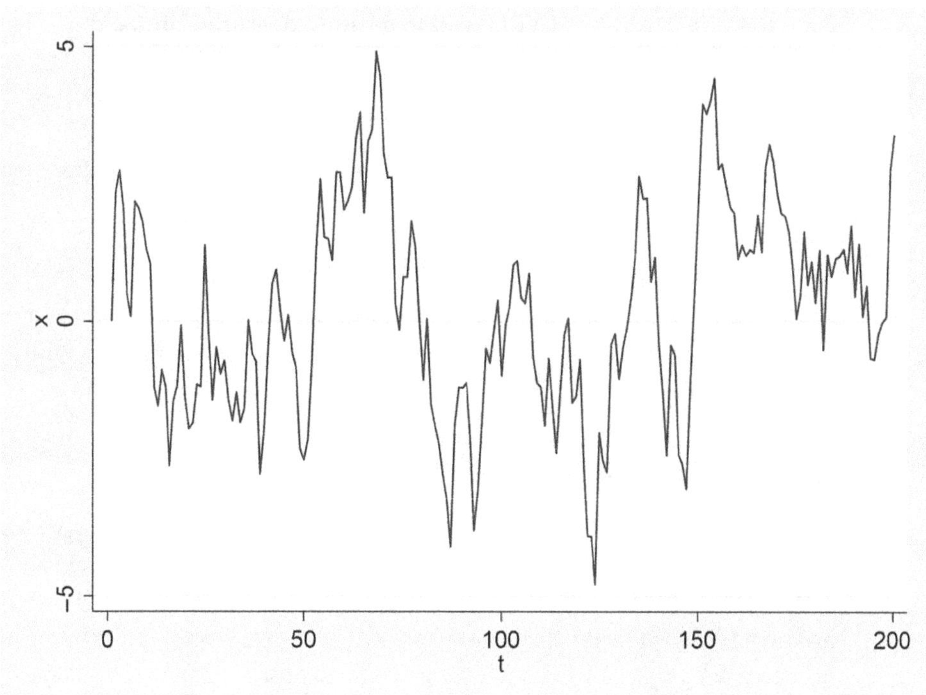

Figure 7.2a. AR(1) with $\beta_1 = 0.9$

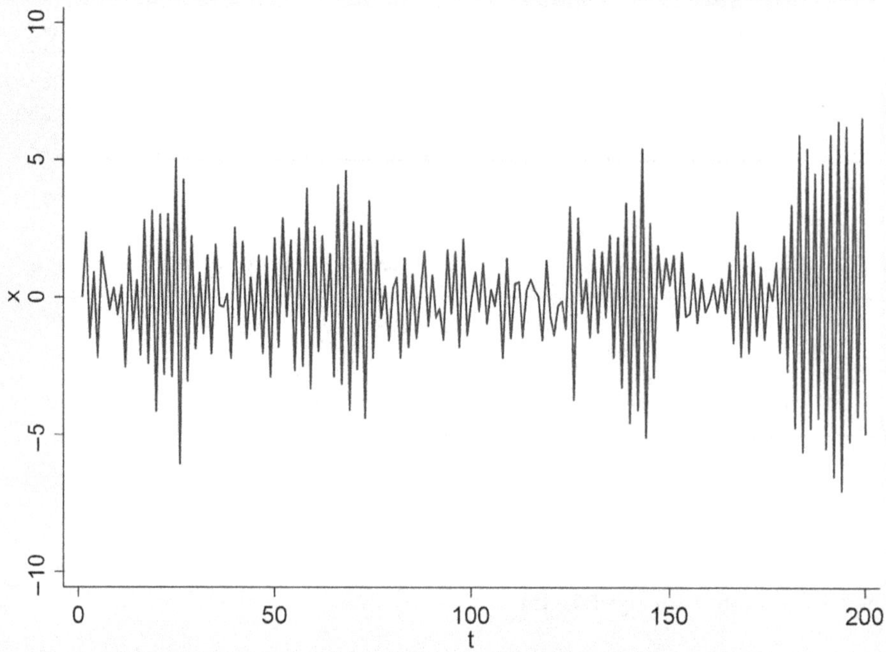

Figure 7.2b. AR(1) with $\beta_1 = -0.9$

common approach that will take care of autocorrelation in the data. The MA(1) model can be written as follows:

$$y_t = \beta_0 + \gamma_1 e_{t-1} + e_t, \tag{7.10}$$

and a moving average model with q lags, MA(q), would be as follows:

$$y_t = \beta_0 + \sum_{i=1}^{q} \gamma_i e_{t-i} + e_t. \tag{7.11}$$

Figure 7.3 gives two examples of univariate MA(1) with $\gamma_1 = 0.9$ and $\gamma_1 = -0.9$.

Although the mean reversion is faster in Figure 7.3b, MA(1) with $\gamma_1 = 0.9$ in Figure 7.3a seems to account for autocorrelation.

7.1.2.4 Autoregressive Moving Average Model

It is also possible to combine these two models by including lagged values of the dependent variable (AR) and lagged values of the residuals (MA), so-called ARMA models. A model with p autoregressive terms and q moving average terms, ARMA(p,q), can be written as follows:

$$y_t = \beta_0 + \sum_{i=1}^{p} \beta_i y_{t-i} + \sum_{i=1}^{q} \gamma_i e_{t-i} + e_t. \tag{7.12}$$

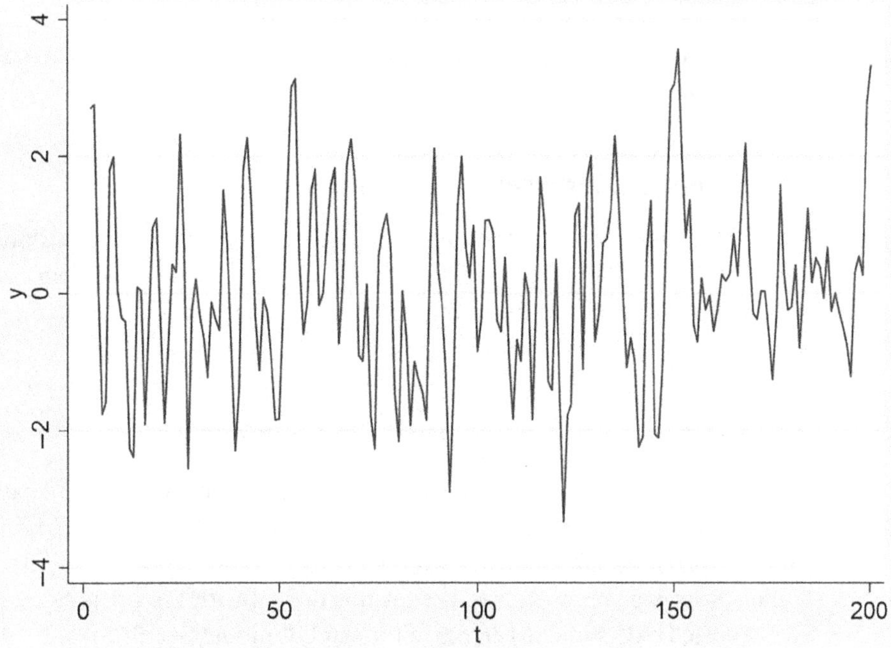

Figure 7.3a. MA(1) with $\gamma_1 = 0.9$

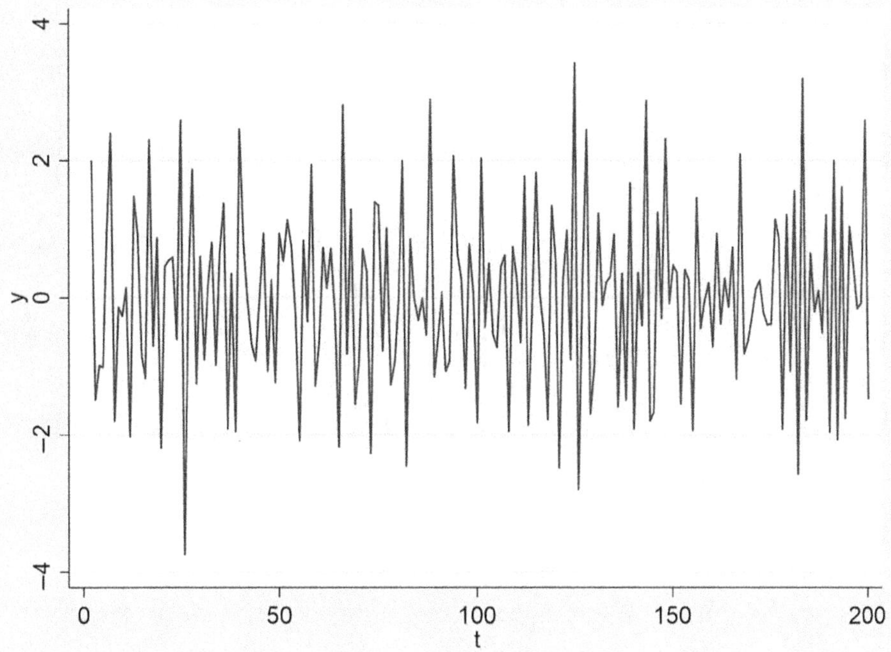

Figure 7.3b. MA(1) with $\gamma_1 = -0.9$

Figure 7.4 presents two examples of an ARMA(1,1) process, one with $\beta_1 = 0.9$ and $\gamma_1 = 0.9$ and the other with $\beta_1 = -0.9$ and $\gamma_1 = -0.9$.

The ARMA (1,1) process in Figure 7.4b with $\beta_1 = -0.9$ and $\gamma_1 = -0.9$ has a faster degree of mean reversion than the ARMA (1,1) process in Figure 7.4a.

7.1.2.5 Autoregressive Distributed Lagged Model

In ARDL models, both the lagged values of the dependent variable and the lagged values of the independent variables are included as regressors in the model. Equation (7.13) gives an example for the ARDL with lag 1, but it can be extended to a model with higher order of the lags, depending on the research question:

$$y_t = \beta_0 + \beta_1 y_{t-1} + \beta_2 x + \beta_3 x_{t-1} + e_t. \tag{7.13}$$

One reason for including higher-order lags of the dependent and independent variables in the model is that, if the autoregressive term is large enough, it may capture the autocorrelation in y_t, then e_t would not be autocorrelated. If you cannot include higher-order lags because, say, it does not fit well with the research question, then you can use HAC standard errors in the ARDL model (see Brooks, 2019 and Mills, 2019 for details).

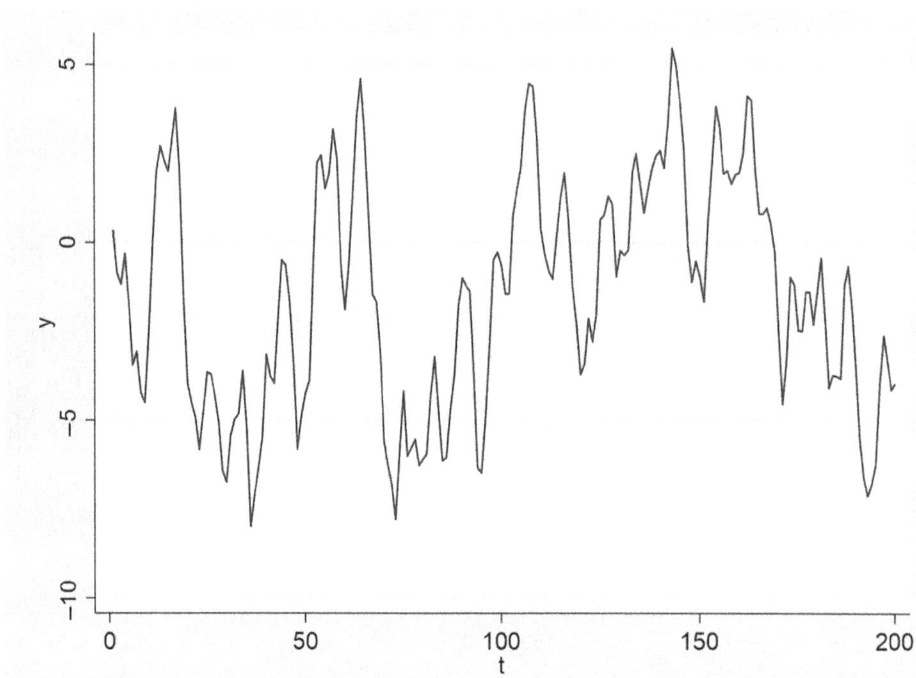

Figure 7.4a. ARMA(1,1) with $\beta_1 = 0.9$ and $\gamma_1 = 0.9$

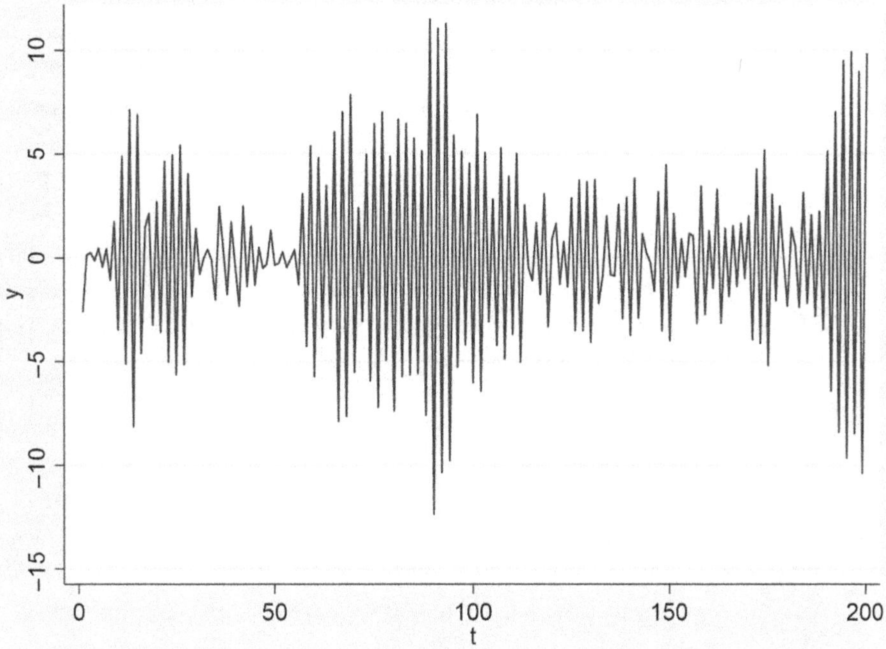

Figure 7.4b. ARMA(1,1) with $\beta_1 = -0.9$ and $\gamma_1 = -0.9$

7.2 Stationarity

So far the focus has been on autocorrelation, but these models require another condition, so-called stationarity. A stationary process has a constant mean $E(e_t) = e$, constant variance $\text{var}(e_t) = \sigma^2 < \infty$, and does not follow a trend. In Equation (7.2) above, $e_t = \rho e_{t-1} + v_t$, if the coefficient $|\rho| < 1$ then the process is stationary, and v_t follows a white-noise process. A strict stationary process satisfies the condition that the probability of series y_t having a value equal to or less than a constant is the same as for the series y_{t+k}. Consider the following joint distribution function F:

$$Fy_{t_1}, y_{t_2}, \ldots, y_{t_T}\left(y_1, \ldots, y_T\right) = Fy_{t_1+k}, y_{t_2+k}, \ldots, y_{t_T+k}\left(y_1, \ldots, y_T\right). \tag{7.14}$$

The process in Equation (7.14) is a strict stationary process, since its joint probability distribution is the same when shifted in time (Brooks, 2019). In other words, the probability measure for the series y_t is the same as that for y_{t+k}, for all values of k.

A weak stationary process satisfies the condition of the constant mean, $E(y_t) = \mu$, the constant variance, $E(y_t - \mu)(y_t - \mu) = \sigma^2 < \infty$, and the covariance that depends on the difference between t_1 and t_2. The latter process is said to be covariance stationary. More formally, the covariance could be written as follows:

$$E\left(y_{t_1} - \mu\right)\left(y_{t_2} - \mu\right) = \gamma_{t_2 - t_1} \forall t_1, t_2. \tag{7.15}$$

The term $\forall t_1, t_2$ means for all values of t_1 and t_2. Let's define $\gamma_{t_2-t_1} = \gamma_s$, which is the autocovariance function. The autocovariance shows how y depends on its past values. If the process is stationary, the autocovariance depends on the difference between the values of y at t_1 and t_2. This means that the covariance γ_s between y_t and y_{t-1} is the same as the covariance between y_{t-2} and y_{t-3}. However, γ_s depends on the unit of measurement and can take very large negative or positive values. Normalizing γ_s will give the autocorrelation function. The normalization is done by dividing γ_s by the variance γ_0, $\pi_s = \frac{\gamma_s}{\gamma_0}$. It is possible to plot π_s against the series $s = 1,2,3,\ldots$ to obtain a correlogram and make two interesting analyses, autocorrelation function (ACF) analysis and partial autocorrelation function (PACF) analysis. The ACF for an m lag is defined as follows:

$$\text{ACF}(m) = \frac{\text{cov}(y_t, y_{t-m})}{\text{var}(y_t)}. \tag{7.16}$$

If the model is A(1) then $\text{ACF}(m) = \pi_m m$, in other words, for larger values of m the function will be decreasing, it tails off. The PACF for an m lag can be written as follows:

$$\pi_m = \text{corr}[y_t - E(y_t \mid y_{t-1}, \ldots, y_{t-m+1}), y_{t-m}], \tag{7.17}$$

where $E(y_t \mid y_{t-1}, \ldots, y_{t-m+1})$ is the minimum mean squared error predictor of y_t, for given $y_{t-1}, \ldots, y_{t-m+1}$. Thus, PACF is the correlation between y_t and y_{t-m} minus whatever is explained by the intervening lags.

We can test for a white-noise process by computing the Box–Pierce statistic. This is another test for autocorrelation and the null hypothesis is that all correlations up to lag m are equal to 0. The Q-statistic asymptotically has a χ^2 distribution with m degrees of freedom. Table 7.1 provides a list of coefficients of ACF, PACF, Q-statistic, and the p-value for the Q-statistic. The analysis is for AR(1) with $\gamma = 0.9$ and for simplicity, up to five lags are examined.

The results from the Box–Pierce statistic show that the null hypothesis that all correlations up to lag k are equal to 0 can be rejected. Corrections up to five lags are tested. The results suggest that this process does not follow white noise (evidence of autocorrelation), as shown by the Prob > Q value that is less than 5% for any lag k. Thus, the null hypothesis that all five lags are not autocorrelated can be rejected. The Box–Pierce test is shown to have poor small-sample properties and thus a

Table 7.1 The Box–Pierce statistic

. corrgram x, lags(5)

LAG	AC	PAC	Q	Prob > Q
1	0.847	0.860	145.670	0.000
2	0.706	−0.048	247.320	0.000
3	0.588	−0.032	318.230	0.000
4	0.499	0.038	369.610	0.000
5	0.421	−0.015	406.370	0.000

modification has been made to the test, the so-called Ljung–Box statistic, used as a general test of autocorrelation. Note also that the ACF and PACF can only be used in stationary series. To examine the ACF and PACF patterns more carefully, Figure 7.5 plots the ACF and PACF of AR(1) with $\gamma = 0.9$. The gray shaded area shows the 95% confidence interval.

In Figure 7.5a, you can reject the null hypothesis of a white-noise process and observe how the ACF tails off. In Figure 7.5b, the PACF analysis shows significant autocorrelation for the first lag only, as PACF removes the effect of the intervening lags; the PACF is the correlation between y_t and y_{t-m}. However, you should be careful with the interpretation of PAC as it can only be used in stationary series. One remedy for a non-stationary process is to detrend the variable, or transform it by taking logs or first differences. The example below examines ACF and PACF for the first difference of the variable.

As can be seen in Figures 7.5c and d, after first differencing the variable you cannot reject the null hypothesis that there is no autocorrelation (up to lag 5) by examining both ACF and PACF. It is also possible to detrend the variable to obtain a stationary process. This is done by regressing the variable on a time trend, an index variable indicating time ($t = 1,2,3,\ldots,T$) and thereby obtaining the residuals from the regression. Note that this is different from including time dummies in a regression. A type of autocorrelation pattern, seasonality, should also be considered to obtain a stationary process. Seasonality means that the pattern is observed in

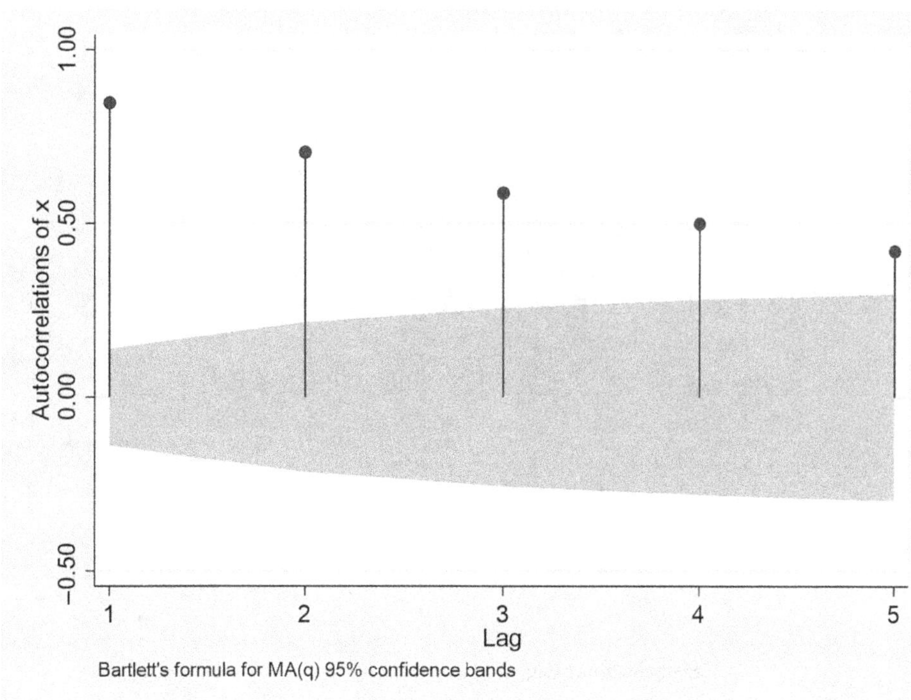

Figure 7.5a. ACF of AR(1) with $\gamma = 0.9$

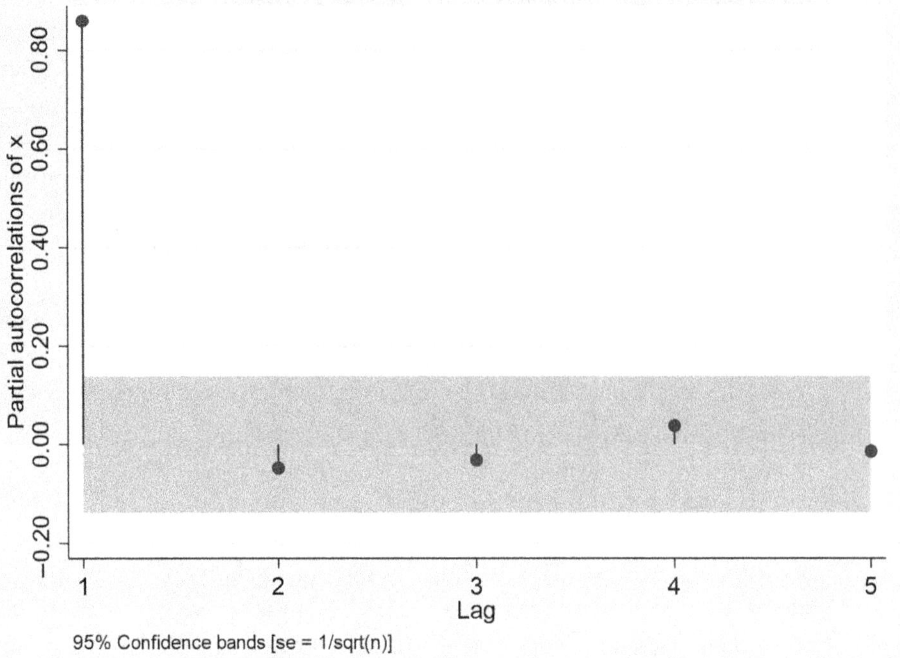

Figure 7.5b. PACF of AR(1) with $\gamma = 0.9$

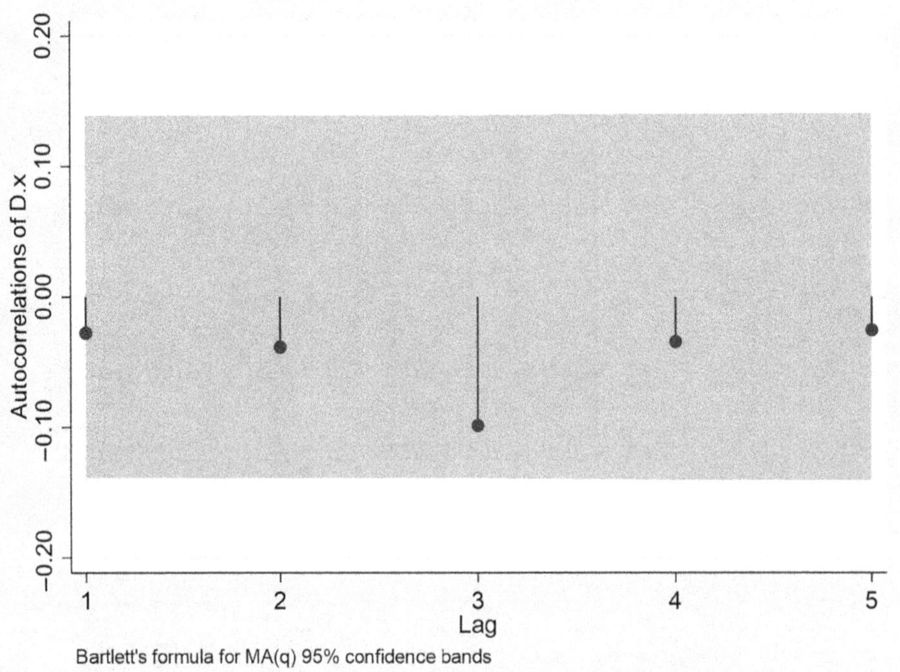

Figure 7.5c. ACF for the first difference

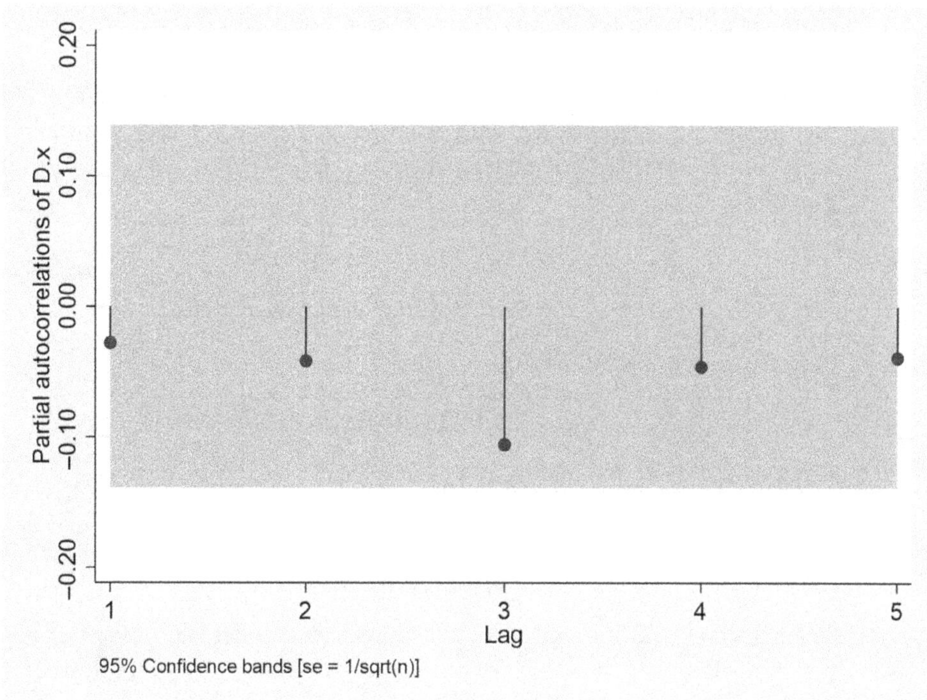

Figure 7.5d. PACF for the first difference

every season, which could be monthly, quarterly, or yearly. For instance, you may observe an increase in revenue in retail businesses around Christmas time every year. Detrending may help with adjusting the seasonality in the time series.

7.2.1 Testing for Stationarity

Consider a simple AR(1) model:

$$y_t = \rho y_{t-1} + e_t. \tag{7.18}$$

In Equation (7.18), if $\rho = 1$, it is said that the model is a random walk and thus y_t has a unit root. If a time series has a unit root, it means that it has a systematic pattern, which is unpredictable. In other words, y_t is non-stationary, which can lead to serious issues in the analysis. One issue is the spurious regressions, meaning that you can obtain high R^2 values despite the data having no correlation. The second issue is errant behavior, meaning that, for example, the t-statistic will not follow a t-distribution.

On the other hand, if $|\rho| < 1$ in the AR(1) model as in Equation (7.18), then y_t is stationary. Stationarity is important because non-stationary variables are not mean-reverting, it does not make sense to analyze their mean. Consider a large sample; a variance depending on time (t * var) would be exploding. In the case of $\rho = |1| < 1$, the effect of shock will disappear eventually and thus y_t will revert to its mean. The closer ρ is to 0, the faster the effect dies out. If $\rho = 0$, y_t will immediately revert to its mean and you are back to a white-noise process.

The Dickey–Fuller (DF) test (Dickey and Fuller, 1979; Fuller, 1976), commonly used to test for stationarity, tests whether the degree of mean reversion is sufficient for stationarity. To see how this test works, subtract y_{t-1} from both side of Equation (7.18):

$$y_t - y_{t-1} = \rho y_{t-1} - y_{t-1} + e_t, \tag{7.19}$$

$$\Delta y_t = (\rho - 1) y_{t-1} + + e_t. \tag{7.20}$$

Let's define $\delta = (\rho - 1)$, then the model is

$$\Delta y_t = \delta y_{t-1} + e_t. \tag{7.21}$$

DF tests the following one-sided hypothesis:

$$H_0 : \delta = 0 \text{ or } H_0 : \rho = 1,$$

$$H_1 : \delta < 0 \text{ or } H_0 : |\rho| < 1.$$

The reason why DF is a one-sided test is that in studies, the case of $|\rho| > 1$ does not make much sense. The standard t-statistic is calculated as a DF statistic, $t_{\mathrm{DF}} = \frac{\hat{\delta}}{Se_{\hat{\delta}}}$. However, the distribution is no longer normal and thus new critical values are calculated, which depend on whether the model includes an intercept only or an intercept and a trend. The software programs often provide critical values when the test is conducted.

Unit-root tests are specific to the choice of lag length and the inclusion of constant and trend. Depending on your research question, you have to choose the relevant form of the test and motivate it. Reporting the details of these choices in your research will allow for reproducibility of your results. In the analysis, you should explicitly state that the alternative hypothesis in the intercept-only model is that the variable is stationary around the intercept and the alternative in the intercept and trend model is that the variable is stationary around a linear time trend.

This test works well if the residuals e_t are serially uncorrelated, but if they are correlated then the DF statistic is not valid since the assumption of zero autocorrelation in OLS is violated. Because the null hypothesis is unit root, $\delta = 0$, Equation (7.21) becomes $\Delta y_t = e_t$. This feature can be used to augment Equation (7.21) by substituting Δy_t for e_t and iterating it for further lags. The augmented DF (ADF) tests the stationarity of the following model:

$$\Delta y_t = \delta y_{t-1} + \theta_1 \Delta y_{t-1} + \cdots + \theta_p \Delta y_{t-p} + e_t. \tag{7.22}$$

The next section briefly presents some standard models used when the data are non-stationary. Readers are referred to Brooks (2019) and Mills (2019) for excellent details of these models, as well as a detailed review of other time-series models.

7.2.2 Models for Non-stationary Data

7.2.2.1 Autoregressive Moving Average Models with Differenced Variable

The ARIMA (p,d,q) model is an ARMA model with p autoregressive lags, q moving average lags, and difference on the order of d. Taking the first difference of the variable may lead to a stationary process. It is then said that the variable is integrated of order 1, expressed as I(1). Figure 7.6 revises the simulated ARMA(1,1) with $\beta_1 = 0.9$ and $\gamma_1 = 0.9$ (see Figure 7.4a) and produces an ARIMA(1,1,1) process instead.

Compare Figure 7.4a with Figure 7.6 and observe how the process has become more stationary when the ARIMA model is used. The series resembles more a stationary process now, and exhibits some random walk-like behavior, although it is difficult to see without knowing how the data is generated (simulated data). This analysis makes more sense with real data where the data-generating process is known.

7.2.2.2 Exponential Smoothing

One concern that may arise when using the lagged values as regressors is the weight assigned for the previous observations. Usually, recent observations are more influential in predicting future observations. Equation (7.23) summarizes a simple exponential smoothing model:

$$y_t^s = \alpha y_t + (1-\alpha) y_{t-1}^s, \tag{7.23}$$

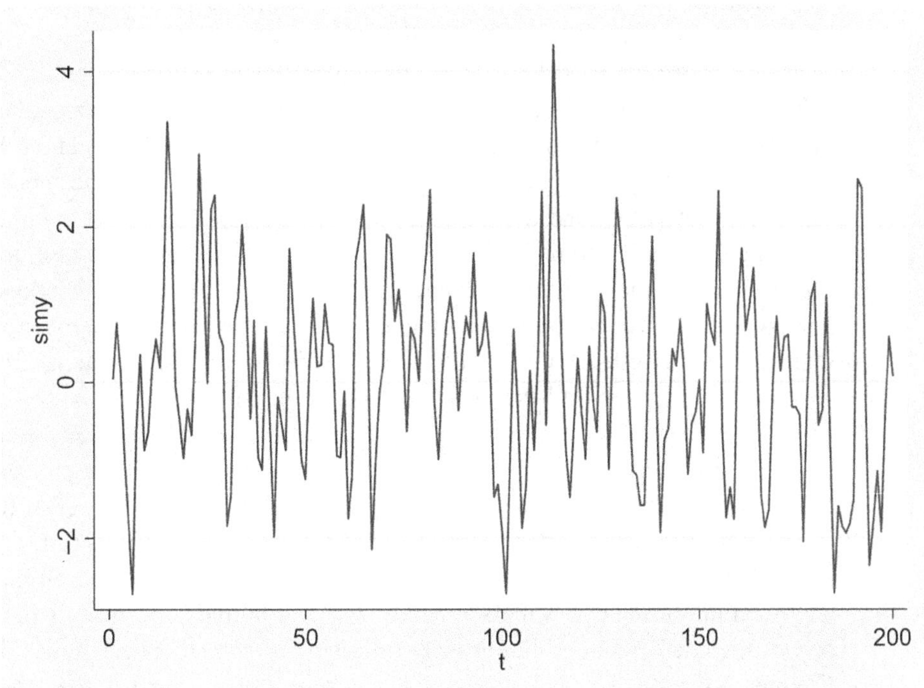

Figure 7.6. ARIMA(1,1,1)

where y_t^s is the smoothed value of the variable at time t, y_t is the actual value at time t, and y_{t-1}^s is the smoothed value at time $t-1$. The coefficient α is known as the smoothing constant and it ranges between 0 and 1. You can iterate Equation (7.23) by substituting for y_{t-1}^s in further lags and arrive at a general equation for exponential smoothing (see Brooks, 2019 for more details):

$$y_t^s = \left(\sum_{i=0}^{T} \alpha (1-\alpha)^i \, y_{t-1} \right) + (1-\alpha)^T \, y_0^s. \tag{7.24}$$

The effect declines exponentially over time, since the exponential constant is defined as $0 \le \alpha \le 1$. Equation (7.24) is an ARIMA(0,1,1) model with MA coefficient $(1-\alpha)$. You can modify this simple exponential smoothing model by allowing for trends and seasonality (see Brooks, 2019 and Mills, 2019 for details).

7.2.2.3 Vector Autoregressive Models

Vector autoregressive (VAR) models are systems of regression models that can be seen as a kind of hybrid model between univariate time-series models and simultaneous equation models, covered in Chapter 6. VAR models have more than one dependent variable. Suppose we have the case with only two variables whose current values depend on different combinations of past values of both variables and residuals. Thus, each of these variables has a regression equation where the residuals are assumed to follow a white-noise process. This feature also allows one to use OLS separately on each equation, because the variables on the right-hand side are predetermined, meaning that their values are known at time t.

The model can be extended by including other variables, first-difference terms, and cointegrating relationships. Thus, VAR models are flexible. For example, a VAR model can be extended to include a number of lags of each variable and first-difference as well as cointegrating relationships (to be discussed shortly). The model is then called a vector error correction model (VECM). In these models it is important to select the lag length optimally. Section 7.2.3 will cover the methods. Also, there is no need to specify which variables are endogenous, since all are assumed endogenous.

However, there are also some problems with the VAR models, for example, determining the lag lengths. Another important issue is that the individual parameters are so many and have limited theoretical interpretation in VAR models. It is common to find some lagged values of the coefficients that have different signs than others. Thus, instead of interpreting the individual coefficients, the block significance tests, or impulse responses, or variance decompositions are used. However, if the aim is to forecast, perhaps the interpretation of the individual coefficients is not relevant.

The block significance test is a joint hypothesis test, testing the null that all the lagged values of the coefficients are zero. The alternative hypothesis is that at least one of the coefficients is significantly different from zero. The F-test, covered in Chapter 5, is used. This is also a type of causality test. In some studies, the focus is on the sign of the relationship or on the horizon of these effects. In these situations, the F-test cannot be used. Instead, the study can explore the impulse responses and variance decompositions.

Impulse responses show how the dependent variable responds to the unit shocks applied to residuals in each of the equations in the VAR system. In this way, the VAR model is expressed as the vector moving average model. Studies often plot the impulse response functions; the applied work in this chapter provides an example. The last approach is variance decomposition, which provides the proportion of changes in the dependent variables based on their own shocks versus shocks to the other variables. The dynamic structure of VAR leads to a shock being transmitted to the other variables as well. The variance decomposition explains how much forward forecast error variance of a given variable is explained by the innovation of each independent variable. Thus, it provides similar information as impulse response (see Brooks, 2019 for details).

7.2.2.4 Granger Causality

Granger causality (Granger, 1969) means that if, say, the variable y_1 causes y_2, then the lag of y_1 should be significantly related to y_2 but not vice versa. If true, then it is said that y_1 Granger causes y_2. Moreover, if y_2 causes y_1, the lag values of y_2 should be significantly related to y_1. If this relation holds for both y_1 and y_2, then there is a bidirectional causality. It is important to note that Granger causality means there is a correlation between the current value of, for example, y_2 and past values of y_1. This is different from the causality argument in Chapter 6; changes of one variable cause changes of another variable.

7.2.3 Goodness of Fit for Model Selection

The most commonly used information criteria for model selection are the Akaike information criterion (AIC) and the Bayesian information criterion (BIC), which measure the trade-off between model fit and the complexity of the model:

$$\text{AIC} = -2\ln(L) + 2k, \tag{7.25}$$

$$\text{BIC} = -2\ln(L) + \ln(N)k, \tag{7.26}$$

where L represents the value of the likelihood function, N is the number of observations, and k is the number of parameters being estimated. A lower value of AIC or BIC indicates a lower loss of information, and hence a better model fit. There are also other goodness-of-fit measures, such as the Hannan–Quinn information criterion (HQIC), but they are used to a lesser extent in corporate finance studies. If they all indicate the same model then you simply choose that model, but the problem arises if these different information criteria indicate different models as best fit. Although AIC and BIC are the most used information criteria, they have their own specification issues. For instance, AIC is not consistent. The more parameters the model has, the lower AIC tends to be. Thus, there is a trade-off between the number of parameters in a model and the model fit. The second term in AIC is for an adjustment (penalty) for adding more parameters. BIC applies greater adjustment for the number of parameters added to the model than AIC (see the second term in Equation (7.26)). However, imposing greater adjustment could be unnecessary. Burnham and Anderson (2002) give theoretical arguments in favor of AIC over BIC, particularly in the case of multivariate regression models.[1]

7.3 Cointegration

Recall the ARIMA models, the additional letter I in the acronym stands for integrated. For example, taking the first difference of the variable will lead to a process that is integrated of order 1, I(1). If two variables that are I(1) are linearly combined, the combination will also have an order of integration 1, I(1). Suppose that we have a time-series model with one independent variable and both y and x are I(1). The residuals obtained from this linear model will be a linear combination of the variables and will also be I(1). However, it is desirable to obtain residuals that are I(0), in other words stationary. The residuals, the linear combination of the variables, will be I(0) if the variables are cointegrated.

Let's examine this more formally by assuming that we have a time-series model with one independent variable x that is stationary, I(0), but a dependent variable y that has a unit root, non-stationary, assume I(1). Thus, the variance for x is $\text{var}(x) = \sigma_x^2$ and the variance for y is $\text{var}(y) = \sigma_y^2 * t$. The linear combination of the model is given by the residuals:

$$e_t = y_t - \beta_0 - \beta_1 x_t. \tag{7.27}$$

In Equation (7.27), because the variance of the residuals, $\text{var}(e_t)$, depends on t through y that is I(1), the residuals are likely non-stationary. However, the variables y and x are defined as cointegrated if the residuals, the linear combination of the variables, are stationary. If true, then in Equation (7.27) the term $(1 - \beta_1)$ is called a cointegrating vector. That is, the stationary, linear combination of non-stationary variables is the cointegrating vector. The interpretation is then that the variables y and x are cointegrated with cointegrating vector $(1 - \beta_1)$. Financial data is often non-stationary but they may move together over time. There could be some underlying mechanism that could affect the variables, implying that the two series have some relationship in the long run. Thus, cointegration can also be seen as a long-term or equilibrium relationship (see Brooks, 2019).

7.3.1 Testing for Cointegration

The cointegration test is basically a test for whether the residuals are stationary. In the above example, the residuals will be non-stationary if the variables are not

[1] See Fabozzi et al. (2014) for more details.

cointegrated. Thus, it is necessary to test the residuals for stationarity. The Engle–Granger (EG) test is used to test for stationarity in the residuals. It is a two-step procedure: first you test whether y and x are stationary using the ADF test; second you regress y on x and then test whether the residual term ($e_t = y_t - \beta_0 - \beta_1 x_t$) is stationary using the ADF test. Engle and Granger (1987) provide a set of critical values for the application of the EG test. The reason is that the test is made on residuals of an estimated model. When calculating the residuals, the sampling errors in the coefficient estimates will affect the distribution of the test statistic and thus standard critical values cannot be used, the standard t-statistic is not valid. Phillips and Ouliaris (1990) provide the asymptotic distribution of the EG test (residual-based test).

The null hypothesis in this test is that potentially cointegrating residuals have a unit root, I(1). The alternative hypothesis is that residuals are stationary, I(0). If the null hypothesis can be rejected, there is cointegration, which is evidence of a stationary linear combination of the non-stationary variables. The test is often applied to specifications in first differences, and hence I(1) represents the unit root in the test.

7.3.2 Autoregressive Conditionally Heteroskedastic Models

This chapter has mostly focused on autocorrelation and stationarity by introducing basic concepts and models in time-series data. However, there could still be a problem with heteroskedasticity in time-series data. In fact, in most corporate finance studies it is difficult to assume that the variance of the errors is constant over time. ARCH models incorporate a non-constant variance of the error term in the autoregressive model, in which the assumption is that the current value of the variance of the errors depends on previous squared error terms:

$$\sigma_t^2 = \beta_0 + \beta_1 e_{t-1}^2. \tag{7.28}$$

As in Equation (7.28), if you use the first lag of squared error terms, the model is known as ARCH(1). If you use further lags of squared error terms, say up to q lags, then the model is known as ARCH(q). How to test for ARCH effects? First, you run the model and save the residuals. Second, you square the residuals and run a regression on q own lagged squared residuals, or more formally:

$$\hat{e}_t^2 = \beta_0 + \beta_1 \hat{e}_{t-1}^2 + \beta_2 \hat{e}_{t-2}^2 + \cdots + \beta_q \hat{e}_{t-q}^2 + u_t, \tag{7.29}$$

where u_t are i.i.d. residuals. You obtain R^2 from this regression and calculate the test statistics as TR^2, where T is the number of observations. The statistic has a χ^2 distribution with q degrees of freedom. The null hypothesis in the test is that all the coefficients (excluding the intercept) are jointly equal to 0. The alternative hypothesis is that at least one of the coefficients is different from 0. Deciding on the number of lags, q, is arbitrary and sometimes you may need large lag values in the models. Thus, a more general formula for ARCH is implemented, a so-called generalized ARCH (GARCH) model.

7.3.3 Generalized Autoregressive Conditionally Heteroskedastic Models

GARCH is similar to the ARMA model since the lagged values of the conditional variance are included in the regression model as a regressor. This allows the conditional variance to be dependent on the own past lags:

$$\sigma_t^2 = \beta_0 + \beta_1 \hat{e}_{t-1}^2 + \beta_2 \sigma_{t-1}^2. \tag{7.30}$$

The dependent variable in the model is conditional because it is a one-period-ahead estimate for the variance calculated using past information. The calculated (conditional) variance can be interpreted as a weighted function of a long-term average value (based on the intercept), volatility in the previous period, and the estimated variance from the previous period. The GARCH model is often preferred over the ARCH model as the GARCH tends to avoid overfitting (see Brooks, 2019 for details).

Equation (7.30) is a GARCH(1,1) model but can be extended to a GARCH(p,q) model by including further lagged squared error terms and conditional variance in the model:

$$\sigma_t^2 = \beta_0 + \sum_{i=1}^{q} \beta_i \hat{e}_{t-i}^2 + \sum_{j=1}^{p} \gamma_j \sigma_{t-j}^2. \tag{7.31}$$

Although the linearity assumption of the CLRM is about linearity in the parameters, not in the variables, in the model in Equation (7.31) the parameters are more likely non-linear. Thus, you use another estimation model called maximum likelihood, where the log-likelihood function of the model is maximized. We will cover this technique when discussing the non-linear models in Chapter 10.

Studies often use a GARCH(1,1) model to capture the volatility clustering in the data but if the volatility clustering is still evident, higher-order models can be estimated. Another related issue is non-stationarity in the variance. If the coefficients obtained from a GARCH model imply non-stationarity in the variance, then a conditional variance forecast will not converge to the long-run average value of the variance as the horizon of the prediction increases. This GARCH process that has non-stationarity in the variance is called integrated GARCH (IGARCH).

7.4 Application on Mortgage Rate

This section examines the relation between the weekly US mortgage rate and maturity rates.[2] The data begin in 2016 week 2 and end in 2021 week 48. Figure 7.7 plots mortgage rate and maturity rate over time, as well as providing a scatterplot between the two rates. Table 7.2 provides descriptive statistics on these variables.

[2] The maturity rate is referred to as the rate, determined by the bank, at which debt comes due and all principal and interest must be repaid to the bank.

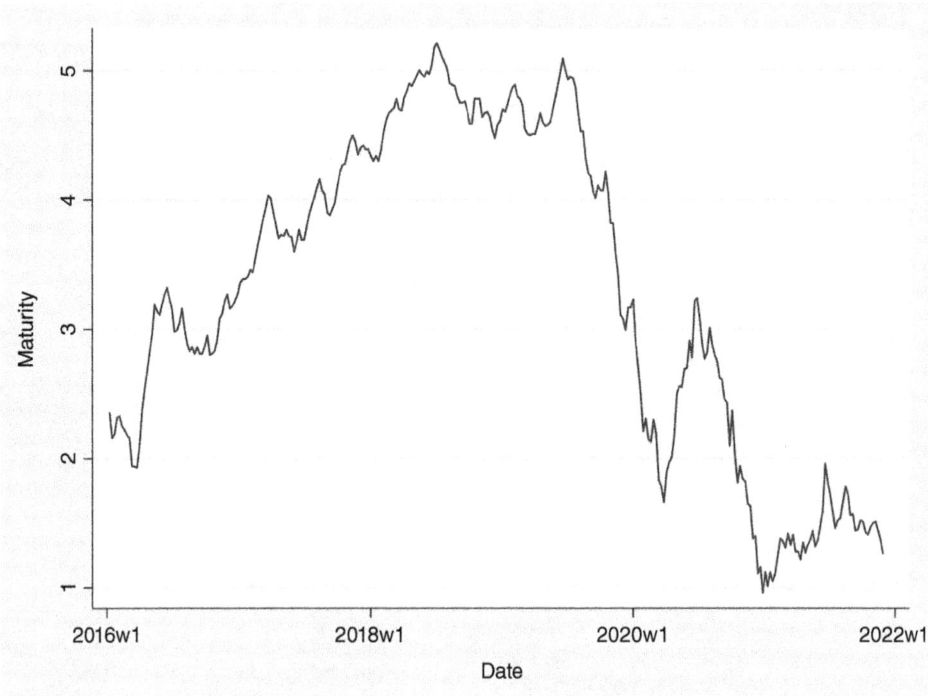

Figure 7.7a. Maturity rate over time

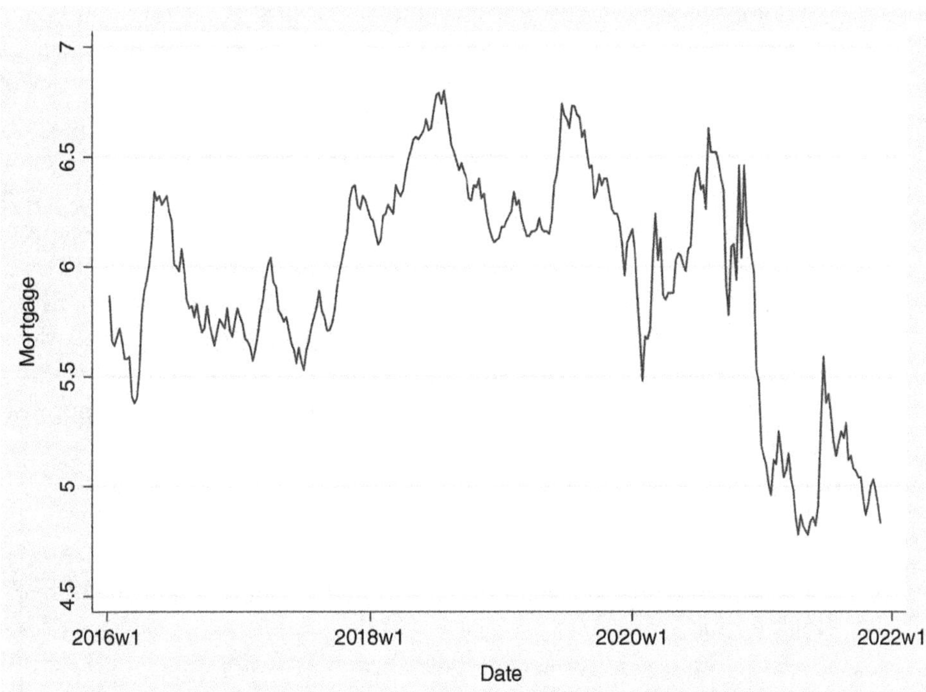

Figure 7.7b. Mortgage rate over time

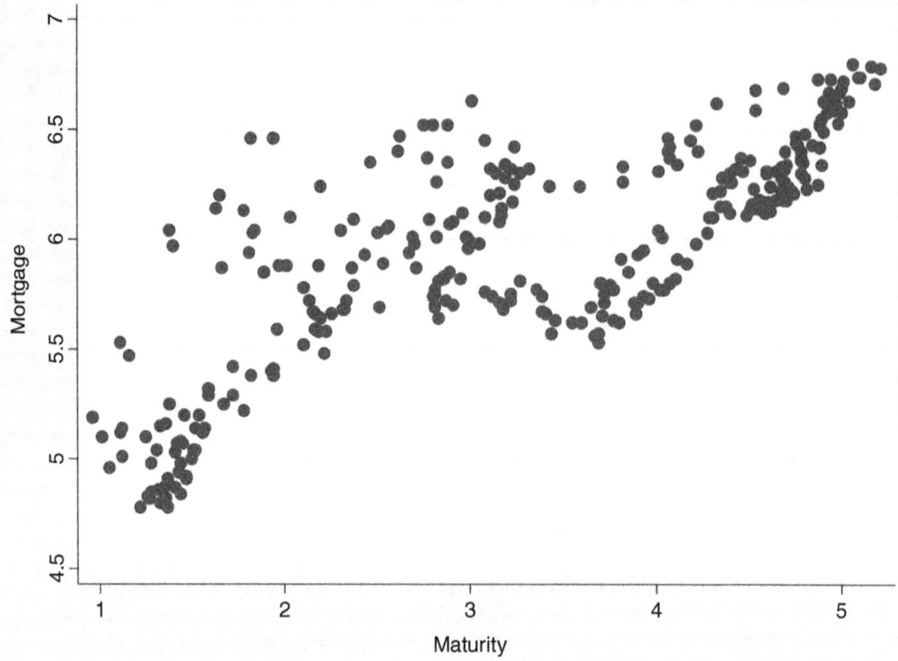

Figure 7.7c. Scatterplot of mortgage rate and maturity rate over time

Figure 7.7 shows that both rates increased until 2019, followed by a decrease. It also shows more variation in mortgage rate until 2019, but when looking at the whole period the variation in mortgage rate seems to be higher, which is also confirmed by the descriptive statistics in Table 7.2. The standard deviation of the mortgage rate is about 0.50%, whereas the standard deviation of the maturity rate is 1.25%. The observed lower standard deviation of the mortgage rate is consistent with the idea of its stickiness. The scatterplot shows a positive correlation between the two rates.

Table 7.3 confirms the results from the scatterplot and shows a positive relation between the mortgage rate and the maturity rate. Figure 7.8 plots the predicted residuals over time.

It is evident in Figure 7.8 that the degree of mean reversion is not fast enough, indicating a problem with autocorrelation.

7.4.1 Test for Autocorrelation

Let's test for autocorrelation by calculating the Durbin–Watson d-statistics (Figure 7.9).

The computed d-statistic is 0.09, which is lower than the d_l critical value of approximately 1.4, indicating a positive autocorrelation. Table 7.4 shows that the Breusch–Godfrey LM test also rejects the null hypothesis of no autocorrelation.

Table 7.2 Descriptive statistics

Variable	Obs.	Mean	Std. Dev.	Min	Max
Mortgage	307	5.940	0.498	4.780	6.800
Maturity	307	3.283	1.249	0.960	5.210

Table 7.3 OLS results

. reg mortgage maturity

Source	SS	df	MS		No. obs.	307
Model	46.843	1	46.843		F(1, 305)	494.030
Residual	28.919	305	0.095		Prob > F	0.000
Total	75.762	306	0.248		R-squared	0.618
					Adj R-squared	0.617
					Root MSE	0.308

mortgage	Coeff.	Std. Err.	t	P > |t|	[95% conf. interval]	
maturity	0.313	0.014	22.230	0.000	0.286	0.341
_cons	4.912	0.050	99.220	0.000	4.814	5.009

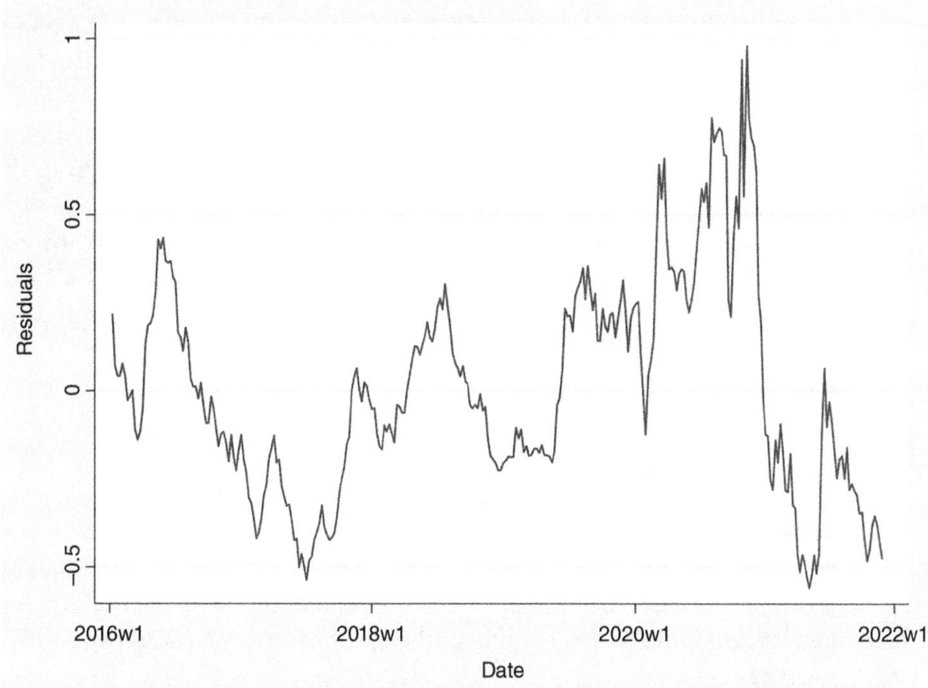

Figure 7.8. Residuals over time

.estat dwatson

Durbin-Watson d-statistics (2, 307)= .086259

Figure 7.9. Durbin–Watson test

Table 7.4 The Breusch–Godfrey LM test

. estat bgodfrey

lags(*p*)	chi2	df	Prob > chi2
1	280.796	1.000	0.000

H0: no serial correlation

Table 7.5 The Breusch–Godfrey LM test for further lags

. estat bgodfrey, lags (1/5)

lags(*p*)	chi2	df	Prob > chi2
1	280.796	1.000	0.000
2	281.151	2.000	0.000
3	281.881	3.000	0.000
4	282.028	4.000	0.000
5	282.029	5.000	0.000

The default is the first lag in the Breusch–Godfrey LM test, but you can also test for further lags. The Durbin–Watson test only tests for autocorrelation in the first lag, while the Breusch–Godfrey LM test can be used to test for autocorrelation up to further lags. This might be important as there may be a reason to suspect autocorrelation in higher orders, for instance in data that have a seasonal pattern. The null hypothesis is that the residuals do not have autocorrelation up to the chosen lag. Table 7.5 provides an example for five lags.

The data are weekly. If you are interested in examining autocorrelation for 1 month, use four lags plus one. As can be seen in the table, up to lag 5 you can reject the null hypothesis of no autocorrelation. This is unsurprising, as there is already autocreation in the first lag and the Breusch–Godfrey LM test is a joint test.

7.4.2 HAC Standard Errors

Table 7.6 shows results from the regression with Newey–West standard errors, which correct both heteroskedasticity and autocorrelation in the standard errors (HAC) up to the fourth lag. As before, the choice of the number of lags is arbitrary and it requires an understanding of the order of autocorrelation and the pattern in the time-series data.

When comparing these results with the OLS regression results in Table 7.3, it can be observed that the point estimations of the coefficients are the same but the standard errors and hence the *t*-values differ once you use HAC standard errors in the regression. The standard errors have become larger and hence lower *t*-values. In the OLS estimation with HAC standard errors, the conventional standard errors are

Table 7.6 Regression with Newey–West standard errors

. newey mortgage maturity, lag(4)

Regression with Newey–West standard errors				No. obs.		307.000
Maximum lag = 4				F(1, 305)		110.780
				Prob > F		0.000
mortgage	Coeff.	Newey–West Std. Err.	t	P > |t|	[95% conf. interval]	
maturity	0.313	0.030	10.530	0.000	0.255	0.372
_cons	4.912	0.120	40.810	0.000	4.675	5.148

multiplied by an adjustment term for autocorrelation. The adjustment term tends to increase with the magnitude of the autocorrelation in the error terms. This means that greater autocorrelation leads to a greater upward adjustment of the conventional error terms in the OLS regression.

7.4.3 Test for Stationarity

Since autocorrelation is evident in the data, it is likely that the data are non-stationary. You can use an ADF test to test the null hypothesis that the variables have a unit root that is non-stationary. Figure 7.10 shows the results for each variable up to the fifth lag.

In absolute terms, the ADF test statistics for mortgage rate (−1.318) and maturity rate (−0.718) are lower than the critical DF value of −2.878 at the 5% level. This is also reflected in the MacKinnon approximate *p*-value, which is larger than 5% for each variable. These results indicate that you cannot reject the null hypothesis that each of these variables have a unit root, they are non-stationary when testing up to the fifth lag.

7.4.4 Remedy for Non-stationarity

One way to remedy the problem of non-stationarity is to take the first difference of the variables. Let's look at the ADF results for the first difference of these variables. Figure 7.11 confirms that taking the first difference makes them stationary. For each of the variables you can reject the null hypothesis of a unit root.

The results suggest that the original variables have a unit root but not the first differences. Table 7.7 shows the results from the OLS regressions on the first difference of the variables.

The results show that the change in maturity rate is still positively related to the change in mortgage rate, as in level regressions, but the coefficient has increased from 0.31 to 0.60 as well as the *t*-values improving.

Table 7.7 Results from OLS on first difference of the variables

. reg d.mortgage d.maturity

Source	SS	df	MS		No. obs.	306
Model	1.424	1.000	1.424		F(1, 304)	199.17
Residual	2.173	304.000	0.007		Prob > F	0.000
Total	3.597	305.000	0.012		R-squared	0.3958
					Adj R-squared	0.3938
					Root MSE	0.08455

D.mortgage	Coeff.	Std. Err.	t	P > |t|	[95% conf. interval]	
maturity D1.	0.596	0.042	14.110	0.000	0.513	0.679
_cons	−0.001	0.005	−0.260	0.795	−0.011	0.008

```
. dfuller mortgage, lags(5)

Augmented Dickey-Fuller test for unit root

Variable: mortgage                          Number of obs  = 301
                                            Number of lags =   5

H0: Random walk without drift, d = 0

                                          Dickey-Fuller
                   Test        ——————— critical value ———————
              statistic              1%           5%          10%
---------------------------------------------------------------------
 Z(t)            -1.318          -3.456       -2.878       -2.570
---------------------------------------------------------------------
MacKinnon approximate p-value for Z(t) = 0.6211.

. dfuller maturity, lags(5)

Augmented Dickey-Fuller test for unit root

Variable: maturity                          Number of obs  = 301
                                            Number of lags =   5

H0: Random walk without drift, d = 0

                                          Dickey-Fuller
                   Test        ——————— critical value ———————
              statistic              1%           5%          10%
---------------------------------------------------------------------
 Z(t)            -0.718          -3.456       -2.878       -2.570
---------------------------------------------------------------------
MacKinnon approximate p-value for Z(t) = 0.8420.
```

Figure 7.10. Results from ADF test

```
. dfuller d.mortgage, lags(5)

Augmented Dickey-Fuller test for unit root

Variable: D.mortgage                     Number of obs  = 300
                                         Number of lags =   5

H0: Random walk without drift, d = 0

                                       Dickey-Fuller
                   Test      -------- critical value ---------
              statistic           1%           5%          10%
--------------------------------------------------------------
 Z(t)            -6.750       -3.456       -2.878       -2.570
--------------------------------------------------------------
MacKinnon approximate p-value for Z(t) = 0.0000.

. dfuller d.maturity, lags(5)

Augmented Dickey-Fuller test for unit root

Variable: D.maturity                     Number of obs  = 300
                                         Number of lags =   5

H0: Random walk without drift, d = 0

                                       Dickey-Fuller
                   Test      -------- critical value ---------
              statistic           1%           5%          10%
--------------------------------------------------------------
 Z(t)            -5.723       -3.456       -2.878       -2.570
--------------------------------------------------------------
MacKinnon approximate p-value for Z(t) = 0.0000.
```

Figure 7.11. ADF test results for the first difference of the variables

7.4.5 Test for Cointegration

To test whether the mortgage rate and the maturity rate are cointegrated, the Engle–Granger two-step method can be used. You first regress the mortgage rate on the maturity rate (using the original variables) in an OLS regression. These results were presented in Table 7.3. You then predict the residuals, call them ehat, and finally run an ADF test on the predicted residuals. You use one lag for the test. But first, for the first-difference regression you can examine the information criteria to choose

Table 7.8 Information criteria for lag-order selection

. varsoc d.maturity d.mortgage, maxlag(5)

No. obs. = 301

* optimal lag

Lag	LL	LR	df	p	FPE	AIC	HQIC	SBIC
0	541.034				0.000	−3.582	−3.572	−3.557
1	553.327	24.587	4	0.000	0.000	−3.637	−3.607	−3.563
2	568.890	31.126	4	0.000	0.000	−3.714	−3.664*	−3.590*
3	571.929	6.078	4	0.193	0.000	−3.707	−3.638	−3.535
4	576.274	8.690	4	0.069	0.000	−3.709	−3.621	−3.488
5	581.616	10.684*	4	0.030	0.00008*	−3.718*	−3.610	−3.447

Table 7.9 Cointegration test

. dfuller ehat, lags(5)

			No. obs.	301
			No. lags	5
H0: Random walk without drift, d = 0				
			Dickey–Fuller	
	Test statistic		critical value	
		0.01	0.05	0.1
Z(t)	−2.285	−3.456	−2.878	−2.57
MacKinnon approximate *p*-value for Z(t)				
0.1769				

an optimal lag. Table 7.8 shows these results, while Table 7.9 shows the results from the cointegration test.

The different information criteria models suggest a different number of optimal lags, but following AIC you should choose the model with five lags in the difference regression. Let's examine whether these variables are cointegrated, using the results from the cointegration test in Table 7.9.

The results from the cointegration test suggest that you cannot reject the null hypothesis that predicted the residuals, ehat, having a unit root. In absolute terms, the test statistic (−2.285) is lower than the DF critical value of −2.878 obtained from Phillips and Ouliaris (1990), and hence the MacKinnon approximate *p*-value is greater than 5%. Thus, you can conclude that the mortgage rate and the maturity rate are not cointegrated, suggesting no long-run equilibrium relationship between the variables.

7.4.6 Results from the Vector Autoregression Model

To examine whether the past values of first differences can predict a change in variables, you can implement a vector autoregression (VAR) model. Figure 7.12 shows the results from the VAR model.

```
. varbasic d.maturity d.mortgage, lags(1/5)

Vector autoregression

Sample: 2016w8 thru 2021w48                    Number of obs     =        301
Log likelihood =   581.6157                    AIC               =  -3.718377
FPE            =   .0000832                    HQIC              =  -3.609954
Det(Sigma_ml)  =   .0000719                    SBIC              =  -3.447425

Equation           Parms      RMSE     R-sq      chi2     P>chi2
----------------------------------------------------------------
D_maturity           11     .110153   0.1086   36.66832   0.0001
D_mortgage           11     .102001   0.1493   52.81476   0.0000
----------------------------------------------------------------

------------------------------------------------------------------------------
             | Coefficient  Std. err.      z    P>|z|     [95% conf. interval]
-------------+----------------------------------------------------------------
D_maturity   |
    maturity |
         LD. |   .2304876   .0734706     3.14   0.002     .0864878    .3744873
        L2D. |   .2936003   .0758246     3.87   0.000     .1449868    .4422139
        L3D. |  -.0107917   .0772126    -0.14   0.889    -.1621257    .1405422
        L4D. |   .0526123   .0753231     0.70   0.485    -.0950183    .2002428
        L5D. |   .0643026   .0761755     0.84   0.399    -.0849988    .2136039
             |
    mortgage |
         LD. |  -.1897681    .078246    -2.43   0.015    -.3431274   -.0364088
        L2D. |  -.1409231   .0791213    -1.78   0.075    -.2959979    .0141517
        L3D. |   -.056624    .080556    -0.70   0.482    -.2145108    .1012628
        L4D. |  -.0325522   .0801407    -0.41   0.685    -.1896251    .1245207
        L5D. |  -.0917339   .0778211    -1.18   0.238    -.2442604    .0607927
             |
       _cons |  -.0027285   .0062408    -0.44   0.662    -.0149603    .0095032
-------------+----------------------------------------------------------------
D_mortgage   |
    maturity |
         LD. |    .335218    .068033     4.93   0.000     .2018758    .4685603
        L2D. |   .0869802   .0702128     1.24   0.215    -.0506344    .2245947
        L3D. |  -.1415208   .0714981    -1.98   0.048    -.2816544   -.0013871
        L4D. |  -.1164957   .0697484    -1.67   0.095      -.2532    .0202086
        L5D. |    .170302   .0705377     2.41   0.016     .0320506    .3085535
             |
    mortgage |
         LD. |  -.2600525   .0724549    -3.59   0.000    -.4020616   -.1180434
        L2D. |    .152381   .0732654     2.08   0.038     .0087834    .2959787
        L3D. |   .1597362    .074594     2.14   0.032     .0135347    .3059377
        L4D. |   .0043131   .0742094     0.06   0.954    -.1411348    .1497609
        L5D. |  -.2237179   .0720615    -3.10   0.002    -.3649559   -.0824799
             |
       _cons |   -.002224   .0057789    -0.38   0.700    -.0135505    .0091025
------------------------------------------------------------------------------
```

Figure 7.12. Results from a VAR model

As there is no theoretical explanation for the point estimates, you examine the R^2 value from each regression that is presented at the top of the table. The R^2 value in the models varies between 10% and 15%, showing how much of the variation in the change in mortgage rate and change in maturity rate is explained by their own first lagged differences.

Figure 7.13 shows the VAR model's dynamic behavior by using an impulse response analysis. The term IRF means the impulse and response variables. The subfigures show how a (one-standard-deviation) shock in the variable on the X axis influences the variable on the Y axis, and how long (how many weeks in this case) this response continues. For instance, in the top-right panel, in the initial period a positive shock on the change in mortgage rate increases the change in maturity rate, and thus the initial value is approximately 0.6. As time passes, a shock to change the mortgage rate decreases the change in maturity for about 3 to 4 weeks, and you observe a decay to 0 as both variables are stationary.

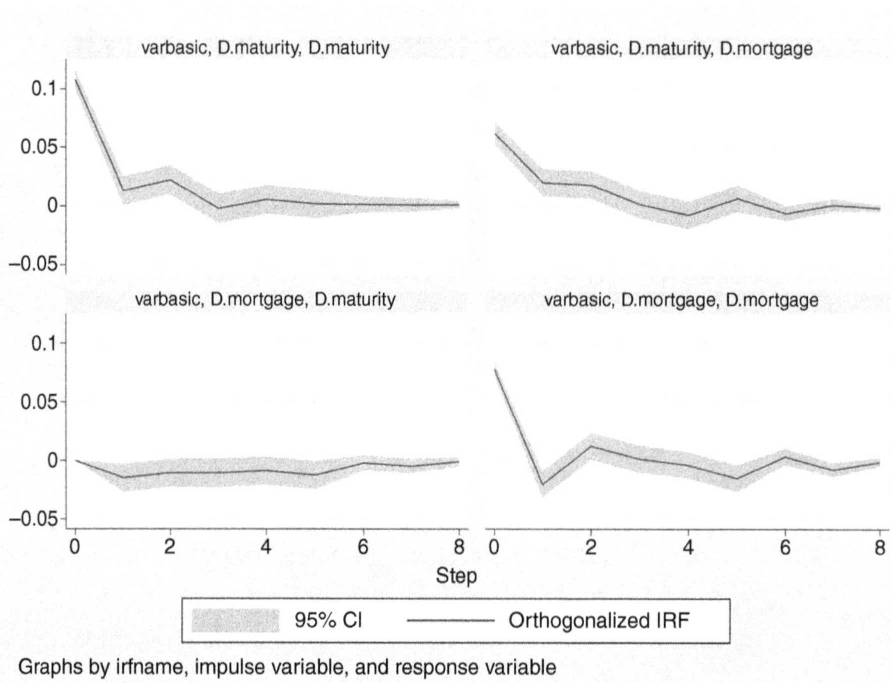

Figure 7.13. Impulse and response analysis

7.4.7 Results from the Granger Causality Test

Table 7.10 shows the results from the Granger causality test.

In the table, for instance, D.maturity refers to the test of the null hypothesis that all coefficients on lagged values of the change in maturity are equal zero against

Table 7.10 Results from the Granger causality test

. vargranger

Equation excluded	chi2	df	Prob > chi2
D_maturity D.mortgage	12.302	5	0.031
D_maturity ALL	12.302	5	0.031
D_mortgage D.maturity	37.107	5	0.000
D_mortgage ALL	37.107	5	0.000

the alternative that at least one of the coefficients is not zero. The result shows that the lagged change in maturity rate affects the change in mortgage rate (p-value less than 5%), indicating that the change in maturity rate Granger causes the change in mortgage rate.

7.4.8 Results from the ARCH and GARCH Models

If you find volatility clustering in the data, which seems to be evident in Figure 7.8, you could use a generalized autoregressive conditional heteroskedasticity (GARCH) model. Table 7.11 applies a GARCH(1,1) model to the change in mortgage rate and the change in maturity rate.

Table 7.11 Results from the GARCH(1,1) model

. arch d.mortgage d.maturity, arch(1) garch(1)

					No. obs.	306
					Wald chi2(1)	360.680
Log-likelihood	400.746				Prob > chi2	0.000
D.mortgage	Coeff.	Std. Err.	z	P > |z|	[95% conf. interval]	
mortgage maturity D1.	0.642	0.034	18.990	0.000	0.576	0.708
_cons	−0.003	0.003	−0.940	0.346	−0.010	0.004
ARCH						
arch L1.	0.111	0.023	4.760	0.000	0.065	0.157
garch L1.	0.880	0.018	48.040	0.000	0.844	0.916
_cons	0.000	0.000	2.540	0.011	0.000	0.000

The model is a maximum likelihood estimation, which will be discussed in the forthcoming chapters. In addition to the coefficient on the change in maturity, the model produces autoregressive conditionally heteroskedasticity ARCH(1) and GARCH(1) coefficients, which are β_1 and β_2 in Equation (7.28). The results show that even after accounting for the volatility effect, there is still a positive and significant relation between change in maturity and change in mortgage rate. The ARCH coefficient shows how the lagged squared errors affect the variance, and the GARCH coefficient shows how the previous values of variance affect the variance

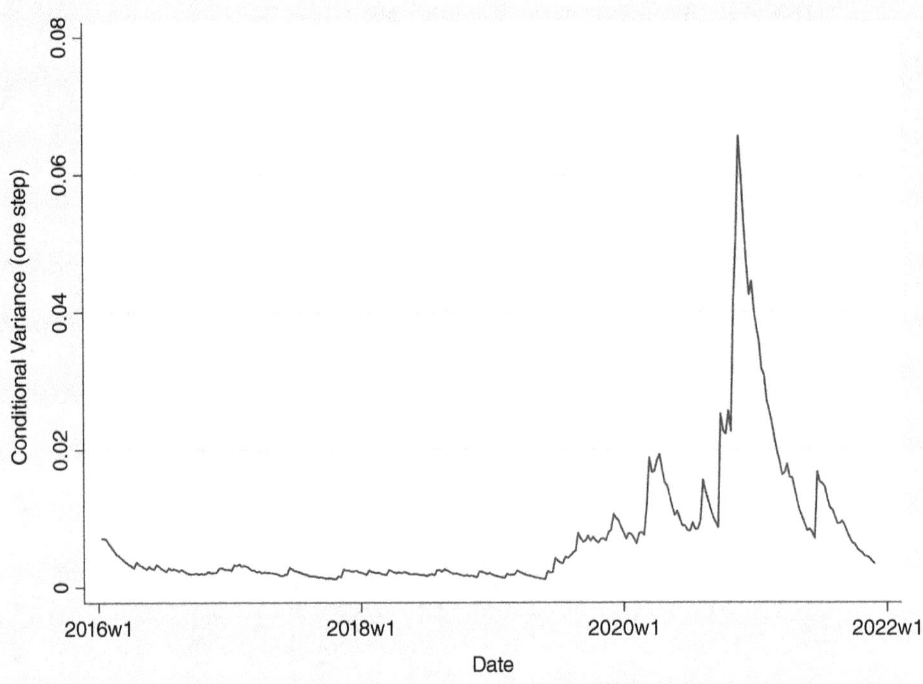

Figure 7.14. Predicted variance from GARCH

at time t. The sum of these coefficients is slightly less than 1, indicating (weak) stationarity.

Both ARCH and GARCH terms are positive, enabling us to correctly avoid predicting negative volatility. Negative volatility does not make sense. You can predict the in-sample variance and plot it over time.

Figure 7.14 shows high variance around 2021, which the GARCH model has picked up. This is evidence of volatility clustering or volatility spiking, providing valuable information for out-of-sample variance prediction. However, the high variance around 2021 also indicates a unit root in variance, also termed IGARCH (integrated GARCH). This is problematic since for stationary GARCH models, conditional variance forecasts tend to converge to the long-term average value of the variance as the prediction horizon increases, but for IGARCH the convergence will not be achieved. Perhaps a GARCH model applied to a different time window, removing observations after 2020, will generate coefficients that show stationarity.

7.5 Lab Work: Time-Series Analysis

In this lab work you will examine the potential relationship between the daily US market return, Rm, and the daily closing price of the Chicago Board Options

Exchange's CBOE Volatility Index (VIX). All the provided data are simulated in this lab work (due to permission reasons) and hence the figures and analysis may not represent the real data. The simulated data at hand cover the period between January 02, 1990 and May 27, 2022. However, those of you who are interested in downloading the variables can obtain the VIX data from VIX Index Historical Data (cboe.com) and the daily US market return from Kenneth R. French – Data Library (dartmouth.edu). It would be interesting to observe the analysis using a real dataset and compare the results with the results obtained from this simulated data.

Use Chapter_7_VIX.dta (available at www.cambridge.org/Mavruk) to answer the following questions.

Declare your data as time series.
Stata code:

```
tsset date
```

Problem set

1. Plot Rm and VIX over time and interpret the figures.
   Stata code:

   ```
   twoway line Rm date
   twoway line VIX date
   ```

2. Regress Rm on VIX using OLS and interpret your results.
   Stata code:

   ```
   reg Rm VIX
   ```

3. Predict and plot the residuals from Problem 2 and interpret your results.
   Stata code:

   ```
   predict ehat, resid
   twoway line ehat date
   ```

4. Test for first-order autocorrelation using a Durbin–Watson test. Explain how this test works and interpret your results.
   Stata codes:

   ```
   reg Rm VIX
   estat dwatson
   ```

5. Test for autocorrelation for order AR(p) using the Breusch–Godfrey LM test. Include the lags that are significant. Do you have a problem with autocorrelation for higher lag orders than AR(1)? Explain your steps. Compare your results to those from the Durbin–Watson test.

   ```
   estat bgodfrey
   estat bgodfrey, lags (1/5)
   ```

   Examine the further lags.

6. Estimate the model using the Newey–West standard errors. Use the appropriate lag from the results in Problem 5. Compare and discuss the results with those you obtained from OLS in Problem 3. Explain the Newey–West standard errors.

   Stata code:

```
newey Rm VIX, lag(5) force
```

7. Explain the problem with non-stationary time-series data used in a regression. What is an augmented Dickey–Fuller test?
8. Test for the unit root in Rm and VIX using the augmented Dickey–Fuller test with a constant but no time trend. You can add as many significant lags plus one. Explain the steps and interpret the results.

   Stata code:

```
dfuller Rm, lags(1)
dfuller VIX, lags(1)
```

9. Test for the unit root in the first difference of Rm and the first difference of VIX using the augmented Dickey–Fuller test with a constant but no time trend. Explain the steps and interpret the results. Regress the first difference of Rm on the first difference of VIX. Interpret your results.

   Stata code:

```
dfuller d.Rm, lags(1)
dfuller d.VIX, lags(1)
reg d.Rm d.VIX
```

10. What does cointegration mean? When can two variables be cointegrated? Test whether Rm and VIX are cointegrated. Explain the test and interpret your results.

    Stata code:

```
reg Rm VIX
predict ehat, residual
dfuller ehat, noconstant lags(1) /*Cointegration linear
combination of x is stationary. Run e=b*e_t-1, H0: b=0*/
dfuller ehat, lags(1) /*Cointegration linear combination
of x is stationary. Run e=b*e_t-1, H0: b=0*/
dfuller ehat, lags(2)
```

    Note: If ehat is already defined in the problem sets above. Just drop ehat and rerun the code above.

11. What is a vector autoregressive model (VAR)? Briefly explain. What is the Akaike information criterion? Use the Akaike information criterion to decide the appropriate lag length in the VAR model. Interpret the results.

    Stata code:

```
varsoc d.Rm d.VIX, maxlag(3)
```

12. Run a VAR regression using the first difference Rm as the dependent variable and the lagged first difference of Rm and the lagged first difference of VIX as the independent variable. Interpret the results from R^2. Explain whether Rm Granger causes VIX and whether VIX Granger causes Rm. Interpret the impulse and response graphs (automatically provided after running the code).
   Stata code:

```
varbasic d.Rm d.VIX, lags(1/3)
vargranger
```

13. What is a GARCH model? Briefly explain. Run a GARCH (1,1) model to examine the change in Rm and the change in VIX. Predict the in-sample variance and plot it over time. Interpret the figure.
   Stata code:

```
arch d.Rm d.VIX, arch(1) garch(1)
predict var, variance
tsline var
```

Good luck!

7.6 Mini Case

Webb (2020) examines the cost of sanctions for a sanctioning state. The study connects sanctions to stock market uncertainty with the motivation that sanctions and sanctions threats may create market uncertainty that is reflected in stock price volatility for firms with commercial interests in targeted states. The stock price data are compared within sectors at the same point in time, within sectors over time, and across sectors over time. Thus, the analysis in the paper applies various time-series models. The main message in the paper is that talks, warnings, and signals are costly. While it may take some time to impose sanctions, international financial markets may respond to the news immediately. The study focuses on firm-level estimates to evaluate the economic cost of sanctions, because economic sanctions are likely only costly for firms that have commercial interests in targeted states. The study uses US firm data from the S&P 500 stock market index based on their Morgan Stanley Capital International (MSCI) Global Industry Classification Standard (GICS) codes.

TASK

1. Go to the link: Replication Data for: Re-examining the Costs of Sanctions and Sanctions Threats Using Stock Market Data – Harvard Dataverse
   Download the dataset: rcs.tab
   Download the do file: table1.do

2. Go to the link: Full article: Re-examining the costs of sanctions and sanctions threats using stock market data (tandfonline.com)

   Download the paper. Alternatively, you can download an earlier version of this paper published in Clayton McLaughlin Webb's dissertation: https://oaktrust.library.tamu.edu/bitstream/handle/1969.1/155228/WEBB-DISSERTATION-2015.pdf?sequence=1&isAllowed=y

   The full dissertation is publicly available on the link.
3. Replicate Table 1 in the published paper (Table 2.1 in the dissertation is an earlier version of the model that provides sufficient information for replication). Present and explain your results.
4. Interpret the results from the MA coefficients.
5. Interpret the results from the AR coefficients.
6. Interpret the results from the ARCH coefficients.
7. Interpret the results from the GARCH coefficients.

7.7 Summary

A time series contains values of a dataset sampled at different points in time. Some examples in financial research include asset prices, volatility index, inflation rate, and so on. Time-series analysis is concerned with dependence and correlation structures in a time-series dataset. The aim is to describe the pattern and trend in the data and develop a predictive model. Many different mathematical and statistical techniques are applied to model time-series data. These models tend to predict future values (of asset prices, for example) for a given asset's price time series. Such analysis is essential for evaluating investments and firm decision-making, and it has many applications in (corporate) finance studies. Some examples include the CAPM, stochastic volatility models, forecasting revenues, cash flows, and so on.

This chapter briefly covers the basic methods used in time-series analysis. While presenting the models, the chapter also briefly discusses the main issues with time-series data. Some of these issues are whether the time-series data have equally spaced intervals, noise or error, how quickly the series grows, and whether the series has missing values. The chapter begins by testing for autocorrelation and a remedy for autocorrelation. It then presents some standard tests for stationarity and cointegration, by briefly covering random walk and unit root tests. The models covered, among others, include autoregressive distributed lag (ARDL), autoregressive moving average (ARMA), autoregressive integrated moving average (ARIMA), generalized autoregressive conditional heteroskedasticity (GARCH), and vector autoregressive (VAR). The chapter provides an application on the mortgage rate and ends with lab work and a mini case.

KEY TERMS

Time-series analysis; autocorrelation; remedy for autocorrelation; autoregressive (AR) model; moving average (MA) model; ARMA; ARIMA; Newey–West variance estimator; stationarity; cointegration; vector autoregressive (VAR) model; Granger causality test; GARCH; application on mortgage rate.

REFERENCES

Baum, C. F. 2006. *An Introduction to Modern Econometrics Using Stata*. Stata Press, College Station, TX.

Breusch, T. S. 1978. Testing for autocorrelation in dynamic linear models. *Australian Economic Papers*, 17, 334–355.

Brooks, C. 2019. *Introductory Econometrics for Finance* (4th ed.). Cambridge University Press, Cambridge.

Burnham, K. P. and Anderson, D. R. 2002. *Model Selection and Multimodel Inference* (2nd ed.). Springer Science+Business Media, New York.

Dickey, D. A. and Fuller, W. A. 1979. Distribution of estimators for time series regressions with a unit root. *Journal of the American Statistical Association*, 74, 427–431.

Engle, R. and Granger, C. (1987). Cointegration and error correction representation, estimation and testing. *Econometrica*, 55, 251–276.

Fabozzi, F. J., Focardi, S. M., Rachev, S. T., and Arshanapalli, B. G. 2014. *The Basics of Financial Econometrics: Tools, Concepts, and Asset Management Applications.* Wiley, New York.

Fuller, W. A. (1976) *Introduction to Statistical Time Series*. Wiley, New York.

Godfrey, L. G. 1978. Testing against general autoregressive and moving average error models when the regressors include lagged dependent variables. *Econometrica*, 46, 1293–1301.

Granger, C. W. J. 1969. Investigating causal relations by econometric models and cross-spectral methods. *Econometrica*, 37, 424–438.

Mills, T. C. 2019. *Applied Time Series Analysis*. Academic Press, New York.

Newey, W. K. and West, K. D. 1987. A simple, positive semi-definite, heteroskedasticity and autocorrelation consistent covariance matrix. *Econometrica*, 55, 703–708.

Phillips, P. and Ouliaris, S. 1990. Asymptotic properties of residual based tests for cointegration. *Econometrica*, 58, 165–193.

Stock, J. and Watson, M. 2019. *Introduction to Econometrics: Global Edition*. Princeton University Press, Princeton, NJ.

Webb, C. 2020. Re-examining the costs of sanctions and sanctions threats using stock market data. *International Interactions*, 46, 749–777.

8 Event Studies

INTRODUCTION

The application of event studies in corporate finance has grown tremendously over time. A simple search of the phrase "event studies" in Google Scholar provides millions of hits, indicating how popular the method has become over the years. Event studies measure the effects of an event on some outcome variable, such as stock returns, firm value, and so on (MacKinlay, 1997). The underlying assumption of the method, in the case of market studies, is that the market reacts immediately to the event. Thus, examining stock prices (or common equity) over a short period is the most appropriate measurement used in event studies. Particularly central to an event study is the measurement of an abnormal stock return (see Fama, 1970, 1998). Event windows of 1 year or more are generally accepted as long horizon, although the definition is arbitrary (Kothari and Warner, 2007).

Short-horizon methods examining the effects of an event seem to provide more reliable results than long-horizon methods, although both methods depend on the event sample size and firm/stock characteristics such as volatility. Long-horizon methods have some limitations, partly because of issues with the measurement of stock returns over a longer period (Kothari and Warner, 2007). The models use the ordinary least squares (OLS) estimator, covered in Chapter 5, and it is more likely that the classical linear regression model (CLRM) assumptions about the cross-sectional or time-series dependence of (abnormal) returns are violated in the long run. Inference from long-horizon methods is also more difficult, mainly because most of the event studies in (corporate) finance are concerned with tests of market efficiency. In a sense, the test is about how quickly the market responds to a particular event (MacKinlay, 1997).

In long-horizon event studies it is also more problematic to determine the exact event date, making the models poorly specified. Long-horizon models tend to be more sensitive to the choice of benchmark, while this is less problematic in short-horizon event study models. In the long run, it is less clear whether the chosen model tests market efficiency or the model is correctly chosen, a so-called joint hypothesis problem (see Kothari and Warner, 2007). Accordingly, long-horizon models tend to have low power. Long-horizon models have improved over the years, but some limitations remain.

Events can be either firm-specific or economy-wide. For example, insider trading, mergers and acquisitions, earnings announcements, equity issuance, dividends announcements, share repurchase, stock splits, and CEO turnover are typical events examined in corporate finance studies. Some examples of economy-wide events include regulations (see, e.g., Hamberg, Mavruk, and Sjögren, 2013). MacKinlay (1997) refers to Dolley (1933) as the researcher who first applied event studies in corporate finance by examining the effects of stock splits on stock prices. Dolley (1933) examined 95 stock splits between 1921 and 1931 and reported a price increase in 57 of the stocks and a decline in 26 of the stocks. Fama et al. (1969) examined stock splits in more recent time by removing the effects of simultaneous dividend increases. Models introduced by Fama et al. (1969), as well as by studies examining the effects of earnings announcements on stock prices (Ball and Brown, 1968), are still in use today. Some adjustments to the standard models have been made as the applications of the models extend to different research questions, across time periods and geography. The adjustments relate to the violations of the statistical assumptions behind the standard models (see Brown and Warner, 1980).

In some studies, regression discontinuity design (RDD), covered in Chapter 6, is also used as an event study estimating treatment effects in a quasi-experimental setting, although it is not a standard event study method. However, RDD could be used to strengthen the validity of an event study. It is believed that RDD is more than an evaluation strategy as it leads to more credible causal inferences than other standard event study methods (see Lee and Lemieux, 2010). Thus, in this book, RDD is covered in Chapter 6 along with endogeneity discussions. This chapter reviews the standard event study methods with a focus on short-term event studies and discusses some of the modifications for these models. Since events related to corporate finance mostly require time-series data, Chapter 7, which covers time-series analysis, is essential to understand event study methods. However, there are also some event study techniques that require panel data, for example, the difference-in-differences model, which will be covered in Chapter 9. This chapter ends with an application of mainly short-term event studies, lab work, and a mini case.

8.1 Basic Event Study Model

Event studies provide a powerful method for estimating dynamic treatment effects. Broader examples of event studies can be observed in the labor economics literature (Jacobson, LaLonde, and Sullivan, 1993). This study examines the loss of income after being displaced from a current job. In the study, event time zero indicates the time of job displacement. The time-zero event is the treatment, that is the policy that affected the job displacement. The outcome variable is the income for each period (quarter) relative to a baseline comparison period, which is more than 5 years before the job displacement. The focus is on the change after the event time zero, but it is also interesting to examine the changes in the income before the event. The study finds that income decreases significantly after being displaced.

In a clean event study, you would expect that the income pattern before the event shows no trend, otherwise you would have problems with the model used. Observing a trend before the event would suggest that the treatment is expected or there are other factors affecting the event (Miller, 2023). In the mentioned study, one factor could be that the demand for the output of the industry may have affected the earnings before the event, and in turn caused the displacement. An alternative explanation is that if the displacement was predicted and thus resulted in discouragement, it could decrease labor supply and thus yield a pre-event trend. The analysis in Jacobson et al. (1993) shows a pre-event trend and a sudden drop in earnings at the event time of displacement. This is followed by an increase over the next 2 years that eventually levels off at about $500.

In business studies, the standard event study models were first applied to finance. MacKinlay (1997) provides a survey of earlier event studies with finance applications. The application of event studies in corporate finance is mostly concerned with the market efficiency hypothesis. This section first provides an overview of this hypothesis before presenting the standard event study models.

8.1.1 Background

It is said that a market is efficient if prices fully reflect all available information. If prices only reflect some information but not all, the market is then inefficient. There are two immediate implications of efficient markets. First, since all information is reflected immediately in prices, investors should not expect abnormal returns. Second, firms should expect a value that equals the present value of future cash flows (see Hillier et al., 2021). If markets are efficient, the price instantaneously responds and adjusts to the event, fully reflecting new information in the event. Further, there should be no subsequent increases and decreases in prices.

If the markets are inefficient, you may observe two different responses by market participants. One is the slow response, where prices adjust slowly to the new information in the event. It is unlikely that this will continue for long, since the market will learn this new information eventually and then the prices will reflect it completely. The second one is overreaction, where prices over-adjust to the new information. However, since the market will learn about it over time, you would expect a reversal in the prices, eliminating the overreaction. If the information in the event affects the fundamentals of the firm, then the price reversal will not revert to the initial price observed before the event. Instead, you will observe a new equilibrium but the overreaction will be eliminated (see MacKinlay, 1997).

The underlying assumptions behind the market efficiency hypothesis are that investors react rationally to all new information because they consider risk diversification and return. It is not possible to predict price fluctuations because new information is released randomly. There will be some deviations from rationality, but the assumption is that the deviations are independent. Finally, there are rational arbitrageurs in the market and any irrational investor behavior is completely offset by them. You only need a subset of rational arbitrageurs to take advantage of arbitrage opportunities (Fama et al., 1969; MacKinlay, 1997).

There are three types of market efficiency. The weak form suggests that current prices reflect all information in past prices. The semi-strong form suggests that current prices reflect all the information in past prices and public information (e.g., annual reports). Finally, the strong form suggests that current prices reflect all the information in past prices, public information, and inside information (see Fama, 1970, 1998 for details).

8.1.2 Event Study Model

The focus is on the stock return response to a particular event throughout the example models. Suppose an event occurs at time t and the following return equation is given:

$$R_{jt} = E(R_{jt}) + e_{jt}, \tag{8.1}$$

where R_{jt} is the period's stock return and $E(R_{jt})$ is the expected stock return. The period can be daily, weekly, monthly, and so on. The residual term e_{jt} is the difference between the actual stock return and the expected stock return, and is given by

$$e_{jt} = R_{jt} - E(R_{jt}), \tag{8.2}$$

$$\text{AR}_{jt} = e_{jt}. \tag{8.3}$$

This difference is known as the abnormal stock return, AR, as presented in Equation (8.3); a return beyond what is expected for a given event. One question that arises directly is the measurement of $E(R_{jt})$. How do you know what the expected return is? To answer this question, this chapter will use different models to measure the expected return. Event studies test two things, a so-called joint hypothesis. They test whether abnormal returns are significantly different from 0 and at the same time whether the chosen model is correct for the abnormal return tests. The second question relates to the definition of a normal period. In Equation (8.2) all the returns are measured at time t but the interest is often in the outcome after the event. In other words, how does the stock return respond to an event ex post? To answer this question, you need to measure the expected returns in a normal time when the event has not yet occurred (i.e., ex ante) and compare the expected return to the actual return after the event, or more correctly said, in the event period. To be able to establish whether the actual return systematically deviates from the expected return for a given event, you need to test whether the observed abnormal return is significantly different from 0. To calculate the test statistics, you need to aggregate the abnormal returns. This is done either cross-sectionally (for different firms) or in a time series (for the same firm), or both as the focus is to examine the mean of abnormal returns. Thus, the test is whether the mean abnormal return is significantly different from 0. If there are N stocks, then the average abnormal return, AAR, at time t is given by

$$\text{AAR}_t = \frac{1}{N}\sum_{j=1}^{N} \text{AR}_{jt}. \tag{8.4}$$

It is also customary to examine if the abnormal returns over a period around the event time t are significant. This so-called cumulative abnormal return (CAR) over a period is a time-series aggregation and can be examined for an individual firm. CARs can also be aggregated across firms. Suppose that the event time $t = 0$ and you want to aggregate abnormal returns over a period of $t-1$ and $t+1$, denoted $[-1; +1]$. In this case, the horizon length is $L = t_2 - t_1 + 1$, also known as the event window, where in this example $t_1 = -1$ and $t_2 = +1$. More formally, the CAR is given by

$$\text{CAR}_j(t_1,t_2) = \sum_{t=t_1}^{t_2} \text{AR}_{jt}. \tag{8.5}$$

A significant CAR would indicate abnormal returns around the event. The event window is 3 days in the example. Observing abnormal returns over this period would be inconsistent with the market efficiency hypothesis holding. However, Equation (8.5) gives only the CAR. To test whether it is significant you need to calculate the standard error and the test statistics, t-value, also known as standardized CARs:

$$t = \frac{\text{CAR}_j(t_1,t_2)}{\left[\sigma^2 \text{CAR}_j(t_1,t_2)\right]^{1/2}}, \tag{8.6}$$

where the variance of the CARs is given by

$$\sigma^2 \text{CAR}_j(t_1,t_2) = L\sigma^2(\text{AR}_{jt}) \tag{8.7}$$

and the variance of abnormal returns is given by

$$\sigma^2(\text{AR}_{jt}) = \frac{1}{T-2}\sum_{t=2}^{T} e_{jt}^2. \tag{8.8}$$

Equation (8.7) suggests that the variance of abnormal returns depends on L; the longer the horizon length, the larger the variance. Also note that the variance is constant, computed as a one-period variance of abnormal return, where time-series independence is assumed. If you observe event time clustering in the data, then the time-series independence assumption for the variance is violated, which would lead to downward bias in the estimation of standard errors and hence higher t-values (see Kothari and Warner, 2007 for details). One remedy for event time clustering is to use the calendar-time portfolio approach, which will be discussed shortly.

8.2 Estimation of Expected Return

This section examines the five most commonly used methods in the estimation of expected returns: market-adjusted model; market model; capital asset pricing model (CAPM); Fama–French three-factor model (Fama and French, 1993); and Carhart (1997) four-factor model. Since you need to compare the effects of an event on the returns with the returns during normal periods, or at least in periods where the effect of this event is absent, the estimation period and event period should be different. The event period should be an out-of-sample period. Note that the calendar time for the event for each firm is different, and thus data must be arranged so that event time 0 represents the time of the event for each firm regardless of the calendar time of the event. Consider the timeline in Figure 8.1 representing days when an event occurs at time (day) 0.

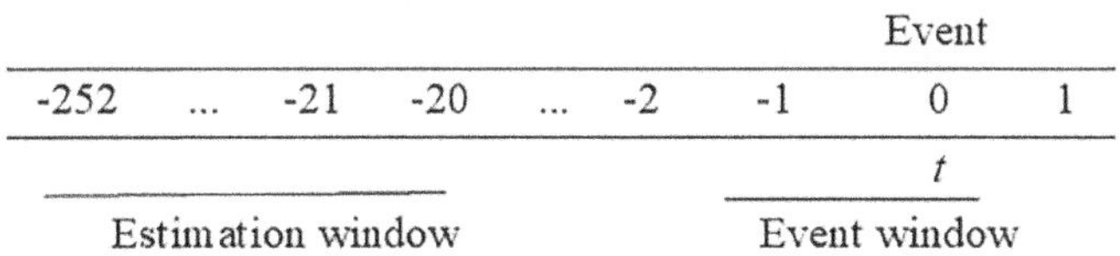

Figure 8.1. Event timeline

It is customary to leave some gap between the estimation window and the event window to avoid any overlap between expected returns (what should be normal returns for a given model) and the actual returns observed during the event window. This is also done to avoid the effect of any other event(s) that may or may not be related to the event that is being examined. This time gap is arbitrary but there is a generally accepted standard. The example above follows this standard period in an event study. The estimation window above is [−252; − 20], which represents the interval between −252 and −20 days before the event occurs. The days represent the trading days, so the total estimation period is 232 trading days, and the estimation period ends 1 month (20 trading days) before the event occurs on trading day 0. Following an asset pricing model, you estimate the parameters during this period, often using OLS. The estimation window can also be thought of as the in-sample period. Since it is usually an OLS estimation, you obtain constant parameters from the estimation along with the mean squared error of the model.

These parameters are then used to measure the expected return during the event window, [−1; +1]. This is the out-of-sample estimation. The choice of event window is also arbitrary, depending on the research question, but the standard (e.g., measuring the effect of a particular company news) is 3 days: 1 day before the event, the event day, and 1 day after the event. In Figure 8.1, the period (days in this example) greater than +1 is known as the post-event period. You can also look at the effects of an event during the post-event period (an arbitrary choice of number of days depending on the research question). The reason for including a short period, here 1 day before the event in the event window, is because the market may already have anticipated the news of the event. Also, it is difficult to exactly know the event day. You usually look for a particular announcement in the media, but the same news could be published earlier in another media outlet. It is difficult to establish when exactly the scoop news about the event is published (see Mavruk, 2021), and whether the market has already absorbed the news. Thus, it is customary to include some days before the event in the event window. You could also falsely assign another date before the actual event date, which would make a valid robustness analysis.

Once the expected return is calculated, following Equation (8.2) you calculate the abnormal return as the difference between the actual return during the event window and the expected return during the event window. The models presented below will provide different ways of estimating the parameters during the estimation window.

8.2.1 Market-Adjusted Model

This model is not an estimation model. It assumes that the expected return of a security is the return on the market, $E(R_{jt}) = R_{mt}$, and uses historical market returns. The model also has a theoretical assumption that the intercept from an estimated market model (described below) is 0 and the slope is 1. Thus, the abnormal return can simply be calculated as the difference between the actual return and the market return during the event window:

$$\mathrm{AR}_{jt} = R_{jt} - R_{mt}. \tag{8.9}$$

There are two issues with this model, or more correctly, with all models that use market return as expected return. First, the usual implementation of this model is to use the historical return on the market, but expected returns are about future returns. Some studies use the outcome of survey studies that ask both professionals and academics what they think the market return would be in the future (see Fernandez and de Santos, 2022). However, the outcome of these surveys is usually a cross-sectional, one-period market return. For an event study model to work you need time-series information. Second, you typically do not know what the true market portfolio is. Put differently, it is not possible to construct a portfolio that contains all the securities. This critique is known as Roll's (1977) critique and implies that calculation of abnormal returns is not feasible because the underlying portfolio is unobservable. The standard remedy for this problem is to use a proxy for a market portfolio: Nasdaq OMX30, S&P500, and so on. A related, but perhaps less serious, issue is how one should best weight the proxy for a market portfolio: value-weighted, equally weighted, or price-weighted? The most used measure is the value-weighted market portfolio, but it is also common to observe other applications of weighting schemes without much motivation for choosing one over another.

8.2.2 Market Model

This is similar to the general model presented in Equation (8.1), where you also insert an intercept in the market model and assume that the expected returns are equal to the market return:

$$R_{jt} = \alpha_j + \beta_j R_{mt} + e_{jt}. \tag{8.10}$$

One difference between the market model and the market-adjusted model is that you estimate the parameters in the market model to calculate ARs, whereas you take the difference between the stock return and the market return to calculate the ARs in the market-adjusted model. In other words, you let the empirical data determine the intercept and slope. You estimate the market model during the estimation window to obtain intercept and slope parameters, and then use them in the event window to calculate the abnormal returns. ARs in the market model are given by

$$\mathrm{AR}_{jt} = R_{jt} - \hat{\alpha}_j - \hat{\beta}_j R_{mt}. \tag{8.11}$$

8.2.3 Capital Asset Pricing Model

The CAPM is a theoretical model that was developed in the early 1960s by Treynor (1962), Sharpe (1964), Lintner (1965), and Mossin (1966). It is derived from the mean–variance analysis. The model predicts the expected return for a security given the risk-free rate, the expected return on the market portfolio, and the asset's relative risk to the market portfolio (β_j). The OLS estimation method to determine the CAPM is given by

$$R_{jt} - R_{ft} = \alpha_j + \beta_j \left(R_{mt} - R_{ft} \right) + e_{jt}. \tag{8.12}$$

The difference between the market model and the CAPM is that in the CAPM we subtract the risk-free rate from both the return on the stock and the return on the market to obtain the risk premium on the stock and the risk premium on the market, which indicates the premium investors expect for entering the specific risky asset market, most often the equity market. The risk-free rate in this equilibrium model is thought of as a return from an alternative investment that investors can earn instead of investing in the risky (often equity) market. The parameter β_j measures the relation between systematic risk and expected return. If all the return data are sampled correctly, the estimated beta should equal the covariance between the stock return and the market return divided by the variance of the market return: $\beta_j = \frac{\operatorname{cov}(R_j, R_m)}{\sigma^2_{R_m}}$, which is a measure of systematic risk. According to the theory, the expected return (excess of risk-free rate) is only explained by the return on the market (excess of risk-free rate) and by some random error, reflecting the trading mistakes, cognitive ability, non-cognitive ability, and so on of investors. This random error is known as idiosyncratic risk, unsystematic risk, or firm-specific risk. $\beta_j = 1$ indicates that the stock follows the market. Following the CLRM assumptions, the error term is normally distributed with zero mean, implying that you do not expect trading mistakes, or idiosyncratic risk, on average; there is no systematic deviation from the market return. It is said that portfolio diversification will satisfy this assumption by averaging out the idiosyncratic risk in the portfolio. This particular assumption opens many discussions by behavioral economists, arguing against the application of this theoretical model in real investment data. Since, on average, trading mistakes are not expected to occur, the model builds on a representative agent where every investor in the market behaves as this representative agent. The argument raised by behavioral economists is whether the trade behavior of market participants is homogenous (do all investors look like Jones, walk like Jones, and talk like Jones?).

Since the risk-free rate is seen as an alternative investment, the market return is supposed to explain beyond what is earned by this alternative investment. Thus, the theoretical presentation of the model is such that the risk-free asset is on the right-hand side of the equation $R_{jt} = R_{ft} + \beta_j (R_{mt} - R_{ft})$. To estimate this equation, you move R_{ft} to the left-hand side and hence obtain Equation (8.12) presented above. This also means that you should not have an intercept in the model. If, on average, the error term is 0, then the expected return on the stock is only explained by the expected market return. Any deviation from the expected market return will be picked by the intercept α_j. We get back to the interpretation of α_j when we discuss the calendar-time portfolio approach. Using Equation (8.12), during the estimation window, you estimate α_j and β_j and then use these parameters to calculate the abnormal return, AR_{jt}, in the event window:

$$\text{AR}_{jt} = \left(R_{jt} - R_{ft}\right) - \hat{\alpha}_j - \hat{\beta}_j\left(R_{mt} - R_{ft}\right). \tag{8.13}$$

8.2.4 Fama–French Three-Factor Model

The CAPM is a theory that posits a linear relationship between the beta (systematic risk) of a stock and its expected return. The average return on the market has historically been higher than the risk-free rate of return, so it is plausible to assume that the risk premium on the market is positive. Hence, you would expect a positive relationship between the beta of a stock and its expected return. It is reasonable to elaborate on this relationship by considering the boundaries. For instance, assume that the stock has no systematic risk, beta is 0, then according to the CAPM the expected return is equal to the risk-free rate. Investors do not get compensated if they do not take any systematic risk. The alternative is then the risk-free rate. Instead, assume now that the stock follows the market perfectly so that beta is 1, then the expected return on the stock is equal to the expected return on the market. The model provides an intuitive explanation for the efficient sets of securities.

One critique of the CAPM is that the model allows correlation among the securities, but it does not explain the underlying factors causing the correlation among these securities. It is thus not a straightforward task to understand how including a sufficient number of securities in a portfolio reduces the unsystematic risk if the securities are correlated. The argument is that the unsystematic risk could be correlated across securities as well. Thus, specifying the factors that cause the correlation among the securities may better help us understand why the unsystematic risk would reduce when you include a sufficient number of securities in a portfolio. This critique against the CAPM caused the rise of an alternative view of risk and return, the arbitrage pricing theory (APT) (see Ross, Westerfield, and Jaffe, 2005), which assumes that the returns of securities depend on a number of market-wide and industry-wide factors. In other words, the same factor or factors can cause correlation among the securities (see Ross et al., 2005 for more details).

The Fama–French three-factor model is developed based on APT and adds the size risk factor SMB_t and value risk factor HML_t to the CAPM, suggesting that these additional factors provide more explanatory power. The size risk factor is the difference in returns on equities of small and large capitalized firms and represents the additional return investors have historically gained by investing in equities with relatively small firms. The size of the firms is determined by the statistical distribution and calculated as the average return on the equities of the smallest 30% of firms minus the average return on the equities of the largest 30% of firms. A positive coefficient on SMB_t would indicate that small firms outperformed large firms. The value risk factor is the difference in the returns of high and low book-to-market equities.

The factor is computed as the average return on the equities of the 50% of firms with the highest book-to-market ratio, minus the average return on the equities of the 50% of firms with the lowest book-to-market ratio. A positive coefficient on the HML_t factor would indicate that the value firms outperformed the growth firms and vice versa. The estimation model is formally given as

$$R_{jt} - R_{ft} = \alpha_j + \beta_j\left(R_{mt} - R_{ft}\right) + \gamma_j \text{SMB}_t + \delta_j \text{HML}_t + e_{jt}. \tag{8.14}$$

Similar to the CAPM and the market model, Equation (8.14) is run during the estimation window and then the parameters α_j, β_j, γ_j, and δ_j are obtained, which are used in the event window to calculate the abnormal return, AR_{jt}:

$$\text{AR}_{jt} = \left(R_{jt} - R_{ft}\right) - \hat{\alpha}_j - \hat{\beta}_j\left(R_{mt} - R_{ft}\right) - \hat{\gamma}_j \text{SMB}_t - \hat{\delta}_j \text{HML}_t. \tag{8.15}$$

8.2.5 Carhart's Four-Factor Model

The model adds the fourth factor, momentum returns, to the CAPM (Carhart, 1997). The factor is calculated as the difference between the period returns on diversified portfolios of the winners and losers from the previous year. The idea with momentum returns is that past winners (over some short period, e.g., 3–18 months) tend to continue to win over the next 3–18 months (see Jegadeesh and Titman, 1993). More formally:

$$R_{jt} - R_{ft} = \alpha_j + \beta_j\left(R_{mt} - R_{ft}\right) + \gamma_j \text{SMB}_t + \delta_j \text{HML}_t + \pi_j \text{MOM}_t + e_{jt}. \tag{8.16}$$

The model is estimated during the estimation window to obtain the parameters which are then used to calculate abnormal returns in the event window:

$$\text{AR}_{jt} = \left(R_{jt} - R_{ft}\right) - \hat{\alpha}_j - \hat{\beta}_j\left(R_{mt} - R_{ft}\right) - \hat{\gamma}_j \text{SMB}_t - \hat{\delta}_j \text{HML}_t - \hat{\pi}_j \text{MOM}_t. \tag{8.17}$$

8.3 Aggregation of Abnormal Returns Across Firms

Measuring abnormal returns or cumulative abnormal returns over a period of time for an individual firm is useful if the aim is to use them in a model in a cross-sectional analysis. It is more common to calculate CARs for an individual firm and then regress the CARs on some explanatory variables to examine whether these variables explain the CARs. However, as a first step, to draw meaningful conclusions on how the market responds to a particular event, you need to examine how a sample of firms respond to the event. Thus, you need to aggregate abnormal returns across firms. The average abnormal return across N firms at time t is defined by

$$\text{AAR}_t = \frac{1}{N}\sum_{j=1}^{N} \text{AR}_{jt}. \tag{8.18}$$

The conventional test statistic is given by

$$t = \frac{\text{AAR}_t}{[\sigma^2(\text{AAR}_t)]^{1/2}}, \tag{8.19}$$

where the variance of the average abnormal returns is calculated as

$$\sigma^2(\text{AAR}_t) = \frac{1}{N^2}\sum_{j=1}^{N}\sigma^2(\text{AR}_{jt}). \tag{8.20}$$

The variance of the individual-firm abnormal return is given in Equation (8.8): $\sigma^2(\text{AR}_{jt}) = \frac{1}{T-2}\sum_{t=2}^{T} e_{jt}^2$.

It is more common to use average CARs across firms in the descriptive analysis. Once you calculate the average abnormal return at time t, AAR_t, you can accumulate it over an event window and compute the cumulative average abnormal return (CAAR):

$$\text{CAAR}(t_1, t_2) = \sum_{t=t_1}^{t_2}\text{AAR}_t. \tag{8.21}$$

Alternatively, first accumulate CARs for individual firms over the event window and then take the average of the CARs across firms. The result from each approach would be identical.

The conventional t-statistic of the CAAR is defined as

$$t = \frac{\text{CAAR}_t}{[\sigma^2(\text{CAAR}_t)]^{1/2}}, \tag{8.22}$$

where the variance of the CAAR is defined as

$$\sigma^2(\text{CAAR}_t) = \frac{1}{N^2}\sum_{j=1}^{N}\sigma^2(\text{CAR}_j(t_1, t_2)). \tag{8.23}$$

The variance of the CAR for an individual firm is defined in Equation (8.7): $\sigma^2\text{CAR}_j(t_1, t_2) = L\sigma^2(\text{AR}_{jt})$.

8.4 Long-Term Event Studies

All the models presented above measure the market response to an event over a short-term event window. If you want to measure whether the event still has an effect on stock returns over a long-term event window, you need to use a different model. One possibility is to accumulate abnormal returns over a longer period in the event window, but this approach will not correctly incorporate risk in the measurement of abnormal returns. This is because CARs use arithmetic returns and hence do not allow compounding of returns. Particularly for long-term stock performance measures, you need to compound returns to account for the effective interest rate, the return on return at the end of the compounding period. CARs measure the simple interest earned on a stock and do not capture the effective rate. In the short run, the difference between the simple interest rate and the compound interest rate is negligible, but in the long run compound interest can grow faster than simple interest, and hence there will be a difference between the two ways of calculating returns. To incorporate compound interest, you use buy-and-hold abnormal returns (BHARs), given by

$$\text{BHAR}_j = \left[\prod_{t=t_1}^{t_2}(1+R_{jt})-1\right]-\left[\prod_{t=t_1}^{t_2}(1+E(R_{jt}))-1\right], \tag{8.24}$$

where $E(R_{jt})$ is often the return on a market. The other factors, such as the Fama–French three-factor model and Carhart's (1997) four-factor model, are not used in the calculation of BHAR. As a benchmark, it is also common to use the return of a matched portfolio that has not gone through the event. The matching is based on size, value, industry, and so on. Similar to the CAAR, you can also calculate the average BHARs across firms in the cross-section (see Barber and Lyon, 1997; Lyon, Barber, and Tsai, 1999).

8.5 Calendar-Time Portfolio Approach

It is possible to examine the effects of an event by studying a portfolio of stock returns after the event has occurred. This also reflects long-horizon event studies. In this approach, for each calendar time, you form an event portfolio that contains all the firms that have gone through the event within a predetermined period prior to the calendar time t. Consider, for instance, initial public offerings (IPOs). Suppose the aim is to measure the long-run performance of a stock after the IPO using monthly return data. One approach is to calculate the BHAR for each IPO, but you could also build a portfolio of IPO stocks that have been listed, say, 1 month prior to the calendar month t and calculate the average monthly returns of all event firms in the portfolio, $R_{pt} = \sum_{j=1}^{N} w_{jt}R_{jt}$. Here the assumption is a value-weighted, w_{jt}, portfolio return, but you could calculate an equally weighted, $1/N$, portfolio return or use another weighting scheme, depending on the research question. You could then regress the portfolio return against one of the market models presented above in a time-series regression to observe whether the IPO of stock portfolio has earned abnormal returns over the chosen period. For instance, the Fama–French three-factor model would formally be presented as follows:

$$R_{pt} - R_{ft} = \alpha_p + \beta_p\left(R_{mt} - R_{ft}\right) + \gamma_p\text{SMB}_t + \delta_p\text{HML}_t + e_{pt}, \tag{8.25}$$

where the coefficients are constant and measured for the calendar-time portfolio. α_p indicates whether IPO firms outperformed or underperformed against the market and the other three factors of portfolios. Although Lyon et al. (1999) suggest that the Fama–French calendar-time approach seems to be a valid representation of long-run event studies, Loughran and Ritter (2000) argue that the calendar-time portfolio approach has low power because the approach assigns equal weight to each month regardless, whether the month's portfolio includes firms with "hot" or "cold" event activities. However, the approach seems to work well in random samples, although BHARs tend to provide more robust results in long-run event studies (see Lyon et al., 1999).

8.6 Details with Aggregation of Returns

The critique raised by Loughran and Ritter (2000) targets the calendar-time portfolio approach, since it gives equal weight to each month regardless of whether the month's portfolio has heavy or light event activities. However, the weighting scheme can be an issue when aggregating ARs or CARs across the firms as well. One remedy for this problem is to standardize abnormal returns by dividing them by their standard deviation, so-called SARs, and then aggregate them across firms.

8.6.1 Assumption of Independent Events

Another important consideration with the aggregation of abnormal returns is the assumption that the events are independent of one another. But events may be clustered over time, leading to a violation of the assumption of independent returns in the aggregation. This will affect the calculation of standard errors and hence the conventional test statistics for the aggregated abnormal returns across firms will not be valid. Brooks (2019) suggests constructing test statistics on an event-by-event basis and then presenting their descriptive statistics. He also suggests forming portfolios of firms that experience the event in the same period. The standard deviation can then be calculated using the returns of the event firms in the cross-section, in the same period, allowing a cross-sectional correlation of returns of these firms. The latter approach is less preferred as it does not allow different variance for each event firm in the portfolio.

8.6.2 Concern with the Calculation of Variance of Returns

Another concern with the calculation of the variance of the returns has been raised (see Boehmer, Musumeci, and Poulsen (1991); Brooks, 2019). In the presented models above, you calculate the variance based on the estimation window and use it to compute the test statistics in the event window. However, it is likely that the underlying factor that caused the event will also increase the uncertainty of returns over the event window. Thus, you would expect a higher variance of returns in the event window than in the estimation window. Accordingly, the variance from the estimation window will be lower, leading to a higher test statistic and hence a more frequent rejection of the null hypothesis that the event does not affect the stock returns. To remedy this problem, Boehmer et al. (1991) suggest using a cross-sectional variance of returns across firms in the event window. One disadvantage of this approach is that the variance would be constant for all firms in the event study, whereas the variance calculated from the estimation window will be unique to each firm.

8.6.3 Fewer Events

In the case of too few events or too short an estimation window, the test statistics that are based on asymptotic properties (that are true when the sample size becomes larger) are not valid because of non-normality. It is therefore common to conduct and present non-parametric tests for such events. The non-parametric test in the event-study context tests whether the event affects the proportion of positive abnormal returns.

It is also important to consider the exogeneity of the events. The event studies in corporate finance are often based on corporate decisions, which are endogenously determined. Although the underlying factors for the event are market-based, managers of the firm may decide to time the market. Indeed, this is a hot topic in the IPO literature; firm managers tend to decide to go public when the overall market is doing well, although the IPO process can take some time. Similarly, capital restructuring, dividend payments, and so on are all decided by firm managers/directors. Using such events without discussing the exogeneity of the events in the studies might be too naïve.

8.7 Application of Short-Term Event Studies

This exercise examines how stock prices respond to the news of a CEO's departure. The exercise follows the literature focusing on whether CEOs matter and whether CEO ability has an effect on firm value and performance (see, e.g., Chang, Dasgupta, and Hilary, 2010; Homroy, Mavruk, and Nguyen, 2023). Since CEOs are not randomly assigned to firms, it is difficult to find a valid answer to these questions in a cross-sectional study without considering the dynamics of labor market participation of CEOs. Chang et al. (2010) suggest that the market response to the news of a CEO's departure is one possible way of examining the ability of the CEO and how a CEO contributes to firm performance. If CEOs have high ability, then the market reaction to the departure news should be negative. Using data from Sweden, Homroy et al. (2023) follow a similar methodology to proxy a measure of CEO ability and then relate it to firms' environmental, social, and corporate governance (ESG)-linked compensation. They examine whether the ESG-linked pay is higher in firms with generalist CEOs. This exercise will replicate some of their analysis with a small random sample of news on 35 CEO departures. The event is the announcement of CEO departure, not the effective CEO departure date, as the market may already have anticipated the CEO departure news.

This study uses Carhart's (1997) four-factor model in an estimation window of $[-250; -20]$ to estimate the parameters in the four-factor model (using the CAPM or Fama–French three-factor model, the results qualitatively hold). It then uses these parameters to calculate the expected return in the event window of $[-3; +3]$ and hence to calculate the abnormal returns over the event window. Cumulative abnormal returns are then calculated, along with their conventional test statistics. Table 8.1 presents the average abnormal returns and Table 8.2 presents the average cumulative abnormal returns over different event windows. Asterisks ** indicate significance at the 5% level. Figure 8.2 summarizes the results from cumulative abnormal returns.

Table 8.1 Average abnormal returns

t	NoFirms	AAR	*t*-test
−3	35	0.0033	1.211
−2	35	0.0003	0.101
−1	35	−0.0020	−0.724
0	35	−0.0084**	−3.050
1	35	−0.0025	−0.896
2	35	−0.0017	−0.625
3	35	−0.0005	−0.193

Table 8.2 Average cumulative abnormal returns

t	NoFirms	CAAR	*t*-test
[0; 1]	35	−0.0109**	−2.777
[−1; 1]	35	−0.0129**	−2.686
[−2; 2]	35	−0.0143**	−2.311
[−3; 3]	35	−0.0115	−1.569

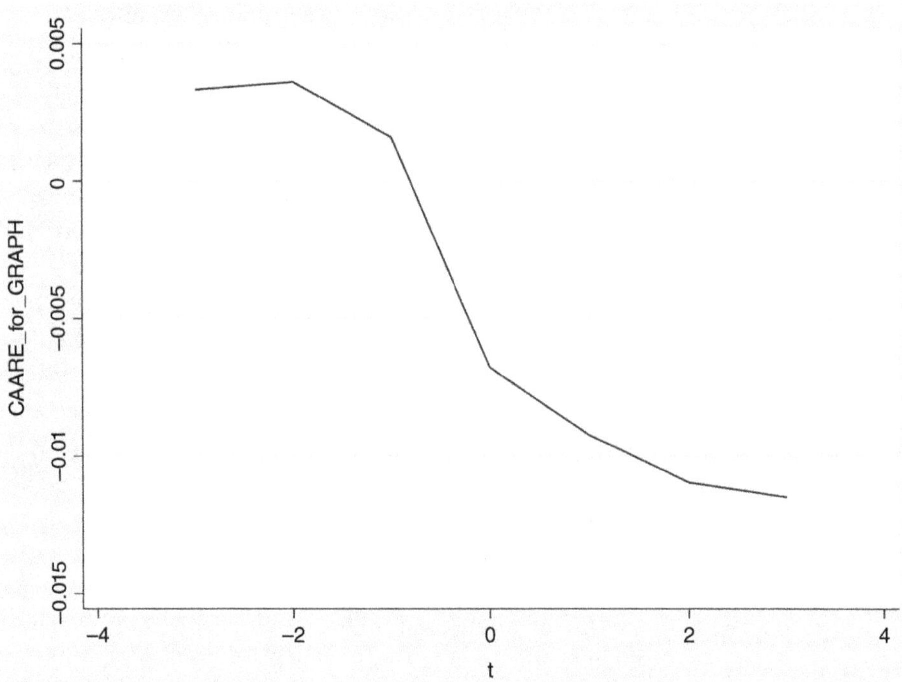

Figure 8.2. CARs over time

The results show that on the announcement day of the CEO's departure, the average abnormal return across firms is significantly negative (0.8%), which verifies the results from Chang et al. (2010) and Homroy et al. (2023), indicating that CEOs have high ability on average. In Table 8.2, the average CARs are negative and significant (about 1%) for the event windows [0; +1],[−1; +1],[−2; +2], however, most of the effect comes from the announcement day. Figure 8.2 verifies the declining CAARs over the event window.

Table 8.3 presents results from the average BHARs during a different window and Figure 8.3 plots the average BHARs over time.

Table 8.3 Average buy-and-hold abnormal returns

t	NoFirms	BHAR	SkewAdjT
[−250; −20]	35	0.0230	0.472
[−250; −3]	35	0.0208	0.395
[−250; −1]	35	0.0142	0.277
[−20; −1]	35	0.0044	0.337
[−20; 3]	35	−0.0063	−0.371
[−3; 3]	35	−0.0098	−1.412
[0; 3]	35	−0.0097**	−1.990

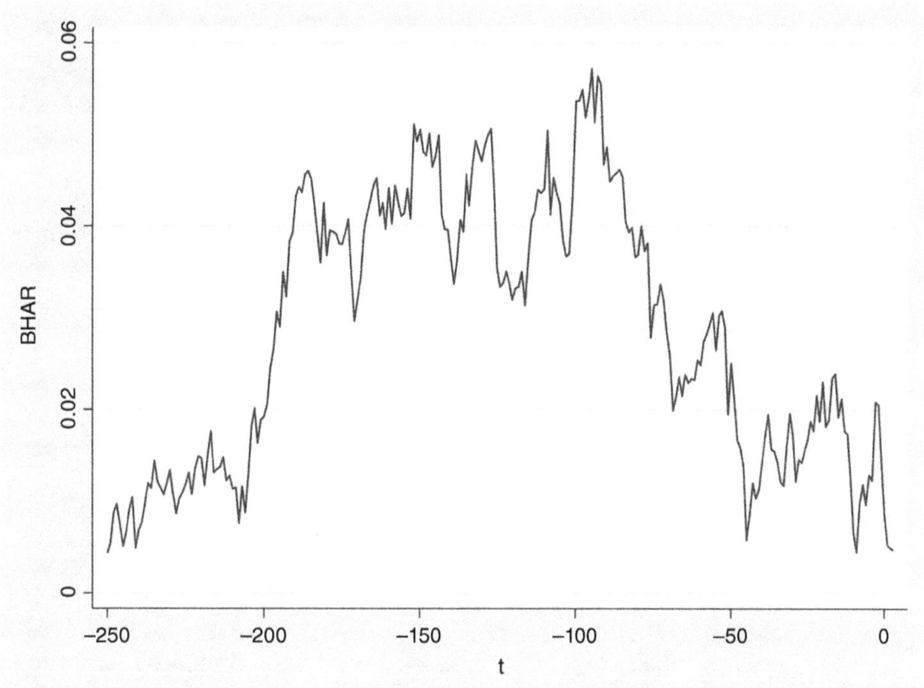

Figure 8.3. BHARs over time

Table 8.3 shows that the average BHAR is positive for the period in which CEOs are still in the job, but they are insignificant using the current sample. In the table, the test statistics are the skewness-adjusted t-statistics, which adjust the cross-sectional t-test for a potential skewed abnormal return distribution (see Hall, 1992 for more details). The average BHAR turns negative when the event period is included in the calculation period, [–20; +3] and beyond. It turns significantly negative on the announcement of the departure day and three trading days after, [0; +3]. Figure 8.3 confirms these results.

8.8 Lab Work: Event Studies

In this lab work you will use the same data, CEO departure data, as in Section 8.7 and examine the robustness of the results using different event-study models and by changing estimation and event windows. The variables market return, Fama–French factors, momentum factor, and Treasury-bill rate (proxy for risk-free rate) are simulated (due to permission reasons) and thus do not reflect the real data. Those of you who are interested in downloading the original variables can obtain them from Kenneth R. French – Data Library (dartmouth.edu). It would be interesting to observe the analysis using a real dataset and compare the results with the results obtained from this simulated data.

In the lab work you will elaborate on different ways of measuring standard errors for the CARs. You are given the full code, eventstudy2 in Stata, for the event study on this book's webpage (www.cambridge.org/Mavruk). To use the code, you need to install it in Stata. For detailed explanations, see "findit eventstudy2" in Stata where you will also find some examples. For each question, run the code to produce the results. You should focus on the following output files.

(i) graphfile: click on it and interpret the figure.
(ii) aarfile: average abnormal returns file. The focus is on the following variables:

```
t, NoFirms, AARE, NAAREt_test
```

t: time
NoFirms: the number of firms used to calculate abnormal returns in each t
AARE: the average abnormal returns
NAAREt_test: the t-test assuming cross-sectional independence.

(iii) carfile: cumulative abnormal returns file. The main focus is on the following variables:

```
t NoFirms CAARE NCAAREt_test
```

t: time
NoFirms: the number of firms used to calculate cumulative abnormal returns
CAARE: the average cumulative abnormal returns
NCAAREt_test: the t-test assuming cross-sectional independence.
In this file you should also elaborate on the other t-value calculations.

Problem set

For Questions 1–6, calculate AAR and CAAR for given CEO departure news and test their significance. Use an estimation window of [–250; – 20] and varying event window within the interval [–3; + 3].

1. Use the constant mean model. Explain how this model works and interpret your results.
2. Use the market-adjusted model. Explain how this model works and interpret your results.
3. Use the market model. Explain how this model works and interpret your results.
4. Use the CAPM. Explain how this model works and interpret your results.
5. Use the Fama–French three-factor model. Explain how this model works and interpret your results.
6. Use the Fama–French four-factor model. Explain how this model works and interpret your results.
7. Compare your results from models 1–6 above. Do your results hold when using these different models? Which model would you suggest using? Motivate your answers.
8. In the carfile (output file) you obtain a NCAAREt_test, which is the t-test assuming cross-sectional independence. But there are also other t-values computed. Briefly explain what they are. Which t-value would you suggest using? Motivate your answer (see Stata's help file for eventstudy2).
9. Use the Fama–French four-factor model again and alter your estimation window to [−125; − 20] and a varying event window within the interval [−3; +3]. Compare your results to those obtained in model 6. Do your results hold? Explain. In a new exercise, alter your event window (your own choice) as well. What do you observe?
10. Calculate BHARs and their significance using varying windows within the interval [−125; +3]. This is a replication of the BHAR results in Section 8.7 with a different window. Compare your results to those obtained in Section 8.7.

Good luck!

8.9 Mini Case

Greenwoods, Laaritz, and Wurgler (2023) examine how stimulus checks were spent. During the pandemic, the US government provided stimulus checks, sizable economic impact payments, in three rounds between March 2020 and March 2021. The first round was in mid-April 2020, the second in early January 2021, and the last in March 2021. These stimulus checks reached approximately $814 billion in payments directly to US taxpayers. The study shows that these stimulus checks led to growth in retail trading accounts and affected stock prices. Retail investors used some portion of the stimulus checks to invest in stocks, but these investments seemed to drive up the prices of the stocks purchased. In their main analysis, Greenwoods et al. (2023) carefully examine how the distribution of the stimulus checks was related to retail trading and whether these trading effects increased abnormal returns. The authors conduct standard event studies to examine the abnormal returns within a few days of the first, second, and third rounds of stimulus checks.

Task

1. Go to the link: Replication Data for: Stock Market Stimulus – Review of Financial Studies Dataverse (harvard.edu)
   Download the zip file that includes both data and do files: stock_market_stimulus.zip
2. Go to the link: Stock Market Stimulus | The Review of Financial Studies | Oxford Academic (oup.com)
   Download the paper. Alternatively, you can download the working paper version from the following link: www.nber.org/papers/w29827
3. Replicate Panel A of Table 5 in the paper. Present and explain your results.
4. Replicate Panel B of Table 5 in the paper. Present and explain your results.
5. Revise your analysis in Panel A of Table 5 by using the constant mean model. Present and explain your results. Do your results differ from Part 3? Explain.
6. Revise your analysis in Panel A of Table 5 by using the Fama–French three-factor model. Present and explain your results. Do your results differ from Part 3? Explain.
7. Revise your analysis in Panel A of Table 5 by using the Fama–French four-factor model. Present and explain your results. Do your results differ from part 3? Explain.

Note that Table 5 in the working paper version corresponds to Table 5 in the published version.

8.10 Summary

Event studies are commonly applied in corporate finance, with the focus on testing the market efficiency hypothesis and evaluating the effects of corporate decisions on firm value, stock prices, and other outcome variables. These studies provide valuable insights into investor behavior, firm value, and shareholder wealth by exploring market response to corporate events such as mergers and acquisitions, stock splits, share repurchases, and dividend payments. It is also common to apply the event-study methods to examine the effects of regulatory and policy changes. For example, studies can explore the effects of the introduction of new regulations, such as International Financial Reporting Standards, on investor behavior and firm value, and so on. Some event studies also examine investment strategies by trying to identify trading opportunities based on market response to previous events. These studies try to identify patterns from past events and develop some investment strategies to be used in future similar events. Overall, the results from event studies have been essential to understand the consequences of the changes in market behavior and provide insight into market efficiency theories and corporate decision-making, among other corporate and investment behavior.

The chapter discusses the event-study model using examples from: (i) return predictability literature, examining the weak form of market efficiency; (ii) the effects of firm-level and macro news on stock returns, testing semi-strong efficiency; as well as (iii) insider trading, testing the strong form of efficiency. In short-term event studies the chapter reviews abnormal (AR) and cumulative abnormal return (CAR) calculations and discusses statistical tests of ARs and CARs. It also covers long-term event studies and discusses buy-and-hold abnormal returns as well as the calendar-time portfolio approach. The chapter provides an application of a short-term event study by examining how stock prices respond to the news of a CEO's departure. The chapter ends with lab work and a mini case.

KEY TERMS

Short-horizon event studies; long-horizon event studies; calendar-time portfolio approach; abnormal returns; cumulative abnormal returns; market-adjusted model; market model; CAPM; Fama–French three-factor model; Carhart's four-factor model; aggregation; application of short-horizon event studies.

REFERENCES

Ball, R. and Brown, P. 1968. An empirical evaluation of accounting income numbers. *Journal of Accounting Research*, 6, 159–178.

Barber, B. M. and Lyon, J. D. 1997. Detecting long-run abnormal stock returns: The empirical power and specification of test statistics. *Journal of Financial Economics*, 43, 341–372.

Boehmer, E., Musumeci, J., and Poulsen, A. B. 1991. Event-study methodology under conditions of event-induced variance. *Journal of Financial Economics*, 30, 253–272.

Brooks, C. 2019. *Introductory Econometrics for Finance* (4th ed.). Cambridge University Press, Cambridge.

Brown, S. J. and Warner, J. B. 1980. Measuring security price performance. *Journal of Financial Economics*, 8, 205–258.

Carhart, M. M. 1997. On persistence in mutual fund performance. *Journal of Finance*, 52, 57–82.

Chang, Y. Y., Dasgupta, S., and Hilary, G. 2010. CEO ability, pay, and firm performance. *Management Science*, 56, 1633–1652.

Dolley, J. C. 1933. Characteristics and procedure of common stock split-ups. *Harvard Business Review*, 11, 316–326.

Fama, E. 1970. Efficient capital markets: A review of theory and empirical work. *Journal of Finance*, 25, 383–417.

Fama, E. 1998. Market efficiency, long-term returns, and behavioral finance. *Journal of Financial Economics*, 49, 283–306.

Fama, E. and French, K. 1993. Common risk factors in the returns on stocks and bonds. *Journal of Finance*, 33, 3–56.

Fama, E. F., Fisher, L., Jensen, M. C., and Roll, R. 1969. The adjustment of stock prices to new information. *International Economic Review*, 10, 1–21.

Fernandez, P. and de Santos, T. G. 2022. Survey: Market risk premium and risk-free rate used for 95 countries in 2022. Working Paper. IESE Business School.

Greenwood, R., Laarits, T., and Wurgler, J. 2023. Stock market stimulus. *Review of Financial Studies*, 36, 4082–4112.

Hall, P. 1992. On the removal of skewness by transformation. *Journal of the Royal Statistical Society. Series B: Methodological*, 54, 221–228.

Hamberg, M., Mavruk, T., and Sjögren, S. 2013. Investment allocation decisions, home bias and the mandatory IFRS adoption. *Journal of International Money and Finance*, 36, 107–130.

Hillier, D., Ross, A. S., Westerfield, R. W., Jaffe, J. F., and Jordan, B. D. 2021. *Corporate Finance* (4th ed.). McGraw-Hill Education, London.

Homroy, S., Mavruk, T., and Nguyen, V. D. 2023. ESG-linked compensation, CEO skills, and shareholders' welfare. *Review of Corporate Financial Studies*. https://doi.org/10.1093/rcfs/cfad012

Jacobson, L. S., LaLonde, R. J., and Sullivan, D. G. 1993. Earnings losses of displaced workers. *American Economic Review*, 83, 685–709.

Jegadeesh, N. and Titman, S. 1993. Returns to buying winners and selling losers: Implications for stock market efficiency. *Journal of Finance*, 48, 65–91.

Kothari, S. P. and Warner, J. B. 2007. Econometrics of event studies. In B. E. Espen (ed.), *Handbook of Corporate Finance: Empirical Corporate Finance*. Elsevier, North-Holland, pp. 3–36.

Lee,D. S. and Lemieux, T. 2010. Regression discontinuity designs in economics. *Journal of Economic Literature*, 48, 281–355.

Lintner, J. 1965. The valuation of risk assets and the selection of risky investments in stock portfolios and capital budgets. *Review of Economics and Statistics*, 47, 13–37.

Loughran, T. and Ritter, J. 2000. Uniformly least powerful tests of market efficiency. *Journal of Financial Economics*, 55, 361–389.

Lyon, J., Barber, B., and Tsai, C. 1999. Improved methods of tests of long-horizon abnormal stock returns. *Journal of Finance*, 54, 165–201.

MacKinlay, A. C. 1997. Event studies in economics and finance. *Journal of Economic Literature*, 35, 13–39.

Mavruk, T. 2021. Cross-regional differences in news tone and local stock ownership. *Management Science*, 67, 3276–3298.

Mavruk, T. 2022. Analysis of herding behavior in individual investor portfolios using machine learning algorithms. *Research in International Business and Finance*, 62, 101740.

Miller, D. L. 2023. An introductory guide to event study models. *Journal of Economic Perspectives*, 37, 203–230.

Mossin, J. 1966. Equilibrium in a capital asset market. *Econometrica*, 34, 768–783.

Roll, R. 1977. A critique of the asset pricing theory's tests. Part I: On past and potential testability of the theory. *Journal of Financial Economics*, 4, 129–176.

Ross, A. S., Westerfield, R. W., and Jaffe, J. F. 2005. *Corporate Finance: International Edition*. McGraw-Hill Education, Singapore.

Sharpe, W. F. 1964. Capital asset prices: A theory of market equilibrium under conditions of risk. *Journal of Finance*, 19, 425–442.

Treynor, J. L. 1962. Toward a theory of market value of risky assets. Unpublished manuscript.

9 Panel-Data Analysis

INTRODUCTION

The focus of this chapter is the panel-data analysis that can also be seen as a pooled time series of cross-sections. The unit of analysis can be, among others, individual, stock, firm, CEO, and so on, and the key distinction that makes such an analysis more detailed than a single cross-sectional data analysis (covered in Chapter 5) or a time-series data analysis (covered in Chapter 7) is that you can follow the behavior of these units over time. Panel data provide a richer source of variation, allowing a more efficient estimation of the coefficients of interest compared to cross-sectional data. By following the units over time, you can learn more about their behavior, which makes it possible to relax some of the assumptions about the characteristics of the units. This means that you can study and control for individual heterogeneity in panel data.

Consider a study of CEO compensation. Many of the CEO characteristics can be observed and included in a regression model, examining the determinants of CEO compensation. However, how should you measure CEO ability, which is unobserved, in relation to analysts, investors, and the firm? If you cannot control for this individual specific characteristic, it will lead to a biased estimate. Panel-data analysis provides some advanced methods that make it possible to control for the unobserved CEO ability, although some assumptions about the distribution of this individual specific effect are still necessary. Note that CEO ability is difficult to identify in cross-sectional data, or time-series data, unless you can find a sophisticated measure for ability. For instance, Custódio, Ferreira, and Matos (2013) collect some variables related to CEOs' previous experience and use this information in a principal component analysis (PCA) to build a general measure of ability index. This index is then used to identify more generalist CEOs and specialist CEOs.

Such a sophisticated ability measure can be used in a cross-sectional analysis. The authors relate this ability measure to CEO pay and find that total compensation to generalist CEOs is higher than to specialist CEOs. Although this measure can be obtained in the cross-section, the study uses panel data to examine this challenging research question. In sum, panel data can make it possible to control for unobserved heterogeneity and to study the dynamic behavior of units over time.

This means that you can study the change in the behavior of observed units as well. Thus, panel data makes it possible to test more complicated models than purely cross-sectional or time-series data.

There are also some limitations of panel data. The data collection problem, including incomplete information on the units over time, is one of the main limitations. This is similar to the problems with designing surveys: non-response, frequency of interviewing, measurement errors, self-selectivity, attrition, and survivorship bias are some of the concepts covered in Chapter 2. But it is more problematic in a panel-data setting, because the data need to be collected over time. Short time-series dimension is particularly problematic in corporate finance studies that examine firm-level (micro) panels, involving annual firm characteristics. Increasing the time dimension in such panels may help but it will also increase the likelihood of survivorship bias. Cross-sectional dependence is also problematic as there are many studies related to geography of investments in corporate finance. If, for instance, cross-regional dependence (in particularly long panels) is not considered, it will affect the inference. Readers should consult Hsiao (2003) and Baltagi (2008) for more details on the benefits and limitations of panel data.

This chapter reviews some basic linear panel-data models and then covers the selection between these models. Although some non-linear models are covered in Chapter 10, non-linear panel-data models are beyond the scope of this book. The chapter also discusses dynamic panel-data models. It ends with an application of panel-data analysis to provide an example of how the panel-data techniques are used in research. Lab work is given for further practice at the end of the chapter. Finally, a mini case is provided.

9.1 Error-Components Model

We begin by presenting the error-components model to explain panel-data analysis. In Equation (9.1), the variables in the model are indexed as *i* for individual and *t* for time, and the standard linear regression is given as a panel-data model:

$$y_{it} = \beta_0 + \beta_1 x_{1,it} + \beta_2 x_{2,it} + \cdots + \beta_n x_{n,it} + e_{it}, \tag{9.1}$$

where the index *i* may represent an individual, stock, or firm, and so on, and there are x_n independent variables in the example. The index *it* represents that the individual units are observed over time in the panel data. It is a linear model, so the intercept β_0 and slope coefficients β_n are constant for all individuals and over time. The residual term e_{it} varies for each individual and time and picks up all unobservable factors that are not controlled in the model by the independent variables x_n. You estimate this model using ordinary least squares (OLS) and thus the standard classical linear regression model (CLRM) assumptions also apply to the linear panel-data models. One limitation of the model presented is that it is difficult to assume that the residuals for the same individual are uncorrelated over time. Thus, conventional standard errors based on i.i.d. residuals will be misleading, and hence further assumptions about the residuals are necessary (Stock and Watson, 2019). To begin with, the structure of the panel standard errors is examined:

$$e_{it} = \alpha_i + u_{it}, \tag{9.2}$$

where u_{it} is assumed to be i.i.d., just as the standard OLS residuals. The term α_i is the individual effect, which is time-invariant; in other words, it is individual-specific. The reason for assuming that u_{it} is homoskedastic and serially uncorrelated is that these features can be attributed to the individual effect α_i. However, you still need to assume exogeneity of the independent variables, $\text{cov}(x_n, e_{it}) = 0$, in Equation (9.1). It may be less strong to assume that the independent variables are uncorrelated with the model residuals u_{it}, $\text{cov}(x_n, u_{it}) = 0$, but assuming that the independent variables are uncorrelated with the individual effects will be very strong. It is often the case that unobserved characteristics of the individuals are correlated with observed characteristics $\text{cov}(x_n, \alpha_i) \neq 0$. Consider the previous example of CEO ability, which may well be correlated with the CEO's level of education, which can be observed and included in the model. One aim in this chapter is to explore how panel data can relax such strong assumptions.

Panel-data techniques can solve such issues (to a certain extent), since panel data tend to be larger than cross-sectional data or time-series data alone. This also implies that observed variables vary not only in one dimension, but across both individuals and over time, leading to more efficient estimators because you can better examine the changes in the behavior of units over time. In the error-components model, the individual-specific effect stays constant across time for each individual α_i. Different panel-data techniques are used to estimate this individual-specific effect. For example, the fixed-effects model gives an intercept for each individual and estimates this effect. In the random effects model, the individual-specific effect follows a random distribution with parameters that are estimated in the regression analysis. These models will be covered in detail next.

The argument here holds for panel data, where the same individual can be followed over time, rather than a pooled (independent) cross-section or pseudo panels. In the latter datasets you can examine the changes in behavior at an aggregate level, as you cannot follow the individual units over time. However, one advantage of examining pooled cross-sectional data is that observing different individuals in each time period implies more variation in the independent variables.

Most corporate finance studies use panel data. The main reason is that data often suffer from omitted-variable bias in corporate finance, and panel-data techniques seem to be efficient in reducing identification problems with omitted variables. Consider again the example with CEO ability. In panel data, you can include a manager-specific effect and assume this is a fixed unknown parameter that is unique to the manager. This treatment will reduce the effects of omitted variables as they will be captured by this manager-specific effect. This means that the estimations from a panel-data model will be more consistent than using an incomplete model that ignores the omitted variables totally.

Along this line, panel data can also make it possible to include internal instruments for the endogenous regressors and those variables with measurement errors.

For instance, lagged values of the variables can in some research designs be assumed uncorrelated with the error term at time t, but the lagged values are correlated with the values of the variable itself at time t. Thus, the lagged values may provide a valid internal instrument for the endogenous variables. Having time-series information on the individual units, you could also use transformations of the variables as an internal instrument. For instance, the deviation from the time average of the variable for the same individual, also called demeaning, can be assumed uncorrelated with the individual effect, $\text{cov}(x_{it} - \bar{x}, \alpha_i) = 0$, and thus can be used as an internal instrument for x_{it}. Note that such a transformation of the data eliminates the individual effect as α_i is unique to the individual and constant over time. This means that the transformation will eliminate the endogeneity problem. This chapter will cover this specific panel-data model next. See Nijman and Verbeek (1990), Hsiao (2003), and Baltagi (2008) for more detailed discussions on the differences and similarities between panel data and pooled cross-sectional data.

9.2 Fixed-Effects Model

The fixed-effects model is a special case of a linear model where the intercept varies over the individual units α_i. More specifically, the model is given as

$$y_{it} = \alpha_i + \beta_1 x_{1,it} + \beta_2 x_{2,it} + \cdots + \beta_n x_{n,it} + u_{it}, \tag{9.3}$$

where the error term is assumed i.i.d. as individual effects α_i are included in the model as intercept, rather than being embedded in the residuals. This also means that you can assume the x_n are exogenous, $\text{cov}(x_n, u_{it}) = 0$, as the residuals do not include the individual effects α_i. This is, of course, on the condition that endogeneity is not caused by any other bias. A simple model that captures the individual effects is known as the least squares dummy variable (LSDV) estimator. In this model you replace α_i with a dummy variable for each individual unit. Thus, the coefficients of these dummy variables estimate the individual effects. If data have a large N, a large number of individual units, then you have to insert $N-1$ number of dummy variables to control for the individual effects. This approach may not be feasible in samples with large N, as we lose one degree of freedom each time a regressor is included in the model.

Instead of including a dummy variable for each individual, you can transform the data to eliminate the individual effects, a so-called within transformation. Consider Equation (9.3) again and take the average of the variables for each individual unit. More formally:

$$\bar{y}_i = \alpha_i + \beta_1 \bar{x}_{1,i} + \beta_2 \bar{x}_{2,i} + \cdots + \beta_n \bar{x}_{n,i} + \bar{u}_i. \tag{9.4}$$

Next, transform the data by calculating the deviation of the variable (Equation (9.3)) from the average for each individual unit (Equation (9.4)), so-called demeaning of the variables. This is given by

$$(y_{it} - \bar{y}_i) = \beta_1(x_{1,it} - \bar{x}_{1,i}) + \beta_2(x_{2,it} - \bar{x}_{2,i}) + \cdots + \beta_n(x_{n,it} - \bar{x}_{n,i}) + (u_{it} - \bar{u}_i). \tag{9.5}$$

Note that the variables that are constant, time-invariant, are eliminated in this transformation. Thus, the individual effects α_i get eliminated. The results from this model would be identical to the results from the LSDV approach. Since the model takes into account individual effects, the estimated betas β_n are unbiased estimators. Here you assume that $\text{cov}(x_{it} - \bar{x}_i, u_{it}) = 0$. If x_{it} is already uncorrelated with u_i to begin with, then $\bar{x}_i$ is also uncorrelated with the residuals, $\text{cov}(x_{it}, u_{it}) = 0$. You can replace u_{it} with some lag or lead values of the residuals u_{is} and if you can assume that x_{it} is uncorrelated with even u_{is}, $\text{cov}(x_{it}, u_{is}) = 0$, it is said that x_{it} is strictly exogenous, meaning that current, past, and future values of residuals are not correlated with x_{it}. Since the fixed-effects model is estimated with OLS, the test statistics are the standard t-statistics or Wald statistics. Under some conditions it can be assumed that the fixed-effects estimator β_{FE} is asymptotically normal (Baltagi, 2008). Because the transformation refers to the within transformation, deviation of the variable from its own mean for each unit, the interpretation of the estimation should refer to the within dimension of the data, within individual units, not between individual units.

It is important to emphasize that by prioritizing the fixed effects, you narrow the analysis to a particular dimension of the data, for example, within-firm variation. This means you forgo the opportunity to explain between-firm variation. Therefore, it is also crucial to identify exactly which units vary over time. In some analyses, the choice of the fixed-effects model is plausible as it is more difficult to argue that between-unit variation will result in estimates of a causal effect. This chapter will cover some techniques for choosing between these models.

9.3 First-Difference Model

Equation (9.5) eliminated the individual effects by calculating the deviation from the average, by demeaning the variable for each individual unit. Alternatively, you can transform the model by taking the first difference for each individual unit:

$$\begin{aligned}(y_{it} - y_{i,t-1}) = \beta_1(x_{1,it} - x_{1,i,t-1}) + \beta_2(x_{2,it} - x_{2,i,t-1}) + \cdots \\ + \beta_n(x_{n,it} - x_{n,i,t-1}) + (u_{it} - u_{i,t-1}).\end{aligned} \tag{9.6}$$

Again, the individual effects α_i are eliminated and OLS is used to estimate the first-difference parameters β_{FD}. Thus, a standard t-test can be applied but the serial correlation in the residuals should be considered when computing standard errors. The assumption here is that the first-differenced variables and the first-differenced residuals are uncorrelated:

$$\text{cov}(x_{it} - x_{1,i,t-1}, u_{it} - u_{i,t-1}) = 0. \tag{9.7}$$

Note that this assumption is only about the first-differenced values, values at time t and $t-1$. So it allows a correlation between x_{it} and further lags of u_{it}, for instance. In this sense, it is less restrictive than the strict exogeneity assumption made in the fixed-effects model.

9.4 Difference-in-Differences Model

Examining single cross-sectional differences after some treatments has been discussed in Chapter 6 when dealing with endogeneity bias. The outcome for the treated group is compared with the outcome of the untreated (control) group. If the treatment concerns some time period (e.g., a regulation posed in a certain period), you could assign a dummy for the treatment period and regress the outcome, dependent variable on this dummy to examine the slope differential before and after the treatment period. If you have more observations for some post-treatment period (and/or pre-treatment period), you can either assign a dummy for these periods or take the average of the values during the pre- and post-treatment periods. You can then use OLS to estimate the cross-section of unit averages (see Bertrand, Duflo, and Mullainathan, 2004). The description of the treatment effects below draws on Roberts and Whited (2013).

The treatment-effects analysis of cross-sectional comparison examines the differences in the outcome by comparing treated and control groups in the same time period. Time-series comparison examines the same unit before and after treatment, enabling us to control for the unobserved differences between treated and untreated groups. The difference-in-differences (DiD) model combines these two cross-sectional and time-series models. The model is given by

$$y_{it} = \beta_0 + \beta_1 d_{\text{treated}} + \beta_2 d_{\text{post}} + \beta_3 d_{\text{treated}} \times d_{\text{post}} + e_{it}, \tag{9.8}$$

where the dummy d_{treated} indicates the individual groups that are treated (dummy equals 1 for treated and 0 for untreated individuals). It controls for the overall differences between the treated and untreated groups. The dummy d_{post} indicates the period after the treatment (1 for post-treatment period and 0 for pre-treatment period). It controls for trends common to both treatment and control groups. The coefficient β_3 on the interaction variable of $d_{\text{treated}} \times d_{\text{post}}$ is the DiD estimator. It compares the outcome of treated and untreated groups before the treatment with the outcome of treated and untreated groups after the treatment. In other words, the DiD estimator captures the variation generated by the change in the outcome of the treated group, relative to the change in the outcome of the untreated group.

9.4.1 Expected Outcomes of DiD Estimators

You can also estimate DiD coefficients using differences of the variables. The equations below examine the expected outcomes of DiD estimators:

$$\begin{aligned} E\left(y \mid d_{\text{treated}} = 1, d_{\text{post}} = 1\right) &= \beta_0 + \beta_1 + \beta_2 + \beta_3, \\ E\left(y \mid d_{\text{treated}} = 1, d_{\text{post}} = 0\right) &= \beta_0 + \beta_1, \\ E\left(y \mid d_{\text{treated}} = 0, d_{\text{post}} = 1\right) &= \beta_0 + \beta_2, \\ E\left(y \mid d_{\text{treated}} = 0, d_{\text{post}} = 0\right) &= \beta_0. \end{aligned} \tag{9.9}$$

Given these expected outcomes, Table 9.1 summarizes the pre-treatment and post-treatment effects for treated and control groups, respectively.

Table 9.1 Conditional mean estimates from DiD regressions

	Post-treatment	Pre-treatment	Difference
Treated	$\beta_0 + \beta_1 + \beta_2 + \beta_3$	$\beta_0 + \beta_1$	$\beta_2 + \beta_3$
Untreated	$\beta_0 + \beta_2$	β_0	β_2
Difference	$\beta_1 + \beta_3$	β_1	β_3

The hypothesis is usually tested for the DiD estimator of β_3, but it is also interesting to examine the average outcome for the treated group during the post- and pre-period, or the average difference in the outcome for the treated group before and after the treatment ($\beta_2 + \beta_3$).

9.4.2 Control Variables in a DiD Model

Corporate finance studies often include control variables in a DiD model because treatments are hardly exogenous. The control variables may help reduce the error variance caused by non-randomized treatments. Thus, you can more efficiently estimate the DiD effect, β_3, if you include control variables in the model when you are uncertain about the randomized assignment of treated and control groups. If the groups are randomly assigned, adding control variables will not alter the result on β_3. Hence, it is a good exercise to compare the results from a DiD model with and without control variables.

9.4.3 Assumption of Parallel Trends

Recall from Chapter 6 that the control variables should not be affected by the treatment itself. This condition is also related to the assumption of parallel trends. In the absence of treatment, the average change in the outcome variable would have been the same for the treated and the control groups. Note that the parallel trend assumption is not about the level of the outcome but the changes in the outcome should be the same, implying that any trends in the outcomes for these groups prior to treatment should be the same. However, if there is a large difference in the level of outcome variable between the treated and control groups in the pre-treatment period, you should be extra careful with the functional form of the regression equation when estimating the DiD parameter. For instance, the DiD estimator will be more sensitive to the inclusion of control variables. Overall, if the included control variables are correlated with the treatment, the parallel-trend assumption is less likely to hold.

The parallel-trend assumption can be tested by following some simple techniques. The easiest one is to do a falsification test, where you can falsely assign a treatment period and revise the DiD analysis. There should be no significant DiD effect then. As mentioned above, the control variables should not be affected by the treatment. One simple way to test this is to replace the dependent variable with a control variable and observe the DiD estimator. Again, the effect should be insignificant. You can repeat this exercise for the other control variables as well. If there are multiple treatment and control groups in the data, this may assist with more comparisons and thus examine any potential bias in the DiD estimator further. Understanding the source of bias will better help reduce it. Moreover, you can examine whether the treatment and control groups are balanced, meaning that these groups should be similar on observable characteristics. If the groups are different along observable characteristics, then it is likely that they will be different along unobservable characteristics as well. See Roberts and Whited (2013) for more discussions on the parallel-trend assumption.

9.5 Random-Effects Model

In contrast to the fixed-effects model, in the random-effects model the assumption is that the unobservable individual characteristics α_i are random. Thus, there are two random error terms in the model:

$$y_{it} = \beta_0 + \beta_1 x_{1,it} + \beta_2 x_{2,it} + \cdots + \beta_n x_{n,it} + \alpha_i + e_{it}, \tag{9.10}$$

where both individual characteristics (random effects) α_i and the model residuals e_{it} are assumed i.i.d. The model has a two-component error term with α_i, the individual specific random effect which is constant over time, and e_{it}, the standard error term which varies across individuals and over time.

9.5.1 Assumptions and Link Between Random-Effects and Fixed-Effects Models

The random-effects and the fixed-effects models have similarities, since they both capture the unobserved heterogeneity in the data. However, it is also helpful to cover the differences behind the assumptions of these models to better understand and compare the estimates from each model. This will also help with the robustness of the analysis; what to expect from these different estimates depends on these assumptions.

The random-effects model has stronger assumptions than the fixed-effects estimator. The random effects α_i and residuals e_{it} are assumed independent. In addition, these two error components should be independent of all the variables in the model, $x_{n,it}$, to satisfy the CLRM assumption of exogeneity. This condition also counts for all lead and lag values of the independent variables in the model. If these assumptions hold, then the OLS estimator of a random-effects model is unbiased and consistent. However, it is still not efficient because the two-component error term model tends to suffer from autocorrelation. This means that it is necessary to correct for the standard errors by transforming the model and hence using a generalized least squares (GLS) estimator. The transformation has been done by calculating the observation's deviation from the individual mean (within variation) and by calculating the deviation between the individual mean and the overall mean in the data (between variation). The within variation and between variation in the data is then weighted by an adjustment factor, given by $\gamma = \frac{\sigma_u^2}{\sigma_u^2 + T\sigma_\alpha^2}$. That is, the ratio of the variance in the residuals to the total variance coming from the residuals and random effects multiplied by the number of time periods in the data. If there is no individual effect then the adjustment factor γ is 1, which leads back to the OLS estimator. For a large T, the adjustment factor γ will go to 0, meaning that for a large T the results from fixed-effects and random-effects estimators will converge.

Taken together, the random-effects model has a stronger assumption than the fixed-effects model regarding the correlation between unobserved individual effects and independent variables; they are assumed uncorrelated. This feature leads to narrow conditions under which the assumptions of the random-effects model hold. Thus, the random-effects model is rarely properly used.

9.5.2 Combination of Within Estimator and Between Estimator

The random-effects estimator for this transformation that uses both within and between variation, along with the adjustment factor, is thus a combination of the fixed-effects (within) estimator and the so-called between estimator. The between estimator is an OLS estimator for individual means that averages out time-series information (see Verbeek, 2004 for more details). The transformed random-effects model can be written as

$$(y_{it} - \theta\bar{y}_i) = \beta_0(1-\theta) + \beta_n(x_{n,it} - \theta\bar{x}_{n,i}) + v_{it}, \tag{9.11}$$

where $\theta = 1 - \gamma^{\frac{1}{2}} = 1 - \sqrt{\frac{\sigma_u^2}{\sigma_u^2 + T\sigma_\alpha^2}}$ and $x_{n,it}$ represents the number of independent variables included in the model. If $\gamma = 0$ then $\theta = 1$, which leads to the within estimator of the fixed-effects model. Since γ is a proportion, θ is bounded between 0 and 1, $0 \le \theta \le 1$. As long as $\gamma > 0$, the random-effects estimator tends to be more efficient than the fixed-effects estimator because it uses between variation in the data. The transformation is done for each independent variable, which will have a β_n estimate each. The error term v_{it} is i.i.d. across individuals and time, as this transformation can now be estimated by OLS. However, one complexity is that σ_u^2 and σ_α^2 are unknown and have to be estimated first using the so-called feasible GLS estimator.

9.6 Choice Between Fixed-Effects and Random-Effects Model

As mentioned above, if T is large in the data, the difference between fixed-effects and random-effects estimators is negligible. However, if T is small, there could be substantial differences in the results from these estimators and thus you need to carefully determine which model to rely on, which is not an easy task. The first aspect to consider is the way the data are sampled. If the individuals are randomly sampled, then assuming that their unobserved characteristics are randomly distributed might be plausible. The correct choice is then to use the random-effects model, which will allow you to make inference on the population of the study units, for instance, firms. However, if the aim is to make a prediction of a particular type of firm, then assuming that the unobserved individual characteristics are fixed and specific to the firm is more appropriate. This is useful if identification of firm-specific characteristics is important for the study. You can then use a fixed-effects model, permitting inference to be made on firms in the collected sample of firms.

Besides these intuitive explanations, the functional forms are also important. Recall that random-effects models have a stronger assumption regarding the correlation between unobserved individual effects and the independent variables; they are assumed uncorrelated. In contrast, fixed-effects models allow correlation between independent variables and unobserved individual effects. If they are uncorrelated, the fixed-effects model also works since it eliminates the effects of individual effects from the model, but in this aspect it is more flexible than the random-effects model.

Hausman (1978) provides a more formal test of the correlation between individual effects and the independent variables in a model. The null hypothesis in this test is that the independent variables and the individual effects are uncorrelated. The test examines the difference in the results from the fixed-effects estimator and the random-effects estimator. Under the null hypothesis there should be no difference between the fixed-effects estimator and the random-effects estimator, since both models provide efficient estimates if the individual effects are uncorrelated with the independent variables. Here the assumption is that there is no other misspecification in the functional form of the model. However, the alternative hypothesis suggests that there is a difference in the results from these estimators if there is a correlation between the independent variables and the individual effects. If true, the correct model should be the fixed-effects model as it allows such a correlation. The Hausman test statistic evaluates the difference in these two estimates by computing their variance–covariance matrix. The statistic has an asymptotic χ^2 distribution with K degrees of freedom, where K is the number of parameters in the model.

9.7 Explained Variation in Panel Data

The standard R^2 is used and interpreted in the OLS method. In a panel-data setting you need to consider both within variation and between variation. The total variation is the sum of these two variations. Table 9.2 provides an example.

Table 9.2 Overall variation

Id	Period	Variable	Individual mean	Overall mean	Within variation	Between variation	Overall variation
i	t	y_{it}	$\overline{y}_i$	$\overline{y}$	$y_{it}-\overline{y}_i$	$\overline{y}_i-\overline{y}$	$y_{it}-\overline{y}$
1	2020q1	0.070	0.020	0.011	0.050	0.009	0.059
1	2020q2	−0.037	0.020	0.011	−0.057	0.009	−0.047
1	2020q3	0.057	0.020	0.011	0.037	0.009	0.046
1	2020q4	−0.010	0.020	0.011	−0.030	0.009	−0.021
2	2020q1	−0.041	0.008	0.011	−0.048	−0.003	−0.051
2	2020q2	−0.015	0.008	0.011	−0.023	−0.003	−0.026
2	2020q3	0.026	0.008	0.011	0.018	−0.003	0.015
2	2020q4	0.061	0.008	0.011	0.053	−0.003	0.051
3	2020q1	−0.074	0.004	0.011	−0.078	−0.006	−0.085
3	2020q2	0.053	0.004	0.011	0.048	−0.006	0.042
3	2020q3	0.050	0.004	0.011	0.046	−0.006	0.039
3	2020q4	−0.012	0.004	0.011	−0.016	−0.006	−0.022

Suppose you can observe individuals 1, 2, and 3 over four quarters during 2020 in the data, thus the dataset is a balanced panel. While a balanced dataset is preferred, unbalanced panel datasets – where data for some individuals are missing over some time periods – seem to be more common in empirical settings (see Baltagi and Song, 2006 for more discussions). In Table 9.2, the variable y_{it} shows the values of the individual observations over time, $\overline{y}_i$ are the individual means of the observations for individuals 1, 2, and 3, and $\overline{y}$ is the overall mean in the data. The deviation of each observation from its mean, $y_{it}-\overline{y}_i$, is the within deviation. The deviation of each individual mean from the overall mean, $\overline{y}_i-\overline{y}$, is the between variation. Finally, the deviation of each observation from the overall mean is the total variation, $y_{it}-\overline{y}$, which is the sum of the within and between variation in the data.

In terms of R^2, the average total variation can be written as

$$\frac{1}{NT}\sum\nolimits_{i=1,t=1}^{N,T}(y_{it}-\overline{y})^2=\frac{1}{NT}\sum\nolimits_{i=1,t=1}^{N,T}(y_{it}-\overline{y}_i)^2+\frac{1}{N}\sum\nolimits_{i=1}^{N}(\overline{y}_i-\overline{y})^2. \tag{9.12}$$

9.7.1 Which R^2 Should be Presented?

If the model is a fixed-effects model, thus examining within variation, you may present within R^2, which is given by $R^2_{\text{within}}=\rho^2(\hat{y}_{it}-\hat{y}_i, y_{it}-\overline{y}_i)$, where ρ is the correlation coefficient that maximizes the correlation between the fixed-effects estimator and the deviation of observations from the individual mean. If the model is a random-effects model, then you may present the between R^2, that is $R^2_{\text{between}}=\rho^2(\hat{y}_{it},\overline{y}_i)$. The overall R^2 is the one that the standard OLS estimator maximizes, $R^2_{\text{overall}}=\rho^2(\hat{y}_{it},y_{it})$. However, regardless of which estimator is used, these three R^2 measures can be presented in the analysis.

9.8 The Hausman–Taylor Random-Effects Instrumental-Variable Method

In your study, if you want to examine the effect of one of the time-invariant variables on the dependent variable, and if the Hausman test described above consistently favors the fixed-effects model, it is necessary to use a more flexible model. The Hausman–Taylor IV estimator (Hausman and Taylor, 1981) can be used to estimate the coefficients on the time-invariant variables. The model allows both time-invariant and time-variant variables, as well as allowing these variables to be correlated with the individual specific effects. The variables in the model can be summarized into the following categories: (i) time-invariant exogenous variables; (ii) time-invariant endogenous variables; (iii) time-variant exogenous variables; and (iv) time-variant endogenous variables. The condition for the model to work is that the number of time-variant exogenous variables should be equal to or greater than the number of time-invariant endogenous variables. The Hausman–Taylor IV estimator is given by

$$y_{it} = \beta_0 + \beta_1 x_{1,it} + \beta_2 x_{2,it} + \beta_3 w_{1,i} + \beta_4 w_{2,i} + \alpha_i + e_{it}, \tag{9.13}$$

where x_1 and x_2 are time-varying and w_1 and w_2 are time-invariant variables. The variables x_1 and w_1 are assumed to be exogenous, uncorrelated with α_i and e_{it}, while the variables x_2 and w_2 are assumed to be correlated with the individual effects α_i, but not with e_{it}. The Hausman–Taylor IV estimator uses the exogenous variables as their own instruments. The endogenous variable x_2 is instrumented by its deviation from the individual means, $x_{2,it} - \bar{x}_{2i}$, and the endogenous variable w_2 is instrumented by the individual average, $\bar{x}_{1i}$. This approach will make it possible to estimate the coefficients on the time-invariant variables, even if the Hausman test favors the fixed-effects model in the presence of a correlation between time-variant variables and individual effects. There is no need to use external instruments in the model, as individual means of time-variant variables that are uncorrelated with the individual effects are used as internal instruments. However, the model allows the use of additional external instruments. Despite its easy implementation, the model has not been picked up by corporate finance research (see Verbeek, 2004 for more details).

9.9 Inference in Panel Data

As mentioned earlier, the fixed-effects model allows correlation between α_i and unobservable individual effects, whereas the random-effects model does not allow this correlation. Both models assume α_i and the model residuals e_{it} are uncorrelated. So, if the independent variables are exogenous, there is no problem with consistency of the coefficient estimates. However, it is likely that panel data suffer from both heteroskedasticity and autocorrelation, which will lead to inefficient tests for significance of the coefficients, and thus the wrong conclusions. One simple approach to remedy this problem with inefficiency of the OLS estimation is to use heteroskedasticity and autocorrelation-consistent standard errors (see Chapters 5 and 7). Another approach is to use a feasible GLS estimator, but the application of this approach is relatively uncommon in corporate finance studies. See Baltagi (2008) for more details on the GLS approach. Arellano (1987) suggests that the fixed-effects estimator might be more appropriate to use than the random-effects estimator, as it might be difficult to assume that independent variables are uncorrelated with the unobserved individual effects in the presence of heteroskedasticity and autocorrelation.

Another reason why the fixed-effects estimator might be a better choice is that it is relatively easier to test the presence of autocorrelation in a fixed-effects model. For instance, similar to OLS, a simple application of the Durbin–Watson test can be used to test for the first-order autocorrelation in a fixed-effects model. One difference from OLS is that the test assumes that autocorrelation is constant across the individuals in the fixed-effects model. Verbeek (2004) presents a lower and upper bound for 5% critical values of the Durbin–Watson statistic. For heteroskedasticity, a variant of the Breusch–Pagan test can be applied in a random-effects model, in terms of a Lagrange multiplier (LM) test, where the null hypothesis is that there are no individual effects (see Baltagi, 2008).

It is also common to use clustered standard errors to remedy heteroskedasticity and autocorrelation problems in panel data. In this case the assumption is that the observations are clustered into groups, allowing correlation of errors within the cluster but not across them. One example is clustering on geographical region in local bias studies (see Mavruk, 2021). Here the model assumes that investors' choice within a geographical region is correlated, but investment choices across regions are not. Standard errors can also be clustered on time, by assuming that an individual's investment choice over time is correlated, but the investment choices across individuals are independent. Clustered standard errors tend to be larger than conventional standard errors in the presence of heteroskedasticity and autocorrelation. The consequence of not accounting for heteroskedasticity and autocorrelation in panel-data models is that standard errors will be too low, leading to narrow confidence intervals and thus large t-statistics and low p-values (see Cameron and Miller, 2015).

9.10 Stationarity in Panel Data

Testing stationarity (a process with constant mean, variance, and autocorrelation structure) in panel datasets is important, particularly in panels with large T and small N. Testing stationarity in panels with small T and large N is relatively uncommon and does not seem to provide powerful results, as the aim in examining stationarity and cointegration is to explore long-run relationships. For instance, in an international corporate finance study, if the aim is to estimate regression coefficients separately for each group of firms from different countries, time-series models could be used (as discussed in Chapter 7). This would make the analysis less complicated. However, having this option also means that the model has heterogeneity in the parameter estimates when estimating panel data of many different firms. It is likely that parameters differ across international firms, so-called heterogenous panels (see, e.g., Pesaran and Smith, 1995). The bias introduced by heterogenous panels might be large, particularly in non-stationary panels, emphasizing the importance of tests for stationarity in panel data.

Suppose that you test stationarity of the dependent variable in Equation (9.1) where the first-order autoregressive model is given by

$$y_{it} = \alpha_i + \beta_i y_{i,t-1} + e_{it}. \tag{9.14}$$

Insert $y_{i,t-1}$ in both sides of the equation to give

$$\Delta y_{it} = \alpha_i + (\beta_i - 1) y_{i,t-1} + e_{it}, \tag{9.15}$$

where $(\beta_i - 1)$ can be defined as γ_i. The null hypothesis in this unit-root test is $\gamma_i = 0$ for all i. The alternative hypothesis is that the dependent variable y is stationary for all i, $H_1 : \gamma_i < 0$ (see Choi, 2001; Im, Pesaran, and Shin, 2003; Maddala and Wu, 1999). This alternative hypothesis allows the mean-reversion parameter γ_i to be different for at least one i. If you want to impose that the mean-reversion parameter is constant for all i, then the alternative hypothesis would take the form $H_1 : \gamma < 0$ (Harris and Tzavalis, 1999; Levin, Lin, and Chu, 2002; Quah, 1994). The difficulty in these tests is that rejection of the null does not mean that all the time series is stationary, as the null hypothesis would be rejected even if only one of the γ_i is stationary. The literature discusses further issues related to the cross-sectional dependents of the residual terms e_{it}, serial correlation, potential heteroskedasticity in e_{it}, and the asymptotic properties of the test statistics that depend on the distribution of N and T (see Maddala, Wu, and Liu, 2000; Phillips and Moon, 1999).

The discussion above concerns the stationarity in one series, dependent variable. If there is more than one variable, for instance, when running a multivariate panel regression, you could examine the long-run relationships between the variables. Similar to the time-series analysis, the cointegration test in panel data is based on the residual term from the panel regression. The same complexities discussed above also count for the panel cointegration test, particularly the issues with heterogeneity in the parameters of the cointegrating relationships and that multiple cointegrating relationships may exist (see Baltagi, 2008; Hsiao, 2003). The alternative tests for stationarity in panel data are beyond the scope of this book; readers are referred to the detailed review of Baltagi (2008).

9.11 A Short Review of the Generalized Method of Moments

This section briefly describes the generalized method of moments (GMM) estimation for linear models. Using the sample moment conditions, GMM provides a class of estimators for the unknown population parameters. Since GMM uses assumptions about specific moments of the random variables instead of using the entire distribution, it is widely applicable. Another advantage of using GMM is that the model seems to perform better when the data have heteroskedasticity and the source of it is unknown (Hansen, 1982). The presence of heteroskedasticity in the models leads many identification tests to provide invalid results. For instance, the IV estimator (e.g., 2SLS) might be consistent but it is inefficient in the presence of heteroskedasticity (Baum, Schaffer, and Stillman, 2003).

GMM uses orthogonality conditions to better capture the heteroskedasticity in panel-data models. The conventional IV technique is a special case of GMM estimators. The short description of GMM below draws on Baum et al. (2003).

Suppose $x_{1,it}$ and $x_{2,it}$ in Equation (9.1) are endogenous with parameters K, $E(x_{1,i},e_i) \neq 0$, and $E(x_{2,i},e_i) \neq 0$, and that you have a set of instrumental variables Z given by an $n \times L$ matrix. The instruments in a set of L called L_1 (instruments Z_1) are exogenous, excluded instruments, $E(Z_1,e_i) = 0$, and the remaining $L - L_1$ instruments (Z_2) are exogenous, included instruments. For the order condition to hold you must have the number of excluded instruments in L equal to or greater than the number of endogenous regressors K, $L \geq K$. It is said that if $L > K$ then the equation is overidentified and if $L = K$ then the equation is exactly identified. So far this is the same as the conventional description of the IV estimator in 2SLS described in Chapter 6. Instrumenting the endogenous variables with instruments in L will lead to the IV estimator of $\hat{\beta}$.

The idea with GMM is that each instrument will produce a moment condition. So, if you have L number of instruments, they will produce L number of moment conditions, so-called orthogonality conditions, since each instrument is assumed to be independent of the residual term:

$$g_i\left(\hat{\beta}\right) = Z_i e_i = Z_i\left(y_i - X_i\hat{\beta}\right), \tag{9.16}$$

where g_i is $L \times 1$ and the orthogonality condition means that you have $E[g_i(\beta)] = 0$. Note that the residuals are unknown to begin with and thus estimated; the assumption is $e_i \equiv \hat{e}_i$. Each set of L conditions are sample conditions, given by

$$\bar{g}\left(\hat{\beta}\right) = \frac{1}{n}\sum_{i=1}^{n} g_i\left(\hat{\beta}\right) = \frac{1}{n}\sum_{i=1}^{n} Z_i e_i = \frac{1}{n}\sum_{i=1}^{n} Z_i\left(y_i - X_i\hat{\beta}\right). \tag{9.17}$$

In the GMM framework, these sample moment conditions are used to find a β that solves $\bar{g}(\hat{\beta}) = 0$. If you have as many L moment conditions as the endogenous regressors K, $L = K$, you can find β that solves $\bar{g}(\hat{\beta}) = 0$ and the estimator $\hat{\beta}$ is the IV estimator. However, if the equation is overidentified, $L > K$, then it is not possible to find β that sets all L moment conditions to zero, $g_i(\hat{\beta}) = 0$. It is then common to use a weighting matrix of W in the moment conditions, $L \times L$, to obtain the objective function given by

$$J\left(\hat{\beta}\right) = n\bar{g}\left(\hat{\beta}\right)' W \bar{g}\left(\hat{\beta}\right). \tag{9.18}$$

The GMM estimator is then β that minimizes this objective function $J(\hat{\beta})$, given by

$$\hat{\beta}_{\text{GMM}} = \left(X'ZWZ'X\right)^{-1} X'ZWZ'y. \tag{9.19}$$

Equation (9.19) may provide as many GMM estimators as the choices of weighting matrix W, and therefore you choose the efficient GMM estimator as the one with an optimal weighting matrix that minimizes the asymptotic variance of the estimator. For further details on how to choose the optimal weighting matrix and GMM estimator with heteroskedastic errors, readers may consult Hansen (2000) and Baum et al. (2003). In particular, Baum et al. (2003) emphasize that in the presence of heteroskedasticity you should choose GMM over the simple IV estimator. If the data do not suffer from heteroskedasticity, GMM would asymptotically produce similar results as the simple IV estimator. One caveat with the GMM estimator, however, is the choice of the optimal weighting matrix (a function of fourth moments). You may need a relatively large sample to obtain a reasonable estimate of fourth moments (Baum et al., 2003; Hayashi, 2000). Thus, the efficient GMM estimator may work well in large samples but produce poor results in small samples; the model may produce very large Wald test statistics when over-rejecting the null hypothesis too often. In sum, if the data do not suffer from heteroskedasticity, you should prefer the simple IV technique. It is possible to test for the presence of heteroskedasticity when you have endogenous regressor(s) by following a method introduced by Pagan and Hall (1983). Baum et al. (2003) provide the application of this test in Stata by implementing the "ivhettest" command.

9.12 Dynamic Panel-Data Models

Dynamic panel-data models probably deserve a book of their own, but this section will discuss them briefly. Consider a fixed-effects model and insert a lagged dependent variable on the right-hand side of the equation:

$$y_{it} = \beta_1 y_{i,t-1} + \beta_2 x_{1,it} + \beta_3 x_{2,it} + \cdots + \beta_n x_{n+1,it} + \alpha_i + e_{it}, \tag{9.20}$$

where the parameter β_1 is sometimes called the persistency rate or state dependency. By construction (since y_{it} is a function of the fixed effect), the lagged dependent variable $y_{i,t-1}$ is correlated with the individual effects α_i, which introduces an endogeneity bias in the estimation (see Baltagi, 2008). When doing a within transformation (demeaning the data), the fixed effects are eliminated, but correlation between the demeaned lagged dependent variable and the transformed error term $\left(e_{it} - \overline{e}_i\right)$ will remain, since $\overline{e}_i$ includes $e_{i,t-1}$. If the data have a large T panel, the endogeneity bias would decrease because the lagged values of the error term would contribute to the average to a lesser extent in long panels, decreasing the correlation between the lagged dependent variable and the regression residuals, and hence reducing the endogeneity bias. However, corporate finance studies rarely have long-panel datasets. For instance, the average firm listed on the Nasdaq OMX is observed for 12 years. Increasing the frequency of the data points may help, but firm characteristics are often observed yearly or quarterly.

Another possibility is to take the first difference of the model to eliminate the individual effects:

$$\Delta y_{it} = \beta_1 \Delta y_{i,t-1} + \beta_2 \Delta x_{1,it} + \beta_3 \Delta x_{2,it} + \cdots + \beta_n \Delta x_{n+1,it} + \Delta e_{it}, \tag{9.21}$$

however, there could still be a problem with correlation between $\Delta y_{i,t-1}$ and Δe_{it} because $y_{i,t-1}$ depends on $e_{i,t-1}$, which is used to calculate Δe_{it}. To remedy this endogeneity bias, one approach is to implement a 2SLS model using further lags of Δy_{it} as an instrument for $\Delta y_{i,t-1}$. You could also use the lagged levels of y_{it} as an instrument for $\Delta y_{i,t-1}$, a so-called difference GMM or Arellano–Bond estimator (Arellano and Bond, 1991). The models presented so far assume serially uncorrelated residuals. If this assumption does not hold, the lagged levels of the dependent variable may provide weak instruments for $\Delta y_{i,t-1}$ (Arellano and Bover, 1995; Blundell and Bond, 1998). Thus, an alternative model, a GMM system estimator, suggested by Blundell and Bond (1998), uses both lagged first differences $\Delta y_{i,t-2}$ and lagged levels of the dependent variable $y_{i,t-2}$ as instruments for $\Delta y_{i,t-1}$. The described GMM system estimator provides unbiased coefficients if residuals exhibit first-order autocorrelation. However, for higher orders of autocorrelation, you may need to use a long difference (higher than the first difference) of the dependent variable as instruments (LDIV) (Baltagi, 2008; Hahn, Hausman, and Kuersteiner, 2007).

The model assumes balanced panels with large T, which is less common in corporate finance studies. Kiviet (1995) suggests a different remedy for the fixed-effects bias in short panels by imposing data-dependent correction, a so-called bias-corrected least-squares dummy variable estimator (LSDVC). The model can also be applied to unbalanced dynamic panels, allowing, for instance, firms to enter and leave the dataset during the study period (see Bruno, 2005). For further details on how the LSDVC model works with multiple independent variables, missing or censored data, and in the presence of serially correlated errors, see the studies by Huang and Ritter (2009) and Flannery and Hankins (2013).

9.13 Application of Linear Panel-Data Models

This section will apply simple linear panel-data models on a partial adjustment model of capital structure by following Flannery and Hankins (2013). The control variables deviate a little from those in the paper, and the current study will avoid dividing the panel into subsamples as the data already have a relatively short panel.

9.13.1 Background

The empirical literature in corporate finance has tested Modigliani and Miller's (M&M's) (1958) irrelevance proposition (I). The proposition suggests that the value of the company is irrelevant to the company's capital structure. "In a perfect capital market, the total value of a firm's securities is equal to the market value of total cash flows generated by its assets and it is not affected by its choice of capital structure" (Berk and DeMarzo, 2020, p. 529). However, empirical literature examining firms' decisions about how to finance their operations seems to disagree about this proposition. One interesting finding is that companies tend to choose a target debt-to-equity ratio, trading off their costs and benefits of leverage (Flannery and Rangan, 2006). In a survey study, Graham and Harvey (2001) verify this view by documenting that 81% of firms use a specific target when making their debt decisions. Alternative theories to the trade-off theory have also been proposed, such as the pecking-order theory (Donaldson, 1961; Myers, 1984), suggesting that issuing equity is costly because the market often underprices shares in the presence of information asymmetry. Thus, firms may choose to finance their investments first with internally generated funds, then issue debt if the funds are insufficient. Finally, firms choose equity financing as a last resort. In this theory, firms do not have target debt-to-equity ratios.

Another capital structure theory that rejects the trade-off theory is the market timing hypothesis proposed by Baker and Wurgler (2002). Their findings suggest that firm managers tend to issue shares, and thus finance their projects, when the firm's market-to-book ratio is high. This is different from the pecking-order theory, since the market-timing hypothesis claims that firm managers exploit information asymmetries to benefit existing shareholders and the managers do not have target debt-to-equity ratios. Finally, Welch (2004) documents that managers have inertia to issue and repurchase debt and equity to counteract the effects of stock price changes on their firms' capital structures, which is a notion that also rejects the theory of target debt-to-equity ratios.

The latter-mentioned theories of capital structure are consistent with M&M's irrelevance theory that there are no leverage effects on firm value and that is why firm managers do not spend effort to reverse changes in leverage. However, the trade-off theory rejects M&M's proposition I of irrelevance theory by suggesting that market imperfections influence the relationship between leverage and firm value. M&M's proposition I holds under a set of conditions known as perfect capital markets. M&M have another proposition (II) for the capital structure of firms, which states that the cost of equity is directly related to the percentage of debt in capital structure. M&M's proposal II considers market imperfections, such as tax payments, transaction costs, agency costs, information asymmetries, and so on. The existence of a tax shield will lead to some savings from the debt cost of capital, although this relationship is not linear. Firms cannot keep borrowing and save on the debt cost of capital because of the increase in default probability with increases in debt. This means that although debt is cheaper, it increases the risk and thus increases the cost of equity. Taken all together, M&M's proposal II suggests that savings from the low cost of debt will be offset by a higher cost of equity, and thus firm value will be unaffected by the leverage.

9.13.2 Standard Partial-Adjustment Model of Capital Structure

Flannery and Rangan (2006) and Flannery and Hankins (2013) examine the trade-off theory and suggest that the speed with which firms reverse deviations from their target debt ratios is related to the firms' adjustment costs of leverage. On the one hand, if the adjustment costs are zero, there should be no deviation from firms' optimal leverage. On the other hand, the existence of large transaction costs will deviate firms from their target debt-to-equity ratios. The results in Flannery and Hankins (2013) suggest that firms select a target debt-to-equity ratio by trading off their cost and benefits of leverage over time. The model proposed by Flannery and Rangan (2006) and Flannery and Hankins (2013) is important when testing these competing theories as it provides a dynamic partial-adjustment model of capital structure.

9.13.3 Application

This section examines the standard partial-adjustment model of capital structure, which is given by

$$\mathrm{MDR}_{i,t+1} - \mathrm{MDR}_{i,t} = \lambda\left(\mathrm{MDR}^{*}{}_{i,t+1} - \mathrm{MDR}_{i,t}\right) + \tilde{\delta}_{i,t+1}, \tag{9.22}$$

where MDR is the market debt ratio calculated by the book value of firms' interest-bearing debt divided by the value of the firm defined as the book value of firms' interest-bearing debt plus the market value of equity. MDR* denotes the target market debt ratio and $\tilde{\delta}$ is the residual term. The theory suggests that firms adjust their target debt ratio and actual debt ratio by a proportion of λ over time. Since the target is specific to each firm, it depends on some firm characteristics. More formally:

$$\mathrm{MDR}^{*}{}_{i,t+1} = \boldsymbol{\beta}\mathbf{X}_{i,t}, \tag{9.23}$$

where **X** represents a vector of firm characteristics related to costs and benefits of operating with suboptimal leverage. The firm characteristics include revenue scaled by total assets (REV_TA), market-to-book ratio (MTB), the natural log of total assets (LN_TA), fixed assets (net PPE) scaled by total assets (PPE_TA), an indicator for positive research and development (Dummy_R&D), and the industry mean debt ratio for the firm (Ind_Mean_MDR).[1] Some additional variables are also included in the model, such as firm age, defined as the natural logarithm of the number of years from IPO. FO is foreign ownership in the firm, and the standard deviation of stock returns is calculated based on the daily stock returns within a quarter. Substituting Equation (9.23) into Equation (9.22) gives the regression equation

$$\mathrm{MDR}_{i,t+1} = (\lambda\beta)\mathbf{X}_{i,t} + (1-\lambda)\mathrm{MDR}_{i,t} + \tilde{\delta}_{i,t+1}. \tag{9.24}$$

Equation (9.24) suggests that managers make decisions to close the gap between the actual debt ratio ($\mathrm{MDR}_{i,t}$) and their target debt ratio ($\beta\mathbf{X}_{i,t}$). Eventually, the actual debt ratio converges to the target debt ratio. The long-run effects of firm

[1] Flannery and Hankins (2013) use EBIT, but the number of observations decreases when EBIT is used in the current sample. However, the main results remain the same. It is similar in terms of depreciation and R&D expense: the number of observations decreases when included in the model, but including these variables produces similar results. Using the industry median debt ratio instead of the industry mean debt ratio has no effect on the results. There is not much variation over time in the variable in the current sample.

characteristics $\mathbf{X}_{i,t}$ on the capital ratio are given by its estimated coefficient divided by λ. Since λ is constant, all firms have the same adjustment speed.

In the regression equation, firm-year dummies are also included and standard errors are clustered on firms. In the dynamic panel-data models, robust standard errors are used. The regression table presents results from OLS, the fixed-effects model (FE), Arellano and Bond's (1991) difference GMM estimates, Blundell and Bond's (1998) system GMM estimates (BB), and the least-squares dummy variable correction (LSDVC) model with initial values from the AB estimator, which corrects the biased FE-estimated coefficients. Note that standard errors are not produced in the LSDVC model. The Hausman test results strictly reject the null hypothesis of no difference between the coefficients obtained from random-effects and fixed-effects models, indicating that unobserved firm-specific effects are correlated with MDR and the observed firm characteristics. Thus, the regression table does not show results from the random-effects model. Figure 9.1 provides the test results. Table 9.3 provides descriptive statistics for the variables and Table 9.4 shows the results from various panel-data models. Figure 9.2 shows the output from specification tests after the AB model.

Table 9.3 shows that the average MDR is low, 0.16, and firms' revenue constitutes 23% of the total assets, on average. Firms have 19% foreign ownership and return volatility is about 22%, on average. Table 9.4 shows that the estimated speed of adjustment varies depending on which panel-data technique has been used. OLS

Table 9.3 Descriptive statistics

. sum MDR REV_TA mtb_w LN_TA PPE_TA Dummy_rd Ind_Mean_MDR firm_age fo return_sd

Variable	Obs.	Mean	Std. Dev.	Min	Max
MDR	20388	0.161	0.211	0.000	0.995
REV_TA	22166	0.233	0.302	0.000	22.769
mtb_w	20576	3.953	5.924	−5.952	40.045
LN_TA	22616	6.299	2.616	1.469	12.736
PPE_TA	20512	0.124	0.179	0.000	0.995
Dummy_rd	47712	0.023	0.148	0.000	1.000
Ind_Mean_MDR	47712	0.153	0.124	0.000	0.778
firm_age	22792	1.966	1.128	0.000	4.984
fo	25790	0.186	0.154	−0.001	1.000
return_sd	23690	0.224	0.177	0.000	1.319

```
Test of H0: Difference in coefficients not systematic

   chi2(22) = (b-B)'[(V_b-V_B)^(-1)](b-B)
            = 1021.40
Prob > chi2 =  0.0000
```

Figure 9.1. Hausman test result

Table 9.4 A partial-adjustment model of capital structure

Variables	(1) F_MDR OLS	(2) F_MDR FE	(4) F_MDR AB	(5) F_MDR BB	(6) F_MDR LSDVC
MDR	0.9197***	0.7977***	0.8018***	0.6405***	0.8436
	(118.449)	(55.961)	(36.836)	(18.572)	
REV_TA	0.0026	−0.0241**	0.0018	0.0147	−0.0233
	(0.837)	(−2.146)	(0.315)	(1.032)	
MTB	−0.0003***	−0.0001	−0.0005***	−0.0001	−0.0001
	(−3.680)	(−1.169)	(−3.797)	(−0.408)	
LN_TA	0.0012***	0.0025	0.0031***	0.0014	0.0035
	(3.236)	(1.166)	(3.997)	(0.260)	
PPE_TA	0.0016	0.0444***	0.0032	0.0106	0.0407
	(0.366)	(3.377)	(0.367)	(0.322)	
Dummy_RD	−0.0037**	−0.0001	−0.0052*	0.0006	0.0002
	(−2.285)	(−0.027)	(−1.645)	(0.069)	
Ind_Mean_MDR	0.0703***		0.1781***	0.6471***	
	(8.085)		(8.372)	(4.049)	
Firm_Age	−0.0013**	0.0057**	−0.0019	0.0017	0.0061
	(−2.168)	(2.446)	(−1.582)	(0.195)	
FO	0.0072	−0.0068	0.0099	−0.0007	−0.0055
	(1.547)	(−0.641)	(1.145)	(−0.017)	(.)
Return_Sd	−0.0042	−0.0092**	0.0027	−0.0063	−0.0099
	(−1.119)	(−2.042)	(0.470)	(−0.503)	
Year dummies	Yes	Yes	Yes	Yes	Yes
Constant	−0.0113***	0.0028	−0.0249***	−0.0636*	
	(−3.135)	(0.228)	(−4.653)	(−1.863)	
Obs.	15,912	15,912	15,912	15,912	15,912
No. firms		625	625	625	625
Wald statistics			19590.7	1922.33	
F-value	4080.04	368.14			
R2-overall/within	0.9036	0.6693			

```
------------------------------------------------------------------------------
Arellano-Bond test for AR(1) in first differences: z =  -8.23  Pr > z =  0.000
Arellano-Bond test for AR(2) in first differences: z =   1.80  Pr > z =  0.072
------------------------------------------------------------------------------
Sargan test of overid. restrictions: chi2(1537) =4413.21  Prob > chi2 =  0.000
  (Not robust, but not weakened by many instruments.)
Hansen test of overid. restrictions: chi2(1537) = 513.96  Prob > chi2 =  1.000
  (Robust, but weakened by many instruments.)

Difference-in-Hansen tests of exogeneity of instrument subsets:
  GMM instruments for levels
    Hansen test excluding group:     chi2(1483) = 480.36  Prob > chi2 =  1.000
    Difference (null H = exogenous): chi2(54)   =  33.60  Prob > chi2 =  0.987
  iv(REV_TA_w mtb_w LN_TA PPE_TA_w Dummy_rd Ind_Mean_MDR_w firm_age fo_w return_sd_w y2 y3
y4 y5 y6 y7 y8 y9 y10 y11 y12 y13 y > 14)
    Hansen test excluding group:     chi2(1515) = 458.38  Prob > chi2 =  1.000
    Difference (null H = exogenous): chi2(22)   =  55.57  Prob > chi2 =  0.000
```

Figure 9.2. Specification tests after AB model

with clustered standard errors provides an adjustment speed of 8% (1−0.9197), which is slightly lower than the 13% shown in Flannery and Hankins (2013) (see their Table 1, Panel A). Consistent with Flannery and Hankins (2013), OLS provides the lowest adjustment speed while the highest adjustment speed estimate, 36% (1–0.6405), is obtained in the BB regression. In contrast, the FE model in Flannery and Hankins (2013) provides the highest adjustment speed estimate (25%). Correcting the FE-estimated coefficients in the LSDVC model gives an adjusted speed estimate of 16%.

Taken together, if the assumption that the independent variables are exogenous holds, and that the second-order autocorrelation is absent, the result from the LSDVC model would be the most accurate panel-data estimator across the models, when faced with data limitations of short and unbalanced panels. The test results using the AB model in Figure 9.2 confirm that the second-order autocorrelation is not significant at the 5% level. The Hansen test of overidentification suggests that you cannot reject the null hypothesis of joint validity of the full instrument set. However, this test is prone to some weakness, as it tends to grow weaker the more moment conditions you have in the model. Intuitively, you first aim to obtain that $\frac{1}{n}\sum_{i=1}^{n} Z_i e_i = 0$ by using an optimal weighting matrix that minimizes the asymptotic variance of the estimator, and then test whether it is 0; this makes less sense (see Roodman, 2009 for further discussion).

Indeed, the unreliably good *p*-values of 1.00 obtained in the Hansen test indicate that the test is weakened with the problem of too many instruments (see Ruud, 2000). This means that the endogenous variable, MDR, has been overfit. Unfortunately, there does not seem to be any clear guidance on how many instruments would be too many as it is an empirical question. For instance, Windmeijer (2005) documents that reducing the number of instruments from 28 to 13 seems to reduce the average bias in the two-step estimate of the parameter of interest by 40%. Indeed, the default number of instruments in the AB model in this exercise turns out to be huge, 1561. In a further analysis you could reduce the number of instruments and test the robustness of the results.

9.14 Lab Work: Panel-Data Analysis

Use Chapter_9_MTB.dta (available at www.cambridge.org/Mavruk) for this problem set. This is the same dataset as you have used in the Basic Data Analysis in Stata session. You will examine the determinants of the market-to-book value as well as ROA, using panel-data techniques.

Begin by declaring the data as panel data:

```
egen isin_id = group(isin)
tab isin_id
xtset isin_id period
```

Problem set

1. Present panel descriptive statistics of the variables that are included in the model (mtb, mean_return, vol, liquidity, mktcap, tangibility, beta). The basic features you should focus on are: how many firms the variable covers; how many firm-year observations the variable has; what the T-bar represents; what is the average value of the variable in the overall sample. Also interpret the overall, between, and within variation. It is enough if you choose two variables from the table and interpret these statistics.

   Useful Stata commands:

   ```
   xtsum
   ```

2. Regress the market-to-book value (mtb) on the firm characteristics (mean_return vol liquidity mktcap tangibility beta) and include year fixed effects using OLS. Revise your analysis by regressing ROA on the same firm characteristics and include year fixed effects in OLS. (i) Use robust standard errors. (ii) Use standard errors that are clustered on firm id (isin_id). Interpret and compare your results.

   Useful Stata commands:

   ```
   xi: reg Y X i.year, robust
   xi: reg Y X i.year, cluster(isin_id)
   ```

   Note that "xi:" and "i.year" combined will generate year fixed effects (dummy variables) automatically.

3. Revise your analyses for both MTB and ROA and estimate a random-effects model. Cluster the standard errors on firm id. Interpret your results. Test for random effects using the Breusch–Pagan LM test. Should you choose a random-effects model or the CLRM using the OLS estimator? Explain your steps and interpret the test results.

   Useful Stata commands:

   ```
   xtreg, xttest0
   ```

4. Revise your analyses for both MTB and ROA and estimate a fixed-effects model. Test for individual effects. Interpret your results. Note that you can only test for individual effects when you do not cluster the standard errors.

   Useful Stata commands:

   ```
   xtreg
   ```

5. Test for endogeneity of the variables using the Hausman test. Do not include time dummies and do not cluster the standard errors in this specification. This test will also show whether random effects or fixed effects should be used. Explain and interpret your results. Which model should you use to examine the determinants of MTB? Which model should you use to examine the determinants of ROA?

Useful Stata commands:

```
xtreg mtb mean_return vol liquidity mktcap tangibility
  beta, fe
est store fixed
xtreg mtb mean_return vol liquidity mktcap tangibility
  beta, re
hausman fixed
xtreg roa mean_return vol liquidity mktcap tangibility
  beta, fe
est store fixed
xtreg roa mean_return vol liquidity mktcap tangibility
  beta, re
hausman fixed
```

6. Estimate the MTB and ROA regressions by using the first-differenced OLS. Explain how this model works and what the difference is between this model and the fixed-effects model. Interpret your results.
   Useful Stata commands:

```
xi: reg d.mtb d.mean_return d.vol d.liquidity d.mktcap
d.tangibility d.beta, cluster(isin_id)
xi: reg d.roa d.mean_return d.vol d.liquidity d.mktcap
d.tangibility d.beta, cluster(isin_id)
```

7. DiD analysis: Examine the hypothesis whether firm managers have been taking unnecessary idiosyncratic risk to boost their revenues after endowment insurance accounts in Sweden became popular in 2012.

```
_rsq_: idiosyncratic risk
```

   Run the DiD estimator below and interpret your findings. Do the results support the hypothesis?
   Stata code:

```
gen treated=0
replace treated=1 if _rsq_> .1720151 /*you assume high
idiosyncratic risk if it is greater than average*/
replace treated=. if _rsq_==.
tab treated
gen event_period=0
replace event_period=1 if year>=2012
replace event_period=. if year==.
tab event_period
gen did=treated*event_period
tab did
reg mtb treated event_period did, cluster(isin_id)
```

```
reg roa treated event_period did, cluster(isin_id)
reg mtb treated event_period did mean_return vol
liquidity mktcap tangibility beta, cluster(isin_id)
reg roa treated event_period did mean_return vol
liquidity mktcap tangibility beta, cluster(isin_id)
```

8. To practice dynamic panel-data models, regress the dependent variables MTB and ROA on one-period-lagged dependent variables and on the other control variables. For this question, use Arellano and Bond's (1991) difference GMM estimates (AB). Explain how this model works and interpret your results.

   Stata code:

```
xtabond2 mtb l.mtb mean_return vol liquidity mktcap
tangibility beta i.year, robust gmm(l.mtb) iv(mean_
return vol liquidity mktcap tangibility beta i.year)
xtabond2 roa l.roa mean_return vol liquidity mktcap
tangibility beta i.year, robust gmm(l.mtb) iv(mean_
return vol liquidity mktcap tangibility beta i.year)
```

9. Use Blundell and Bond's (1998) system GMM estimates (BB). Explain how this model works and interpret your results.

   Note that the model does not allow factor variables (i.year). Instead, we generate year dummies (y1–y5) and include them (minus one dummy) in the model.

   Stata code:

```
tab year, gen(y)
xtdpdsys mtb l.mtb mean_return vol liquidity mktcap
tangibility beta y2-y5, vce(robust)
xtdpdsys roa l.roa mean_return vol liquidity mktcap
tangibility beta y2-y5, vce(robust)
```

10. Use the least-squares dummy variable correction (LSDVC) model with initial values from the AB estimator in Question 8. Explain how this model works and interpret your results.

    Note that the model does not allow factor variables and time-series operators, so you need to generate a one-period-lagged dependent variable instead.

    Stata code:

```
gen lmtb=l.mtb
xtlsdvc mtb lmtb mean_return vol liquidity mktcap
tangibility beta y2-y5, initial(ab)
gen lroa=l.roa
xtlsdvc roa lroa mean_return vol liquidity mktcap
tangibility beta y2-y5, initial(ab)
```

Good luck!

9.15 Mini Case

Using detailed data on large asset managers' capital market assumptions, Dahlquist and Ibert (2023) examine the relationship between subjective equity premium expectations, equity valuations, and financial portfolios. The dataset in the study is interesting. Large asset managers seem to disclose their return expectations across different asset classes on their websites. The authors use this information to evaluate whether large asset managers' portfolios reflect their expectations. The results show that the managers' equity premium expectations are heterogenous and countercyclical. Their equity premium expectations are high when valuations are low, and vice versa. In the main analysis the authors use equity premium (over yield and over cash) and equity return (nominal) as dependent variables. The main independent variable of interest is the log of the cyclically adjusted price-to-earnings ratio (CAPE). The regressions are run by considering equity premium expectations for all horizons and for a given date, only one equity premium expectation per asset manager (the one closest to a horizon of 10 years). All regressions include a manager × horizon fixed effect. Standard errors in the regressions are clustered by year-month and manager.

Task

1. Go to the link: Dahlquist_Ibert_replication.zip – Review of Financial Studies Dataverse (harvard.edu)
   Download the dataset: asset_manager_return_expectations_modified.dta
   Download the do file: Tables 1-4.do
2. Go to the link: Equity Return Expectations and Portfolios: Evidence from Large Asset Managers by Magnus Dahlquist, Markus Ibert :: SSRN https://papers.ssrn.com/sol3/papers.cfm?abstract_id=3763796
   Download the paper. The full text is publicly available at the link.
3. Replicate Panel A of Table 2 in the paper. Present and explain your results.
4. Replicate Panel B of Table 2 in the paper. Present and explain your results.
5. Revise your analysis in Panel B of Table 2 with only manager fixed effects. Present and explain your results.
6. Revise your analysis in Panel B of Table 2 by clustering only on manager. Present and explain your results.

9.16 Summary

Panel data consists of multiple observations for each unit in the data. The units could be investors, firms, households, and so on. Panel datasets that allow us to follow these units over time provide intuitive understanding of the unit's behavior. However, in some situations where the units cannot be followed over time, panel data can also be generated by pooling time-series data across some cross-sectional cohorts. The analysis made using panel data tends to outperform the analysis based on cross-sectional datasets, mainly because panel-data analysis is better at addressing the causality issues in research than cross-sectional data. The main reason is that cross-sectional analysis provides inference on the relationship at the time of measurement in the cross-sectional datasets. However, time-series information on the unit in panel datasets allows us not only to model observed unit behavior over time, but also to make some assumptions as well as model the unobserved unit behavior over time. This helps to draw more reliable causal relationships from panel-data analysis than from a cross-sectional analysis, although the endogeneity issue may not be totally eliminated using only panel-data analysis.

This chapter provides a wide range of examples of panel-data techniques, with a main focus on linear panel-data models. It covers the pooled OLS estimator, fixed-effects model, least-squares dummy variable estimator, difference-in-differences model, between estimator, random-effects model, Hausman–Taylor random-effects instrumental variable method, and briefly, dynamic panel-data models. The chapter discusses inference and stationarity in panel data and briefly reviews the generalized method of moments (GMM). An application of linear panel-data models, as well as lab work and a mini case, are provided at the end of the chapter.

KEY TERMS

Panel-data analysis; error-components model; fixed-effects model; random-effects model; first-difference model; difference-in-differences model; Hausman–Taylor random-effects model; inference in panel data; stationarity in panel data; GMM; dynamic panel-data models; application of linear panel-data models.

REFERENCES

Arellano, M. 1987. Computing robust standard errors for within-groups estimators. *Oxford Bulletin of Economics and Statistics*, 49, 431–434.

Arellano, M. and Bond, S. 1991. Some tests of specification for panel data: Monte Carlo evidence and an application to employment equations. *Review of Economic Studies*, 58, 277–294.

Arellano, M. and Bover, O. 1995. Another look at the instrumental variable estimation of error-components models. *Journal of Econometrics*, 68, 29–51.

Baker, M. and Wurgler, J. 2002. Market timing and capital structure. *The Journal of Finance*, 57, 1–32.

Baltagi, B. H. 2008. *Econometric Analysis of Panel Data*. Wiley, Chichester.

Baltagi, B. H. and Song, S. H. 2006. Unbalanced panel data: A survey. *Statistical Papers*, 47, 493–523.

Baum, C. F., Schaffer, M. E., and Stillman, S. 2003. Instrumental variables and GMM: Estimation and testing. *The Stata Journal*, 3, 1–31.

Berk, J. and DeMarzo, P. 2020. *Corporate Finance* (5th ed.). Pearson Education, London.

Bertrand, M., Duflo, E., and Mullainathan, S. 2004. How much should we trust differences-in-differences estimates? *Quarterly Journal of Economics*, 119, 249–275.

Blundell, R. and Bond, S. 1998. Initial conditions and moment restrictions in dynamic panel data models. *Journal of Econometrics*, 87, 115–143.

Bruno, G. S. F. 2005. Approximating the bias of the LSDV estimator for dynamic unbalanced panel data model. *Economic Letters*, 87, 361–366.

Cameron, A. C. and Miller, D. L. 2015. A practitioner's guide to cluster-robust inference. *Journal of Human Resources*, 50, 317–372.

Choi, I. 2001. Unit root tests for panel data. *Journal of International Money and Finance*, 20, 249–272.

Custódio, C., Ferreira, M. A., and Matos, P. 2013. Generalists versus specialists: Lifetime work experience and chief executive officer pay. *Journal of Financial Economics*, 108, 471–492.

Dahlquist, M. and Ibert, M. 2023. Equity return expectations and portfolios: Evidence from large asset managers. Swedish House of Finance Research Paper No. 21-1. https://ssrn.com/abstract=3763796 or http://dx.doi.org/10.2139/ssrn.3763796

Donaldson, G. 1961. *Corporate Debt Capacity: A Study of Corporate Debt Policy and the Determination of Corporate Debt Capacity*. Harvard University Press, Boston, MA.

Flannery, M. J. and Hankins, K. W. 2013. Estimating dynamic panel models in corporate finance. *Journal of Corporate Finance*, 41, 41–73.

Flannery, M. J. and Rangan, K. P. 2006. Partial adjustment toward target capital. *Journal of Financial Economics*, 41, 41–73.

Graham, J. and Harvey, C. 2001. The theory and practice of corporate finance: Evidence from the field. *Journal of Financial Economics*, 60, 187–243.

Hahn, J., Hausman, J., and Kuersteiner, G. 2007. Long difference instrumental variables estimation for dynamic panel models with fixed effects. *Journal of Econometrics*, 140, 574–617.

Hansen, B. E. 2000. *Econometrics*. University of Wisconsin, Madison, WI. www.ssc.wisc.edu/~bhansen/notes/notes.htm.

Hansen, L. 1982. Large sample properties of generalized method of moments estimators. *Econometrica*, 50, 1029–1054.

Harris, R. D. F. and Tzavalis, E. 1999. Inference for unit roots in dynamic panels where the time dimension is fixed. *Journal of Econometrics*, 91, 201–226.

Hausman, J. A. 1978. Specification tests in econometrics. *Econometrica*, 46, 1251–1271.

Hausman, J. A. and Taylor, W. E. 1981. Panel data and unobservable individual effects. *Econometrica*, 49, 1377–1398.

Hayashi, F. 2000. *Econometrics*. Princeton University Press, Princeton, NJ.

Hsiao, C. 2003. *Analysis of Panel Data* (2nd ed.). Cambridge University Press, Cambridge.

Huang, R. and Ritter, J. 2009. Testing theories of capital structure and estimating speed of adjustment. *Journal of Financial and Quantitative Analysis*, 44, 237–271.

Im, K., Pesaran, M. H., and Shin, Y. 2003. Testing for unit roots in heterogeneous panels. *Journal of Econometrics*, 115, 29–52.

Kiviet, J. F. 1995. On bias, inconsistency, and efficiency of various estimators in dynamic panel data models. *Journal of Econometrics*, 68, 53–78.

Levin, A., Lin, C.-F., and Chu, S.-S. J. 2002. Unit root tests in panel data: Asymptotic and finite-sample properties. *Journal of Econometrics*, 108, 1–24.

Maddala, G. S. and Wu, S. 1999. A comparative study of unit root tests with panel data and a new simple test. *Oxford Bulletin of Economics and Statistics*, 61, 631–652.

Maddala, G. S., Wu, S., and Liu, P. C. 2000. Do panel data rescue purchasing power parity (PPP) theory? In J. Krishnakumar and E. Ronchetti (eds), *Panel Data Econometrics: Future Directions*. North Holland, Amsterdam, pp. 35–51.

Mavruk, T. 2021. Cross-regional differences in news tone and local stock ownership. *Management Science*, 67, 3276–3298.

Modigliani, F. and Miller, M. 1958. The cost of capital, corporation finance, and the theory of investment. *American Economic Review*, 48, 655–669.

Myers, S. 1984. The capital structure puzzle. *The Journal of Finance*, 39, 575–592.

Nijman, Th. E. and Verbeek, M. 1990. Estimation of time dependent parameters in linear models using cross sections, panels or both. *Journal of Econometrics*, 46, 333–346.

Pagan, A. R. and Hall, D. 1983. Diagnostic tests as residual analysis. *Econometric Reviews*, 2, 159–218.

Pesaran, M. H. and Smith, R. P. 1995. Estimation of long-run relationships from dynamic heterogeneous panels. *Journal of Econometrics*, 68, 79–113.

Phillips, P. C. B. and Moon, H. R. 1999. Linear regression limit theory for nonstationary panel data. *Econometrica*, 67, 1057–1111.

Quah, D. 1994. Exploiting cross-section variation for unit root inference in dynamic data. *Economics Letters*, 44, 9–19.

Roberts, M. R. and Whited, T. M. 2013. Endogeneity in empirical corporate finance. In *Handbook of the Economics of Finance*. Elsevier, New York.

Roodman, D. 2009. How to do xtabond2: An introduction to difference and system GMM in Stata. *The Stata Journal*, 9, 86–136.

Ruud, P. A. 2000. *An Introduction to Classical Econometric Theory*. Oxford University Press, Oxford.

Stock, J. and Watson, M. 2019. *Introduction to Econometrics: Global Edition*. Princeton University Press, Princeton, NJ.

Verbeek, M. 2004. *A Guide to Modern Econometrics* (2nd ed.). Wiley, Chichester.

Welch, I. 2004. Capital structure and stock returns. *Journal of Political Economy*, 112, 106–131.

Windmeijer, F. 2005. A finite sample correction for the variance of linear efficient two-step GMM estimators. *Journal of Econometrics*, 126, 25–51.

10 Selection of Models with Limited Dependent Variables

INTRODUCTION

The ordinary least squares (OLS) estimation methods examining the cross-sectional data in Chapter 5 or panel data in Chapter 9 assume that the dependent variable is continuous, measured quantitatively, while independent variables may or may not be continuous. Some corporate finance decisions are based on qualitative measures and it is important to model them to better understand firm managers' (or institutions') decisions, although qualitative measures would provide somehow less information than quantitative measures. Readers are referred to Chapter 2 for a definition of the level of variables and the distinction between quantitative and qualitative variables. Some examples for such decisions could be as follows:

- Decision to pay dividends.
- Decision to engage in stock splits.
- Decision to engage in repurchase of shares.
- Decision to issue equity or bonds.
- Decision to list the stock on an exchange.
- Decision to provide credits.
- Decision to invest, expand, abandon, or contract.

These are binary, yes or no, questions and can be coded as a 0–1 dummy variable since there are only two possible outcomes. These binary variables are used as dependent variables in the regression models. There are also some examples of decisions that are based on categories and may take more than two values. For example, studies that use category-dependent variables could be those examining the determinants of firms' credit ratings (Poon, 2003) or determinants of Morning Star's fund ratings (Fang, Holmen, and Mavruk, 2021). Categorical variables are discrete or qualitative variables, but in studies they are quantified and coded just as the binary variables described above.

The binary or category-dependent variables lead to non-linear relationships between the dependent and the independent variables. A non-linear relationship can be interpreted as, for example: a one-unit change at the lower levels of an independent variable may increase the dependent variable, but a one-unit change at the higher levels of the same independent variable may not be related to or may even decrease the dependent variable. This means, in non-linear models, that a change in the independent variable does not always have the same effect on the dependent variable. In linear models, a change in the independent variable always has a constant effect (or no relation at all) on the dependent variable, regardless of the level of the independent variable used to calculate the change (Stock and Watson, 2019).

Examining non-linear relationships in a regression model is more complex. Thus, instead of using linear models, which are covered in Chapters 5–9, this chapter emphasizes the use of non-linear models to capture such complex non-linear relationships. However, the chapter also presents the linear probability model (LPM), which disregards the binary nature of the dependent variable and uses OLS estimation (see Chapter 5). This chapter discusses the advantages and disadvantages of the LPM.

Although non-linear models are the main focus of this chapter, it is essential to note that both the implementation and the economic interpretation of non-linear models are challenging. Since the book is applied in nature, the focus is more on applications and interpretations. Readers will benefit from the Stata code provided (Python and R are also available on the online resources page: www.cambridge.org/mavruk) for the implementation of the non-linear models. The chapter emphasizes the interpretation of the results from the non-linear models by focusing on the calculations and interpretation of marginal effects. The chapter provides a review of various econometric methods to examine binary or categorical classifications from linear probability models, logit or probit models, to more advanced tobit and sample-selection models for the outcome variable used to make decisions. In this sense, the chapter is in the style of a survey presenting a list of micro-econometric models that are commonly used in corporate finance studies. Readers are referred to Wooldridge (2002) and Stock and Watson (2019) for more (technical) details and derivations of the models. The chapter ends with an application of selected non-linear models, lab work, and a mini case.

10.1 Linear Probability Model

The linear probability model (LPM) is a simple approach to examine the limited dependent-variable models. It assumes that the probability of an event occurring is linearly related to the independent variables. Since the probabilities are not observed, the dependent variable in the model is the 0–1 dummy variable and the independent variables can be continuous or categorical. This is a linear model estimated by OLS. The predicted values from the estimation would provide the estimated probabilities of the occurrence of the event for each observation (or unit). The major advantage of the LPM is that it is easier to interpret the estimated coefficients. Studies may also use the LPM, to begin with, in order to obtain some sort of benchmark and compare the results to those obtained from the non-linear models.

The coefficients obtained from the LPM are interpreted as the marginal effect (if the independent variable is continuous) of X on the probability of an event. That is, the percentage point change in the probability of an event for a one-unit change in X, holding the effect of all other independent variables constant. The model is given by

$$P_i = \beta_0 + \beta_1 x_{1,i} + \beta_2 x_{2,i} + \dots + \beta_n x_{n,i} + e_i, \tag{10.1}$$

where $P_i = y_i$ takes the value 1 for occurrence of an event, and 0 otherwise.

10.1.1 Shortcomings of the LPM

Although the LPM is straightforward to estimate and interpret, there are some important shortcomings. Since it is an OLS estimate, the standard assumptions of the classical linear regression model (CLRM) on the residual term should hold. However, the dependent variable is binary and hence most of the assumptions on the standard errors will be violated. In particular, the heteroskedasticity assumption will not hold with the binary variable. Since the dependent variable is binary, residuals will take only two values conditional on the independent variables. Relatedly, the residuals will not be normally distributed, implying that the OLS point estimates are unbiased but inference in small samples cannot be based on the conventional *t*-test, which has a normality-based distribution.

There are other flaws with the linear probability model as well. When predicting the dependent variable and examining its distribution, it may be that the predicted dependent variable extends below 0 and above 1. This is not reasonable, as the predicted dependent variable is the probability of an event occurring (by definition, the probability cannot be below 0 or above 1). Literature using the limited dependent-variable model tends to truncate the values at 0 and 1, but this solution implies knowing ex-ante that the event will either not occur or will occur with certainty. It is similar to the argument of whether the future can be predicted.

A closely related issue is the interpretation; it does not make sense to expect a linear relationship between the probability of an outcome and a continuous independent variable for all possible values. The interpretation may hold for the average value of the independent variable, but it is difficult to argue that the effect on the probability will be constant for very high or very low values of the independent variable. Because of these flaws in the linear probability model, researchers favor non-linear models. The LMP can be used as a pilot study, but it is difficult to argue that you are modeling the probability of an event. If used, it is good to know that the LPM provides more robust estimates of the marginal effects on the probability of an event near the center of the distribution of the independent variable. The brief description of the non-linear models below draws on Wooldridge (2002), Stock and Watson (2019), and Söderbom (2022).

10.2 Logit and Probit Models

Logit and probit models are used especially when you have binary dependent variables. These models remedy the above-mentioned problems in the LPM. Consider the following model:

$$P(y_i = 1 \mid x_i) = g(\beta_0 + \beta_1 x_{1,i} + \beta_2 x_{2,i} + \dots + \beta_n x_{n,i}) = G(\mathbf{x}\boldsymbol{\beta}), \tag{10.2}$$

where G is a function that takes values between 0 and 1. This model is referred to as an index model, as the probability of an event is a function of independent variables through an index that is bounded between 0 and 1. This setting addresses the main problems with LPM. The function G is known as a cumulative density function (CDF), which is monotonically increasing in the index. If $P(y_i = 1 \mid x_i) \to 1$ then $\mathbf{x}\boldsymbol{\beta} \to \infty$ and if $P(y_i = 1 \mid x_i) \to 0$ then $\mathbf{x}\boldsymbol{\beta} \to -\infty$. This makes $G(\mathbf{x}\boldsymbol{\beta})$ a non-linear function. The model will not produce a constant parameter estimate for $\mathbf{x}$, meaning that OLS cannot be used. The assumption on the distribution of the function G determines the choice of the non-linear model. The most commonly used distributions are the logistic distribution and the standard normal distribution. The former assumption allows us to use the logit model, while the latter assumption leads to the probit model. The logit function is given by

$$G(\mathbf{x}\boldsymbol{\beta}) = \frac{\exp(\mathbf{x}\boldsymbol{\beta})}{1+\exp(\mathbf{x}\boldsymbol{\beta})} = \Lambda(\mathbf{x}\boldsymbol{\beta}), \tag{10.3}$$

where again $\Lambda(\mathbf{x}\boldsymbol{\beta})$ is a CDF for the logistic distribution that is bounded between 0 and 1. Instead, if the standard normal distribution is assumed for $G(\mathbf{x}\boldsymbol{\beta})$, the CDF is given by

$$G(\mathbf{x}\boldsymbol{\beta}) = \Phi(\mathbf{x}\boldsymbol{\beta}) = \int_{-\infty}^{\mathbf{x}\boldsymbol{\beta}} \phi\,(v)\,dv, \tag{10.4}$$

where $\phi(v)$ is the normal density function, given by

$$\phi(v) = \frac{1}{\sqrt{2\pi}} \exp\left(-\frac{v^2}{2}\right). \tag{10.5}$$

Both logit and probit functions increase in $\mathbf{x}\boldsymbol{\beta}$, but at the extreme value of $\mathbf{x}\boldsymbol{\beta}$ the effect on the function G is 0, implying that the marginal effects of continuous independent variables are non-linear and hence rejecting the use of OLS.

10.2.1 Latent-Variable Model

The logit and probit models would help solve many problems in the LPM, however, modeling the dependent variable is the same in these binary choice models. The dependent variable takes 0 or 1, which is the observed outcome, the action that the firm manager takes or makes a decision. However, the underlying reason is not observed. For instance, a firm manager makes a capital structure decision after many cost and benefit analyses and eliminates the alternative decision on whether to pay dividends. This net utility to the manager, or to the firm, of paying dividends is not directly observed in such models. In this example, net utility can be a continuous variable, which is unobserved. Such a variable is called a latent variable y^* and is given by

$$y_i^* = \beta_0 + \beta_1 x_{1,i} + \beta_2 x_{2,i} + \cdots + \beta_n x_{n,i} + e_i = \mathbf{x}\boldsymbol{\beta} + e_i. \tag{10.6}$$

The latent variable y_i^* is not observed, but the binary decision made by the firm manager y_i is observed:

$$y_i = 1 \text{ if } y_i^* > 0, \qquad (10.7)$$
$$y_i = 0 \text{ if } y_i^* \leq 0.$$

If you can obtain data on y_i^*, the net utility to managers, then you can simply use OLS. Part A of the Appendix for Chapter 10 at the end of the book provides a derivation of logit and probit models from a latent variable framework for a binary response model.

10.3 Maximum-Likelihood Estimation

Unlike the LPM, logit and probit models are non-linear and thus you need to use maximum-likelihood (ML) estimation instead of OLS when estimating such models. Suppose that you have an independent variable, **x**, in the population and the objective is to estimate the vector of unknown parameters, β, thus the function is $f(\mathbf{x},\beta)$. You draw a random sample from the population, $\{x_{1,i}, x_{2,i}, \ldots, x_{n,i}\}$, to estimate the parameters of β. ML is the estimator $\hat{\beta}_{\text{ML}}$ that provides the greatest likelihood of obtaining the sample $\{x_{1,i}, x_{2,i}, \ldots, x_{n,i}\}$, more formally:

$$L(\beta; x_{1,i}, x_{2,i}, \ldots, x_{n,i}) = \prod_{i=1}^{n} f(\mathbf{x};\beta), \qquad (10.8)$$

where the product of individual likelihoods is $f(x_1;\beta) \times f(x_2;\beta) \times \cdots \times f(x_n;\beta)$. The value of β is the maximum-likelihood value of the function and thus the $\hat{\beta}_{\text{ML}}$ estimator. It is easier to work with sums than products, and hence the log-likelihood function is used instead:

$$\ln L = (\beta; x_{1,i}, x_{2,i}, \ldots, x_{n,i}) = \sum_{i=1}^{n} \ln f(\mathbf{x};\beta). \qquad (10.9)$$

To estimate logit and probit models, the ML estimation can be written as follows:

$$L(y \mid \mathbf{x};\beta) = \prod_{i=1}^{n} G(\mathbf{x}\beta)^{y_i} \left[1 - G(\mathbf{x}\beta)\right]^{(1-y_i)}, \qquad (10.10)$$

where the maximized $\hat{\beta}_{\text{ML}}$ would provide the greatest likelihood of observing the sample of $\{y_1, y_2, \ldots, y_n\}$. The probability of observing $y_i = 1$ is $G(\mathbf{x}\beta)$ and the probability of observing $y_i = 0$ is $[1 - G(\mathbf{x}\beta)]$. The log-likelihood function is given by

$$\ln L(y_i \mid \mathbf{x};\beta) = \sum_{i=1}^{n} \left\{ y_i \ln G(\mathbf{x}\beta) + (1 - y_i) \ln\left[1 - G(\mathbf{x}\beta)\right] \right\}. \qquad (10.11)$$

If you assume a logistic distribution for $G(\mathbf{x}\beta)$, you can replace the function with $\Lambda(\mathbf{x}\beta)$ and if you assume a standard normal distribution for $G(\mathbf{x}\beta)$, you can replace it with $\Phi(\mathbf{x}\beta)$.[1]

[1] See Wooldridge (2002) for how these functions are derived.

10.4 Interpretation of the Logit and Probit Models

The crucial part of the analysis is to interpret the marginal effect (of continuous variables) and the relative effect (of dummy variables) on the probability of decision or response, $P(y_i = 1)$. The marginal effect of a continuous variable $x_{1,i}$ in the LPM is its estimated parameter β_1, which is constant. However, it is not that simple in logit or probit models. The marginal effect in non-linear models is the partial derivative given by

$$\frac{\partial P(y_i = 1)}{\partial x_{1,i}} = \frac{\partial G(\mathbf{x}\boldsymbol{\beta})}{\partial x_{1,i}} = g(\mathbf{x}\boldsymbol{\beta}) \times \beta_1, \tag{10.12}$$

where $g(\mathbf{x}\boldsymbol{\beta})$ is the probability density function of $G(\mathbf{x}\boldsymbol{\beta})$. The sign of the marginal effect will be the same as the estimated parameter β_1, since the probability density is non-negative. The non-linearity is about the parameter: because $g(\mathbf{x}\boldsymbol{\beta})$ will be different for each value of $x_{1,i}$, you will have different values of the marginal effect and hence it is the non-linear effect. The software usually uses the mean values to evaluate the marginal effects, although you may use a different value for $x_{1,i}$.

How about when the independent variable is discrete? You can examine the relative effect (RLE) of a discrete independent variable (i.e., $x_{2,i}$):

$$\text{RLE} = G(\beta_0 + 1x_{1,i} + \beta_2 x_{2,i} + \cdots + \beta_n x_{n,i}) - G(\beta_0 + 0x_{1,i} + \beta_2 x_{2,i} + \cdots + \beta_n x_{n,i}), \tag{10.13}$$

where the values of the other coefficients are also needed to compute the RLE. Similar to the marginal effects, the sign of the RLE is the same as the sign of the estimated coefficient (β_2 in this example).

10.4.1 Odds Ratio for the Logit Model

It is not uncommon to interpret the estimates from a logit model in terms of the odds ratio. The odds ratio measures the probability of $y_i = 1$ relative to the probability of $y_i = 0$, $\frac{P(y_i=1)}{1-P(y_i=1)}$:

$$P(y_i = 1) = \frac{\exp(\mathbf{x}'\boldsymbol{\beta})}{1 + \exp(\mathbf{x}'\boldsymbol{\beta})}, \tag{10.14}$$

$$\frac{P(y_i = 1)}{1 - P(y_i = 1)} = \exp(\mathbf{x}'\boldsymbol{\beta}),$$

$$\ln \frac{P(y_i = 1)}{1 - P(y_i = 1)} = \mathbf{x}'\boldsymbol{\beta}.$$

For instance, if the odds ratio is 2, the interpretation is that the outcome $y_i = 1$ is twice as likely as the outcome $y_i = 0$.

10.5 Likelihood Ratio Test

To examine how the overall model performs given the independent variables, the likelihood ratio test (LRT) is used. The LRT is executed in logarithms, hence the difference of log-likelihoods is used, which then follows a χ^2 distribution under certain conditions. You first compute the log-likelihood ratio as the difference between the log-likelihood value for the unrestricted model, L_{ur}, and the log-likelihood value for the restricted model, L_r. The unrestricted model is the one that includes a full set of independent variables. The restricted model is the one that includes the number of independent variables, whose effects on the dependent variable are being tested. The number of restrictions depends on the number of individual hypotheses that are of interest. For instance, if the aim is to test whether $\beta_1 = 0$ in the model above, then the restricted model is $G(\beta_0 + \beta_1 x_{1,i})$, whereas the unrestricted model is the full one, $G(\beta_0 + \beta_1 x_{1,i} + \beta_2 x_{2,i} + \cdots + \beta_n x_{n,i})$. You obtain two log-likelihood values from these models and then compute the following log-likelihood ratio (LR) statistic:

$$\text{LR} = 2(\ln L_{\text{ur}} - \ln L_r). \tag{10.15}$$

The resulting LR value is compared with a critical value that is χ^2 distributed, with the loss in the number of degrees of freedom equal to the number of restrictions imposed. In this example, it is 1. If the computed LR value is greater than the critical value, you can reject the null hypothesis that the model is a bad fit. Since ML maximizes the log-likelihood function, lower values of log-likelihood indicate a better fit. In the example above, if β_1 turns out to be significant, then the log-likelihood value obtained from the restricted model will be lower. If you test more hypotheses, imposing more restrictions, and find that these tested coefficients are significant, then the log-likelihood value from the restricted model will be even lower, allowing larger differences between $\ln L_{\text{ur}} - \ln L_r$ and thus a higher LR.

10.6 Inference in Non-linear Models

To make an inference you need to estimate the standard errors, which is less complicated to do in linear models. In non-linear models, computation of the variance–covariance matrix, which is used to estimate standard errors, depends on the inverse of the negative Hessian matrix; that is, the matrix of the second-order derivates of the log-likelihood function (see Wooldridge, 2002). Once you compute the variance–covariance matrix, standard errors can be calculated by taking the square root of the diagonal elements of the covariance matrix. Dividing the parameter estimates by their standard errors will give the *t*-values.

The second-order derivative with respect to the parameter of interest gives the curvature of the log-likelihood function. The more curvature you have, the lower the variance will be. Recall that the aim is to obtain a lower log-likelihood value from the restricted model, to have a higher LR ratio and reject the null hypothesis of a bad fit. If you have a higher degree of curvature, you will not need a large deviation between the parameter value and its ML estimate. However, if the curvature is low, you need to move the parameter value quite far from its ML estimate to obtain a lower log-likelihood value from the restricted model, and thus a higher LR.

So far, the discussion has been about standard errors for the parameter estimates. But you also need to compute the standard errors for the marginal effects, which are easily calculated in Stata using the `mfx` command after probit or logit. The command uses the delta method to transform the standard errors for the ML parameter estimate to the standard errors for the marginal effects by implementing a Taylor series approximation.[2]

One problem with non-linear models such as probit and logit is that the heteroskedasticity affects the functional form of the model. This means that the parameter estimate obtained from, for instance, the probit model will be an inconsistent estimate of the parameter in the latent-variable model. Further, in the case of the CLRM, the endogeneity problem arises when missing (omitted) variables are correlated with the included independent variables. As discussed in Chapter 6, this biases the estimates of the linear coefficients as a result. However, if the omitted variables are not correlated with the included variables, the coefficients are not biased (due to the omitted-variable bias problem) in the CLRM. In this case, the omitted variables lead to an increase in the variance of the residuals (caused by unobserved heterogeneity), which is less of a concern. This is more problematic in non-linear models because the variance of the residuals (unobserved heterogeneity) affects the estimates of the coefficients in non-linear models (see Cramer, 2007; Wooldridge, 2002).

Most studies use robust standard errors in non-linear models for reliable inferences. As discussed in Chapter 5, robust standard errors consistently estimate the true standard errors and thus provide a basis for valid inferences about the coefficient estimates. Although unlikely for the non-linear models since they tend to be heteroskedastic by construction, if the model is nearly correct, the conventional standard errors are likely to be valid. Thus, the differences between the conventional and robust standard errors can be examined to validate the coefficient estimates. If it turns out that homoskedasticity-only and heteroskedasticity-robust standard errors are the same, there is no problem in using heteroskedasticity-robust standard errors. If they differ, you are better off using heteroskedasticity-robust standard errors. In general, economic theory does not give a convincing reason to assume that the residuals are homoskedastic. It is therefore more plausible to assume that the residuals are heteroskedastic, unless you have reason to believe otherwise (Stock and Watson, 2019). Thus, the simplest approach is to use heteroskedasticity-robust standard errors.

There are also some studies that address this source of inconsistency by modeling the heterogeneity. Alvarez and Brehm (1995) propose a model for the functional form of the heterogeneity based on Harvey's (1976) multiplicative

[2] See Wooldridge (2002) for details.

heteroskedasticity approach. This so-called heteroskedastic probit (hetprobit) model introduces variables accounting for alternative explanations in the error variance, making it somehow a generalized probit model.

Another problem with non-linear models is testing if the coefficient of the non-linear model has an interaction term. The calculation and significance test of the marginal (or relative) effect of an interaction term is not straightforward in non-linear models, and readers are referred to the method introduced by Ai and Norton (2003) and Norton, Wang, and Ai (2004). In particular, the latter study provides Stata codes for computation of the mean marginal effect and the mean z-value.

10.7 Goodness of Fit

To examine how the overall model performs, we observe the goodness-of-fit statistics. Non-linear models rely on two standard measures of goodness of fit: percentage correctly specified and pseudo R^2. For the first method, you begin by computing the estimated probability that $y_i = 1$. Note that the estimated probability is a continuous variable. To determine the predicted outcome $\hat{y}_i$, you have a threshold value of 0.5 and decide that $\hat{y}_i = 1$ if the estimated probability is greater than 0.5, else $\hat{y}_i = 0$. The percentage correctly specified is defined as the percentage of times the predicted outcome $\hat{y}_i$ matches the actual outcome y_i. It is informative to present the percentage correctly specified for both outcomes, 0 and 1.

The most often used pseudo R^2 measure is given as follows:

$$R^2 = 1 - \frac{\ln L_{\text{ur}}}{\ln L_r}, \tag{10.16}$$

where $\ln L_{\text{ur}}$ is the log-likelihood value obtained from the model that includes all the independent variables and $\ln L_r$ is the log-likelihood value obtained from the model with only an intercept. In Equation (10.16), if $\ln L_{\text{ur}} = \ln L_r$ then $R^2 = 0$. If $\ln L_{\text{ur}} \to 0$ then $R^2 \to 1$.

10.8 Multinomial Logit and Probit Models

In cases where the dependent variable has more than two categories, you cannot use a binary choice model (unless you transform the dependent variable to a binary one). Multinomial logit models are suitable if the dependent variable has more than two outcomes and these outcomes cannot be ordered in a natural way. One good example is the traveling choice models in transport economics, where you study the choice of traveling by train (1), bus (2), car (3), or bicycle (4). In this example, the dependent variable y_i takes on four categories j. You can code these categories as given within parentheses above. Here, the ordering of these numbers does not matter, you could just as well have coded train as $j = 4$. However, this coding will be helpful when interpreting the results, particularly for the choice of a reference category. Suppose you have some independent variables **x** that can explain this choice, then the conditional probability of choosing a category of transport is given by

$$P(y_i = j \mid \mathbf{x}) = \frac{\exp(\mathbf{x}'\beta_j)}{\sum_{k=1}^{m} \exp(\mathbf{x}'\beta_k)}, \tag{10.17}$$

where m indicates the total number of categories so the denominator is the sum of all categories. Since Equation (10.17) is a relative measure, the sum of the probabilities for each category must be 1, $\sum_{j=1}^{m} P_{ij} = 1$. One of the categories is used as a reference category, implying that you estimate $j-1$ parameters. You then interpret the parameters relative to the reference category. The software programs often choose the most frequent category as the reference category, but you can also impose a reference category. The derivation of marginal effects (MEs) is more complicated than the MEs in binary choice models, because the MEs in multinomial logit models do not depend just on the parameter of interest, but also on parameters for the other categories. This fact is one reason why the MEs may have a different sign than the estimated parameters. The parameter estimates will be different depending on the chosen reference category, but MEs for each category do not alter if you choose another reference category. MEs are given as a percentage and, unlike the parameter estimates, they are not interpreted relative to the benchmark, implying that the sum of the MEs will be zero.

Similar to the choice of logit and probit in binary choice models, you can also run a multinomial probit (Mprobit) model, which uses standard normal CDF. This would then examine the probability that the individual will choose alternative j. The parameter estimates from Mlogit and Mprobit might differ by a scale factor, but the MEs from these two models will be very similar. The same argument also holds for probit and logit in binary choice models. There will be very small differences in MEs, but it is good practice to run both models and observe the similarities in results.

Although the applications in corporate finance are not common, one extension to multinomial logit models is the conditional logit models that are used when the choice among the alternatives depends not only on the characteristics of the individuals, but also on the characteristics of the alternatives. Part B of the Appendix for Chapter 10 at the end of the book provides some details and examples of the conditional logit models.

10.8.1 Independence from Irrelevant Alternatives

The assumption of independence from irrelevant alternatives (IIA) suggests that when individuals choose among many alternatives, their odds of choosing, for example, A or B should not depend on some other alternative C. To provide an intuition, suppose that you aim to compare the probability of choosing train (1) to bus (2) in the multinomial logit model:

$$\frac{P(y_i = 1 \mid \mathbf{x})}{P(y_i = 2 \mid \mathbf{x})} = \frac{\dfrac{\exp(\mathbf{x}'\beta_1)}{\sum_{k=1}^{m} \exp(\mathbf{x}'\beta_k)}}{\dfrac{\exp(\mathbf{x}'\beta_2)}{\sum_{k=1}^{m} \exp(\mathbf{x}'\beta_k)}} = \frac{\exp(\mathbf{x}'\beta_1)}{\exp(\mathbf{x}'\beta_2)}. \tag{10.18}$$

The ratio of the probabilities in Equation (10.18) depends on β_1, β_2, and the independent variables $\mathbf{x}$, meaning that the parameters of the other categories are irrelevant when comparing the probability of choosing train and the probability of choosing bus. The commonly referred to red bus/blue bus problem in IIA examples suggests that if the individual has an alternative of choosing red bus, blue bus, or train, and the aim is to compare the probabilities of choosing red bus and train, the alternative of blue bus is NOT irrelevant to the individual's decision-making. Thus, the assumption of IIA will not hold, so the multinomial logit model will be mis-specified.

10.9 Ordered-Response Models

It is not uncommon to have a category-dependent variable that has a natural ordering. Credit rating studies are standard examples of ordered-response models. In these studies, a bond falls into a particular credit rating category if its underlying factors are within a certain range (see Brooks, 2019; Poon, 2003). Thus, the limited dependent variable in this case has ordinal meaning. The underlying factors are not directly observed, so they are latent. Such studies use ordered probit or ordered logit models and, as in binary choice models and multinomial response models, the results from these two models will be similar. This section provides a short review of the ordered probit model derived from a latent-variable model:

$$y_i^* = \beta_1 x_{1,i} + \beta_2 x_{2,i} + \cdots + \beta_n x_{n,i} + e_i = \mathbf{x}\boldsymbol{\beta} + e_i. \tag{10.19}$$

The latent-variable model is the same as in Equation (10.6), but it does not have an intercept. To define the categories, you have j cut-off points. For instance, $y = 6$ if y^* is AA or above, $y = 5$ if y^* is A, $y = 4$ if y^* is BB, and so on. The probabilities of observing each category are then defined. In some studies, the estimated parameters are directly interpreted relative to the reference category (see, e.g., Poon, 2003). However, since this is a non-linear model, you can compute and interpret the marginal (partial) effects of these probabilities of observing a certain category. The standard interpretation of the marginal effects (assume positive) is that a one-unit increase in independent variable $\mathbf{x}$ increases the probability of observing the jth alternative by the ME expressed as a percentage. MEs are not interpreted relative to a benchmark and the sign of the coefficient estimates and MEs may differ.

10.10 Corner-Solution Models, Tobit Model

In some studies, the dependent variable is bounded but continues within the bounds. Consider, for instance, a firm investment that has a lower bound of 0, but the upper bound is unlimited. You may consider such variables in two parts. One is the decision to invest, which is a binary 0–1 variable. The other is the continuous part, providing the level of investment. Such variables are called corner-solution variables and are studied in hybrid models between OLS for the continuous part and probit for the binary choice part. Applications of such models to corporate finance studies are not uncommon (see, e.g., Brezigar-Masten, Masten, and Volk, 2021), but they can also be observed in other fields of business studies, for example, accounting (Gallani and Krishnan, 2017) and marketing research (Franses and Paap, 2001). Using only OLS for the corner-solution variables is not efficient, for the same reasons we discussed in the linear probability models above.

One alternative to OLS for corner-solution models is the tobit model, which again can be derived from the latent-variable model:

$$y_i^* = \mathbf{x}\boldsymbol{\beta} + e_i, \tag{10.20}$$

where $y_i = y_i^*$ if $y_i^* > 0$ and $y_i = 0$ if $y_i^* \leq 0$. If you observe the entire distribution of y_i^*, you can simply use OLS given that e_i satisfies the CLRM assumptions. In the investment example above, negative investment can be considered as investment with negative static net present value (NPV) with growth option (so the expended NPV is positive). Consider, for instance, the pharmaceutical industry, where additional investment is required and cash flows are generated in the future if a proposed drug development gets approved by the U.S. Food and Drug Administration (FDA). The equation for the probit part of the tobit that models the probability of zero investment is given in Part C of the Appendix for Chapter 10 at the end of the book. Because only $y_i^* > 0$ is observed, OLS cannot be used, and the estimation becomes more complicated. The ML method is used for the estimation of a tobit model that combines these two parts of the regression equation (e.g., probability of zero investment and level of investment).

How to interpret the result from the tobit model? Suppose that you are interested in the marginal effect of a continuous independent variable ($\boldsymbol{\beta} = \beta_j$, where $j = 1,2,3,\ldots,k$). The marginal effect in the latent-variable model is given by

$$\frac{\vartheta E(y_i^* \mid \mathbf{x})}{\vartheta x_j} = \beta_j. \tag{10.21}$$

If x_j is discrete then the relative effect is the difference between the expected values of y_i^* when $x_j = 1$ and when $x_j = 0$. However, β_j in Equation (10.21) is the marginal effect on the latent variable, it is not the expected actual outcome of y_i, which is more complicated as this variable has two parts and hence you need to compute two MEs for the expected actual outcome. The reader is referred to Wooldridge (2002) for the derivation of these marginal effects. Only the final equations are given below. The first marginal effect is conditional on positive values of y_i:

$$E(y_i \mid y_i > 0, \mathbf{x}) = \mathbf{x}\boldsymbol{\beta} + \sigma_e \frac{\phi\left(\frac{\mathbf{x}\boldsymbol{\beta}}{\sigma_e}\right)}{\Phi\left(\frac{\mathbf{x}\boldsymbol{\beta}}{\sigma_e}\right)}, \tag{10.22}$$

where the conditional expectation can be written as

$$E(y_i \mid y_i > 0, \mathbf{x}) = \mathbf{x}\boldsymbol{\beta} + \sigma_e \lambda\left(\frac{\mathbf{x}\boldsymbol{\beta}}{\sigma_e}\right), \tag{10.23}$$

with λ known as the inverse Mills ratio, given as

$$\lambda(z) = \frac{\phi(z)}{\Phi(z)}. \tag{10.24}$$

The first-order derivative of the conditional expectation with respect to x_j (assume continuous) is the conditional marginal effect

$$\begin{aligned} \frac{\vartheta E(y_i|y_i > 0, \mathbf{x})}{\vartheta x_j} &= \beta_j \sigma_e \frac{\vartheta \lambda\left(\frac{\mathbf{x}\boldsymbol{\beta}}{\sigma_e}\right)}{\vartheta x_j} \\ &= \beta_j \left[1 - \lambda\left(\frac{\mathbf{x}\boldsymbol{\beta}}{\sigma_e}\right)\left[\frac{\mathbf{x}\boldsymbol{\beta}}{\sigma_e} + \lambda\left(\frac{\mathbf{x}\boldsymbol{\beta}}{\sigma_e}\right)\right]\right], \end{aligned} \tag{10.25}$$

where the conditional marginal effect of x_j depends on β_j, other parameters in $\boldsymbol{\beta}$, and all the independent variables in $\mathbf{x}$. The term $\left[\frac{\mathbf{x}\boldsymbol{\beta}}{\sigma_e} + \lambda\left(\frac{\mathbf{x}\boldsymbol{\beta}}{\sigma_e}\right)\right]$ is known as the adjustment factor that is greater than 0 and less than 1.

The second marginal effect is unconditional on y_i:

$$\frac{\vartheta E(y_i \mid \mathbf{x})}{\vartheta x_j} = \beta_j \Phi\left(\frac{\mathbf{x}\boldsymbol{\beta}}{\sigma_e}\right), \tag{10.26}$$

which again depends not only on β_j but also on other parameters and independent variables in the tobit model. The term $\Phi\left(\frac{\mathbf{x}\boldsymbol{\beta}}{\sigma_e}\right)$ is the probability that $y_i > 0$ and since the probability is less than 1, the unconditional marginal effect of x_j is less than its ML estimate of β_j. You can interpret this marginal effect as the marginal effect of x_j on the expected value of y_i (given the other independent variables), which is the ML estimate of β_j times the probability that $y_i > 0$.

As in the other non-linear models described above, heteroskedasticity and non-normality will lead to the wrong calculation of the marginal effects. You can test for heteroskedasticity and non-normality in the residuals. One easier remedy for the heteroskedasticity problem is to use robust standard errors. A more valid approach is to reconsider the functional form of the tobit model and perhaps include higher-order terms or interaction terms in the model. Another issue with the tobit model is that the same independent variables potentially explain, for instance, both the probability of zero investment and the level of investment conditional on that investment being decided. It may not be realistic to assume that a *single mechanism* determines both of the outcomes. If you are not willing to make this strong assumption, you can instead use hurdle models (see Cragg, 1971) that separate the decision to invest and how much to invest once the investment decision is made. In hurdle models, the decision to invest is examined in a probit model and OLS is run to examine how much to invest conditional on that investment being undertaken.

10.11 Censored and Truncated Models

The censored and truncated models are similar to the corner solution models discussed above, however, these models are often used due to problems with data. For instance, a censored variable is defined as the values of the dependent variable capped at a constant if the values beyond this constant are not observed by the analyst. This is similar to the winsorization that was studied in previous chapters. The difference is that in a censored variable you do not know about the values beyond the constant. The censoring may occur both at the lower end and the upper end, depending on the study. Consider, for instance, a study of donation, where some individuals donate and some individuals receive from charity. Since in such a study you often observe only people who donate, those people who receive donations will be coded as 0. Another example is duration data with beginning and end dates for some specific state, for instance unemployment. Duration data are often censored mostly to the right. You often know more about when the unemployment of individuals begins, but have fewer observations on when the unemployment ends.

Brooks (2019) provides an example of a corporate finance study that examines demand for initial public offering (IPO) shares, using investors' demographic characteristics as determinants. In the example, the number of shares allocated to each investor is capped at 250. If the demand is capped at 250, but you observe all the values of the independent variables, even for those individuals who actually have a demand greater than 250, the dependent variable is censored not truncated. In this example, the values for demand will be inserted as 250 in the rows for those who had a larger demand, so you will have observations for other variables for these individuals in the data. In contrast, if the dependent variable is truncated, you will not observe these individuals in the data at all. The rows for both dependent variable and independent variables will be dropped if the demand for IPO shares exceeds 250.

If the dependent variable is censored, you can use a tobit model with a slightly different focus on the marginal effects. Section 10.10 discussed different marginal effects after the tobit regression. In the censored models, the main interest for the marginal effect is the expected value of the unobserved or censored variable y_i^*, which means that the marginal effect is simply β_j.

The truncated data are often related to the sample-selection problems, because you do not know, for instance, those who have a demand for IPO shares that exceeds 250, when the sample is not representative of the population. Ignoring truncation in the data results in biased estimates, but with some assumptions you can correct this bias. Wooldridge (2002) suggests that you can assume normality for the truncated part of the data and derive the expected value of y_i conditional on y_i being observed and conditioned on some independent variables (see Equation (10.22)). You can then compute the marginal effects for the inference (see Equation (10.25)).

10.12 Heckman Selection Model

This section will emphasize the importance of random sampling again. Truncated data is one evidence of sample-selection bias, leading to wrong inferences on population as the truncated sample is not representative of the population. The IPO study discussed above is a good example, but the problem can be even more serious if, for instance, you examine only the active firms in a study, those who have survived, leading to so-called survivorship bias. The Heckman selection model (Heckman, 1976, 1979) is a standard approach to deal with sample-selection bias. The section begins by writing the structural equation to describe the Heckman selection model:

$$y_{1,i} = \mathbf{x}\boldsymbol{\beta} + e. \tag{10.27}$$

In addition, there is a selection equation $y_{2,i}$, which is 1 if $y_{1,i}$ is observed and 0 otherwise. More formally:

$$y_{2,i} = \begin{cases} 1, \text{ if } \mathbf{X}\boldsymbol{\delta} + u_i \\ 0, \text{ otherwise} \end{cases}, \tag{10.28}$$

where $\mathbf{X}$ includes more variables than $\mathbf{x}$ to explain the selection equation. This is one difference compared to the tobit model, which allows a *single mechanism* explaining both the decision and the level equations. If you have at least one variable that determines the selection equation, $y_{2,i}$, but is unrelated to the structural equation, $y_{1,i}$ (exclusion restriction), you would avoid the collinearity problem that may lead to inconsistent estimates.

The standard Heckman model assumes exogeneity for all the independent variables in the population and the normality of the residuals. The sample-selection bias is evident if the two residual terms e_i and u_i are correlated. It is then said that the sample-selection bias generates a type of endogeneity in the (non-randomly) selected sample. If e_i and u_i are uncorrelated, then sample selection would not cause an endogeneity problem and you could rely on OLS. Given the structural and selection equations above, you can write the resulting expected value of $y_{1,i}$ conditional on all the independent variables (that explain both equations) $\mathbf{x}$ and the selection itself, $y_{2,i} = 1$:

$$E\left(y_{1,i} \mid \mathbf{x}, y_{2,i} = 1\right) = \mathbf{x}\boldsymbol{\beta} + \gamma\lambda\left(\mathbf{X}\boldsymbol{\delta}\right), \tag{10.29}$$

where the expected value is $\mathbf{x}\boldsymbol{\beta}$ plus an additional term determined by λ, the inverse Mills ratio. It is not wrong to use OLS if the term $\lambda(\mathbf{X}\boldsymbol{\delta})$ is uncorrelated with $\mathbf{x}$, because this term will end up in the residual term in the OLS method. However, it is often the case that these two terms are correlated and the exogeneity assumption in the CLRM will not hold. If you have some observed explanatory variables that control for the sample selection, then you can run OLS. If you do not have the control variables for the sample selection, you can use the Heckman selection model, also known as Heckit (Heckman, 1976).

Heckman suggests that since it is difficult to observe and include the term $\lambda(\mathbf{X\delta})$ in the model, it could be estimated. You know about the functional form of the inverse Mills ratio λ and have all the $\mathbf{X}$ variables explaining both the selection and the level equations. The difficulty is that for this model to work, you need to have values of all the $\mathbf{X}$ variables for both selected and unselected observations. This is not often the case, but assume that you have these observations, then the only parameter that is unknown to us is δ, which can be estimated using a probit model.

Thus, the Heckit model uses two regression equations. First, a probit model where the dependent variable $y_{2,i}$ is regressed on all the $\mathbf{X}$ variables, using all the observations. From the probit model you estimate the unknown parameters δ,which are then used to calculate the inverse Mills ratio for each observation:

$$\lambda\left(\mathbf{X}\hat{\delta}\right) = \frac{\phi\left(\mathbf{X}\hat{\delta}\right)}{\Phi\left(\mathbf{X}\hat{\delta}\right)}. \tag{10.30}$$

Second, you run an OLS estimation method where $y_{1,i}$ is regressed on all the $\mathbf{x}$ variables plus the estimated inverse Mills ratio $\lambda\left(\mathbf{X}\hat{\delta}\right)$:

$$y_{1,i} = \mathbf{x}\beta + \gamma\lambda\left(\mathbf{X}\hat{\delta}\right) + v_i. \tag{10.31}$$

The estimated β will be consistent since you have corrected for the sample-selection bias by including the estimated inverse Mills ratio in the model. The coefficient γ measures the degree of sample-selection bias, or in other words, gives the covariance between residual terms e_i and u_i. Thus, you can test the existence of selection bias: the null hypothesis of no selection bias is rejected if γ is significantly different from 0.

How about the marginal effects? Similar to the tobit model, you might be interested in more than one marginal effect. First, the marginal effect of say x_1 (that is included in $\mathbf{x}$) on $y_{1,i}$ in the population. This is simply the OLS estimate of β_1. Second, you might be interested in the marginal effect of x_1 on $y_{1,i}$ in the population, where $y_{1,i}$ is observed for selected individuals:

$$\frac{\partial E\left(y_{1,i} \mid \mathbf{x}, y_{2,i} = 1\right)}{\partial x_1} = \beta_1 - \delta_1\gamma\lambda\left(\mathbf{X\delta}\right)\left[\mathbf{X\delta} + \lambda\left(\mathbf{X\delta}\right)\right]. \tag{10.32}$$

Finally, you might also be interested in the marginal effect when the 0s in $y_{1,i}$ are considered, which is more complicated.[3]

[3] Readers are referred to Wooldridge (2002) and Cameron and Trivedi (2005) for derivation of the marginal effects.

10.13 Selected Count-Data Models

In models where the dependent variable is a non-negative integer, you are interested in determining the average count of the dependent variable conditional on the values of the dependent variable being positive. Some examples include: Ginarte and Park (1997) and Allred and Park (2007), who examine the effects of patent strength on the number of granted patents using international patent applications; Hausman, Hall, and Griliches (1984), who examine the number of patents granted by US firms for given R&D expenditures; and Grogger (1990), who examines the effects of capital punishment on daily homicides.

In such studies, you are interested in the exponential conditional mean function that produces intensive margin effects of the relative change in the expected outcome associated with a unit change in the dependent variable. Thus, in such a research design, count-data models become useful when expected counts are modeled as an exponential function of the independent variables:

$$E(y \mid \mathbf{X}) = \exp(\beta \mathbf{X}), \tag{10.33}$$

where y is the dependent variable and $\mathbf{X}$ includes all the independent variables. One alternative approach to the specification in Equation (10.33) is to log-transform the dependent variable and then estimate a linear regression model, which would make it possible to interpret the coefficients as semi-elasticity estimates. However, this model requires that the standard errors are homoskedastic, which hardly holds in real-life data (see Santos Silva and Tenreyro, 2006). In corporate finance studies there are two common econometric models used to estimate count-data models: the Poisson regression model and the negative binomial regression model (see Cohn, Liu, and Wardlaw, 2022). These models are briefly covered next.

10.13.1 Poisson Regression Model

An alternative to estimating a linear regression of a transformed outcome is to estimate a Poisson regression model (Cohn et al., 2022). In this model the probability of a count is determined by a Poisson distribution and thus it is assumed that the conditional mean of the outcome is equal to the conditional variance. Also, the counts (events) are assumed independent. If an event occurs, it does not affect the probability of the event occurring in the future. Unlike a linear regression model, a Poisson regression model can accommodate outcomes with a value of zero and requires no assumption about the relationship between the independent variables and higher-order model error moments (Santos et al., 2006). Another advantage of a Poisson regression model is that it allows group fixed effects in a panel-data setting, which is commonly applied in corporate finance studies. The key difference between a log-linear regression model and a Poisson regression model is that the Poisson regression applies an exponential model rather than transforming the outcome to fit a linear model. Since there are no other restrictions than $y \geq 0$

in the dependent variable, a Poisson regression can be used even if the dependent variable is continuous.

In corporate finance studies the interest is often in the interpretation of the percentage change in the expected count. For example, if x is continuous, the interpretation is as follows. For a one-unit change in x, the expected count changes by $100\times[\exp(\beta)-1]\%$, holding other variables constant.

10.13.2 Negative Binomial Regression Model

The count-data model can also be estimated by the negative binomial regression model if the assumptions of a Poisson regression model do not hold. For example, if the number of counts in the dependent variable is unlikely to occur completely randomly over time with constant probability. Such underlying randomness may not be satisfying if many of the counts depend on the previous occurrences. This is particularly problematic if the model suffers from omitted-variable bias; the influences of unobserved variation in the model may lead to overdispersion in the conditional model. Put differently, the variance may increase proportionally with the mean (see Cameron and Triverdi, 1996).

You can examine whether the data suffer from such a problem by testing the significance of the overdispersion parameter in the regressions. If the results show a significant overdispersion parameter, then the assumption behind a Poisson model (equality of conditional mean and variance) is not satisfied. Thus, using a Poisson model may lead to predicting a lower proportion of zeros than a negative binomial model with the same mean. Consequently, a zero-truncated negative binomial regression model should yield better predictions of the outcome probabilities of the dependent variable. This approach avoids the problems of zero counts and bias caused by heterogeneity (Cohn et al., 2022). The interpretation of a coefficient from a negative binomial regression model based on the expected count is the same as that for a Poisson regression model, since the mean structures of these models are the same but the conditional variance differs.[4]

10.14 Application of Selected Limited Dependent-Variable Models

This section will replicate some of the findings from Harris (2018), who documents that US IPOs in more concentrated industries are more underpriced than other IPOs. This higher underpricing of IPOs in industrial districts seems to represent investor compensation for the location premium associated with more isolated (rural) areas in which information costs tend to be higher than in urban areas. These findings are similar to the results of Hong, Kubik, and Stein (2008), who show that

[4] See Cameron and Triverdi (1996) and more recently Cohn et al. (2022) for details on count-data models.

firms located in areas with a lower concentration of other local listed firms exhibit a location premium via an "only game in town" effect.

This study will use a randomly selected 25% of the data, between the years 2006 and 2009, from a study on IPOs in Sweden (Mavruk and Wermers, 2023) in which the authors examine the interplay between ownership, investor heterogeneity, and corporate social responsibility-related information in business descriptions in IPO prospectuses. This exercise will focus on the industry concentration in a given location and underpricing of IPOs. The literature on local IPOs finds that local firm clustering affects IPO underpricing (Baschieri, Carosi, and Mengoli, 2015). Isolated firms tend to increase in value when they cluster due to local IPOs. There is also evidence that issuers headquartered in rural areas are associated with lower IPO underpricing relative to urban firms (Nielsson and Wójcik, 2016).

Following Harris (2018), this study measures industry concentration in a given location by the geo-industry cluster ratio (GICR), computed as the number of firms in a given industry and the same area scaled by the total number of firms within the industry. Accordingly, higher GICR values indicate more industry concentration in a locality. To apply the selected models presented in this chapter, the study will first treat the dependent variable, IPO underpricing, as a binary variable: 1 for underpricing and 0 otherwise. Then it will truncate the dependent variable, IPO underpricing, to practice some additional limited dependent-variable models. The study also matches the control variables to the model in Harris (2018) as best as possible.

10.14.1 Descriptive Statistics

Table 10.1 presents descriptive statistics for all the variables that are used in this study. The dependent variable, underpricing (51.3%), is determined based on the first-day return, 1 for positive first-day return and 0 for zero or negative first-day return. The first-day return (mean: 14.1%, std: 66.5%) is computed as the percentage difference between the offer price (obtained from prospectuses) and the first-day closing price. Foreign IPO (9.7%) is a dummy indicating if the IPO is headquartered outside Sweden. Hot IPO period (52.8%) is determined if the number of IPOs in a given year is greater than the average number of IPOs in the data. Ln offer size (mean: 4.8, std: 1.70) is the natural logarithm of pre-market value (in MSEK) of the IPO. HHI is the pre-market high ownership concentration of IPO (24%) that is determined if the pre-market Herfindahl index (HHI) of an IPO is greater than the median HHI in the data. Insider ownership after IPO (11.3%) is a dummy indicating whether the IPO is held by the insiders after the introduction. The dummy variable VC backed (14.9%) indicates whether the IPO is backed by venture capital (VC) before the introduction. Popular advisor (9.7%) is a dummy indicating whether the underwriter/advisor of the IPO covers the top 25% of the distribution of IPOs in the data. Geo-industry cluster ratio, GICR (mean: 23.1, std: 22.7) is computed as the number of firms in a given industry and the same area scaled by the total number of firms within the industry. Urban (57.9%) is a dummy indicating whether the IPO is headquartered in an urban area according to definitions of Statistics Sweden

Table 10.1 Descriptive statistics

Variable	N	Min	p25	Mean	p50	p75	Max	SD
first_day_return	195	−0.819	−0.218	0.141	0.010	0.229	3.500	0.665
under_pricing	195	0.000	0.000	0.513	1.000	1.000	1.000	0.501
foreing_ipo	195	0.000	0.000	0.097	0.000	0.000	1.000	0.297
hot_ipo_period	195	0.000	0.000	0.528	1.000	1.000	1.000	0.500
ln_offer_size	195	1.643	3.481	4.780	4.419	5.769	9.770	1.704
hhi	195	0.000	0.000	0.244	0.188	0.310	1.000	0.282
insideo_afteripo	195	0.000	0.000	0.113	0.000	0.000	1.000	0.317
vc_backed	195	0.000	0.000	0.149	0.000	0.000	1.000	0.357
popular_advisor	195	0.000	0.000	0.097	0.000	0.000	1.000	0.297
gicr	195	0.005	0.056	0.231	0.123	0.357	0.750	0.227
urban	195	0.000	0.000	0.579	1.000	1.000	1.000	0.495
cum_rm	195	−0.246	−0.017	0.033	0.046	0.084	0.284	0.085

(see Lista Kommungruppsind 2017 – SCB; www.scb.se). Cum rm is the 90 days of pre-market cumulative market return that is calculated using the return on the OMX Stockholm 30 index and obtained from the webpage of the National Data Center at Stockholm School of Economics.

10.14.2 Results

The study first runs a linear probability model using underpricing as the dependent variable and GICR as the main independent variable. The research hypothesis is that firms going public in more concentrated industrial districts are more underpriced than other IPO firms. If the results show a positive relationship between GICR and underpricing, controlling for other observable determinants of IPO underpricing, the research hypothesis will be supported. In other words, the null hypothesis that there is either no relationship or a negative relationship between GICR and underpricing will be rejected.

The results in Table 10.2 seem to support the hypothesis, as firms going public in concentrated industrial districts seem to be 45.5 percentage points more underpriced than other IPO firms. There are also some other interesting results in the table. The probability of underpricing is 6.1 percentage points higher for larger IPOs. If the IPOs are held by insiders after the introduction, the probability of underpricing increases by 24.2 percentage points. There is some weak evidence (significant at the 10% level) that the probability of underpricing decreases by 24.4 percentage points if the IPOs are introduced by a popular advisor. Finally, there seems to be a 127 percentage point higher probability of underpricing for a percentage point higher 90 days pre-market cumulative market return. Notice that this coefficient is huge and may indicate some issues with the linear probability model. However, excluding this variable from the model, the other results remain the same. So far, these results confirm those obtained in Table 5 of Harris (2018), although Harris treats underpricing as a continuous variable.

Table 10.2 Linear probability model

regress under_pricing gicr urban foreing_ipo hot_ipo_period ln_offer_size hhi insid i.bransch_id, r

No. obs.	195
F(22, 172)	4.970
Prob > F	0.000
R-squared	0.148
Root MSE	0.491

under_pricing	Coeff.	Robust Std. Err.	t	P > |t|	[95% conf.	interval]
Gicr	0.4553406	0.230	1.980	0.049	0.002	0.909
Urban	−0.0259741	0.093	−0.280	0.781	−0.210	0.158
foreing_ipo	−0.0479888	0.133	−0.360	0.719	−0.311	0.215
hot_ipo_period	−0.0573242	0.074	−0.780	0.439	−0.203	0.089
ln_offer_size	0.0613944	0.024	2.530	0.012	0.013	0.109
Hhi	−0.134898	0.144	−0.940	0.349	−0.419	0.149
insideo_afteripo	0.242353	0.119	2.040	0.043	0.008	0.477
vc_backed	−0.0761085	0.111	−0.680	0.495	−0.296	0.144
popular_advisor	−0.2445265	0.138	−1.780	0.077	−0.516	0.027
cum_rm	1.273517	0.445	2.860	0.005	0.396	2.151
bransch_id1						
	0.4899006	0.209	2.340	0.020	0.077	0.903
2	0.9297668	0.207	4.500	0.000	0.522	1.338
3	0.4539283	0.272	1.670	0.097	−0.084	0.991
4	0.1510638	0.258	0.590	0.558	−0.357	0.660
5	0.2947136	0.261	1.130	0.260	−0.220	0.810
6	0.4374731	0.236	1.860	0.065	−0.028	0.903
8	0.3960271	0.328	1.210	0.229	−0.251	1.043
9	0.4038329	0.212	1.900	0.059	−0.015	0.823
10	0.3149162	0.411	0.770	0.445	−0.497	1.127
13	0.211461	0.270	0.780	0.434	−0.321	0.743
16	0.1881318	0.306	0.620	0.539	−0.415	0.791
17	0.1983442	0.213	0.930	0.354	−0.223	0.620
_cons	−0.2124533	0.226	−0.940	0.348	−0.658	0.233

. predict yhat
. sum yhat

Variable	Obs.	Mean	Std. Dev.	Min	Max
yhat	195	0.513	0.193	−0.196	1.070

As mentioned earlier, the linear probability model may predict the dependent variable beyond the range of 0 and 1 (probability bounds). The summary statistics show that the predicted probabilities range between −19.6% and 1.07%, which raises an issue with the validity of the linear probability model, although F-statistics and R^2 seem reasonable.

10.14.3 Marginal Effects After Logit and Probit

Next, the study examines the marginal effects after a logit model in Table 10.3. The results do not alter that much when logit is used instead. The probability of underpricing increases by 49.4 percentage points for a one-unit increase in GICR. The marginal (relative) effects of the control variables mentioned above remain with similar magnitude. Notice also in Figure 10.1 that the percentage correctly specified in the logit model is 68.54%, which seems to be plausible as it is larger than 50%, but you could always improve the performance of the model by better specifying it.

Table 10.4 presents the marginal effects after the probit model, as the observed results are similar to those from the logit model. The probability of underpricing increases by 50 percentage points for each unit increase in the ratio of GICR. The results from the control variables remain the same. There is a slight improvement with the percentage correctly specified though, 64.06% (see Figure 10.2), indicating that the probit is doing slightly better than the logit in this sample.

10.14.4 Results from the Tobit Model

The original data (or sample at hand) may not be suitable for the tobit model, but for the sake of practice and to provide the software codes, the study treats positive values in the dependent variable as continuous and values of 0 remain 0 in the tobit model. So, the dependent variable is censored at the lower end and continues (equal to first-day return) for positive return values. Table 10.5 shows results from the tobit model. The marginal effect in the latent-variable model is given by the ML estimate of the tobit. It shows that the probability of underpricing increases by 87.9 percentage points for a unit increase in GICR, but it

Table 10.3 Marginal effects after logit

margins, dydx(gicr urban foreing_ipo hot_ipo_period ln_offer_size hhi insideo_afteripo vc_backed popular_advisor cum_rm)

N: 192

	dy/dx	Delta-Method Std. Err.	z	P > |z|	[95% conf. interval]	
gicr	0.494	0.242	2.040	0.041	0.020	0.968
urban	−0.032	0.087	−0.360	0.716	−0.202	0.139
foreing_ipo	−0.051	0.121	−0.420	0.675	−0.287	0.186
hot_ipo_period	−0.052	0.069	−0.760	0.449	−0.187	0.083
ln_offer_size	0.061	0.023	2.650	0.008	0.016	0.106
hhi	−0.138	0.135	−1.020	0.307	−0.402	0.126
insideo_afteripo	0.242	0.114	2.130	0.034	0.019	0.466
vc_backed	−0.080	0.109	−0.740	0.462	−0.295	0.134
popular_advisor	−0.241	0.133	−1.820	0.069	−0.500	0.019
cum_rm	1.288	0.431	2.990	0.003	0.443	2.134

```
. estat classification

Logistic model for under_pricing

              ——————— True
Classified |     D          ~D  |  Total
-----------+--------------------+-----------
     +     |    68          39  |    107
     -     |    29          56  |     85
-----------+--------------------+-----------
   Total   |    97          95  |    192
Classified + if predicted Pr(D) >= .5
True D defined as under_pricing != 0

Sensitivity                     Pr( +| D)   70.10%
Specificity                     Pr( -|~D)   58.95%
Positive predictive value       Pr( D| +)   63.55%
Negative predictive value       Pr(~D| -)   65.88%

False + rate for true ~D        Pr( +|~D)   41.05%
False - rate for true D         Pr( -| D)   29.90%
False + rate for classified +   Pr(~D| +)   36.45%
False - rate for classified -   Pr( D| -)   34.12%

Correctly classified                        64.58%
```

Figure 10.1. Classification tests after logit

Table 10.4 Marginal effects after probit

margins, dydx(gicr urban foreing_ipo hot_ipo_period ln_offer_size hhi insideo_afteripo vc_backed popular_advisor cum_rm)

N: 192

	dy/dx	Delta-Method Std. Err.	z	P > |z|	[95% conf. interval]	
Gicr	0.501	0.228	2.200	0.028	0.055	0.947
Urban	−0.031	0.086	−0.360	0.718	−0.199	0.137
foreing_ipo	−0.047	0.123	−0.380	0.702	−0.287	0.193
hot_ipo_period	−0.051	0.069	−0.740	0.458	−0.187	0.084
ln_offer_size	0.062	0.023	2.730	0.006	0.017	0.106
Hhi	−0.137	0.131	−1.040	0.296	−0.393	0.120
insideo_afteripo	0.249	0.112	2.210	0.027	0.028	0.469
vc_backed	−0.076	0.105	−0.730	0.466	−0.281	0.129
popular_advisor	−0.245	0.132	−1.860	0.064	−0.505	0.014
cum_rm	1.279	0.419	3.050	0.002	0.458	2.101

```
. estat classification

Probit model for under_pricing

              -------- True --------
Classified |         D            ~D  |      Total
-----------+--------------------------+-----------
     +     |        68            40  |        108
     -     |        29            55  |         84
-----------+--------------------------+-----------
   Total   |        97            95  |        192

Classified + if predicted Pr(D) >= .5
True D defined as under_pricing != 0

Sensitivity                     Pr( +| D)   70.10%
Specificity                     Pr( -|~D)   57.89%
Positive predictive value       Pr( D| +)   62.96%
Negative predictive value       Pr(~D| -)   65.48%

False + rate for true ~D        Pr( +|~D)   42.11%
False - rate for true D         Pr( -| D)   29.90%
False + rate for classified +   Pr(~D| +)   37.04%
False - rate for classified -   Pr( D| -)   34.52%

Correctly classified                        64.06%
```

Figure 10.2. Classification tests after probit

is only partially significant. However, since the focus is on the upper side of the distribution, a one-sided test, testing whether GICR increases the underpricing, it should be reasonable to interpret this marginal effect.

The table also shows the marginal effect that is conditional on positive values of underpricing. It is significant only at the 10% level. Examining the other marginal (relative) effects in the table, the effects of the above-mentioned control variables in LPM and binary choice models still remain. There are also some other interesting results. For instance, underpricing seems to decrease with foreign IPOs, pre-market high ownership concentration, and if the IPO is VC-backed. These latter results should be interpreted only if the hypothesis is one-sided, testing whether the variable decreases underpricing.

10.14.5 Results from the Heckman Selection Model

Finally, the study will apply the Heckman selection model to the data. Again, the sample at hand may not be suitable for the model, but the study will assume that the sampling is not random and first-day return values are not observed for IPOs with small offer sizes, smaller than 5% of the Ln offer size distribution. Thus, the

Table 10.5 Results from the tobit model

Panel A. Regression output

. tobit under_pricing_1 gicr urban foreing_ipo hot_ipo_period ln_offer_size hhi insideo_afteripo vc_backed popular_advisor cum_rm i.bransch_id, ll vce(robust)

					No. obs.	195
					Uncensored	100
					Left-censored	95
					Right-censored	0
					F(22, 173)	1.58
					Prob > F	0.0552
Log pseudo likelihood	−175.42769				Pseudo R2	0.1022

under_pricing_1	Coeff.	Robust Std. Err.	t	P > |t|	[95% conf. interval]	
Gicr	0.879	0.495	1.780	0.077	−0.097	1.855
Urban	−0.142	0.191	−0.740	0.459	−0.518	0.235
foreing_ipo	−0.383	0.208	−1.840	0.067	−0.793	0.027
hot_ipo_period	−0.011	0.148	−0.070	0.943	−0.302	0.281
ln_offer_size	0.093	0.042	2.220	0.028	0.010	0.177
Hhi	−0.421	0.223	−1.880	0.061	−0.862	0.020
insideo_afteripo	0.234	0.173	1.350	0.178	−0.108	0.577
vc_backed	−0.333	0.195	−1.710	0.089	−0.717	0.051
popular_advisor	−0.598	0.236	−2.540	0.012	−1.064	−0.133
cum_rm	2.579	1.003	2.570	0.011	0.599	4.559
bransch_id1	0.470	0.710	0.660	0.509	−0.931	1.872
2	1.481	0.764	1.940	0.054	−0.028	2.989
3	0.946	0.970	0.980	0.331	−0.968	2.860
4	−0.447	0.760	−0.590	0.557	−1.947	1.052
5	0.179	0.778	0.230	0.818	−1.357	1.716
6	0.139	0.734	0.190	0.850	−1.309	1.587
8	0.020	0.792	0.020	0.980	−1.543	1.582
9	0.071	0.722	0.100	0.922	−1.354	1.496
10	−0.052	0.799	−0.060	0.948	−1.629	1.526
13	−0.276	0.765	−0.360	0.719	−1.786	1.235
16	−0.300	0.804	−0.370	0.709	−1.888	1.287
17	−0.466	0.724	−0.640	0.521	−1.895	0.964
_cons	−0.654	0.676	−0.970	0.335	−1.989	0.681
var(e.under_pricing_1)	0.654	0.161			0.402	1.063

Panel B. Marginal effects in the latent-variable model
. margins, dydx(gicr urban foreing_ipo hot_ipo_period ln_offer_size hhi insideo_afteripo vc_backed popular_advisor cum_rm) predict(e(0,.))

N: 195

	dy/dx	Delta-Method Std. Err.	z	P > |z|	[95% conf. interval]	
gicr	0.307	0.172	1.780	0.075	−0.030	0.645
urban	−0.049	0.067	−0.740	0.459	−0.181	0.082
foreing_ipo	−0.134	0.074	−1.820	0.069	−0.278	0.010
hot_ipo_period	−0.004	0.052	−0.070	0.943	−0.105	0.097
ln_offer_size	0.033	0.015	2.230	0.025	0.004	0.061
hhi	−0.147	0.078	−1.880	0.061	−0.301	0.007
insideo_afteripo	0.082	0.061	1.350	0.176	−0.037	0.201
vc_backed	−0.116	0.068	−1.700	0.088	−0.250	0.017
popular_advisor	−0.209	0.083	−2.510	0.012	−0.372	−0.046
cum_rm	0.902	0.349	2.580	0.010	0.217	1.586

dependent variable, underpricing, will be truncated for Ln offer size smaller than 5% of the distribution. The Heckman selection model allows different independent variables in the selection equation (probability of underpricing) and in the structural equation of the level of underpricing, OLS. Suppose that the study did its homework well and identified whether the IPO has not been listed elsewhere before the years 2006–2009. Thus, the additional variable in the structural equation is the first-time IPO that is not a change of stock market list. Moreover, to better identify the model, the study omits two dummy variables (that showed insignificant results in the previous models), urban and hot IPO period, in the structural equation, but keeps these variables in the selection equation.

Table 10.6 shows the results from the Heckit model along with the marginal effects. The first result to notice is that the significant coefficient on λ in the table indicates the sample-selection problem as the null hypothesis of no selection bias is rejected. The first marginal effects are for the selection equation of probit. The second marginal effects are for the level of underpricing conditional on the positive values of underpricing (positive first-day return). The results from the selection equation (probit) are similar, there is a 1.46 percentage point increase in the probability of underpricing for each unit increase in GICR. The results from the control variables seem to be weaker than what was observed in the previous models, but the sign of the marginal effects tends to hold. Turning to the conditional marginal effects, the results are different. The sign on GICR is negative but partially significant. Insider ownership after the introduction, and whether the IPO is introduced during the hot period, seem to increase underpricing. If the IPO is VC-backed, pre-market high ownership concentration (but significant only at the 10% level), and if a popular advisor introduced the IPO, underpricing seems to decrease.

Table 10.6 Results from the Heckit model

Panel A. Heckit output

						No. obs.	186
						Selected	98
Log likelihood	−160.548					Non-selected	88
test of indep. eqns. (rho = 0)						Wald chi2(21)	41.800
chi2(1)	75.730					Prob > chi2	0.005
Prob > chi2	0.000						

	Coeff.	Std. Err.	z	P > |z|	[95% conf. interval]	
gicr	0.399	0.455	0.880	0.380	−0.491	1.290
foreing_ipo	−0.341	0.231	−1.480	0.139	−0.794	0.111
ln_offer_size	0.063	0.046	1.360	0.174	−0.028	0.153
hhi	−0.401	0.238	−1.690	0.092	−0.868	0.065
insideo_afteripo	0.239	0.209	1.140	0.253	−0.171	0.649
vc_backed	−0.273	0.184	−1.490	0.137	−0.633	0.087
popular_advisor	−0.556	0.283	−1.960	0.049	−1.111	−0.001
cum_rm	1.858	0.820	2.260	0.024	0.250	3.466
first_time_ipo	−0.185	0.090	−2.050	0.041	−0.362	−0.008
bransch_id1	Yes	Yes	Yes	Yes	Yes	Yes
_cons	−0.030	0.503	−0.060	0.952	−1.016	0.955
gicr	1.456	0.612	2.380	0.017	0.257	2.655
urban	−0.053	0.161	−0.330	0.742	−0.369	0.262
foreing_ipo	−0.392	0.348	−1.130	0.260	−1.073	0.290
hot_ipo_period	−0.205	0.108	−1.890	0.059	−0.417	0.007
ln_offer_size	0.094	0.064	1.460	0.144	−0.032	0.219
hhi	−0.527	0.328	−1.610	0.108	−1.169	0.115
insideo_afteripo	0.180	0.281	0.640	0.521	−0.370	0.731
vc_backed	−0.256	0.258	−0.990	0.322	−0.762	0.250
popular_advisor	−0.620	0.374	−1.660	0.098	−1.354	0.113
cum_rm	3.173	1.126	2.820	0.005	0.966	5.380
bransch_id1	Yes	Yes	Yes	Yes	Yes	Yes
_cons	−0.991	0.655	−1.510	0.131	−2.275	0.294
/athrho	18.368	1520.066	0.010	0.990	−2960.907	2997.644
/lnsigma	−0.302	0.098	−3.070	0.002	−0.494	−0.109
rho	1.000	0.000			−1.000	1.000
sigma	0.739	0.073			0.610	0.897
lambda	0.739	0.073			0.597	0.882

Panel B. Marginal effects for the selection equation of probit
. margins, dydx(gicr urban foreing_ipo hot_ipo_period ln_offer_size hhi insideo_afteripo vc_backed popular_advisor cum_rm) atmeans predict(xbsel)

N: 186

	dy/dx	Delta-Method Std. Err.	z	P > |z|	[95% conf.	interval]
Gicr	1.456	0.612	2.380	0.017	0.257	2.655
foreing_ipo	−0.392	0.348	−1.130	0.260	−1.073	0.290
ln_offer_size	0.094	0.064	1.460	0.144	−0.032	0.219
Hhi	−0.527	0.328	−1.610	0.108	−1.169	0.115
insideo_afteripo	0.180	0.281	0.640	0.521	−0.370	0.731
vc_backed	−0.256	0.258	−0.990	0.322	−0.762	0.250
popular_advisor	−0.620	0.374	−1.660	0.098	−1.354	0.113
cum_rm	3.173	1.126	2.820	0.005	0.966	5.380
Urban	−0.053	0.161	−0.330	0.742	−0.369	0.262
hot_ipo_period	−0.205	0.108	−1.890	0.059	−0.417	0.007

Panel C. Marginal effects for the level of underpricing conditional on the positive values of underpricing
. margins, dydx(gicr urban foreing_ipo hot_ipo_period ln_offer_size hhi insideo_afteripo vc_backed popular_advisor cum_rm) atmeans predict(ycond)

N: 186

	dy/dx	Delta-Method Std. Err.	z	P > |z|	[95% conf.	interval]
gicr	−0.304	0.156	−1.950	0.052	−0.610	0.002
foreing_ipo	−0.152	0.149	−1.020	0.307	−0.444	0.140
ln_offer_size	0.017	0.018	0.990	0.323	−0.017	0.052
Hhi	−0.147	0.084	−1.740	0.081	−0.311	0.018
insideo_afteripo	0.152	0.072	2.110	0.035	0.011	0.293
vc_backed	−0.150	0.065	−2.320	0.020	−0.276	−0.023
popular_advisor	−0.257	0.137	−1.880	0.060	−0.524	0.011
cum_rm	0.324	0.405	0.800	0.423	−0.469	1.118
urban	0.026	0.078	0.330	0.743	−0.127	0.179
hot_ipo_period	0.099	0.050	1.960	0.050	0.000	0.198

Taken all together, using IPO data from Sweden in a more recent period, the overall results from GICR are supportive of the evidence provided from the United States by Harris (2018). IPOs in more concentrated industries tend to be more underpriced than other IPOs. Two explanations are offered for this result. First, a competitive business environment within industrial districts increases the riskiness of IPOs and decreases the voluntary disclosure of value-relevant information, owing to higher proprietary costs. Second, the higher underpricing of IPOs in industrial districts partly stems from compensation to investors for the location premium enjoyed by firms in more rural areas. In particular, the latter explanation is consistent with an "only game in town" effect (Hong et al., 2008).

10.15 Lab Work: Selected Limited Dependent-Variable Models

10.15.1 Equity Local Bias

This assignment concerns the equity home/local bias puzzle. You will study the determinants of firm-level local bias by applying non-linear models. Home bias means that investors are reluctant to invest in international markets. Finance theory-based models, such as the capital asset pricing model, which address the homogenous expectations of investors and assume that investors should hold a market portfolio of risky assets in order to maximize risk-adjusted return, do not predict the home-bias phenomenon.

Accordingly, a large body of home-bias studies is concerned with questions such as: Do investors hold the optimal portfolio? Do investors benefit from diversification and hedging risks? The answers to these questions have implications for resource allocation and are central for understanding how the economy behaves. It is in the best interest of investors that the resources are allocated to their most efficient uses. According to finance theory, this objective is obtained if the investors hedge risk optimally. If they do not, then many other questions arise, such as: What are the underlying reasons for not hedging unnecessary exposure to idiosyncratic (i.e., home country-specific) risks? Why would investors forgo opportunities for diversification of risk? What are the implications of not hedging risk optimally for resource allocation? How do the possible reasons for not hedging unnecessary risk influence the economy? Home-bias studies try to provide an answer to these questions by examining the underlying reasons for home bias.

10.15.2 Data

The dataset Chapter_10_Local_Bias.dta used in this assignment (available at www.cambridge.org/Mavruk) contains information on 282 stocks listed on various stock markets in Sweden on 30-12-2014. Information on investors' holdings of the stocks is used for local bias measurements and financial information is obtained from Thomson Reuters Datastream. The dataset is just a random sample obtained from the previous research and generated only for the lab.

10.15.3 Variable Specification

$$\text{lb} = 1 \text{ if local bias} > 0, \text{lb} = 0 \text{ otherwise.}$$

The local bias is measured by dividing investors' value-weighted average distances to their own portfolio by their value-weighted average distances to the benchmark (market portfolio). This measure is multiplied by the difference between the investor's benchmark weight applied to each stock and the actual weight that the investor assigns to each stock. This is a standard individual-level local bias measure defined as if investors place their capital primarily into the stocks of locally headquartered firms in comparison with remote domestic firms. However, the lab work is based on the firm-level local bias measure; that is, the weight of investments placed by locals in the firm minus the weight placed by all other investors of the firm (see Lindblom, Mavruk, and Sjögren, 2017; Mavruk, 2010 for further details on this measurement).

market_value: The market value (in billion SEK) of stocks.
vol: Stock volatility is measured as the standard deviation of the continuously compounded historical returns of the stock.
D_E: Debt-to-equity ratio is defined as the ratio of total liabilities to total assets. This measure is a proxy for leverage or firm distress.
ROA: Return on assets.
employees: The number of employees (in thousands) in the firms.
no_stocks: The number of stocks available to invest in the region.
tradable: Tradable dummy equals 1 if the firm has positive foreign sales, 0 otherwise. It shows the effect of firms' output tradability.
industrials: Industry dummy for industrial firms.
goods and services: Industry dummy for goods and services firms.
financials: Industry dummy for financial firms.
current_ratio: Current ratio is defined as a ratio of firms' current assets to current liabilities and measures the short-run financial health of a firm.

Problem set

1. Create the dependent variable (lb). Present a table with descriptive statistics for the variables used in the model and comment on the descriptive statistics. Run a Pearson correlation test on the variables and interpret your results.
   Useful Stata commands:

   ```
   gen, sum, pwcorr
   ```

2. Estimate model 1 using the linear probability model. Discuss advantages and disadvantages of the linear probability model. Calculate the predicted probabilities. Are all predicted probabilities plausible? Discuss how market value, ROA, and number of stocks affect the local bias.
   Useful Stata commands:

   ```
   reg, predict, sum yhat
   ```

3. Estimate model 1 using the logit model. Calculate the marginal effects. Discuss how market value, ROA, and number of stocks affect the local bias. Compare predicted outcome with actual outcome. What percentage of the values are correctly specified?

   Useful Stata commands:

   ```
   logit, mfx, estat classification
   ```

4. Estimate Equation (1) using the probit model. Calculate the marginal effects. Discuss how market value, ROA, and number of stocks affect the local bias. Compare predicted outcome with actual outcome. What percentage of the values are correctly specified?

   Useful Stata commands:

   ```
   probit, mfx, estat classification
   ```

5. Do you have a problem with heteroskedasticty in your probit model? Test. Explain how the test works and interpret your results.

   A Wooldridge approach:

   ```
   Estimate the model by standard probit. Obtain the
   fitted values, x(i)*bhat. Estimate an augmented model
   by probit. Include the original variables x(i) and then
   [x(i)*bhat]*x1(i), where x1(i) is the subset of x(i)
   in the heteroskedastic function. Then test the joint
   significance of the interaction terms using the Wald test.
   ```

   Useful Stata commands:

   ```
   Reg, test
   ```

   Use also hetprobit. Explain how the model works and interpret your results.

   Stata code:

   ```
   hetprobit lb market_value vol D_E ROA employees no_
   stocks tradable industrials goods_services financials,
   het(market_value)
   ```

6. Does the effect of market value, ROA, and number of stocks on the local bias in Sweden 2014 differ between the three different models (linear probability model, logit model, and probit model)? Explain. What are the main differences among these models? Which one would you prefer to use (and why)?

7. Now estimate the following local bias equation by OLS (only for positive values of the local bias). How does D_E, ROA, and number of stocks affect the local bias? Is the least-squares estimator unbiased? Explain.

   Stata code:

   ```
   regress local_bias market_value vol D_E ROA employees
   no_stocks current_ratio if local_bias > 0
   ```

8. Estimate a tobit model with local bias as the dependent variable. Present the marginal effects and discuss your result. How does D_E, ROA, and number of stocks affect the local bias in Sweden in 2014? Compare with the OLS results in Question 7 and Question 2.

   Stata code:

```
gen y=local_bias
replace y=0 if y<0
gen, tobit.
tobit y market_value vol D_E ROA employees no_stocks
current_ratio, ll
```

   Tobit model marginal effects for the censored sample:

```
margins, dydx(*) atmeans predict (ystar(0,.))
```

9. What is the difference between tobit and Heckman two-stage methods? Explain.

10. In small regions there are few (or no) listed firms, so the calculations of local bias are more observable in larger regions where there are more listed firms. Also, investors are more populated around large regions because of greater job opportunities. Thus, neither firms nor the investors are randomly distributed across the regions. This could generate a sample-selection problem in the analysis. Therefore, use the Heckman two-stage method to estimate the decision to invest locally and how much to invest. Present the marginal effects and discuss the results. How do D_E and number of stocks affect local bias?

    Stata code:

```
heckman y market_value vol D_E ROA employees no_stocks
current_ratio, twostep select(lb = market_value vol
D_E ROA employees no_stocks tradable industrials goods_
services financials)
mfx, predict(yexpected)
mfx, predict(ycond)
margins, dydx(*) atmeans predict(e(0,.))
margins, dydx(*) atmeans predict(xbsel)
```

    Ignore if the dummy variables are omitted in the marginal effects calculations.

Good luck!

10.16 Mini Case

Using data on the board of directors in listed firms from China (Cai, Jiang, and Kang, 2023), examine whether board meeting type (i.e., remote vs. face-to-face board meetings) affects the discussion environment and communication processes.

This mechanism may influence board monitoring effectiveness and corporate policy outcomes. The motivation behind the study is that board meeting type can affect independent directors' time constraints to join the meetings, their incentives to participate actively in the discussion and engage in decision-making, thereby influencing board monitoring effectiveness. The study also explores why firms hold remote meetings and how remote meetings influence directors' board meeting attendance behavior, their monitoring, and ultimately firm value. The data include firms listed in the CSI300 stock index from 2005 to 2019, restricted to those firms whose board meeting data are unavailable. The final sample covers 58,133 board meetings (282,553 board meeting proposals) held by 711 firms. The non-linear models, particularly logit and tobit models, which are the focus of this case study are applied to examine the probability of type of board meetings. A remote meeting is where the public notice on the resolution of the board meeting states that the meeting is held via telephone, video, email, or fax, or if it states that the meeting is held via some telecommunication medium but does not specify the exact media type. Otherwise, the meeting is defined as face-to-face. Remote meetings are further classified as synchronous remote meetings, asynchronous remote meetings, and unknown type of remote meetings.

TASK

1. Go to the link: Replication Data for: Remote Board Meetings and Board Monitoring Effectiveness: Evidence from China – Review of Financial Studies Dataverse (harvard.edu)

   Download the zip file that contains all the datasets and the do file: replication code_rfs_upload.do
2. Go to the link: Remote Board Meetings and Board Monitoring Effectiveness: Evidence from China | The Review of Financial Studies | Oxford Academic (oup.com)

   Download the paper. Alternatively, you can download the working paper version from the link: Remote Board Meetings and Board Monitoring Effectiveness: Evidence from China by Xinni Cai, Fuxiu Jiang, Jun-Koo Kang :: SSRN https://papers.ssrn.com/sol3/papers.cfm?abstract_id=3450328

   The full text is publicly available on the link. This is the latest version before publication, so all the table numbers correspond to the table numbers in the published version at *The Review of Financial Studies*.
3. Replicate the logit regression in Table 3 for a subsample of synchronous meetings. Present and explain your results.
4. Replicate the logit regression in Table 3 for a full sample of meetings. Present and explain your results.
5. Replicate the tobit regression in Table 4 for a subsample of synchronous meetings. Present and explain your results.
6. Replicate the tobit regression in Table 4 for a full sample of meetings. Present and explain your results.

10.17 Summary

In regressions where the dependent variable takes limited values such as 0 and 1, or takes some category of values, using OLS estimation will likely provide biased and inconsistent results. Because the dependent variable is either discontinuous or its range is bounded, one of the assumptions of the CLRM – that the standard error is normally distributed conditional on the independent variables – is violated. This assumption implies that the dependent variable can take any real number, positive or negative, which does not apply in the limited dependent-variable models. The heteroskedasticity assumption of the CLRM model does not tend to hold either when the dependent variable is limited. Instead, there are some other models used depending on the limitations of the dependent variable. For example, for 0–1 dependent variables, probit and logit models are proposed. For categorical variables with more than two categories, multinomial logit models are used; for ordered dependent variables, ordered probit and ordered logit models are used; for censored dependent variables, the tobit model is used; for truncated dependent variables, Heckman's model is used; for count (integer)-dependent variables, Poisson and negative binomial regression models are used, and so on.

The main focus of this chapter is on limited dependent-variable models, for example, covering firm decision-making, capital structure decisions, investor decision-making, and so on. The chapter briefly presents and discusses the linear probability model, maximum-likelihood estimator, probit model, logit model, ordered probit and logit models, multinomial logit model, conditional logit model, tobit model, Heckman selection model, and count-data models. It covers the assumptions behind these models and examines how they work. As usual, the chapter provides an application of selected limited dependent-variable models and ends with lab work and a mini case.

KEY TERMS

Limited dependent-variable models; linear probability model (LPM); logit and probit models; latent-variable model; maximum-likelihood estimation; interpretation; multinomial logit and probit models; independence from irrelevant alternatives; conditional logit models; ordered-response models; tobit model; Heckman selection model; applications.

REFERENCES

Ai, C. and Norton, E. C. 2003. Interaction terms in logit and probit models. *Economics Letters*, 80, 123–129.

Allred, B. B. and Park, W. G. 2007. Patent rights and innovative activity: Evidence from national and firm-level data. *Journal of International Business Studies*, 38, 878–900.

Alvarez, R. M. and Brehm, J. 1995. American ambivalence towards abortion policy: Development of a heteroskedastic probit model of competing values. *American Journal of Political Science*, 39, 1055–1082.

Baschieri, G., Carosi, A., and Mengoli, S. 2015. Local IPOs local delistings, and the firm location premium. *Journal of Banking and Finance*, 53, 67–83.

Brezigar-Masten, A., Masten, I., and Volk, M. 2021. Modeling credit risk with a Tobit model of days past due. *Journal of Banking & Finance*, 122, 105984.

Brooks, C. 2019. *Introductory Econometrics for Finance* (4th ed.). Cambridge University Press, Cambridge.

Cai, X., Jiang, F., and Kang, J-K. 2023. Remote board meetings and board monitoring effectiveness: Evidence from China. *Review of Financial Studies*, 36, 4318–4372.

Cameron, A. C. and Trivedi, P. K. 1996. 12 Count data models for financial data. *Handbook of Statistics*, 14, 363–391.

Cameron, A. C. and Trivedi, P. K. 2005. *Microeconometrics: Methods and Applications*. Cambridge University Press, Cambridge.

Cohn, J. B., Liu, Z., and Wardlaw, M. I. 2022. Count (and count-like) data in finance. *Journal of Financial Economics*, 146, 529–551.

Cragg, J. G. 1971. Some statistical models for limited dependent variables with application to the demand for durable goods. *Econometrica*, 39, 829–844.

Cramer, J. S. 2007. Robustness of logit analysis: Unobserved heterogeneity and mis-specified disturbances. *Oxford Bulletin of Economics and Statistics*, 69, 545–555.

Fang, D. Holmen, M., and Mavruk, T. 2021. Meeting new peers: The effects of Morningstar category reassignment on fund flows and star ratings. *International Review of Financial Analysis* 77, 101842.

Franses, P.H. and Paap, R. 2001. *Quantitative Models in Marketing Research*. Cambridge University Press.

Gallani, S. and Krishnan, R. 2017. Applying the fractional response model to survey research in accounting. Harvard Business School Accounting & Management Unit Working Paper No. 16-016. https://ssrn.com/abstract=2642854 or http://dx.doi.org/10.2139/ssrn.2642854

Ginarte, J. C. and Park, W. G. 1997. Determinants of patent rights: A cross-national study. *Research Policy*, 26, 283–301.

Grogger, J. 1990. The deterrent effect of capital punishment: An analysis of daily homicide counts. *Journal of the American Statistical Association*, 85, 295–303.

Harris, O. 2018. The impact of industrial districts on the pricing of IPOs. *The Quarterly Review of Economics and Finance*, 69, 274–285.

Harvey, A. 1976. Estimating regression models with multiplicative heteroscedasticity. *Econometrica*, 44, 461–465.

Hausman, J. A., Hall, B. H., and Griliches, Z. 1984. Econometric models for count data with an application to the patents–R&D relationship. *Econometrica*, 52, 909–938.

Heckman, J. J. 1976. The common structure of statistical models of truncation, sample selection and limited dependent variables and a simple estimator for such models. *Annals of Economic and Social Measurement*, 5, 475–492.

Heckman, J. J. 1979. Sample selection bias as a specification error. *Econometrica*, 47, 153–161.

Hong, H., Kubik, J. D., and Stein, J. C. 2008. The only game in town: Stock price consequences of local bias. *Journal of Financial Economics*, 90, 20–37.

Mavruk, T. 2010. Local bias across regions. *Journal of Money, Investment and Banking*, 18, 40–54.

Lindblom, T., Mavruk, T., and Sjögren, S. 2017. *Proximity Bias in Investors' Portfolio Choice*. Palgrave Macmillan, Cham.

Mavruk, T. and Wermers, R. 2023. Ownership, and underpricing of IPOs with CSR activities. Working Paper. University of Gothenburg.

Nielsson, U. and Wójcik, D. 2016. Proximity and IPO underpricing. *Journal of Corporate Finance*, 38, 92–105.

Norton, E. C., Wang, H., and Ai, C. 2004. Computing interaction effects and standard errors in logit and probit models. *The Stata Journal*, 4, 154–167.

Poon, W. P. H. 2003. Are unsolicited credit ratings biased downward? *Journal of Banking and Finance*, 27, 593–614.

Santos Silva, J. M. C. and Tenreyro, S. 2006. The log of gravity. *Review of Economics and Statistics*, 88, 641–658.

Söderbom, M. 2022. Teaching resources. Available at Mans Söderbom's website. Last visited July 19, 2022.

Stock, J. and Watson, M. 2019. *Introduction to Econometrics: Global Edition*. Princeton University Press, Princeton, NJ.

Wooldridge, J. M. 2002. *Econometric Analysis of Cross-Section and Panel Data*. MIT Press, Cambridge, MA.

11 Writing Empirical Papers in Corporate Finance

INTRODUCTION

The purpose of this chapter is to briefly present an example of a structure of an empirical paper within corporate finance that could be beneficial for undergraduate, Master's as well as PhD students. The structure may vary depending on the type of empirical paper and the research question, but it is a good start to have a general structure of empirical corporate finance papers in mind. To provide an example, the chapter cites some parts of the study by Luo, Manconi, and Schumacher (2024) in sections of the narration. Students are encouraged to download the paper and read it, focusing on the content and also the structure of the writing. The study examines human capital synergies in asset management mergers and finds that more specialized task assignment leads rotated managers to focus on their investment expertise, which in turn enhances firm value. This chapter is oriented towards writing a research paper rather than a student thesis, but emphasizes the similarities between the two structures. It is essential to recognize that there are also some differences in writing, and students should strictly follow their course guideline. One important advantage of writing a thesis in a research paper format is that it can be used for further studies, whereas theses are often not used after the studies are completed.

Note that both theses and research papers are academic texts. They both aim to explain and answer new and interesting research questions. Although the amount of research required to write a research paper might be more, both require detailed research and in-depth analysis. Both will give you an opportunity to develop your knowledge, gain a different perspective, and foster critical and analytical thinking. The key in both types of writing is creativity. To be creative you need to find a research subject that you are passionate about and read many papers within that subject. You should read as many relevant papers as possible and analyze first the content, of course, but also the writing structure of these papers. It will help you to work on your creative thinking and writing.

This chapter assumes that you have already selected an interesting research topic, which is your first challenge. The research is more fun if you are passionate about your topic, so choose a topic because you are really interested in learning about it. At this stage, the directors of thesis courses would suggest reading relevant papers and talking about your research ideas with your friends and professors, to discuss any issues. Here are some standard questions to consider when choosing a topic:

- Why choose this particular topic?
- Who would be interested in reading your research about this topic (besides your supervisors)?
- How relevant is your topic? Does it matter and for who?
- When and where is the topic important? Is it relevant only for now, or can it be generalized to some other time periods? Is it relevant only for one country/place, or can it be generalized to some other places?
- What is the most recent research in your topic?
- How will you contribute to this recent research? Is the contribution marginal, or can you add a significant amount of new knowledge to this research?

Assuming that you have already selected your research topic, this chapter will briefly discuss the standard content of the following sections:

- Title and Abstract
- Introduction
- Theory and Literature Review
- Data/Methods/Model
- Results
- Conclusions
- References and Appendix

The structure above is general, and readers are referred to Cochrane (2005) for more detailed writing tips that also cover academic writing in asset pricing and economics. Chapter 2 in this book will be helpful with writing the theory, literature review, and hypothesis development part. Chapter 3 will be helpful with writing the data section. The models covered in Chapters 4–10 will help with your model selection, interpretation of the results, as well as drawing meaningful and strong conclusions.

11.1 Title and Abstract

The title should be short and spark interest. Keep it simple and concrete. Many researchers leave the title to a later point during the process of writing, simply to observe how the paper develops first, but it is important that an abstract wakes interest. Different journals have different requirements when it comes to length. An abstract of say 150 words maximum seems plausible. It should contain a brief presentation of the research questions, data and methodology, findings, and a few lines about the implications. The abstract is the first part of the study that people read. If it is not well written and does not convey exactly what the study is about, it is unlikely that people will read the whole study. One strategy to write a simple and concrete abstract could be to read the paper carefully again and take notes on the most important findings, the main message of the paper. Writing these main findings in a few short bullet points will certainly be helpful. Then, use these bullet points to build the abstract. Remember that readers want to know what the study is about; they are not interested in fancy words or stories. The example below cites Luo et al. (2024).

Abstract

"We study human capital synergies in asset management mergers that stem from the improved ability to assign fund managers to more specialized tasks in larger firms. More specialized task assignment allows rotated managers to focus on their investment expertise and leads to incremental $54 million of value added per deal per year on average. The effects are concentrated in mergers that lead to a large increase in firm size and in funds whose management appears less specialized prior to the merger. Our results provide direct evidence on the role of firms in the assignment of tasks to fund managers. (JEL G23, J24, G34)" (Luo et al., 2024, p. 384).

11.2 Introduction

The introduction should contain the subject background description, problem description, and problem analysis, and it should also highlight the aims of the study and its main contribution to previous studies. Bear in mind that all the paragraphs in the text are tied together around the main aim and contribution. A study usually follows two or three papers closely and tries to contribute to the knowledge in these papers. Aim to position your paper well in relation to these papers, with a focus on your novel contribution. The intention of this section is to quickly convey your contribution to the reader, but you also need to motivate what you are doing in order to be convincing.

One standard approach is to begin the section by writing what the study is about, followed by the punchline in the paper, and then start motivating the study. This approach makes sure that the reader directly understands what the study is about. The first (opening) paragraph in the introduction should motivate what you are trying to do in the paper. Make sure in particular that this paragraph (and the following) is not vague and meandering. Avoid throwing in many ideas, suggesting that many things can happen in the paper. Instead, use the first paragraph to position the paper better, highlighting what is missing in the literature and trying to be as specific as possible. This will help your following paragraphs provide a roadmap for how you plan to address the issues raised in the opening paragraph, and help the reader understand what question the paper is trying to answer. In this paragraph, avoid the specific description of your setup and findings that starts in your second paragraph. It is a challenging job to decide how best to position your paper; the best advice on this is to focus on minor faults (nitpick) in your text and rewrite the text, redo. This will help you to convey the exact research question you want to ask. It has to be crystal clear to the reader. Thus, the first few paragraphs should do a very good job of describing the paper's unique research question, methodology, and results.

One strategy to achieve this aim is to describe the existing literature briefly and not go into too many details. Talking too much about the existing literature in the introduction makes it difficult to understand your contribution. It will lead you to spend too long on the context and other papers rather than on your own analysis. After motivating the research questions and your contribution, begin describing the regressions you run. Briefly describe the dataset and what variables are run on what regressors to examine the research question(s). Once the method is clear, begin explaining your main results. Make sure you report the economic significance of your results, so the reader has a sense of the economic effects of your results. In a few lines, write the implications of these results.

The introduction usually ends with an outline of the remaining sections in the paper. It has become more common to write the introduction and theory/literature review parts together in one section, but the standard approach is still to write them separately, as outlined in this chapter. The example below cites the first two paragraphs of the introduction section in Luo et al. (2024).

Introduction

"Scale economies have been of central research interest in asset management at least since the theoretical model of Berk and Green (2004) that prominently features diseconomies of scale at the fund level and the empirical evidence of Chen et al. (2004), who document a negative relationship between fund size and fund performance. Diseconomies of scale at the fund level have been the subject of several studies since. However, much less is known about potential economies of scale at the asset management firm level. This is surprising as Chen et al. (2004) also document a positive relationship between firm size and fund performance: funds managed in larger firms outperform funds managed in smaller firms.

In this paper, we study a particular source of firm level economies of scale in the asset management industry: labor specialization. We hypothesize that fund managers can be assigned more specialized tasks in larger than in smaller firms and that such specialized task assignment improves managerial productivity. We examine this conjecture in the context of mergers between asset management firms. We focus on mergers because they increase firm size in a large and discrete fashion, and we ask whether the post-merger reorganizations of the buyer and target firms are characterized by increases in managerial turnover leading to more specialized task assignment for fund managers and, ultimately, improved performance and value creation in the sense of Berk and van Binsbergen (2015)" (Luo et al., 2024, pp. 384–385).

11.3 Theory and Literature Review

This section should include your literature review and an elaboration of the research questions. Motivations should be tied to the economic theory and to the previous literature. It is unlikely that you will develop a new economic theory in an empirical corporate finance paper. Therefore, the economic theory is used to understand the empirical models and results in the paper. Corporate finance studies often develop hypotheses in this section. Before providing any further details of the motivation, begin the section with your contribution. Then provide a short discussion of the most seminal paper in the field before moving on to the most recent development in the area of interest. Here, the findings in most recent empirical papers are discussed and used as a motivation for developing the hypothesis. The focus is on those two or three papers that you closely follow. The contribution to the previous findings in these papers should be crystal clear, as you often intend to test new hypotheses and add new knowledge rather than replicate others. Note that there is nothing wrong with replicating other studies, using a different dataset, or applying it to another geography of interest or time period. However, the research becomes much more interesting if you aim to add *new* knowledge to the field.

The section should be clearly justified with reference to the previous literature. The standard is to avoid piling up all your hypotheses on top of each other at the end. Instead, use theory and previous literature to motivate your hypothesis well and then write your clear and testable hypotheses explicitly. Another approach is where you provide a background for each hypothesis in subsections and then at the end you write and, more importantly, motivate testable predictions from these hypotheses in a subsection. The latter approach is followed by Luo et al. (2024), although the first approach is more standard.

You often have two to four hypotheses in an empirical corporate finance study. More than four hypotheses might be difficult to handle theoretically and less than two may need more justification along the process. Once you have motivated your first hypothesis well and written that explicitly, in a new paragraph or subsection, begin motivating your second hypothesis and write it explicitly, and so on.

Regarding the motivation of your hypotheses, there are usually two approaches to follow. One approach is to develop hypotheses that do not necessarily rely heavily on assumptions and simply report results that, presumably, the reader would find interesting even though you do not draw strong conclusions about underlying economics. This approach is preferable if you think it will ultimately be hard to convince readers that an inference can be reliably drawn based on results that rely heavily on assumptions. A second approach attempts to methodically develop hypotheses that are closely tied to underlying economics. This approach provides a specific presentation of the potential underlying explanations that can affect what the relevant hypotheses are, how you should design tests, and ultimately, what you can conclude about the relevant underlying economics. If properly done, the second approach hedges more, enabling you to draw strong conclusions about the underlying economics.

The hypothesis development, particularly in this second approach, should be compact when linked to economic theories. It must be clear for the reader how the conclusions can be drawn from the analysis testing the hypothesis. For example, it must be clear whether you are testing a correlation, or you have in mind some kind of causality. It is often not recommended to write explicitly which variable is being used when writing the hypothesis, as this may limit the scope and make the hypothesis less interesting. However, the motivation part should make it clear that the hypothesis is testable. Before writing the hypothesis, try to answer and summarize the following questions in two lines: (i) What is the exact question you are asking? (ii) What is the main incremental contribution of your study? To answer these questions, you may take a step back and ask what points you can clearly identify, in an econometric/statistical sense. What parts are more in the spirit of previously undocumented stylized facts, but would be interesting to know and for future research to try to tease out?

In this section it is also important to present and discuss the channels that link the relations (more specifically, between the main variable of interest and the dependent variable). You may offer some potential interpretations of the evidence obtained from your analysis, but it is more credible if you directly test these interpretations against potential alternatives. Thus, this section should also cover some discussion on the alternative hypothesis being tested. For a valuable contribution to the literature, you should try to provide more direct evidence on the potential mechanisms that can explain the main effects. Otherwise, the evidence presented in the study would be suggestive but does not yet allow you to draw strong conclusions, especially on the mechanisms driving the results. One way of examining the channels behind the relations is to provide more direct evidence on the determinants of the main variable of interest that is being used to test the hypothesis.

11.4 Data/Methods/Model

11.4.1 Data

It is often that the data section comes before the methods section in an empirical study, although there are some examples of studies presenting their method before the data. The recommendation here is to describe the sample selection and data-generating process in detail before presenting your method. Explain what the data sources are and motivate why you use these particular data to examine your research questions and test your hypotheses.

The datasets that the universities have access to are often presented on data centers' homepages or the university library's homepage. These are valuable sources for data collections. It is also possible to obtain financial data from stock exchanges' webpages. For specific factors you may use Kenneth R. French – Data Library (dartmouth.edu) and/or Andrea Frazzini's Data Library (nyu.edu). These data are used in many research projects and are available to download for free. Note that you can use them in your own research and studies but cannot publish the datasets on your own webpage. As in the mini cases provided in this book, you can also use publicly available datasets from leading journals, journal archives, and influential papers. See, for example, Harvard Dataverse.

Many of the empirical research questions are data-driven, meaning that you find those questions interesting because you have a unique dataset. Ideally, you should have a theoretically well-motivated research question(s) and hypotheses first and then go ahead and collect appropriate data to examine it. However, if you have unique data you could then try to learn as much as possible from it and consider the possibilities of combining the data at hand with other sources to study new and interesting research questions. So, you could still have the standard chain of well-motivated research questions first (partly driven by the data at hand), and then collect and combine the other sources with the data.

Regardless of how you have collected the data, what data-processing methods you have used and which variables should be clearly stated and well motivated. After reading the hypothesis development and data/methods sections, it should be clear which variable is being used to test which hypothesis. You should end the data section by presenting descriptive statistics for all the variables that you use in the study, clearly specifying the dependent variable, the main variable(s) of interest that are used to test the hypothesis, and the control variables in the model(s). The reader may not be patient enough to wait until the results section to see the descriptive statistics for the variables in the paper. This should be Table 1 of the paper, however, a table that can be placed in the appendix should provide the definition of all your variables (see the Data and Variables section in Luo et al., 2024).

11.4.2 Methods/Model

The data and methods sections are usually combined and presented in subsections. In the methods section, describe the estimation model by specifying the unit of analysis, which tests and analyses are made, and describe the main variables and how they are related to the dependent variable in your hypothesis. Also describe and motivate the control variables. Use the previous literature briefly to motivate your variables, but make sure that it does not look like a literature review again. You may not need many different estimation models to test three or four hypotheses. Thus, motivate well why you chose a particular estimation model. You may need additional models for the robustness of the results, but it is confusing for the reader if you use many different models. In other words, avoid writing a book in econometrics when writing an empirical paper in corporate finance. Some clear test results with fewer but correct estimation models would enlighten the reader's knowledge of the methodology. For the inference, it is important that you explain how you have computed your error terms in the regressions. Although it is less standard, it is also plausible to write the empirical model right before the results for each subsection.

11.5 Results

The results section may begin with a very short reminder of the variables that are used to test the hypothesis and their expected relationship with the dependent variable. This is in order to prepare the reader for the upcoming tables in this section. After a short introduction to the section, present your main results clearly. Since the descriptive statistics for all the variables have already been presented in the data section, the next table in the paper should provide your main findings, the results from your main hypothesis tests. The main focus should be on the sign, statistical significance, and magnitude (economic significance) of the marginal (relative) effects testing your hypothesis. Again, it should be clear which model and which variable is being used to test which hypothesis. You may then move to the results from the control variables. Avoid interpreting results that are significant at the 10% level. Make sure that you can explain your results in an analytical way, implying that you should compare your results to those two or three previous papers that you closely follow. You should also connect your results to the economic theory that you had in mind and described in the theory section. Do not forget to discuss alternative interpretations of the results.

Your main results should be followed by a robustness analysis backed up by figures and additional tables to provide some intuition for the main results. The robustness section is important as results in corporate finance studies, just as in any other social science field, are usually not straightforward. You need to justify your results. In the robustness section, avoid presenting results from different models/variables without motivation. Each analysis in the robustness section should be well motivated. Try to convince the reader why they should trust your results. Do you trust your results to begin with? It is often the case that the most important robustness analyses are placed in a subsection after you have presented your main results, but some of the robustness analysis can be placed in an (internet) appendix.

Critical ability and independence play a crucial role in this section. Critical ability means that you can evaluate the different components of your analysis. For example, it is important to be able to distinguish between findings and assumptions and also to be able to distinguish between your own interpretations and those of others. Critical ability also means that you must ensure that you present and analyze alternatives to the methods or models that you have used, and that you take a critical approach to your sources. Independence means the ability to carry out your own analyses; this is not the same as personal opinion. The analysis should be based on economic theories and reasoning. You should avoid personal opinions and speculation, in the sense of assessments or conclusions which do not have an economic basis. See the results section in Luo et al. (2024).

11.6 Conclusions

This section should be short, since you are supposed to cover the results and analysis in the results section. Briefly describe the nature of the research problem, explain how the aim is achieved, and give a short summary of your findings. Clearly connect the test results to the hypotheses and research questions. Explain how you analyze the results to answer the research questions and to achieve the aim of the study. Specify what your contribution is to the body of knowledge and describe the most important lessons/contributions that can be learned from your analysis.

Avoid listing results and explain what the reader can learn regarding the underlying economics. Think about who will benefit from your paper and write the implications for these groups of readers. You should also mention some of your study's weaknesses. Conclude this section with some suggestions for future research and the most important conclusions. Sure, this section is the only one where you may discuss your results without supporting your statements with references, but do not speculate – readers are interested in your main results and not your personal opinions. The example below cites the conclusion in Luo et al. (2024).

Concluding remarks

"We test the hypothesis that asset management mergers create scale economies because the combined firm is better able to assign fund managers to more specialized tasks, thereby improving productivity. We find that managerial turnover increases significantly following the merger of two asset management firms and that managerial turnover serves to assign more managers to more specialized tasks, especially following mergers that lead to a large increase in firm size. The reallocation of human capital creates additional value, to the tune of $54 million per year for the average merger but $104 million per year following mergers that lead to a large increase in firm size. Our results highlight the important role asset management firms play in the assignment of employees to specialized tasks, the firm's contribution to value creation that is associated with this, and therefore an important source of firm level economies of scale in asset management" (Luo et al., 2024, p. 422).

11.7 References and Appendix

Refer to the relevant background literature. Check your references carefully: who wrote what? Try to find primarily current studies, check the years, page numbers, spelling, and so on, and also make sure that all the references in the text are included in your reference list. On average, it takes about 4–5 years to complete a paper and publish it. During this time, some of the working papers that you have referred to may have been published. Double-check these references and refer to the published versions instead. For those of you who write academic papers, different journals require different reference styles; pay attention to these requirements. Some language editors adjust the references for the target journal, which may save you time, but it is costly. You have been working hard with the entire paper, so you can just as well work hard on the reference list.

Your references should provide sufficient information so that the reader can go to the same sources as you did without too much effort. Direct quotations, where you use the exact wording of your source (or a translation thereof), must be reproduced in your paper in quotation marks. It is important that sources are referenced and that quotation marks are used to mark direct quotations. If not, you may be accused of plagiarism/misrepresentation.

People often do not read appendices, but it is a great place to present those extra analyses to motivate the main results and convince the reader that you have ruled out other alternative explanations and interpretations of the main findings. You can place the appendices at the end of your paper. For those of you who are writing academic papers, pay attention to the journal's recommendations for the format. Some journals publish the appendix on the journal's webpage. Begin the appendix with a short introduction to the tables/figures and so on. You may use a smaller font, roughly 70% the size of the body text font, and single-line spacing. You can describe your data and estimation methods in detail under subheadings.

11.8 Writing

The paper needs to be written clearly and concisely, with proper referencing. Strive to write in an uncomplicated and unambiguous way; keep it simple and short. Avoid repeating the same things in different places in the paper, but short reminders (if important) are fine. Readers are interested in your new results, so keep your models simple but precise, so that you can convince them on your choice of models. Avoid writing long sentences to eliminate complications and keep the paper short, a maximum length of 40 pages including all the tables, figures, and references. You do not need to fill the paper with all the analysis that may potentially give an intuition of your main results, let the reviewers offer some suggestions.

Try to avoid too many subheadings. Also, avoid using subheadings for short paragraphs. Is often that a heading (or subheading) has more than one paragraph. In corporate finance it is common to use the active tense and present tense. Try to avoid other structures (although it might be difficult sometimes) and be consistent with the tense in the whole paper. If it is a single author, avoid writing "we." Use "I," but avoid using it too much. Avoid using adjectives; "the readers are very clever."

11.8.1 Footnotes

For additional references, or if you want to refer to some details of your calculations maybe, the use of footnotes may be a good option. Too many footnotes, however, makes your text difficult to read, so try not to overuse them. Also, readers do not want to take a break from the sentence and read the footnote. So, try inserting footnotes at the end of sentences.

11.8.2 Tables/Figures

Captions for the tables are usually inserted at the top of the table, directly under the table heading. Captions should be self-contained, meaning that captions should provide the necessary information so that the reader understands the details in the table without going back to the text. Corporate finance studies often have (unnecessarily) many control variables in a regression model. When you present your thesis or paper at a seminar/conference, you need to be familiar with the comment "how about this variable, have you thought of controlling for it?" It often works to provide the full results from the main and control variables in the first table of analysis and interpret them in the text. Then, in the upcoming tables, you may skip showing the results from the control variables – although they are included in the regression model. The standard way of presenting such tables is to show the results from the main variables and then write "Control variables" under the column for the variable names and write "YES" under the column presenting the results. Similarly, write for instance "Firm Fixed Effects," "YES"; "Year Effects," "YES"; and so on. Since these results are not shown in the table, you do not need to interpret them in the text. But make sure that you discuss all other results that are presented in the table. For these untabulated results, you may write a sentence as to whether they hold with the results that are presented in the previous table. Present the values with a maximum of three or four decimals in the tables. If the coefficients are large or small, you may consider scaling the variables. The number of digits you use in all the tables and in the text should be consistent.

Table 11.1 provides an example for a presentation of the results from my own working paper on IPO underpricing. The study examines the relation between CSR information in business descriptions of IPOs and the underpricing of IPOs, which is measured as the percentage difference between the closing price on the first day and the offer price. In the first column, only the main variables of interest are related to the dependent variable, IPO underpricing. Column 2 includes industry, stock market list, and IPO year fixed effects in the model. Finally, the third column includes all the control variables in the model. For the sake of completeness, examining the findings in column 3, the results suggest that the negative CSR words in the environment category seem to have a significant impact on first-day returns. In terms of economic significance, a one percentage point increase in negative CSR words related to environment category decreases the first-day returns by 0.40 percentage points.

Similar to the captions in the tables, the captions in the figures should be self-contained but they are usually placed under the figures. Figures may provide insightful information about the data (particularly for data over time) but they can be complicated as well. Again, keep it simple. Figures often present more than one variable, and you may need to use colors for a better presentation, but consider whether the journal prints colored papers. Online versions usually allow for colored figures.

11.8.3 Review

Read and review your draft thoroughly before you submit it. It's a good idea to ask someone else to proofread it and then make any final corrections before submitting. Also, do not forget to get a language review. During those 4–5 years of working with the paper until it gets published, it is not uncommon to rewrite it about 20 times. Below is a list for a final check before you submit your thesis or paper:

Table 11.1 Tone in environment words/bigrams in business descriptions and underpricing of IPOs

VARIABLES	(1) First-day return	(2) First-day return	(3) First-day return
CSR environment pos pct	0.0345	0.0568	0.0456
	(0.566)	(0.871)	(0.688)
CSR environment neg pct	−0.3806***	−0.4159***	−0.4005***
	(−4.179)	(−3.709)	(−3.429)
Control variables	NO	NO	YES
Industry FE	NO	YES	YES
List FE	NO	YES	YES
IPO year FE	NO	YES	YES
Constant	0.0123	−0.4111***	−0.4255**
	−0.399	(−2.673)	(−2.446)
Observations	423	423	423
F-value	9.800	2.030	1.950
Prob > F	0.000	0.001	0.001
R-squared	0.009	0.084	0.095

The table examines the relation between CSR information in business descriptions and the dependent variable of underpricing of IPOs, which is measured as the percentage difference between the closing price on the first day and the offer price. The regression analyses disregard if the IPO changes the stock market list (28 percent of the data). The table shows results from the most relevant CSR category, which refers to 593 (32 percent) words/bigrams related to environment category. It is measured as the percentage of all positive and negative words/bigrams related to environment in business descriptions of IPOs. Three regression models are run; the first column regresses the first-day return on the CSR variables alone. Column 2 includes industry, stock market list, and IPO year fixed effects in the model. The final column includes all the control variables in the model. Robust (White) standard errors are used, and *t*-statistics are presented within parentheses. The significance of the coefficients is marked with asterisks at 1 percent (***), 5 percent (**), and 10 percent (*) significance levels.

- The paper is well written.
- The structure is clear and the language flows.
- The research questions are well motivated and clearly formulated.
- The relevant previous literature has been used in relation to the research questions.
- The previous literature has been critically discussed.
- The correct research method(s) and model(s) have been used.
- The motivation, advantages, and disadvantages of the selected method(s) and model(s) are discussed.
- The results provide answers to the research questions.
- The results are reliable and make sense.
- The analysis of the results is connected to the previous literature that you closely follow and connected to the economic theory.
- Critical evaluation of the results is provided.
- The figures and tables are clear and self-contained.

- Footnotes are kept to a minimum and inserted at the end of sentences.
- All sources referred to in the text are included in the reference list.
- The reference list follows the formal requirements for the journal.
- The whole paper follows the formal requirements for the journal.

Readers should double-check and add more bullets to this list, as there are always some missing parts in the work. These bullets may also provide some general guidelines for a constructive review of a thesis or empirical paper. You will need to review papers/theses/reports at conferences, workshops, and seminars during your career. Reviewing papers is a great learning process that will help both the reviewer and the respondent gain deeper knowledge in the field.

11.9 Summary

Previous chapters aimed to present different research designs and econometric models used in empirical corporate finance studies. Readers learned how to apply different models, depending on the research question, to datasets using statistical packages. In this chapter the focus is on the structure and writing of your research findings. Good writing is key to conveying the findings from your research to readers. You should demonstrate your critical and analytical skills, and discuss the results from your research in a structured way when writing your thesis/paper.

The thesis/paper should begin with a short title followed by a short abstract, briefly stating the objectives of the research, the main results, and the most important conclusions. The introduction should cover your objectives and suitable background, avoiding a detailed survey of the literature or details of your results. The economic theories and literature review should be used to develop your hypothesis in the literature review section. In the data and methods section, indicate where you obtained the data and provide sufficient details to allow others to reproduce your results. The method(s) should be described in a structured way, convincing readers of the accuracy of the models that allow you to test your hypotheses. The results section should clearly present your findings, emphasizing the significance of your results. The results and discussion sections can be combined by connecting your results to theory and the previous literature. In the conclusion section, a short summary should be followed directly by the implications of your findings. This chapter discusses the details of these sections and thus presents a standard example for the structure of an empirical corporate finance paper. The structure is general and may be different depending on the type of empirical paper and the field. However, beginning with the standard content of the sections will help you to better structure your ideas and writing. The chapter ends by providing some writing suggestions.

KEY TERMS

Writing empirical papers in corporate finance; structure; writing tips; review of drafts.

REFERENCES

Berk, J. B. and Green, R. C. 2004. Mutual fund flows and performance in rational markets. *Journal of Political Economy*, 112, 1269–1295.

Berk, J. B. and van Binsbergen, J. H. 2015. Measuring skill in the mutual fund industry. *Journal of Financial Economics*, 108, 1–20.

Chen, J., Hong, H., Huang, M., and Kubik, J. D. 2004. Does fund size erode mutual fund performance? The role of liquidity and organization. *American Economic Review*, 94, 1276–1302.

Cochrane, J. H. 2005. *Writing Tips for Ph.D. Students*. University of Chicago Press, Chicago, IL.

Luo, M., Manconi, A., and Schumacher, D. 2024. Returns to scale from labor specialization: Evidence from asset management mergers. *Review of Corporate Finance Studies*, 13, 384–427.

12 Future Directions: Machine-Learning Methods

Machine learning (ML) is a growing multidisciplinary field that combines statistics, optimization, and the field of computer science. It is an advanced technique behind artificial intelligence, which has broad applications, for example, in face detection, voice recognition, chatbots for quick customer support, and so on. ML methods seek to learn patterns from data and use the information to make predictions. The methods often use big data that contain a large number of observations and variables (Stock and Watson, 2020) to achieve high prediction accuracy and thus outperformance of many traditional methods. Despite ML methods being relatively new in (corporate) finance, the techniques have been applied to many studies in computer vision, financial time-series analysis, and natural language processing. Particularly, the latter field has been popular in studies examining the relationship between textual/content analysis and information asymmetry theories.

This chapter aims to briefly present most common ML techniques used in (corporate) finance studies, their purpose, and their differences from the traditional econometric methods that have been covered in previous chapters. The description and review below draw on Hoang and Wiegratz (2023) but focus more on corporate finance studies. Using traditional models, the main aim is to examine causal relationships between dependent and independent variables, while ML methods allow users to learn unique features of the high-dimensional data. However, ML methods should not be seen as a replacement for traditional methods, as they allow us to learn and extract information from unstructured data such as text, images, and videos, which in turn can be used in further analysis with traditional methods.

There are two major types of ML method. The first type is supervised machine learning, which uses observations associated with known labels or outcomes. In other words, in supervised learning, some independent variables are used to predict the dependent variable. The label in ML methods corresponds to the values of the dependent variable in traditional methods. In supervised learning, the dependent variable is sometimes called the target variable and the independent variables are often called predictor variables and sometimes called features. Similar to traditional methods, using ML methods in supervised learning results in prediction of the target variable, as well as estimates for the predictor variables. These predicted (learned) parameters in the prediction model can then be used out-of-sample to make new predictions of the target variable in the new dataset. Put differently, a machine learns the parameters in one dataset and uses these parameters to predict the target variable in another dataset.

The second type is unsupervised machine learning, which employs observations without known labels or outcomes. So, there is no target (dependent) variable in unsupervised learning. ML methods are used to derive structural information from often unstructured data. For example, you can try to identify whether the data at hand show any clusters, whether there is any correlation between the observations so that they can be grouped together. These clustered data in turn can be used in further analysis.

These approaches serve different purposes, and this chapter discusses the differences between these ML types. There are also other types of ML, but they are less common in (corporate) finance studies and hence will not be covered in this chapter. These types include, for example, reinforcement learning (Sutton and Barto, 2018), semi-supervised learning (Zhu, 2008), and active learning (Settles, 2009).

12.1 Supervised Learning

The main aim with supervised learning is to make out-of-sample predictions of the target variable. The dataset is divided into so-called training data and test data. An ML method is applied to the training data to estimate the parameters of the prediction model. Finally, these parameters from the prediction model are used to predict the target variable out-of-sample and the resulting expected prediction performance is evaluated. The prediction models used to estimate the parameters vary depending on the research question and complexity of the models. More advanced models are used for complex research designs. Although these complex models may yield higher prediction performance, their interpretability is often questioned. Again, depending on the research question, it might be worth keeping the models simple if the aim is to interpret the outcome of these models.

The OLS method (covered in Chapter 5) is the simplest model that provides direct interpretability. Opponents would argue that OLS shows weaker performance in out-of-sample prediction (Hoang and Wiegratz, 2023). This criticism applies particularly for the linear nature of the OLS estimator, and non-linear transformations of the variables have been suggested to improve the predictions. There are also other suggestions to improve the performance of OLS predictions, so-called regularized linear methods that, in a way, introduce bias in the OLS estimation (Hastie, Tibshirani, and Friedman, 2009). These methods aim to shrink the size of the coefficients to achieve a better prediction performance, since there is a bias–variance trade-off in the estimations. Introducing this bias in the coefficient estimates will decrease the variance. The least absolute shrinkage and selection operator (LASSO) is the most common regularized linear method that introduces bias in the OLS coefficients. LASSO introduces bias by penalizing the coefficients with a large variance with little information, and assigning zero for insignificant coefficients. The feature of LASSO also allows for variable selection. Other regularized models include, for example, ridge regression and elastic net regression, which have a different penalty structure in OLS estimation (Zou and Hastie, 2005). These latter models are not commonly used in corporate finance studies.

More complex models that incorporate non-linearity and some interaction effects have also been suggested (Hastie et al., 2009). The most common technique is the decision tree, where the model builds on nodes and often has multiple layers. The decision tree gets split for a given value of a predictor variable. The last node where there is no other split in the tree is called a leaf node. When the tree reaches a leaf node, it produces a prediction value. Since the values are observed at each node, the decision tree model offers high interpretability. The most commonly used decision tree model in corporate finance is random forests, which combine multiple decision trees (Breiman, 2001). The method repeatedly draws bootstrap samples from the data at hand to separately build a decision tree for each sample. Again, when each tree reaches a leaf node, a prediction value is computed. The average of the prediction values obtained from each decision tree is the prediction of a random forest model. Since the prediction value is the average value from each decision tree, random forests yield higher prediction performance than a single decision tree. However, it is more difficult to interpret the predicted values at each node of each decision tree in random forests.

To improve the prediction performance in random forests, boosted regression trees have been suggested (Hastie et al., 2009). The difference in this model is that it builds the trees iteratively instead of combining many independent trees as in random forests. This approach allows the model to consider the observations in the previous trees that are poorly predicted, and hence tends to yield a better prediction performance than random forests. The other advanced ML techniques that consider non-linearity and interaction effects include, among others, neural networks. Yet such models are less commonly applied in corporate finance studies, mainly because the models are applied to unconventional data and they are difficult to interpret, including a complex layer structure (also called hidden layers).

12.2 Unsupervised Learning

The aim of unsupervised learning is to derive and learn structural information from unstructured data. There are many different types – subcategories – of unsupervised learning, but the most commonly used techniques are clustering and dimensionality reduction. The first technique, clustering, groups observations with high and low similarity and different methods of clustering can be applied to group the observations. The most common method is centroid-based, which positions observations around multiple central points, also called centroids. The K-means method (MacQueen, 1967) is the most commonly used method in corporate finance. Moreover, density-based methods – called DBSCAN (Ester et al., 1996) – are commonly used for clustering data. There are also clustering methods based on the statistical distribution of the observations, so-called distribution-based methods. For example, Gaussian mixture models (Rasmussen, 1999) rely on the underlying data being normally distributed. If the underlying data contain a hierarchical relationship, then the initial clusters in the data can be used to build a hierarchy in the data using a method called BIRCH (Zhang, Ramakrishnan, and Livny, 1996).

The second unsupervised learning technique is dimensionality reduction, which reduces the dimension in the data but retains most of the relevant information. The most common method of dimensionality reduction is principal component analysis, already covered in Chapter 4. The second most used method is based on neural networks, particularly the so-called autoencoder neural network (Goodfellow, Bengio, and Courville, 2016).

Along with clustering and dimensionality reduction methods, unsupervised learning also includes outlier detection techniques, which are similar to the techniques covered in Chapters 2 and 3. However, ML methods of outlier detection tend to yield higher performance, particularly in high-dimensional data, than the traditional methods used to manage outliers (Domingues et al., 2018). Other methods in unsupervised learning that focus on synthetic data generation use neural networks to generate synthetic data that closely matches the training data (Goodfellow et al., 2020). For example, data on bank transactions are highly confidential, while anti-money laundering literature that aims to predict and identify money laundering transactions often relies on synthetic anti-money laundering data (Jensen, 2024).

12.3 Limitations of ML

There is no doubt that ML methods have become increasingly useful in corporate finance studies. However, there are also some limitations of these methods. The main limitation is that such methods offer low interpretability, and hence they are sometimes called black-box methods, as the process generating the prediction is often not directly observed. The literature proposes some techniques for interpretability of ML methods (see Burkart and Huber, 2021), the most common being Shap values. This method is used to explain predictions from supervised learning methods, for example random forests. It is a method that originated from coalitional game theory (Shapley, 1953), and it measures the effects of a feature (independent variable) by taking into account its interaction with other features (see Lundberg and Lee, 2017; Strumbelj and Kononenko, 2010).

Computing Shap values can be computationally expensive, but it yields some decision plots and summary plots that are useful and informative about the features. Another advantage of using Shap values is that they offer both global interpretability and local interpretability. If the aim of the study is to explain how much each feature contributes to the target variable, and hence the prediction of the model, then global interpretability (which is at the feature level) is useful. If, instead, the aim is to explore how each observation of the feature contributes to the target variable, then local interpretability (where each observation receives its own Shap values) could be used. This analysis would be more interesting if the plan is to use these individual Shap values in a further analysis.

The second limitation of using ML methods is that ML requires large datasets. Particularly, ML tends to outperform traditional methods if the number of variables is large relative to the number of observations. Since large datasets are often not available, one solution to this problem is to use ML models that have already been trained with data containing large amounts of observations that are comparable to the current (but a smaller) dataset. Such pre-trained ML models can be applied to textual analysis and face recognition, for example. The final limitation of using ML methods is that these methods are computationally expensive. Relative to the OLS method, for example, ML methods take more time and computing power.

12.4 Summary

ML methods are increasingly used in (corporate) finance studies with impressive applications. ML is a part of artificial intelligence that learns from historical data, identifies patterns, and assists with decision-making. ML can be used to construct new measures from unstructured data such as text, images, and videos. One relevant field for corporate finance studies is textual analysis, which focuses on word counts based on specific dictionaries. Such studies mainly focus on the measurement of sentiment, measurement of corporate executives' characteristics, and measurement of firm characteristics, among others. ML methods tend to provide easier access to the information contained in unconventional data, saving time and effort to obtain structured data, as well as quantifying some relevant qualitative information.

ML methods are also applied with the aim of reducing prediction error in the models. Some examples include studies on the prediction of asset prices and trading behavior, prediction of credit risk, prediction of firm outcomes and firm decision-making. Finally, ML methods are also used to extend the existing traditional econometric methods. The performance of ML models depends on the quality (and size) of the input data ("garbage in, garbage out") and the choice of ML model. There are many ML models, but all come with their own details and issues. It is therefore essential to select accurate model(s) for the analysis. This chapter briefly reviews some broad types of ML methods. It covers supervised learning, which tends to achieve superior prediction performance by using more flexible functional forms than OLS in the prediction model. It explains unsupervised ML methods that derive and learn structural information from conventional data. Finally, the chapter discusses some limitations and drawbacks of ML, as well as potential remedies.

KEY TERMS

ML methods; prediction error; supervised learning; unsupervised learning; limitations and drawbacks of ML; potential remedies of such limitations.

REFERENCES

Breiman, L. 2001. Random forests. *Machine Learning*, 45, 5–32.

Burkart, N. and Huber, M. F. 2021. A survey on the explainability of supervised machine learning. *Journal of Artificial Intelligence Research*, 70, 245–253.

Domingues, R., Filippone, M., Michiardi, P., and Zouaoui, J. 2018. A comparative evaluation of outlier detection algorithms: Experiments and analyses. *Pattern Recognition*, 74, 406–421.

Ester, M., Kriegel, H.-P., Sander, J., and Xu, X. 1996. A density-based algorithm for discovering clusters in large spatial databases with noise. *KDD*, 96, 226–231.

Goodfellow, I., Bengio, Y., and Courville, A. 2016. *Deep Learning*. MIT Press, Cambridge, MA.

Goodfellow, I., Pouget-Abadie, J., Mirza, M., Xu, B., Warde-Farley, D., Ozair, S., et al. 2020. Generative adversarial networks. *Communications of the ACM*, 63, 139–144.

Hastie, T., Tibshirani, R., and Friedman, J. 2009. *The Elements of Statistical Learning: Data Mining, Inference, and Prediction* (2nd ed.). Springer, New York.

Hoang, D. and Wiegratz, K. 2023. Machine learning methods in finance: Recent applications and prospects. *European Financial Management*, 29, 1657–1701.

Jensen, R. I. T. 2024. *Machine Learning for Anti-money Laundering*. PhD thesis, Department of Electrical and Computer Engineering, Aarhus University, Denmark.

Lundberg, S. M. and Lee, S.-I. 2017. A unified approach to interpreting model predictions. *Neural Information Processing Systems*, 30, 4768–4777.

MacQueen, J. 1967. Some methods for classification and analysis of multivariate observations. *Proceedings of the Fifth Berkeley Symposium on Mathematical Statistics and Probability*, pp. 281–297.

Rasmussen, C. 1999. The infinite Gaussian mixture model. *Advances in Neural Information Processing Systems*, 12, 554–560.

Settles, B. 2009. Active learning literature survey (Computer Science Technical Report No. 1648). Available at http://digital.library.wisc.edu/1793/60660

Shapley, L. S. 1953. A value for *n*-person games. In H. W. Kuhn and A. W. Tucker (eds), *Contributions to the Theory of Games II*. Princeton University Press, Princeton, NJ, pp. 307–317.

Stock, J. H. and Watson, M. W. 2020. *Introduction to Econometrics* (4th ed.). Pearson, Harlow.

Strumbelj, E. and Kononenko, I. 2010. An efficient explanation of individual classifications using game theory. *Journal of Machine Learning Research*, 11, 1–18.

Sutton, R. S. and Barto, A. G. 2018. *Reinforcement Learning: An Introduction*. MIT Press, Cambridge, MA.

Zhang, T., Ramakrishnan, R., and Livny, M. 1996. BIRCH: An efficient data clustering method for very large databases. *ACM SIGMOD Record*, 25, 103–114.

Zhu, X. 2008. Semi-supervised learning literature survey (Computer Science Technical Report No. 1530). Available at https://pages.cs.wisc.edu/~jerryzhu/pub/ssl_survey.pdf

Zou, H. and Hastie, T. 2005. Regularization and variable selection via the elastic net. *Journal of the Royal Statistical Society: Series B (Statistical Methodology)*, 67, 301–320.

Appendices

Appendix for Chapter 2: Standard Errors for Various Sampling Techniques

This appendix provides standard errors for various sampling techniques covered in Chapter 2.

(i) The standard error for the mean of a simple random sample is given by

$$se_{\text{simple random sample}} = \sqrt{\frac{s^2(N-n)}{n(N-1)}}, \tag{2.6}$$

where s^2 is the variance for the simple random sample, n is the sample size, and N is the population size.

(ii) The standard error for the mean of a stratified random sample is given by

$$se_{\text{stratified random sample}} = \frac{1}{N}\sqrt{\sum\nolimits_{\text{str}=1}^{k} N^2\left(\frac{N-n_{\text{str}}}{N-1}\right)\frac{s^2}{n_{\text{str}}}}, \tag{2.7}$$

where N represents the number of units in the population and n_{str} represents the number of units in the stratum, k is the number of strata, and s is the standard deviation in strata.

(iii) The standard error for the mean of a clustered random sample that assigns equal weights for each cluster is given by

$$se_{\text{clustered random sample}} = \frac{\sqrt{\sum\frac{(\bar{\bar{x}}-\bar{x})^2}{(n_c-1)}}}{\sqrt{n_c}}, \tag{2.8}$$

where $\bar{\bar{x}}$ is the overall mean of the clusters, $\bar{x}$ is the mean of each cluster, and n_c is the number of clusters in the sample. If the clusters are unequally weighted, we replace the numerator in Equation (2.8) with the weighted standard deviation $s_w = \sqrt{\frac{1}{(n_c-1)}\sum((\frac{v}{\bar{v}})^2(\bar{x}-\bar{\bar{x}}_w)^2)}$, where $\bar{\bar{x}}_w$ is the overall weighted mean, v is the weighting unit in the cluster, and $\bar{v}$ is the average cluster size.

(iv) The standard error for the mean of a systematic random sample is given by

$$se_{\text{systematic random sample}} = \sqrt{\left(\frac{N-n}{N}\right)\frac{s^2}{n}}, \quad (2.9)$$

where s is the standard deviation of the systematic random sample, n is the number of units in the sample, and N is the number of units in the population.

Appendix for Chapter 3: Non-parametric Analysis

Non-parametric analysis is a branch of statistical analysis that uses models which impose no functional form assumptions. Parametric analysis uses models that assume a functional form and, typically, parameterize that functional form with one or more parameters. Basically, you could find non-parametric versions of almost all the models in statistics or econometrics. Tests such as z-, t-, and F-tests depend on the assumptions about the parameters of the population and are called parametric tests. Tests that do not make distributional assumptions about the parameters of the population are called non-parametric tests. These tests can also be used to manage outliers in the data. Because these tests are distribution-free, they are easier to implement and interpret, but they also ignore certain information. This appendix covers the most commonly used non-parametric tests in corporate finance and business studies.

- *Matched-pairs sign test.* This test is used to examine the difference in sign of the values in the dataset. The null hypothesis of the test is that the median of the differences is zero. This means that there are no differences between the signs; plus and minus signs are equally likely to occur. The alternative hypothesis in the test is that there are differences between the signs of the values (see Snedecor and Cochran, 1989). Stata code: `signtest var1=var2`.
- *Wilcoxon matched-pairs signed-rank test.* The null hypothesis in this test is that the distributions are the same and the alternative hypothesis is that the distributions are not the same (Wilcoxon, 1945). Stata code: `signrank var1=var2`.
- *Mann–Whitney U-test (Wilcoxon rank sum).* This test compares whether two independent samples have been drawn from two populations which have the same relative frequency distribution. The null hypothesis is that the sum of the ranks of the observations in each sample is equal. This hypothesis is tested against the hypothesis that the sum of the ranks in each sample is not equal. Stata code: `ranksum var, by(group var)`.
- *Kruskal–Wallis test for m independent samples.* This test is similar to the Mann–Whitney U-test and is used when there are more than two independent samples. The null hypothesis in the test is that the samples are drawn from p identical populations, and the alternative hypothesis is that the distributions are not the same. Stata code: `kwallis var, by(group var)`. The dependent variable is continuous, but the group variable could have an ordinal scale.
- *Spearman rank correlation test.* This test is used to examine the relation between the two sets of ranked data and is similar to the parametric version of the Pearson

correlation test. The null hypothesis is that there is no rank correlation, and the alternative hypothesis is that there is a rank correlation between the two variables. Stata code: `spearman var1 var2`.

- *Number-of-runs test.* This test is used to examine the randomness of a series, in other words, the test examines whether the collected dataset is random, serially independent. Thus, the null hypothesis is that the series of observations is random. The alternative hypothesis is that the series is not random. Stata code: `runtest var1`.

Appendix for Chapter 4: Eigenvalues and Eigenvectors of the Variance–Covariance Matrix

Principal components analysis ranks the principal components in decreasing order of importance, so that the components are uncorrelated. The first principal component accounts for as much variance in the data as possible, and each following principal component accounts for the remaining variability in the data. Suppose $\mathbf{x}$ is a random variable with mean μ and variance–covariance matrix Σ. In practice, we need to estimate μ and Σ, but suppose that there is no estimation error and thus $\hat{\mu} = \mu, \hat{\Sigma} = \Sigma$ for simplicity. We define the first principal component as $y_1 = \mathbf{b}_1'(\mathbf{x} - \mu)$, where $\mathbf{b}_1$ is computed so that the variance of $\mathbf{b}_1'(\mathbf{x} - \mu)$ is maximized over all vectors of $\mathbf{b}_1$ by satisfying $\mathbf{b}_1'\mathbf{b}_1 = 1$ (normalization). The maximum value of the variance of $\mathbf{b}_1'(\mathbf{x} - \mu)$ satisfying $\mathbf{b}_1'\mathbf{b}_1 = 1$ is said to be the eigenvalue λ_1, which is the largest eigenvalue of the variance–covariance matrix of Σ. Here, $\mathbf{b}_1$ is an eigenvector of the variance–covariance matrix of Σ and y_1 is the first principal component. The condition $\mathbf{b}_1'\mathbf{b}_1 = 1$ means that the eigenvector of the variance–covariance matrix Σ that is used to define the principal component y_1 is normalized to 1.

We define the second principal component as $y_2 = \mathbf{b}_2'(\mathbf{x} - \mu)$, where $\mathbf{b}_2$ is computed so that the variance of $\mathbf{b}_2'(\mathbf{x} - \mu)$ is maximized over all vectors of $\mathbf{b}_2$ by satisfying $\mathbf{b}_2'\mathbf{b}_2 = 1$. Here, the variance of $\mathbf{b}_2'(\mathbf{x} - \mu)$ is the maximum among all linear combinations of $\mathbf{x}$ that are uncorrelated with the first principal component of y_1. This maximum variance is the second largest eigenvalue, λ_2, of the variance–covariance matrix Σ. Similarly, we can define the remaining principal components. For instance, the ith $(i = 3, 4, \ldots, p)$ principal component is defined by $y_i = \mathbf{b}_i'(\mathbf{x} - \mu)$, where $\mathbf{b}_i$ is computed as satisfying $\mathbf{b}_i'\mathbf{b}_i = 1$ and the variance is a maximum among all linear combinations of $\mathbf{x}$ that are uncorrelated with principal component y_{i-1}. The maximum value of the variance of $\mathbf{b}_i'(\mathbf{x} - \mu)$ is the ith largest eigenvalue, λ_i, of the variance–covariance matrix Σ. The ordered eigenvalues can be represented as $\lambda_1 \geq \lambda_2 \geq \cdots \geq \lambda_p$ and the corresponding $\mathbf{b}_1, \mathbf{b}_2, \ldots, \mathbf{b}_p$ are the normalized eigenvectors of the variance–covariance matrix Σ. It is said that two principal components are uncorrelated if their underlying eigenvectors are uncorrelated. As mentioned, the variance of the ith principal component is the eigenvalue λ_i, and thus to account for the total variation in the data, all the eigenvalues are summed. This would be equivalent to the total amount of variation measured by the original variables. The ratio

$\frac{\lambda_i}{\sum_{i=1}^{p} \lambda_i}$ represents the proportion of the total variability in the data that is accounted for by the ith principal component of y_i.

The principal component scores are the values of the principal components that indicate the location of the observations. Consider the mth observation of the ith principal component; that is, compute the principal component score $y_{m,i}$ for the mth observation of the random variable $\mathbf{x}_m$: $y_{m,i} = \mathbf{b}_i'(\mathbf{x}_m - \mu)$, where $i = 1,2,\ldots,p$ and $m = 1,2,\ldots,N$. The normalization of the eigenvector $\mathbf{b}_i'\mathbf{b}_i = 1$ leads to one interesting result. The elements within the eigenvector are comparable to one another, but those across the eigenvectors are not comparable. Normalization leads to the sum of the squares of the elements in each eigenvector aggregating to 1, meaning that the value of the element is smaller the more non-zero elements the eigenvector has. One way of comparing the elements across the eigenvectors is to compute the component-loading vectors by multiplying the elements in each vector by the square root of the corresponding eigenvalue. More formally, $\mathbf{c}_i = \lambda_i^{1/2} \times \mathbf{b}_i$ for $i = 1,2,\ldots,p$, where the $\mathbf{c}_i$ are component loadings. Just as for $\mathbf{b}_i$, the component loadings $\mathbf{c}_i$ are eigenvectors of the variance–covariance matrix Σ, but $\mathbf{c}_i$ has length $\lambda_i^{1/2}$ instead of 1. Now the elements of $\mathbf{c}_i$ are comparable with each other.

To determine the actual dimensionality (the number of principal components) in the data, you need to seek the number of principal components that have variance greater than zero. The most common method of determining the number of principal components is to plot the eigenvalues, a so-called scree plot. Of course, you could observe the eigenvalues in the output table as well, but a scree plot shows the point at which the eigenvalues level off, indicating that they are close to zero and can be ignored.

Appendix for Chapter 5: Details on CLRM

A. Minimizing Residual Sum of Squares

The aim of this part of the appendix is to minimize the residual sum of squares (RSS). The software program will do this for you, but it might be good to go through how the minimization is done. You first take the partial derivatives of the RSS with respect to b_0 and b_1, then set the partial derivatives equal to 0. Equation (5.21) show the solution for b_0:

$$\begin{aligned} \frac{\partial \text{RSS}}{\partial b_0} &= 2Nb_0 - 2\Sigma y_i + \Sigma b_1 x_i, \\ 2Nb_0 - 2\Sigma y_i + \Sigma b_1 x_i &= 0, \\ \Sigma y_i - Nb_0 - \Sigma b_1 x_i &= 0, \\ \Sigma y_i &= Nb_0 + \Sigma b_1 x_i, \\ b_0 &= \bar{y} - b_1 \bar{x}. \end{aligned} \tag{5.21}$$

Equation (5.22) gives the solution for b_1:

$$\frac{\partial \text{RSS}}{\partial b_1} = 2\sum x_i^2 b_1 - 2\sum x_i y_i + 2\sum x_i b_0, \tag{5.22}$$

$$\sum x_i y_i - \sum x_i b_0 - \sum x_i^2 b_1 = 0,$$

$$\sum x_i y_i = \sum x_i b_0 + \sum x_i^2 b_1.$$

Observe that b_1 enters into both Equation (5.21) and Equation (5.22). To solve b_1, multiply Equation (5.21) by $\sum x_i$ and Equation (5.22) by N and then subtract Equation (5.21) from Equation (5.22):

$$\sum x_i \sum y_i = Nb_0 \sum x_i + \sum b_1 x_i \sum x_i,$$

$$N\sum x_i y_i = N\sum x_i b_0 + N\sum x_i^2 b_1,$$

$$N\sum x_i y_i - \sum x_i \sum y_i = Nb_0 \sum x_i + Nb_1 \sum x_i^2 - Nb_0 \sum x_i + \sum b_1 x_i \sum x_i,$$

$$N\sum x_i y_i - \sum x_i \sum y_i = Nb_1 \sum x_i^2 - b_1(\sum x_i)^2,$$

$$\sum x_i y_i - \frac{\sum x_i \sum y_i}{N} = b_1\left[\sum x_i^2 - \frac{(\sum x_i)^2}{N}\right],$$

$$b_1 = \frac{\sum x_i y_i - \frac{\sum x_i \sum y_i}{N}}{\left[\sum x_i^2 - \frac{(\sum x_i)^2}{N}\right]}. \tag{5.23}$$

The final step is just a presentation of the equation as deviation from the averages:

$$b_1 = \frac{\sum(x_i - \bar{x})(y_i - \bar{y})}{\sum(x_i - \bar{x})^2}. \tag{5.24}$$

B. Illustration of CLRM Assumption 2

To illustrate this, revisit the definition of b:

$$b_1 = \frac{\sum_{i=1}^{N}(x_i - \bar{x})(y_i - \bar{y})}{\sum_{i=1}^{N}(x_i - \bar{x})^2} \text{ and let } w_i \equiv \frac{\sum_{i=1}^{N}(x_i - \bar{x})}{\sum_{i=1}^{N}(x_i - \bar{x})^2}. \tag{5.25}$$

Here the ratio is defined as w_i:

$$b_1 = \sum_{i=1}^{N} w_i (y_i - \bar{y}), \tag{5.26}$$

where using the population parameters β instead of the sample parameters b, $y_i - \bar{y}$ is defined as follows:

$$y_i - \bar{y} = \beta_0 + \beta_1 x_i + e_i - (\beta_0 + \beta_1 \bar{x} + \bar{e}), \tag{5.27}$$

$$y_i - \bar{y} = \beta_1 (x_i - \bar{x}) + e_i - \bar{e}. \tag{5.28}$$

Insert Equation (5.28) into Equation (5.25):

$$b_1 = \sum_{i=1}^{N} w_i \left(\beta_1 \left(x_i - \overline{x} \right) + e_i - \overline{e} \right), \tag{5.29}$$

$$b_1 = \beta_1 \sum_{i=1}^{N} w_i \left(x_i - \overline{x} \right) + \sum_{i=1}^{N} w_i \left(e_i - \overline{e} \right). \tag{5.30}$$

Note that the first term equals $\beta_1 \times 1$, following how w_i is defined in Equation (5.25). It follows that

$$b_1 = \beta_1 + \sum_{i=1}^{N} w_i \left(e_i - \overline{e} \right). \tag{5.31}$$

The second term can be rewritten as follows:

$$\sum_{i=1}^{N} w_i \left(e_i - \overline{e} \right) = \sum_{i=1}^{N} w_i e_i - \overline{e} \sum_{i=1}^{N} w_i. \tag{5.32}$$

Since the sum of the deviation of a variable from its own average is 0: $\Sigma \left(x_i - \overline{x} \right) = 0$, which is the numerator in w_i, the second term in Equation (5.32) is 0, thus

$$\sum_{i=1}^{N} w_i \left(e_i - \overline{e} \right) = \sum_{i=1}^{N} w_i e_i. \tag{5.33}$$

Let's insert Equation (5.33) into Equation (5.31) and take the expectation of both sides:

$$E\left(b_1 \right) = \beta_1 + E\left(\sum_{i=1}^{N} w_i e_i \right), \tag{5.34}$$

$$E\left(b_1 \right) = \beta_1 + \sum_{i=1}^{N} w_i E(e_i). \tag{5.35}$$

Finally, if the assumption of $E(e_i) = 0$ holds, obtain an unbiased estimator of b_1:

$$E\left(b_1 \right) = \beta_1. \tag{5.36}$$

Note that if there is an intercept in the model you cannot test this assumption, as the sum of the estimated residuals will be zero, $\sum_{i=1}^{N} \hat{e}_i = 0$.

C. Semi-parametric Analysis

Semi-parametric models combine parametric and non-parametric analyses. As the name suggests, these models range from being fully parametric to fully non-parametric. In this sense, such models allow more flexibility by avoiding distributional assumptions for some variables, but still impose some structure on the other variables in the model, thereby increasing the precision of the estimates.

One simple example of a semi-parametric model is to use indicator variables to approximate the shape of a relationship within the context of a linear regression in place of a linear relationship. For instance, consider an example of capital structure studies. To examine how ownership is related to a firm's capital structure, defined as the ratio between the market value of long-term debt and total assets, you could replace the ownership with a series of indicator variables for intervals of values of ownership. If the number of indicator variables (the intervals) increases as the sample size increases, then a semi-parametric analysis is being performed. The analysis often includes some control variables (covariates), such as the size of the firm, book-to-market ratio, and so on, to isolate the effect of ownership on capital structure. These control variables are still continuous in the semi-parametric model. If you also create intervals for these covariates and include indicators for corresponding intervals in the model instead of the covariates, then the model becomes non-parametric. The so-called semi-parametric or partially linear model can be more formally presented as follows:

$$\mathrm{CS}_j = f\left(\mathrm{ownership}_j\right) + \beta_k \mathbf{X}_{j,k} + e_j, \tag{5.37}$$

where CS_j is the capital structure of the firm and $f(\mathrm{ownership}_j)$ is an arbitrary function to be estimated using non-parametric methods. Including dummy variables for intervals of values of risk is a special case mentioned above. $\mathbf{X}_{j,k}$ includes all the control variables, such as size, book-to-market, and so on. The model retains the parametric linear form for all $\mathbf{X}_{j,k}$. This means that the dimension of the non-parametric component is 1 in the model, which may help with computation and convergence rates, provided that the approach is other than using dummy variables for interval values of ownership. Our main variable, $\mathrm{ownership}_j$, is the variable of interest in the model, and it is also the variable whose correct functional form is unknown. Various methods can be used to estimate this semi-parametric model; the dummy variable approach has already been mentioned. Another simple approach is called double-residual regression, in which the model regresses both CS_j and $\mathrm{ownership}_j$ on $\mathbf{X}_{j,k}$ in separate regressions and then uses the standard non-parametric regression methods – such as quantile and median regression (see Cameron and Trivedi, 2005) – on the residual terms from these two regressions to estimate the function.

One advantage of the non-parametric regression methods is that the data determine the functional form. If the functional form is non-linear, assuming linearity in the parameter will lead to a poor approximation. The disadvantage of this approach is the loss of degrees of freedom. A single linear regression has one degree of freedom, but a model with five dummy variables (indicators) has five degrees of freedom.

The trade-off between semi-parametric and parametric methods lies in the flexibility of capturing the functional form against the loss of efficiency in the estimation (or specification error against variance). If the relationship is non-linear in the population, failing to impose that structure will mean you lose information in the estimation, leading to less precise estimates. The studies often use non-parametric and semi-parametric analyses for robustness checks, or as a precursor to parametric analysis. These models are perfect candidates in the data management process to learn about the data and underlying patterns.

Appendix for Chapter 6: Derivation of OLS Estimator in the Presence of Endogeneity

Recall that the sum of the deviation of a variable from its own average is 0: $\Sigma(x_i - \bar{x}) = 0$. Thus, we rewrite Equation (6.2) as

$$b_1 = \frac{\Sigma(x_i - \bar{x})(y_i - \bar{y})}{\Sigma(x_i - \bar{x})^2} = \frac{\Sigma(x_i - \bar{x})y_i - \bar{y}\Sigma(x_i - \bar{x})}{\Sigma(x_i - \bar{x})^2}, \tag{6.31}$$

$$b_1 = \frac{\Sigma(x_i - \bar{x})y_i}{\Sigma(x_i - \bar{x})^2} = \Sigma\left[\frac{(x_i - \bar{x})}{\Sigma(x_i - \bar{x})^2}\right]y_i, \tag{6.32}$$

and replace y_i with Equation (6.1):

$$b_1 = \Sigma\left[\frac{(x_i - \bar{x})}{\Sigma(x_i - \bar{x})^2}\right](\beta_0 + \beta_1 x_i + e_i). \tag{6.33}$$

The first multiplication in Equation (6.5) is 0: $\beta_0 * \Sigma\left[\frac{(x_i - \bar{x})}{\Sigma(x_i - \bar{x})^2}\right] = 0$, and the second multiplication is β_1: $\beta_1 * \Sigma\left[\frac{(x_i - \bar{x})}{\Sigma(x_i - \bar{x})^2}\right]x_i = \beta_1 * 1 = \beta_1$ (see Appendix 2D of Hill, Griffiths, and Lim, 2008 for details on this step).

Thus, Equation (6.5) can be rewritten as

$$\text{plim}\,\hat{b}_1 = \beta_1 + \Sigma\left[\frac{(x_i - \bar{x})}{\Sigma(x_i - \bar{x})^2}\right]e_i = \beta_1 + \text{plim}\frac{\Sigma(x_i - \bar{x})e_i}{\Sigma(x_i - \bar{x})^2} = \beta_1 + \text{plim}\frac{\Sigma x_i' e_i}{\Sigma x_i'^2}. \tag{6.34}$$

Note that x_i' is defined as $x_i' \equiv (x_i - \bar{x})$. Thus

$$\text{plim}\,\hat{b}_1 = \beta_1 + \frac{\text{cov}(x_i, e_i)}{\text{var}(x_i)}. \tag{6.35}$$

Appendix for Chapter 7: Durbin–Watson Test for Autocorrelation

An alternative test for autocorrelation of order 1 is the Durbin–Watson test. The test statistic is calculated as

$$d = \frac{\sum_{t=2}^{T}(\hat{e}_t - \hat{e}_{t-1})^2}{\sum_{t=1}^{T}\hat{e}_t^2}. \tag{7.32}$$

The Durbin–Watson statistic d is compared with critical values of the Durbin–Watson statistic for upper (d_u) and lower (d_l) values. From the critical values of Durbin–Watson statistics tables, you can obtain d_u and d_l for a given level of significance and the number of parameters in the model, excluding the intercept. The null hypothesis in this test is that there is no autocorrelation, H_0: $\rho = 0$. Rejecting the null hypothesis means that residuals exhibit a first-order autocorrelation or follow an AR(1) process. You can determine whether there is a first-order autocorrelation by following the rules:

(i) If $d < d_l$ then reject H_0: $\rho = 0$.
(ii) If $d > d_u$ then do not reject H_0: $\rho = 0$.
(iii) If $d_l < d < d_u$ then the test is inconclusive.

Appendix for Chapter 10: Details of Models with Limited Dependent Variables

A. Derivation of Logit and Probit Variables from a Latent Variable Framework

To study how logit and probit models can be derived from a latent variable framework for a binary response model, the section begins by assuming a logistic distribution and uses the logit model to examine the positive outcome $y_i = 1$. The model is given by

$$\begin{aligned} P(y_i = 1) &= P(y_i^* > 0 \mid x_i) \\ &= P(\mathbf{x}\beta + e_i > 0 \mid x_i) \\ &= P(e_i > -\mathbf{x}\beta) \\ &= 1 - \Lambda(-\mathbf{x}\beta) = \Lambda(\mathbf{x}\beta). \end{aligned} \tag{10.34}$$

This last step uses the symmetric property of the logistic distribution.[1] You can apply the same exercise for the probit model by assuming a standard normal distribution for the function $G(\mathbf{x}\beta)$:

$$\begin{aligned} P(y_i = 1) &= P(y_i^* > 0 \mid x_i) \\ &= P(\mathbf{x}\beta + e_i > 0 \mid x_i) \\ &= P(e_i > -\mathbf{x}\beta) \\ &= 1 - N\left(-\frac{\mathbf{x}\beta}{\sigma}\right) = \Phi(\mathbf{x}\beta), \end{aligned} \tag{10.35}$$

where again the last step uses the symmetric properties as well as $\sigma = 1$ for the CDF of the standard normal distribution.

B. Conditional Logit Models

Conditional logit models are used when the choice among the alternatives depends not only on the characteristics of the individuals but also on the characteristics of the

[1] See Wooldridge (2002) for details.

alternatives. The multinomial logit (probit) models allow the individual to choose only one alternative, $y_i = j$. This also means that the data are used in wide format. For conditional and mixed logit models you need to arrange the data in long format, data per individual and alternative. Suppose a CEO has a choice of investing in two projects: the first is more sustainable in terms of environment, but costs more; the second costs less, but is also less environment friendly, all else equal. Suppose also that the CEO receives an incentive scheme that includes sustainability targets (ESG-linked pay). In this example, the CEO will enter the long-format data three times for each period. If the CEO chooses to invest (decision = 1) in the sustainable project, it will be coded as 1. The other alternatives for the CEO will be coded as 0. Suppose also that a second CEO does not receive ESG-linked pay and chooses not to invest in the sustainable project. Table A.1 provides the information for this example.

Table A.1 Data on long format

Project	CEO	Decision	ESG-linked pay
Sustainable	1	1	1
Not sustainable	1	0	1
Neither	1	0	1
Sustainable	2	0	0
Not sustainable	2	1	0
Neither	2	0	0

The variable ESG-linked pay (w_i) varies over CEO i but not over alternatives (decision). You could also have some other independent variables that vary over alternatives and CEO ($x_{i,j}$). For instance, the cost of capital for each alternative investment might differ. The conditional logit model examines the probability that CEO i will choose alternative investment j. More formally:

$$P(y_i = j|\mathbf{x}) = \frac{\exp(\mathbf{x}_{ij}'\beta + \mathbf{w}_i'\gamma_j)}{\sum_{k=1}^{m}\exp(\mathbf{x}_{ik}'\beta + \mathbf{w}_i'\gamma_k)}, \tag{10.36}$$

where you estimate $j-1$ number of coefficients γ_j for alternative invariant variables $\mathbf{w}_i$ and one coefficient β for alternative and individual variant variables $\mathbf{x}_{ij}$ in the conditional logit (clogit) model. The probability sum of choosing each alternative will be 1. The coefficient γ_j is interpreted as an increase in the independent variable increasing/decreasing the probability of choosing alternative j relative to the benchmark category. You interpret β (suppose positive) as an increase in the value of the alternative j increasing the probability of choosing that particular alternative and decreasing the probability of choosing all other alternatives.

You can compute $j \times j$ sets of marginal effects for each alternative variant independent variable $\mathbf{x}_{ij}$ and the sum of these alternative marginal effects will be zero. These marginal effects (assume positive) are interpreted as a one-unit increase in $\mathbf{x}_{ij}$ increasing the probability of choosing the jth alternative and decreasing the probability of choosing other alternatives. MEs are interpreted as a percentage.

One extension to the clogit model is the mixed logit model, which produces random parameters for the independent variable and the standard deviation of the independent variable. The interpretation of the parameters and MEs is similar to that in the clogit model. One advantage of mixed logit models is that the potential significant coefficient on the standard deviation of the independent variable can be interpreted as evidence of heterogeneity across individuals with respect to the effect the independent variable has on the probability of choosing alternative *j*. The use of conditional logit and mixed logit models is not common in corporate finance studies, but there are many decisions in corporate finance that may particularly fit a clogit model.

C. Probit Part of the Tobit Model

The equation for the probit part of the tobit that models the probability of zero investment is given as

$$\begin{aligned} P(y_i = 0|\mathbf{x}) &= P(y_i^* \leq 0), \\ &= P(\mathbf{x}\boldsymbol{\beta} + e_i \leq 0), \\ &= P(e_i \leq -\mathbf{x}\boldsymbol{\beta}), \\ &= \Phi\left(\frac{-\mathbf{x}\boldsymbol{\beta}}{\sigma_e}\right), \\ &= 1 - \Phi\left(\frac{\mathbf{x}\boldsymbol{\beta}}{\sigma_e}\right), \end{aligned} \tag{10.37}$$

where the standard normal distribution is applied and the symmetry property of the normal distribution is used in the last two steps.[2]

REFERENCES

Cameron, A. C. and Trivedi, P. K. 2005. *Microeconometrics: Methods and Applications.* Cambridge University Press, New York.

Hill, R. C., Griffiths, W. E., and Lim, G. C. 2008. *Principles of Econometrics* (3rd ed.). Wiley, Hoboken, NJ.

Snedecor, G. W. and Cochran, W. G. 1989. *Statistical Methods* (8th ed.), Iowa State University Press, Ames, IA.

Wilcoxon, F. 1945. Individual comparisons by ranking methods. *Biometrics* 1, 80–83.

[2] See Wooldridge (2002) for more details.

Index

Introductory Note

References such as '178–79' indicate (not necessarily continuous) discussion of a topic across a range of pages. Wherever possible in the case of topics with many references, these have either been divided into sub-topics or only the most significant discussions of the topic are listed. Because the entire work is about 'quantitative methods' and 'corporate finance', the use of these terms (and certain others which occur constantly throughout the book) as an entry point has been restricted. Information will be found under the corresponding detailed topics.

For EU product safety concerns, contact us at Calle de José Abascal, 56–1°, 28003 Madrid, Spain or eugpsr@cambridge.org.

www.ingramcontent.com/pod-product-compliance
Lightning Source LLC
Chambersburg PA
CBHW082326230425
25634CB00024B/588

* 9 7 8 1 0 0 9 3 0 7 4 1 3 *